CITY
ON THE
LAKE

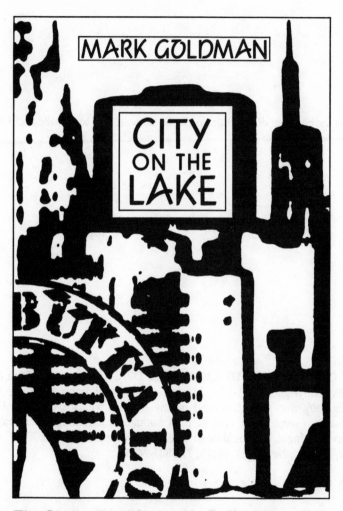

MARK GOLDMAN

CITY
ON THE
LAKE

BUFFALO

The Challenge of Change in Buffalo, New York

Prometheus Books
Buffalo, New York

To the children of the Buffalo public schools, and to Charlie and Lydia

94 93 92 91 90   5 4 3 2 1

Library of Congress Catalog Card Number 90-61329

ISBN 0-87975-579-2

Printed in the United States of America on acid-free paper

TABLE OF CONTENTS

PROLOGUE

The 1970s were a difficult time for Buffalo. Everything was unraveling, particularly for those of us who lived here. The economy was crumbling; both downtown and the neighborhoods were dying; city government was crippled; public institutions were bankrupt.

There was a blizzard too, the worst in history. Clouds and shadows and winds came roaring in off the lake; blinding, relentless waves of snow followed, smothering, paralyzing the city.

Struck by a barrage of steady blows, those who could left. By the tens of thousands they moved away, from the streets and neighborhoods, from the city, from the region, now commonly and condescendingly referred to as the "Rust Belt." Then, one day in the spring of 1976, in the midst of this swirling cycle of decline, Federal District Judge John T. Curtin told the people of Buffalo that they would have to integrate their public schools. History told them it would not be easy.

In cities throughout the nation, court orders similar to Judge Curtin's had led to violence and bitterness. In Boston and New York, Cleveland and Detroit, Chicago and Philadelphia, the middle classes (whites as well as blacks) had abandoned the public schools, writing them off as hopeless, confining them increasingly to the poor.

Most people expected the same to happen in Buffalo. In this melting pot, racial conflict—always heated, sometimes violent—had been the norm as white ethnics and blacks slugged it out at the bottom of the city's long and shaky economic ladder. And now, in the mid-1970s, as industry was drying up and the pie was rapidly dwindling, most predicted the conflict would be greater still. Following Curtin's decision in 1976, fear-filled talk of "another Boston" rippled through the community. Fear and concern escalated and, suspecting the worst, the white exodus from the city grew.

However, despite the prophesies of doom; the beating that Buffalo was taking; the relentless assaults to its wealth, health, and confidence; the community began to respond positively to Judge Curtin's rulings. Sudden and sweeping changes were occurring in the city's public schools. Old schools, magnificent brick and sandstone structures, venerated for decades in neighborhoods throughout the city as vital community institutions, were being closed. And new ones, with new and different names, new programs, and, most significantly, a new, racially mixed student body, were being opened. The citizens of Buffalo, engaged in a process that had undermined and destroyed cities throughout the country, were peacefully and successfully integrating their public schools.

Gradually, word of what was happening in Buffalo spread, and people began to come to the city from all over—from Detroit and Cleveland, from New York and Chicago, from Europe and Japan—to see for themselves how this beat-up, rusty old city on Lake Erie had been able to do what none of them could.

Following the riots on the Crystal Beach Boat on Memorial Day, 1956, no one would have thought it could ever be possible.

1

RIOTS ON THE CANADIANA

Crystal Beach was a large, old fashioned amusement park located on the Canadian shore across Lake Erie from Buffalo. Though dismantled in 1989, it was beloved by many. Scruffy and shabby, with the look of another era, it would have been perfect for a film set in the 1930s or 1940s. There was a large dance hall, an outdoor beer garden, and buildings where the gentle pastel colors of neon lights radiated softly from within glass bricks. Cheap and close, Crystal Beach, like Coney Island in New York City, was the most popular outdoor summer recreation spot in the area for almost a century. There is hardly a local resident alive who hasn't ridden the Comet, the park's huge roller coaster; or nursed "Crystal Beach suckers," multicolored lollipops hand-dipped at the park; or eaten french fries with white vinegar, washed down with loganberry jucie, the rich, dark syrupy concoction that has dripped down the chins of generations of Buffalonians.

Most people got there by car, a twenty-minute ride across the Niagara River via the Peace Bridge. Until 1956, many others took the Crystal Beach boat, the S.S. *Canadiana,* a large, old, three-decked wooden steamer that had been making the hour-long trip up the river and out onto Lake Erie since the amusement park opened at the turn of the century. Not fancy or elaborate, the boat was nonetheless pleasant and the trip relaxing. People sat on deck picnicking and sunning themselves, and in the evening a band played dance music in the rear of the ship.

The 1956 season started, like all summer seasons, on Memorial Day. "That was like the beginning of summer," recalls Bill Robinson, a black man now in his mid-forties. "We all looked forward to it, the boat and all. Back than, if you were in any club or gang or what have you, the thing was to go to the beach on Memorial Day. And you'd go in your gang's clothes. The El Dorados wore matador pants and purple jackets. The El Tones had turquoise jackets with black trim. The Conservative Lovers . . . they were a girl's gang . . . wore dark blue. The Sweethearts had purple jackets with a dragon stitched on the back."

On Wednesday night, May 30, 1956, the last boat back to Buffalo was packed. There were nearly a thousand passengers, most of them teenagers, many of them black. Fighting had broken out at the amusement park earlier in the day, and the Ontario Provincial Police had arrested nine of the troublemakers, four of them white, five black. When the *Canadiana* pulled away from the pier at Crystal Beach at five past nine that night, all seemed well.

It was a rainy night and many passengers were below decks, huddling to keep warm. Then, suddenly, midway through the dark Lake Erie passage, fighting broke out between groups of black and white teenagers. Gangs —the morning paper called them "rampaging gangs"—rushed back and forth over the decks of the ship. It reported further that "switchblade knives were brandished. Youngsters were shoved to the deck. Above deck roving groups of Negroes attacked the outnumbered whites. Girls were beaten mercilessly and youths who attempted to defend themselves were slugged and kicked without feeling." The evening paper reported that black teenage girls started the riot by attacking white girls. " 'All of us white children were sitting together,' [said] the sobbing white girls, being escorted home by their parents and the police. 'They kept laughing at our shorts and began hitting us. They threw some of us to the floor. They were running up and down the decks. The Negro boys joined in . . . the parents were afraid to break it up. . . .' " Buffalo police officer Jeremiah R. Cronin said, "I'd never seen anything like it in all my years in the department."

The next day the local press carried the news in large frightening headlines: "Nightmare Boat Trip from Crystal Beach, Public's Wrath Runs High," said one paper.

"Violence Erupts at Crystal Beach," said another, "Tensions Brewing." The story was repeated in papers throughout the country. The New York *Daily News* reported in a caption under a wire photo that "Youths Riot at Crystal Beach." The *Washington Post* said, "Teens Battle at Amusement Park." Gov. Harriman expressed "grave concern" and urged authorities in Buffalo to investigate. U.S. Attorney John Henderson, worried about "subversive connections with the incidents aboard the S.S. *Canadiana,"* asked the FBI to do the same.

By the middle of June the FBI had identified witnesses. The story they told was one of fear, confusion, and panic. One said that she had seen a "small white boy, about seven years old, being attacked by a colored girl about thirteen or fourteen years old." There were other reports of "Negro girls accosting white girls, pulling their hair, scratching them and causing them to become hysterical." Others thought the fight had been precipitated by "rival Negro gangs in from the Ellicott and Cold Springs neighborhoods." Others were not quite sure what they had seen. One had seen Negro girls attack white girls, but was able to identify neither attackers nor victims. Another said she wasn't sure "whether the victim was Negro or white." One who had sought shelter from the rain below deck said she was not even aware there had been a disturbance aboard the steamer. The captain of the *Canadiana,* Edward Solomonson, was equally nonplussed. He'd never felt the situation was bad enough to call the Coast Guard. "Similar events happened before," he said, "This was just a little bit more than ordinary."

Southern newspapers saw it differently, seeming to relish the news. Under a photograph of policemen struggling with unruly blacks, the Washington *Daily News* wrote that "Holiday Outing Is Day-Long Race Riot." The *Daily News* in Jackson, Mississippi, accused the Northern press, particularly the *New York Times* and the *New York Herald Tribune,* of virtually ignoring what they saw clearly as a "race riot." These same papers, the *Daily News* wrote, who "lather themselves with indignation and accusing headlines when discord rears its ugly head in the South, just can't see, hear or speak of comparable evil when such breaks out at home or just down the road at Buffalo."

Most in Buffalo disagreed. While there were several meetings of politicians, concerned ministers, and lay leaders to discuss the "implications of the riots for race relations," the public stance of community leaders was that the riot aboard the *Canadiana* was caused by juvenile delinquents and was not a "race riot." There were, the *Buffalo Evening News* said, "too many undisciplined punks—male and female—traveling in gangs looking for trouble." The absence of any adult participation, the paper continued, "clearly refutes any too-easy assumptions that the underlying problem was a breakdown in community race relations." The mayor, Chester Kowal, saw the incident as "part and parcel of juvenile hooliganism." King Peterson, the black councilman from the Ellicott district, felt the same way. It was not a race riot, he said, but rather "a fight caused by unruly and dangerous teenagers." L. L. Scruggs, a highly respected black physician, held the same opinion. "It is unanimously agreed by the Negroes in Buffalo that this was not a race riot," he said. The Board of Community Relations, while not discounting "racial tensions" as a cause, agreed with the mayor that the primary problem was indeed "juvenile hooliganism." Police Commissioner Joseph DeCillis and Urban League President Frank Evans reassured the community in a joint statement that there was "no racial problem in Buffalo and there is no cause for alarm on that score."

Some dissented from the consensus. Victor Einach, Buffalo field representative of the State Commission Against Discrimination, said that blacks had "a strong chip on their shoulders." Whites, on the other hand, "refuse to face up to the fact that racial problems exist." The head of the Youth Board agreed. "Anyone who denies that there are tensions in certain areas of this city is blind," he said. Rev. Kenneth A. Bowen, president of the Buffalo branch of the NAACP, was much less sanguine than other spokespersons for the black community. He expressed his sorrow that the summer had opened with this kind of conflagration, "especially since it seems to be between racial groups."

What actually happened on the *Canadiana,* two and a half miles out on Lake Erie that rainy night in May 1956, made little difference to the white people of Buffalo. No matter how hard the press and the politicans tried to convince them otherwise, the great majority of white Buffalonians saw the riots as an outburst of violence by blacks against whites. The white people of Buffalo were frightened, and many of them, particularly the immigrants who had been living in the neighborhoods of the East Side for generations, began to leave.

2

EAST SIDE

Today there are few reminders in downtown Buffalo of the old Exchange Street station. The tracks are still there, partially buried by a highway overpass. But the vast station constructed by the New York Central Railroad—a great cavernous place, the city's Castle Garden, its Ellis Island, where so many thousands of Eastern Europeans made their first, ceremonious entry into the city—simply is no more.

Not all of Buffalo's immigrants had come by train. In the mid-nineteenth century an earlier generation of settlers, Irish and German, had taken a long and slow journey up the Hudson River from New York, turning west at Albany and following the Erie Canal to Buffalo. In the first decades of the nineteenth century a number of laborers, mostly Irish, traveled across the state to build the Erie Canal, a project that virtually created Buffalo by providing the fastest passage to the East for the grain-exporting Midwest.

The area was first settled in substantial numbers in the late eighteenth and early nineteenth centuries by Protestants from New England farms and the small towns of New York State who made their way west on well-traveled overland routes—through the breathtaking Mohawk Valley, the still, quiet majesty of the Finger Lakes, past Rochester, the burgeoning flour-milling capital of the country, and over the windswept flats of Batavia down to Buffalo, a small settlement nestled where the still waters of Lake Erie turn into the fast-moving currents of the Niagara

River. In the beginning almost all of these people lived on the West Side, on Delaware Avenue, on Church, Court, Mohawk, and Huron Streets, and on other broad and radiating streets and boulevards grandly planned by Joseph Ellicott in the early 1800s. Based on designs by European royalty for their capital cities, Ellicott's plans for the streets of this tiny frontier town were incongruously majestic and imperial.

Confined largely to the West Side, near the settlement's waterfront, Ellicott's plan did not cross Main Street to the East Side. Main Street is as old as Buffalo. A broad, six-lane throughfare, it begins near the terminus of the old Erie Canal and runs into the central business district with its office buildings, stores, theaters, and hotels. Beyond the theater district, however, Main Street quickly loses its identity, continuing for several miles with no apparant rhyme or reason, past an inexplicable array of churches, car washes, cheap office buildings, nineteenth-century brick office blocks, a McDonald's, a Burger King, several turn-of-the-century mansions converted into funeral homes, secretarial schools, beauty parlors, and Freddie's, a once-popular but now closed suburban-style drive-in donut shop. It was this street, which many now consider ugly and depressing, that for so many years, like a racial Maginot Line, has served to divide the East Side from the West Side.

For Mabel Dodge, the *fin-de-siecle* debutante of a prominent Delaware Avenue family, the area east of Main Street was where the foreigners lived. The East Side was foreign, exotic, mysterious, and dangerous— a place Dodge wanted to visit but never dared to on her own. It was here, she knew, that Leon Czolgosz, the Polish anarchist who shot President McKinley at the Pan-American Exposition, had stayed on his frequent visits to Buffalo. Immigrants and foreigners—Poles and Germans, Irish and Italians—lived on the East Side by the thousands, squeezed into tightly knit, overlapping neighborhoods, street after street lined with tiny, wooden homes, interrupted only by church steeples: St. Stanislaus and Transfiguration at Broadway and Fillmore Avenues, where the Poles lived; St. Boniface and St. Phillips in the German "Fruit Belt"; St. Lucy and St. Colomba off Swan Street, jam-packed with Italians; and St. Patrick's for the Irish.

There were East European Jews on the East Side too, flourishing in a world virtually unknown to the wealthy, assimilated German Jews on the West Side. Thousands of them lived up and down the side streets off William Street—Hickory, Pratt, Spring, Cedar, Spruce, and Pine Streets. William was lined with Jewish businesses: bakeries, butcher shops, barber shops, bicycle shops, dry goods stores, clothing stores, tailors, and shoe repair shops (until forced out by the Italian competition, shoe-making was quite a Jewish business). Almost a dozen synogogues stood in the area by 1920—Anshe Ames, Brith Sholem, Beth Jacob, the Russische Shul, Ahavas Achem, and the Clinton and Pine Street Shuls. There are traces of Jewish settlements everywhere—Mogen Davids on the Jefferson Street Real Southern Baptist Church, the old Jefferson Street shul; the fading, barely legible names on peeling, wood-painted signs over the storefronts on William Street—Teible's Meats, Goldstein's Dry Goods, Shorenstein's Deli. And on Ken Moody's home at 78 Watson Street there is a mezzuzah, its reliefs felt plainly through the paint that has been layered over it through the years. Among the first African-American families on the street, the Moodys bought their home from a woman named Finkelstein in 1941.

Blacks, however, had been living on the East Side for years, longer than any ethnic group in the city except Native Americans. They started coming in the 1820s: free blacks from downstate in quest of opportunity and fugitive slaves from the South. By mid-century the black community had become a significant center of free black life in America, a hotbed of abolitionism and the final stop on the renowned Underground Railroad to freedom in Canada. A poignant artifact of those first years in the long and tumultous history of Buffalo's black community still stands: the small and graceful brick Michigan Street Baptist Church, built, say the large numerals carved proudly into the stone lintel over the doorway, in 1845. Across Michigan from the Little Harlem, a still-busy nightclub that has been here since the 1920s, the shiny-red Michigan Street Baptist Church today is the repository of materials pertinent to the history of Buffalo's African-American community. The church used to be something else—a secret way station, a stop on the long and circuitous Underground Railroad, a place where fugitive slaves, protected by the blacks of Buffalo, could rest, recover, and plan the final leg of their journey to freedom.

For years Buffalo's black community remained small and hardly noticed, its few thousand members clustered around the Baptist Church on Michigan Street and Vine Alley, site of the AME Church and the Vine Alley Colored School. During World War I, however, their numbers grew considerably. In 1921 a weekly journal called *Buffalo Saturday Night* printed one of the first descriptions of the black East Side. The story, called "Local Color: A Visit to Buffalo's Black Belt," noted tremendous influx of blacks into the city during the war. According to the writer, "Munitions plants, chemical plants and construction work drew them to Buffalo by the hundreds and thousands and one has only to walk through the colored quarter to realize that there are many thousands of colored people here now." In heated, sensuous terms that most of today's readers would find offensive, the writer urged his audience to visit the area. "If you have eyes in your head you cannot but find it interesting. You may find much that is bestial there. You will perhaps get a glimpse of rough, savage beauty, you may hear jangling, drunken, rag-time, you may hear the soft chant of Negro hymns. I do not know what you will see or hear if you visit the Negro colony, but you will always find life there—primitive, uncivilized, passionate life and that is always interesting."

For those who lived in the neighborhood, however, blacks were neither strange nor exotic. East Side Jews, fewer in numbers and free of the stringent ties that bound Catholic immigrants to their parishes, mingled freely with their African-American neighbors. On small, tree-lined streets packed with wooden one-, two-, and three-family homes, they lived together, blacks in one flat Jews in another. Jewish-owned stores on Jefferson Avenue and William Street catered to a mixed clientele of blacks and Jews, and the Jewish Community Center and the Brotherhood of Sleeping Car Porters stood catty-corner from each other. Though now separated by miles of concrete highway and immense gaps of material comfort, many local blacks and Jews in their sixties and seventies talk fondly of a time when they lived together on the streets of the old East Side.

Buffalo's booming wartime economy brought growth and opportunity to Buffalo's African-American community. In a report prepared in 1943, the State Committee on Discrimination reported that 14,506 blacks, 7 percent of the work force, were employed in Buffalo's 104 war-related industries. Lured by the promise of steady, good-paying work, thousands of blacks migrated north. The number of blacks in Buffalo grew from 18,000 in 1940 to 24,000 in 1945. Prospects for blacks remained good even after the war. The State Commission Against Discrimination reported in 1947 that "Buffalo Negroes today enjoy occupational opportunities and more civil rights than in almost any other metropolitan area in the country." The Urban League concurred, saying that, due largely to a stringent anti-discrimination law in effect in New York State since 1945, blacks were holding their own. Of the 14,000 blacks who had found industrial jobs during the war, the league said, 90 percent had either retained them or got better ones. Nonetheless, the Urban League reported, much of Buffalo's economy particularly its nonindustrial sectors, remained off limits to Buffalo's African-American community.

Since it opened in the mid-1920s, the Buffalo chapter of the Urban League had made small but relentless efforts to find jobs for blacks in the local economy. Its progress was extremely slow and painstaking, its rewards small and somehow pathetic. The report of the league's Industrial Department for 1947 reported, "The situation is very encouraging . . . a Negro salesgirl has been placed at Hengerer's. J. N. Adam is next on the list. At Hengerer's there is a Negro forelady supervising ten persons. There are girls doing semi-clerical work as a result of long-range planning and ground work." In addition, "Nurse training has been secured in Meyer Memorial Hospital, after many years of struggle and petition and all hospitals, except the Buffalo General, accept Negro patients." Meanwhile, the Buffalo Bills, then in the All-American Conference, signed their first black player, a man named Edward L. Conwell, a sprinter and member of the 1948 U.S. Olympic Team.

These results were mitigated by the balance of the report. While pleased that there were two blacks on the faculty of the University of Buffalo, there were, the league said, no black professors at State Teacher's College, and no black teachers in any Buffalo high school. What's more, "There has never been a Negro intern in any local hospital and no medical school graduates in the last twenty years."

Gradually, as the industrial economy expanded, blacks began to make economic progress. By 1956 the director of industrial relations for the Buffalo League was pleased to report that "the Niagara Frontier is leading the country in integrating the Negro in industry and commerce." Even so, with their average income lagging far behind whites, black workers had to settle for crumbs. As late as 1957, the appointment of a black sales representative for the Canada Dry Bottling Company was reason to cheer. The *Buffalo Criterion,* one of the city's African-American newspapers, reported that the hiring "marked the first time one of our young men had been given the opportunity to promote sales and advertising for a local soft drink firm."

By 1950 Buffalo's African-American population exceeded 37,000. Seeking out friends and family and a neighborhood that would nurture and sustain them, they descended upon the Ellicott District, long the center of African-American community life in Buffalo. As they did, the white ethnics who had been there for generations—the Germans in the Fruit Belt and Cold Springs, the Jews on Jefferson and William, and the Italians on Swan Street—left.

Some went to more outlying neighborhoods: Italians to South Buffalo, Jews to Humboldt Park and North Buffalo, Germans to various neighborhoods. But most went to the suburbs. Between the end of the war and 1950 whites were leaving the city at the rate of twenty-two a day. Whites were leaving more quickly from Buffalo, said the National

Industrial Conference Board, than from any other city in the country (though followed closely by two other aging industrial cities, Cleveland and Pittsburgh). The exodus gathered momentum during the 1950s and by the end of that decade the U.S. Census reported that more than 80,000 white people, 15 percent of Buffalo's white population, had left their old city neighborhoods for the suburbs.

Overwhelmed by the flood of southern blacks into their community, many of the older, more established African-American families who had lived in the Ellicott District for years also moved out. Excluded from the suburbs by the notoriously discriminatory housing policies of the federal government and the equally discriminatory housing convenents that had been passed throughout suburban America by townships in conjunction with the real estate industry, these blacks moved into the neighborhoods vacated by the white ethnics. Despite its distinctly racist overtone, there was something perversely beneficial about the movement of whites to the suburbs; for had they not left in such large numbers, there would have been no place for blacks to move. Racial conflict would have been exacerbated by conflicts over turf, and race relations would have deteriorated even more than they did.

Blacks, however, were not over-concerned by the departure of whites. Indeed, Rev. Kenneth Bowen, president of the local chapter of the NAACP, was pleased with the progress of the transition. Commenting on the phenomenon in 1956, he said, "The movement of second-generation middle-class Negroes from the Ellicott District to the Cold Springs and the Humboldt Park section has been steady, smooth and successful, devoid of friction." Thus, for those blacks able to afford to buy homes in these suddenly abandoned neighborhoods of the East Side, the white exodus was a blessing, allowing them to escape the deterioration of the old Ellicott District.

Driving around the streets of the Ellicott District today Leland Jones, his voice filled with regret, says wistfully that he never saw anything fall so fast as his own neighborhood. Jones was born here in the early 1920s, shortly after his father, a farmer in Waverly, New York, moved to the Ellicott District and opened Leland Jones' Funeral Parlor, the best and biggest funeral parlor on the black East Side. The community was small then, just beginning to push out from William and Clinton Streets to Jefferson. Even in the Ellicott District blacks were far outnumbered by Jews and Italians. Jones went to School 32 on Clinton Street, today one of jewels in the crown of the city's public schools, re-fashioned as the Bennett Park Montessori Center. He excelled and in 1935 was valedictorian and president of his class, and winner of the highly coveted city-wide Richmond Speaking Contest. Four years later Jones graduated from Buffalo Technical High School (the building that now houses the Buffalo Academy for the Visual and Performing Arts, Buffalo's "Fame school"), where he majored in engineering. As athletic as he was studious, Jones won a football scholarship to the University of Buffalo, out Main Street near the city line, in a neighborhood he had never seen before. UB's first and only black quarterback, Jones led his team to victories that no one thought were possible.

One of those games was against Baltimore's Johns Hopkins. Jones had never been further south than Lackawanna, New York. Now, in Baltimore, he says, he experienced racism—"Southern Style"—for the first time in his life. He checked into the hotel with the rest of his teamates, but was taken aside and told he'd have to stay at the Hotel Royale, a "colored hotel" on the east side of town.

More frightened than angry, alone and segregated in this strange southern city, Jones in desperation called Carl Murphy, the rich and powerful publisher of Baltimore's black daily, the *Baltimore Afro-American*. Jones had known about the *Afro-American* since high school, reading it regularly while hanging out at Baker's, a soda shop and news-stand on William Street. The owner subscribed to black papers from all over the country and after school Jones and his friends read them over a coke, a dish of ice cream, and a piece of pie; papers like the *Afro-American,* New York City's *Amsterdam News,* and the Chicago *Defender.* Jones particularly liked the *Afro-American* and now he reached out to someone he thought might be able to help him. Within an hour Murphy came around to the Royale, picked up Jones, and took him to his home in Silver Springs.

The Murphys liked Jones and he liked them, particularly their daughter Carlita. He came back often to visit and she always showed him a good time. (Once she took him to a dance at Morgan State, the black college in Baltimore Carlita attended. He'd like it, she promised. There'd be lots of Buffalo folk there. If half the blacks who left Buffalo to go to black colleges in the South had returned, Jones says, "Boy, would we have a strong community today.") In 1946, after serving two years in the U.S. Signal Corps, Leland Jones married Carlita Murphy. They moved back to Buffalo, where Jones entered the UB law school. in 1949 he was elected county supervisor from the Ellicott District, the first African-American elected to office in the history of the city.

Meanwhile, conditions in Jones's Ellicott District were getting worse. It was increasingly plagued by overcrowding, high rents, and blight, and black community leaders were becoming concerned. In 1951 the Urban League reported that the "trend toward ghetto living in the Ellicott District is the major social problem in the Negro community." Even the white community could no longer ignore the drastic and dramatic changes that were taking place there. In July 1952 the *Evening News* commented that "the good people of Buffalo who think they live in a sleek, clean, tree-lined city would be shocked beyond description if they could see the conditions in the Ellicott District."

Despite his best efforts, there seemed little that Supervisor Jones could do. Then came the decision by the federal government to designate the Ellicott District an "Urban Renewal Area." In 1952 the city announced that, with the aid of federal urban renewal funds, twenty-nine blocks in the Ellicott District would be demolished and cleared, replaced with a public housing project consisting of a series of seven-story buildings and recreational facilities. Bounded by William and Swan Streets and Jefferson and Michigan Avenues, the area, everybody agreed, was badly run down, packed tightly with hundreds of antiquated frame homes, seedy bars and scruffy factories. It was, as one downtown banker eager to expedite the project said, "a colored slum of the worst kind, and just a stone's throw from our best downtown district." While many in the black community, including Leland Jones and King Peterson, his successor on the Common Council, favored renewal of the area, like many of their constituents they were opposed to the sweeping demolition and clearance project outlined by city and federal authorities. Some of them, particularly the home owners, favored what they called "The Baltimore Plan," whereby federal funds would be used for renovation and restoration of existing homes. Jones, concerned that the public housing projects would only increase the isolation of blacks in the Ellicott District, urged a program of small-scale, scatter-site public housing. But the city would listen to none of these alternatives and in January 1958 demolition and clearance of the Ellicott District began. The residents scattered. Some, the better-off homeowners, moved to Humboldt Parkway. Some vacated to temporary homes nearby, where they waited, hoping to be relocated into the promised Ellicott projects. Most, however, moved north into the Fruit Belt, where they were joined by the crush of blacks moving into Buffalo from the South at a rate of ten a day throughout the 1950s.

Driving around the streets of the old East Side, Joe Tanzella looks for traces of the huge Italian neighborhoods that used to be here. Tanzella is in his mid-forties and he was born and raised here, on Hickory Street, where the swimming pool of the John F. Kennedy Recreation Center was later built. Like most urban renewal projects, the center looks like it belongs in a shopping plaza in the suburbs. Like the high-rise "projects" that were built here as part of the Ellicott Renewal Plan, it sits there, shabby now, and still, after thirty years, not really belonging.

Tanzella is chairman of the annual St. Lucy's banquet that used to be a tradition around here. There are no longer any traces of the old Italian parish in the Ellicott District, and the banquet is held at a place called Samuel's Grande Manor, located in the farthest reaches of suburban Clarence. Tanzella has a painting of the old neighborhood done in the 1940s, a primitive executed by one of the neighbors, like Joe Fasanella's views of New York's Little Italy. Flanked by frame homes, a grocery on one corner, a tavern on the other, a large brick church in the rear, the painting's streets are filled with cars and people. Though probably somewhat idealized, the painting shows a sense of neighborhood that was destroyed by urban renewal.

Tanzella talks about the neighborhood as he drives, reeling off the names of people who lived on his street. There were two churches— St. Columba's, where Joe was baptized, built in the 1890s for the Irish but attended mostly by Italians as early as the 1920s, and St. Lucy's around the corner on Swan Street. Swan was minutes away from downtown and after school, at night, and on Saturdays, neighborhood kids walked there, meeting at the Deco Restaurant or at Woolworths. There were great restaurants: Bocce's, Santora's, and Jacobi's. After the war the Tanzellas moved to his grandmother's "condo," a large brick apartment building on Swan. Today there are only traces of the large Italian community that flourished on Swan, like the sign over the store at Swan and Michigan—five letters, "POTEN," remain where Joe says Potenza the tailor had his shop.

It all ended in the 1950s, with the Ellicott District urban renewal project. Suddenly, Tanzella says, "there were bulldozers at our back door," and overnight, it seemed to him, whole streets were cleared and St. Lucy's came tumbling down—today it is only a vast, empty field on Swan Street.

On the south side of Swan, spread sparsely between and amongst grass-filled empty lots, there are old, decayed wooden homes, where many of Tanzella's friends and family lived. For some reason, Tanzella says, the bulldozers stopped on the north side of Swan, leaving a few houses standing, lone survivors of urban renewal, staring out on the wreckage of their neighborhood. The Tanzellas couldn't stay there after that, and in 1958 they moved. Rev. Msgr. Carl J. Fenice, pastor at

St. Lucy's, was furious. "What galls me most," he said years later, "is that the plot of land where our church was is still empty." Also empty since the early 1980s are the brick towers of the Ellicott Project.

Chef's restaurant remains, surrounded by parking lots in this once-dense Italian neighborhood. Owned by Lou Billitieri, Jr., from the old neighborhood, the restaurant is one of the most popular in Buffalo. Originally one small room in a late-nineteenth-century brick building on the corner of Swan and Chicago Streets, Billitieri has added several rooms in recent years to accommodate the crowds that come here from all over the metropolitan area. The food is great—Chef's specializes in southern Italian and Sicilian dishes; the portions are large, and the place, with its many tables covered with red and white table cloths, is warm and very neighborly. Chef's is always crowded: at lunch-time with business people and politicians from downtown, at night with families headed off to the "Aud" to watch the hockey team, the Buffalo Sabres, or to Pilot Field to watch the baseball team, the Buffalo Bisons. But there is something eerie about Chef's, which, like St. Columba's around the corner on Hickory, is one of the few surviving remnants of the old Italian neighborhood in the Ellicott District. Something about the place, despite its history, lacks neighborhood legitimacy and authenticity.

The story of the Ellicott District is a sad one, and it attracted national attention. An April 1958 article in the *Wall Street Journal* announced that, "Another Northern City Runs into a Race Problem." The paper interviewed William Sims, a local African-American attorney who had just become the president of the local NAACP. Knowing then what others came to realize only much later, Sims considered the worsening problems of Buffalo's growing black ghetto to be the result of faulty public policy as much as any product of changing demographics. Like Jones, Peterson and a handful of other black community leaders, Sims had fought the Ellicott Urban Renewal Project and lost. Sensing the consequences of this ill-conceived project, Sims told the *Journal* that, "Before long most of the city will be Negro and the suburbs white. That will be segregation all over again."

There are few middle-aged African-Americans in Buffalo today who were not in some way affected by the Ellicott Urban Renewal Project. They all talk about it intimately, angrily, and are clearly personally offended by the rash and thoughtless policy that did so much to undermine the neighborhoods of the city's East Side.

Just as deeply etched in the memory of many a Buffalonian is the tragedy of Humboldt Parkway, destroyed during the late 1950s in a heinous act of urbicide. No one who remembers the serene beauty of Fredrick Law Olmsted's magnificent parkway can understand how public officials charged with protecting the public trust could have conceived and then executed a plan so devastating in impact and scale. Today, more than thirty years after it was destroyed, Humboldt Parkway has become part of Buffalo's communal memory, shared even by a new generation of Buffalonians for whom a name is all that remains of this splendid vestige of another time.

For artist Michael Margulis Humboldt Parkway was a glorious avenue of adventure and escape, a peaceful and pleasant route to bike from his home on Goulding to the Buffalo Museum of Science in Humboldt Park or, in the other direction, to the Albright Art Gallery overlooking the Lake in Delaware Park. These childhood experiences are hauntingly suggested in the vision that he reflects today in his graphic designs.

In Europe, Lilly Popper says sadly, cities are destroyed by bombs, not bulldozers. Lilly and Otto Popper arrived in Buffalo in June 1949, ten years almost to the day since fleeing the Nazis in their home town of Pilzen, Czechoslovakia. They spent the war in England and afterward made their way to the city they would call home for the rest of their lives. For eighteen months the couple and their two daughters lived on Fox Street, sharing a three-bedroom upper flat with two women. The street was lovely and quiet, the solid, two-family frame homes shaded by soaring elm trees, like a cathedral over the street, Lilly said. Best of all, the house was around the corner from Humboldt Parkway, a lushly landscaped gift to the city from the great park planner, Fredrick Law Olmsted. In the evenings, particularly on those long, soft, quiet summer evenings that Buffalonians cherish, the family joined their neighbors there, walking, or sitting on the ornamented wood and cast-iron benches that lined the Parkway.

In 1951, the Poppers moved even closer to Humboldt Parkway, to a flat of their own in a two-family home on Norway Park. The Poppers lived upstairs, their landlords, a German butcher and his wife, below. By the early 1950s rumors began to circulate in the neighborhood. People whispered that the parkway was doomed. The state was said to be building a highway over it.

The bulldozers arrived in the late winter of 1958. By then the Poppers, like many others, had left. Those who stayed watched in disbelief as trees, twenty the first week, hundreds over the months that followed, were removed root and branch from the rich soil that was soon to be covered with concrete.

From their home on Humboldt Parkway Dr. Lydia Wright and her husband, Dr. Frank Evans, watched the same sight. Fredrick Law Olmsted had laid out the parkway as a woodsy link joining Humboldt Park to Delaware Park. The parkway, Wright knew, held the neighborhood together. It was the place where the children played, the grownups walked.

Like everybody else in the neighborhood, Wright and Evans came to the parkway to sit, to walk, and to socialize with friends and neighbors. The couple had tried to stop the project, lobbying officials in Buffalo and Albany about the plan to build an intra-urban highway through their neighborhood, but got no response. Planning officials were working on a grand scheme for the construction of highways in and around the whole city. The Niagara Extension of the New York State Thruway linked Buffalo and Niagara Falls. The Kensington Expressway was scheduled to follow, linking the city to the rapidly expanding suburbs east of it. The Humboldt and Scajaquada Expressways cutting through the heart of the city would connect the Niagara Extension and the Kensington.

In the post-war boom years, when cars and suburbs changed forever the way we live, highway building in Buffalo, as in cities throughout the country, was all the rage. No place was spared, not the Niagara riverfront, not Delaware Park, and certainly not the neighborhoods. Few people questioned, let alone protested, when, in the early 1950s the Buffalo shoreline of the Niagara River, one of the world's most breathtaking waterfront vistas, was chosen as the site of the Niagara Extension of the New York State Thruway. Even less was said in the early 1950s when the state built the Scajaquada Expressway, a four-lane, grade-level highway cutting through the heart of Delaware Park and the exclusive residential neighborhood that surrounds it.

But because it was built through the heart of a dense residential neighborhood, the Humboldt Expressway had a far greater impact on the social geography of Buffalo than either the Scajaquada or the Niagara Extension. There was little that Wright, Evans, and their band of neighborhood activists could do. Like many road-building schemes, this one had broad support within the power structure of the community. The Chamber of Commerce liked it and had supported it from the beginning. Buffalo was "on the threshold of a great and unlimited future," it declared. "This is not the time to make little plans. To reject the expressway would be little short of treason." The mayor, a man named Steven Pankow, liked the plan too. Pointing out that most of the funds for the highway network would come from Albany, he said, "Never has Buffalo been offered so much for so little."

There were a handful of other middle-class black families in the Humboldt Parkway neighborhood when Wright and Evans moved there in 1954. The decision to build the highway led still more whites to move and soon more middle-class blacks—teachers and lawyers, account-ants and steel workers, politicians and ministers—replaced them, and by the time construction of the highway began in early 1958 the Humboldt Parkway neighborhood was predominantly black, the best and nicest black neighborhood in Buffalo. This did not stop the highway planners, however, and, like the Poppers down the street and hundreds of their other neighbors, Wright and Evans watched in anguish as their park was destroyed. As the clearing began in front of her house, Lydia Wright, looking out of her living room window, saw for the first time the houses on the other side of the parkway, for so long hidden by the forest-like web of trees that had always lined Humboldt Parkway.

Wright and Evans stayed in their Humboldt Parkway home and today, sitting in their large and comfortable living room, they hardly hear the cars go by anymore. They see them, though, and so they keep their white-lace curtains drawn. The Poppers, however, didn't stay, and shortly after construction began, they, like so many of their neighbors, moved to the suburbs.

Some made other choices. In 1961 Robert Traynham Coles, a young black architect, bought an empty lot near the junction of the Humboldt Expressway and the Kensington Expressway, the planned but still unbuilt highway between downtown and the eastern suburbs. Unlike his neigh-bors, Cole knew how to read surveyors maps. These told him far more than the smooth assurances of state and city officials, who maintained that the highway planned for the area would be "consistent with the contours of Humboldt Parkway." Coles designed and built his home at 321 Humboldt Parkway later that year so that the rear of the house, not the front, would face the six-lane highway that the parkway had become.

3

WEST SIDE

It is eleven o'clock on Sunday morning and the one Italian mass of the week is about to be said at St. Anthony of Padua's Church on Court Street behind City Hall on Buffalo's Lower West Side. A Blazer pickup truck, traces of snow on the hood, pulls hurriedly into the empty parking lot. It is blustery and the drive in from surburban Orchard Park takes more than the usual thirty-five minutes. A healthy-looking man in his late forties, wearing tartan slacks and an Izod sweater, hops down from the cab and runs around to open the passenger door for a short, thin, stooped old lady dressed in black from head to toe. She gets down slowly, cautiously setting her feet on the slippery macadam, takes her son's arm and follows his lead to the arched entrance of the church. He'll be back in an hour, the man tells her, to pick her up.

It's noon on a Friday at Jenny's, up Niagara Street a half mile from St. Anthony's, and the place is packed. It seems that half of the hundreds of Italians who work at City Hall are lined up waiting to get in the door of the small, steamy luncheonette—especially on Fridays, when there's no better homemade macaroni and cheese and deep-fried fish anywhere in Buffalo. (The Poles who work in City Hall would argue that the fish fry at the recently burned down Roosevelt, in their old neighborhood on Broadway, was better.) Like the guy in the Blazer bringing his mother to St. Anthony's Italian mass, these Italians don't live in the neighborhood anymore, but they still come back to Jenny's all the time. A few are still here, living in the ancestral homes their parents found in the neighborhood when they came to town at the turn of the century. The Galuzzos still live on Busti Avenue in the house where Sal Galuzzo was born almost sixty years ago. His son and daughter-in-law live upstairs. Most of his neighbors, though, the people he grew up with, the kids from School 1 across the street, or from Holy Cross around the corner, left years ago, in the late 1960s and early 1970s when urban renewal demolished the old Italian West Side. Most of them live off Hertel Avenue now, in the old Jewish neighborhood in North Buffalo. Others have moved to Tonawanda and West Seneca, northern and southern suburbs of Buffalo.

Urban renewal projects, even the good ones, have a raw, unfinished look. They never quite fit into their surroundings. Take Niagara Street's Shoreline apartments on the Lower West Side: from the observation tower on the twenty-fourth floor of City Hall, the Shoreline project resembles a trailer park plunked arbitrarily into the heart of the city. It wasn't supposed to be like that. Since the beginning of the century Buffalo's mayors and other members of the downtown business and political establishment have fixed their eyes on the waterfront. Whether for a new railroad terminal at the beginning of the century, or for a domed stadium, canal-era theme park, or university campus in our own day, Buffalo's waterfront has been touted as the site for a host of pie-in-the-sky visions and plans, few of which have seen the light of day. The site has always been too tempting to ignore, with its broad, curving shoreline, its clear and unbroken view of Lake Erie, and the dramatic confluence of the lake and the Niagara River. Mayor Frank Sedita, like his predecessors and his successors, had high hopes for the area, for the waterfront, and for Niagara Street.

Like the West End in Boston, demolished in the late 1950s, the area had been an Italian neighborhood since the 1890s, when St. Anthony's, the oldest Italian church in Buffalo, was founded. Sedita was raised in the parish. He couldn't have had much fondness for his old neighborhood, however, because in 1958 he announced that, like the Ellicott District on the East Side, it had been designated an urban renewal area.

From Virginia Street South to below City Hall, from Niagara Street to the Thruway and beyond to the edge of the Niagara River, homes would be demolished, the land would be cleared and, it was promised, the area would be renewed by the construction of new luxury and middle-income townhouses and apartments.

It was a classic story of 1950s urban renewal, the kind that was popular in cities throughout the country. Unfortunately, the plot was always the same, the end predictable. With broad powers conferred on him by the Housing Act of 1949, the mayor of Buffalo, like mayors in cities throughout the country, was able to condemn huge chunks of land, without either relocating the residents or providing relocation allowances to them. What exactly the land was being cleared for nobody, planning officials included, really knew. Some said there would be a stadium. Others, for a brief time during the mid-1960s, said that the new campus of the State University of New York at Buffalo would be built there. Still others talked of new housing, expensive, high-rise apartments that would bring the suburbanites back downtown.

Neighborhood residents knew still less, mostly only that they had to move. Beginning in the early 1960s, thousands of Italians from the waterfront renewal site moved out. Many were bitter, furious at the mayor, their mayor who had turned his back on his people, on his neighborhood, forcing them out of their homes, paying them a fraction of what they felt their property was worth. They had been living in the neighborhood for years. They, their parents, and their children had all gone to St. Anthony of Padua on Court Street, to School 1 on Busti Avenue. And now, with their mortgages long paid up, Mayor Frank Sedita—"Frankie from Efner Street"—was telling them they had to start over in new homes, in new neighborhoods, with new mortgages. Sedita's Efner Street, except for one forlorn little block, was among those destroyed.

The lost housing stock had been amazing, among the oldest and sturdiest in the city: narrow, tall, frame and brick Italianate structures sporting latter-day Eastlake porches and carpenter's gingerbread, built in the 1850s and 1860s and ornamented into the 1890s. The area designated for clearance was an attractive, lively, and interesting neighborhood. Charles Burchfield, Buffalo's great watercolorist, came to know the place while working as a designer in the Birge wallpaper factory around the corner at Niagara and Maryland Streets, where a McDonald's is today. His "Little Italy in Spring," painted in 1927–28, showed the Seventh Street neighborhood below Maryland that was demolished in the 1960s. It has two-and three-story frame Victorian homes with gardens and porches in front; a woman hanging up laundry in an empty lot; others clustered on the corner talking; a man selling fish from a hand-drawn cart; children watching a hurdy-gurdy man play his tunes; tall, bent trees in the foreground; Lake Erie in the background, receding as far as the eye can see.

The people liked their neighborhood, and, like the fruit trees and vineyards they planted in their back yards, they had sunk deep roots into the Lower West Side. But now it was being torn up and destroyed and no one seemed to notice, let alone care, not even the newspapers, which barely touched this horrific story of public policy gone wrong. Joe Ritz, a reporter for the *Courier Express,* was an exception. He had heard about the plans for the renewal of Niagara Street and in June 1966 was given permission to do a piece on it. For the better part of an afternoon Ritz walked around the neighborhood, talking to residents and taking notes. Back in the city room at the *Courier* building on Main Street, Ritz wrote, "Many waterfront residents are still mystified over the use of federal, state and city taxpayer money to buy homes and commercial structures, clear them and sell the land to private developers on the theory that the buildings to be removed from the Waterfront Project area are slums or 'substandard' structures." As far as Ritz could tell, the neighborhood was in good shape. Of Seventh Street he said, "Gardens and fruit trees flourish and the interiors of the homes are well-kept and comfortably furnished." The people in the neighborhood "resent the scattering of neighbors and relatives and their relocation from familiar stores, churches and gathering places. . . . Perhaps to understand the residents' feeling one has to be a gardener. One has to have nursed a cherry tree from a sapling, protected it from insects and diseases, watered it, fed it, worked it so that it is capable of bearing one hundred quarts of fruit and then face the certain knowledge that it will be destroyed one afternoon by a clanking bulldozer." Clearance began in the fall of 1966 and the neighborhood disappeared at a rate of a hundred homes a month.

There was no more excuse for the destruction of this neighborhood than there was for that of the hundreds of others felled by the ax of urban renewal that chopped through cities throughout the United States in the late 1960s. By then people should have known better. Urban renewal was close to twenty years old. Writers like Jane Jacobs in her *Death and Life of American Cities,* published in 1961, and Martin Anderson in his 1964 *The Federal Bulldozer* had provided excellent critiques of "urban renewal" and "slum clearance." The phone call Jacobs made from a pay phone in Boston's West End in a desperate attempt to understand—if not stop—the renewal of that neighborhood could just as easily have been made from Niagara Street almost ten years later. The lessons of failed urban renewal projects were there, but the planners and public officials of Buffalo chose not to see them.

The waterfront land cleared from the area behind City Hall up to Virginia Street remained vacant for almost two years, until the Urban

Development Corporation, a newly created state super-agency, took over in 1969. Under the leadership of Edward Logue, a master planner in the tradition of Robert Moses who had presided over highly praised and publicized clearance and renewal projects in New Haven and Boston, the UDC would take up where the city left off. Logue promised that the company would build an entire community between Niagara Street and the Niagara River, a mixed-use development for ten thousand people with a school, recreation facilities, and high- and low-rise apartments for moderate and low income subsidized housing. There was something thoughtless, tasteless, even obscene about the language the UDC used to describe its project, as if nothing, let alone a community that had struggled to stay alive, had ever been there before. The UDC said it would "create a New Town in Town," a place "arranged in a village atmosphere" where "suburban-style housing joins the urban Renaissance." Today the project sits there. "The Shoreline," it is called. Clustered, sand-colored concrete buildings designed by Logue's hand-picked, internationally known architect Paul Rudolph, it is surrounded, as anyone who had read Jane Jacobs knew that it would be, by grass fields and common areas: an empty, concrete suburban development in the heart of the city, where once there had been a neighborhood.

The trashing of the Lower West Side was compounded by city and state highway planning. Since the end of World War II highways had been seen as the solution not only to the city's transportation problems but, more significantly, to the problem of dealing with the growth of the suburbs. In 1945 and 1946, when the state was planning the Buffalo-area route of the New York State Thruway, many Buffalonians—led by the mayor, members of the City Planning Commission, and a host of other downtown interests—urged a route through rather than around downtown. Citing state construction czar Robert Moses's reports on Baltimore and Portland, Welles V. Moot, the chairman of the City Planning Commission, supported a route that would pass "through the heart of the city," as well as through the residential neighborhoods on the East Side. In a 1945 report that had the support of such downtown groups as the Chamber of Commerce, the Real Estate Board, and a host of neighborhood organizations and businessmen's associations, Moot wrote that the thruway should "come into the center of the city and link up the area's major industrial, commercial and cultural centers. It should connect South Buffalo with the central parts of the city and then pass east of Main Street. It should take the heavy burden of traffic from congested streets on the north side and thus check the economic decline of close-in residential neighborhoods." Downtown groups, apparently, were not alone in thinking that the thruway was meant to generate economic growth as much as it was to be a means of transportation. Indeed, suburban groups opposed a route through downown for the same reason downtowners supported it. Thus began the rivalry between the suburbs and downtown that has characterized so much of the recent history of the metropolitan area. "We in the suburbs," said one petition to the State Department of Transportation, "should not be called upon to sacrifice the life blood of our commercial arteries to supply Buffalo with a transfusion of plasma." The DOT had its own ideas, however, and in 1946 decided on a riverfront route for what is now called the Niagara Thruway. It would be years before it was completed. The main line to Buffalo opened in 1953. The Niagara Extension, which the *Courier Express* once called "a trail of broken promises" and "nightmare alley," was finally completed in 1959. Given the amount of demolition downtown eventually suffered anyway, perhaps it would have been better to run the highway through the downtown area. At least the city's waterfront would have been preserved.

Even as late as 1962 spokesmen for downtown interests continued to support highways as the solution for what ailed the city center. Rapid transit, approved in nearby Toronto nearly ten years before, was rejected by the City Planning Board in 1964. The board supported instead its "Major Trafficways Plan," which called for completion of a long-planned system of intra-urban highways. The Planning Board based its plans on the incredible projection that the city's population would grow by more than 10 percent during the decade. This was optimistic, given the findings of the 1960 census, which showed that Buffalo's population decline since 1950 of 8.2 percent was second only to Detroit's.

Part of the laundry list of projects that made up the board's plan— the Skyway and the Scajaquada Creek Expressway—had been completed. Other elements of it—the Delaware Park Shortway, the North Park Expressway and the East Side Arterial—were never constructed. And on some projects, like the Kensington Expressway, work had finally begun. But two of the planned highways, the Elm-Oak Arterial and the West Side Arterial, remained mere glints in the eyes of the state's road-happy transportation planners. Beginning in the mid-1960s they began to pay attention to them, particularly the West Side Arterial.

The purpose of the West Side Arterial was to join, through the area of downtown now known as the Theater District, the Niagara Section of the Thruway on Buffalo's West Side with the Kensington Expressway on the East Side. There had been a variety of different plans and proposals for the 1.3-mile highway. Nobody seemed to know for sure whether it would be four lanes or six, or what streets it would go under, or over, or on. But no one seemed to question the wisdom of building the road, and throughout the late 1960s—when they should have begun to know better—city, county, and state planning officials were still enthusiastic about the West Side Arterial. In early 1966 the state DOT district engineer Norman Krapf urged the preliminary layout of the highway. "A group of bankers and business people want it," he said, "and they have adopted the plan as originally worked up and have offered all sorts of connectons that would feed the Central Business District." Citing what he said was the rapid rate of development in downtown Buffalo, Krapf said, "It is imperative that we get started on the preliminary layout of a highway that is capable of handling the future highway traffic destined for downtown Buffalo." Krapf was clearly out of touch with the realities of downtown in the 1960s, utterly unaware of its relentless decline as a retail and entertainment center.

A meeting of city and state transportation officials in Albany in August 1968 revealed that concrete plans for the arterial still had not been developed. However, a consensus was developing for a street-level route. It is difficult to understand how the highway was conceived even in that form, but, incredibly, for a while state and local officials were considering the still more appalling alternative of building the arterial as an overhead, elevated highway rising above the city's great north- and south-bound avenues: Elmwood, Delaware, and Franklin. This despite the lessons that should have been learned from the Brooklyn-Queens Expressway and particularly the Lower Manhattan Expressway, which had recently been cancelled because of the outrage of area residents. With callousness and ignorance state and city officials proceeded despite what they conceded was a "closely built-up area with many churches and other costly buildings." They would simply adapt their plans to fit the requirements of this densely developed area. The state would settle, they said, for a fourteen-foot separation between highway and sidewalk instead of the usually required thirty-foot divider. But some of the buildings would have to come down. Among those listed for demolition were some of the city's great turn-of-the-century buildings: the Buffalo Club, the Montefiore Club and the Grosvenor Library. Not too many cared. In an article about the buildings to be demolished, the *Courier Express* noted, apparantly satisfied, that "the buildings . . . will be replaced by grass and trees."

By the middle of the 1969 officials in Buffalo began to hedge their support for the arterial. New ideas about downtown development were, it seemed, being discussed. Downtown merchants had begun to question the wisdom of bisecting Main Street, the primary route to the downtown business district, with a six-lane, grade-level highway. New planning ideas were afoot too. The Niagara Frontier Transportation Authority, having just received a $250,000 grant from the federal Urban Mass Transit Authority, was studying the feasibility of a rapid transit line between downtown Buffalo and Amherst. Mayor Sedita, who had just commissioned a new master plan for the central business district, said he was not willing to proceed until "coordinated plans are available from all parties." He asked the state for a delay of the arterial.

Meanwhile, as planners and politicians seemed to forget about the West Side Arterial, the neighborhoods on the Lower West Side continued to decline, caught in a cycle of abandonment and decay. Realizing the devastating impact the arterial would have on their community, anybody who could began to leave. Some sold their homes, joining those who had left the neighborhood because of the Shoreline urban renewal. Many more moved but held onto their homes, converting them for the short run into income-producing multiple dwellings, holding out in the longer run for a state buyout when construction of the arterial began. Soon absentee ownership, the paradoxical slum condition of overcrowding in some units side by side with high vacancy rates in others, high turnover, and abandonment plagued the area. Efforts by residents to halt the cycle of decay were frustrated by cutbacks in city services and by banks and insurance companies unwilling to invest in a neighborhood destined for condemnation. When in late 1971 the Niagara Frontier Housing Development Corporation applied to the federal Housing and Urban Development Agency for a $2.5-million grant to rehabilitate multiple dwellings on the Lower West Side, its application was denied. HUD responded, "The project is in the probable roadway corridor of the proposed West Side Arterial." Meanwhile, people were leaving, particularly the Italian-Americans who had been in the neighborhood for years. In 1960 there were nineteen hundred families, mostly Italian, attending Immaculate Conception Church on Edward and Elmwood. By 1973 there were five hundred, all but a handful Puerto Rican.

In late 1972 Mayor Sedita reported that the new master plan for downtown Buffalo was completed. It recommended with no apparent awareness of any inconsistency the construction of both the West Side Arterial and a rapid transit line along the Buffalo-Amherst Corridor. A state regional official had told Sedita earlier in the year that the arterial was competing for priority with projects in other cities and might soon lose its place in line. Realizing that it was now or never for the arterial, the mayor, unwilling to say no to even the most dubious capital project, asked that it be reactivated, but as a scaled-down, four-lane surface road. The state complied with the request, but said planning would have to begin from scratch, and with extensive citizen participation.

Since the mid-1960s, when planning for the arterial began in earnest, city and state planners had been reluctant to involve the public in their decisions. In a memo to Edward Ummiker, the city's planning engineer, state District Engineer Krapf said that he had been "advised to proceed swiftly with the development of the plan." Aware that there would be problems with rights-of-way, Krapf told Ummiker to take up the matter with city officials before any citizen involvement. "Let's assume we have their blessing before going ahead with the public hearing," he said. Now, however, in compliance with strict federal guidelines for community participation, the state DOT initiated an elaborate and extensive campaign to elicit the opinions of a broad range of community groups. From an office opened on the Lower West Side it issued a brochure in English, Italian, and Spanish explaining the project and inviting ideas and recommendations. "In keeping with the spirit of community involvement in transportation development studies," it wrote, "the Department is willing to consider any alternatives offered by the local citizens." Eight community meetings were held in the spring of 1973 at churches and schools throughout the Lower West Side. Then eight different citizen's task forces were formed to deal with all aspects of the project. Special groups were formed as liaisons between DOT and neighborhood homeowners, business people, churches, and schools. Finally, in May 1974, the DOT offered nine alternate plans, ranging from no highway to a $30-million proposal to build the original, partially depressed, partially elevated highway. As if looking for a way out, a DOT official told the press, "If at any point in [this] process the local officials and citizens show a definite overwhelming opposition to a project of any kind, the project would be deemed infeasible and removed from the DOT's transportation program."

Opposition to the project was, in fact, growing apparent, particularly among Puerto Ricans. A special task force reported that close to two thousand Puerto Ricans would have to be relocated—but where would they go? There were vacancies at the Shoreline project, but the State Urban Development Corporation said they probably wouldn't do. The problem, a UDC official told DOT, was that "Puerto Ricans will only move into a building in a group of several families. UDC rules do not permit this." The Puerto Ricans in the neighborhood had the most to lose and least to gain by the construction of the arterial. Thus they were its strongest and most vociferous opponents.

There had been a small community of Puerto Ricans in Buffalo since the mid-1940s, when they migrated from the island and from New York City to work in Buffalo's defense industries. Others came later, drifting into the city from surrounding agricultural areas, where many of them worked as seasonal farm laborers. At first Buffalo's Puerto Ricans settled on the East Side, on Swan Street, but with the expansion of the black population there in the 1960s they gradually began to move to Niagara Street and the Lower West Side, where, in midst of the rubble of an area destroyed by decades of failed urban renewal policies, some recognized the promise of creating a new community of their own. But first they had to beat the arterial. The task fell to the Puerto Rican–Chicano Committee, founded by students from the University of Buffalo and led by Francisco Perez and José Pizarro.

Pizarro was from New York City, one of the several dozen New Yorkers who had come to Buffalo in the late 1960s to study at UB. Pizarro was a student activist, organizing cultural and political events for the several hundred Hispanics attracted to the university by its variety of generous incentive programs. Pizarro liked Buffalo and, like many of the others, stayed. Housing was cheap, and though the city lacked the dynamism and vibrancy of New York's Puerto Rican community, life in Buffalo was easier and friendlier. Besides, for an educated Puerto Rican like Pizarro there was a future in Buffalo, particularly in politics and in community organizing, where the block grant program had created so many opportunities at the grassroots level.

Perez was born in the small town of Moca in Puerto Rico. He had come to Buffalo in 1953 when his father, a fruit picker, sent for him, his mother, and his brothers and sisters. By then his father was working at Bethlehem Steel and living on Niagara Street on the Lower West Side. Perez grew up there, graduating from Grover Cleveland High School, which was still mainly Italian. After two years at the University of Puerto Rico, Perez returned to the Lower West Side where, in 1971, he, Pizarro, and a few others formed the Puerto Rican–Chicano Co-ordinating Committee. Having seen how urban renewal on the waterfront had wrecked the Italian community there, Perez and Pizarro began to use their organization to fight the West Side Arterial. By the early 1970s, "far too much Puerto Rican concrete had been poured on Virginia Street," one veteran of the struggle remembers, "for anyone, including New York State, to jackhammer it out without a fight."

A whole community had been created on Virginia Street. Everything came together here. Group after grassroots group, politics heavily on their mind—the Puerto Rican–Chicano Coordinating Committee, Alianza, the Spanish Speaking Political Caucus, the Buffalo Hispanic Association—were all trying to deal with the problems of the Hispanic community. Father Antonio Rodriguez was pastor of Immaculate Conception Church. He was a small, suave Spaniard with a Madrieno lisp. "Father Rod" had worked first at St. Anthony's, the Italian church on Court Street. It was "a wonderful Italian neighborhood," he remembers. It was there that Rodriquez came to see the American immigrant experience with his own eyes. He couldn't understand the American emphasis on the melting pot and remembers how shocked he was when his superior at St. Anthony's told him angrily never to address a parishioner in his native Spanish. Rodriquez was convinced that the real purpose of urban renewal was to purposefully break up the city's ethnic enclaves.

Nearby, Father David Gallivan had pressured his superiors at Holy Cross, the old "Italian church" on Niagara and Maryland to hold Spanish services. "Father Dave" had been a missionary in Peru and his perfect Spanish, combined with his South Buffalo Irishman's political instinct, made him an excellent mediator between his Italian and Spanish parishioners. Alternatingly hosting Italian and Spanish saint's days, Holy Cross, like Immaculate Conception, anchored the Puerto Rican community on the Lower West Side. By the early 1970s, the Virginia Street Festival, with its parade, its ragtag tumble of booths, homegrown salsa, and *son* bands, its profusion of Mexican and Puerto Rican delicacies, and its real air of "Dancin' in the Streets," had become an institution. The neighborhood bodegas, shabby as they might look to outsiders, were a real step in creating community strength and self-confidence. They were community-owned sources of plantains, mangos, aguacate, Cafe Bustelo, and bright green, potent-smelling olive oil, and the people readily accepted higher prices to pay the overhead required to keep the stores in business.

The community had only just begun to acquire political power. The bulk of the Puerto Rican Lower West Side is a small and numerically insignificant part of the Ellicott District. The two blacks who have represented the district over the past twenty years have drawn their political strength from the black voters in the district's east side, while consistently ignoring its Puerto Ricans. Thus neglected, the Puerto Ricans developed their own grassroots community leadership—no one was more effective than Frankie Perez. Perez had lived on the Lower West Side since the early 1950s. He was educated, he told a reporter in 1976, at "the University of Virginia Street." Perez is articulate and widely read, gregarious and comfortable with people, energetic, and passionate about the role of organization and cohesiveness in the life of an ethnic community. "Without a sense of community in a city like Buffalo, you can't make it," he says. Perez grew up on the West Side. He remembers watching *West Side Story* at the Allendale Theater on Allen Street in the adjacent Allentown neighborhood, and dancing all the way home, feeling proud to be Puerto Rican. He went to old School 73 on Seventh Street, torn down as part of the Shoreline renewal project. He remembers the principal who slapped him when she overheard him speaking Spanish to his little sister in the hallway. He remembers also the guidance counselor who steered him to McKinley Vocational School so he could learn carpentry, rather than to Grover Cleveland, the academic high school he eventually graduated from. After school Perez went to college in Puerto Rico, studying archaeology and the pre-Colombian culture of the indigenous Arawak and Taino Indians. There he acquired a sense of racial and ethnic pride hard to find on the streets of the Lower West Side. This pride, along with his acute, seemingly innate political skills, made Perez a powerful and extremely effective leader in his community.

By the mid-1970s Perez had become chairman of the four most important grassroots organizations on the Lower West Side: the Lower West Side Resource and Development Corporation, the Virginia Street Development Corporation, the Virginia Street Festival, and the Puerto Rican–Chicano Coordinating Committee. The leading power broker in the Puerto Rican community ("I was kind of like . . . the LaGuardia of the Lower West Side," he says, referring to the populist mayor of New York City in the 1930s and 1940s). Perez hadn't traveled much, but he had been to Chinatown and Little Italy in lower Manhattan and Bedford-Stuyvesant in Brooklyn, where he visited the comprehensive community renewal project started there by Robert Kennedy during his short tenure as a U.S. senator. Perez was particularly taken by Chinatown and Little Italy, impressed at how ethnic minorities had created dynamic communities. He returned to Buffalo's Lower West Side, eager to replicate what he had seen. But first he would have to kill the proposed West Side Arterial.

By 1974 the Puerto Rican community had strong allies in its fight against the arterial. Both of the councilmembers from the affected areas had joined the fight, as had the powerful Allentown Association, which sensed that its efforts to preserve and revitalize the Allentown community were severely threatened by the arterial. The new mayor, Stanley Makowski, who had succeeded Sedita that year, was also opposed to the arterial. In a letter to the state DOT he wrote, "We should come down to earth, recognize reality, and end the agony which has been caused in the community." The DOT was concerned that it might be held legally responsible for the decaying conditions in the neighborhood as a result of its planning of the arterial, and it too began having second thoughts about the project.

By now both newspapers had changed their minds and in several editorials throughout the spring and summer of 1974 they urged the Common Council to go on record against the arterial. The U.S. Environmental Protection Agency, reviewing the DOT's environmental impact statement for the arterial, strongly condemned it. The agency said the arterial would create more rather than less congestion and would encourage urban sprawl and lead to wasteful and inefficient use of energy and land. Urging the city to forget the arterial and turn instead to public transportation, the EPA concluded, "We believe that the only proposal which would make possible the survival of the city . . . is one which emphasizes alternatives to the automobile."

Still, the Buffalo Common Council refused to act. The DOT was becoming impatient. Now that planning for the Main Street line of the rapid transit system was well along, the DOT was eager to end talk about the West Side Arterial once and for all. DOT Commissioner Raymond Shuler, committed to the new rapid transit line, added his influence, and finally, on October 1, 1975, the Common Council acted, requesting that the state withdraw its plans for the West Side Arterial. On January 12, 1976, the State Assembly unanimously approved a measure introduced by Buffalo Assemblyman William B. Hoyt that would remove the arterial from state highway law.

Frankie Perez threw a party at PRCC headquarters on Virginia Street. Now, finally, he was free to pursue his plans for the revitalization of the area. The neighborhood had defeated the Lower West Side Arterial and now the community at least had a chance.

4

ALL AROUND TOWN

What happened to the cities of the United States during the 1970s was a tragedy—hard times for even the big and glamorous cities, places like New York and Boston, harder still for the dark and dirty industrial cities of the Midwest, for Cleveland and Pittsburgh, Youngstown and Buffalo. With their industries eroded by foreign competition and undermined by disinvestment and poor management, these once-great cities of the "Rust Belt" stared at a gloomy and uncertain future. Their tax bases shrank, their expenses soared, and services everywhere were diminished or dismantled. People left by the thousands. While Buffalo's population had been dropping since the end of World War II, the loss during the 1970s were staggering and unprecedented. Buffalo's population dropped from 462,768 in 1970 to 357,000 in 1980, a decline of almost 23 percent. Between 1970 and 1980, the white population fell by 30 percent. While some of this decline was caused by lower birth rates, many people were leaving, going south to the "Sunbelt" and to the suburbs, which grew at phenomenal rates during the 1970s.

The suburbs drained not only the population of the city's neighborhoods, but its commercial base as well. Seneca Street in Irish South Buffalo, Broadway and Fillmore Avenues on the Polish East Side, Grant and West Ferry Streets on the Italian West Side, Hertel Avenue in Jewish North Buffalo, once-thriving shopping areas all, had become rundown and ghostlike as aging, frightened merchants struggled to stay in business. To many it seemed that the area was on its last legs. The problems in the neighborhoods were great. In some, such as Parkside, Linwood-Oxford, and Fillmore-Leroy, they were caused by racial change. In others, like South Buffalo, they were caused by economic upheaval. In all of them the threat to survival was serious and real.

Blessed Trinity Roman Catholic Church, located just east of Main on Leroy Avenue, is one of the most breathtakingly beautiful churches in all of Buffalo. According to *Buffalo Architectural Guide,* published in 1981, the church is an "extraordinary re-creation of North Italian church architecture." The church was built in the 1920s and designed by a local architect named Chester Oakley. Surrounded by the small, wood-frame singles and doubles that fill the streets of the Fillmore-Leroy neighborhood, Blessed Trinity is set serenely back from the curb. According to a 1940s essay written for the Buffalo Historical Society, "The Architecture of Some Buffalo Churches," the church is "true Lombardic in style, following the Italian conception . . . resembling the beautiful church of San Teodora in Pavia, Italy." Blessed Trinity's façade, an intricate weave of glazed terra cotta and brick, is particularly striking. "The bricks were shipped from Exeter, New Hampshire, where they were made by a colony of French workmen, who use the same antiquated tools and methods that were used centuries ago by French artisans. They are a reddish brownish, antique in appearance, irregular in shape, and when the edifice is first approached, the thought occurs that the bricks appear as though they had been set in place by the parishioners, one by one, as they filed by. . . . The display of symbolism is said to exceed anything in the world."

Walter Kerns, the priest at Blessed Trinity, is particularly proud of the architecture of his church and was instrumental in seeing to its 1985 designation as a National Historic Landmark. Kerns came to Blessed Trinity in 1974, a time when Fillmore-Leroy was in a state of cataclysmic change. He had just completed a twelve-year tour of duty as a parish priest in Clarence, a suburb ten miles east of Buffalo. Born and raised in Lockport, an old canal town north of the city, Kerns was comfortable in Clarence and he liked it. Clarence's history as a farm community and as a stop-over on the overland route between New York City and the West antedates the War of 1812. Even now, overrun by relentless tides of suburbanization that have brought a gargantuan mall and numerous tract developments, "the Village," as its residents persist in calling it, still bears a distinct resemblance to the small, New England-style town it once was.

Needless to say, there are few African-Americans in Clarence. In 1966, Kerns remembers, a black doctor moved into a house on one of the streets in one of the many new and fancy "planned unit developments," the kind where pretentious, chateaux-style homes are artfully placed on quiet cul-de-sacs. Within days, Kerns says, the man was presented with a petition urging him to leave.

Kerns immediately began a petition drive of his own, an "Open Housing" petition that committed its signatories to sell or rent to anyone, regardless of race, color, or creed. Six percent of the people of Clarence signed. It was a meagre number, Kerns acknowledges, but still, he says, a greater proportion than would have signed in any of Buffalo's other suburban communities. Kerns grew tired of Clarence and its haughty distance from the problems of the city, and sick of the racism he sensed in so many of its residents. In 1974, after the death of a priest who'd been there for over forty years, Kerns applied for the position at Blessed Trinity.

Fillmore-Leroy, on the northeast side of Buffalo, is worlds apart from Clarence. Developed as a streetcar suburb early in the century, Fillmore-Leroy, like other adjacent neighborhoods—Genessee-Moselle and Walden-Bailey—was settled originally by first- and second-generation Germans and, to a lesser extent, Polish and Italian families moving away from the old East Side. By the time Kerns got to Fillmore-Leroy, however, the original parishioners were dying and their children were leaving. Blessed Trinity, like the other Catholic churches in the neighborhood— St. Bartholomew's on Grider Street and St. Matthew's on Wyoming Avenue—was on its last legs. Throughout most of the 1950s its membership had held steady at sixteen hundred families. But by the mid-1960s the parish began to hemorrhage. Between 1964 and 1968 four hundred families left the parish. By 1974 two hundred more had gone.

Following the same route out of the inner city the Germans had taken before them, blacks were now pushing into Fillmore-Leroy. As they did, the old residents of the neighborhood left. Many simply ran, frightened by the riots of 1967 and the sudden changes taking place. A mere 5 percent of the neighborhood population in 1960, blacks made up 20 percent of it ten years later. Some whites left because of the Kensington Expressway, whose prolonged, seemingly endless construction had disrupted the neighborhood for years. Many left because they were panicked into selling by block-busting realtors, both black and white.

Kerns sensed the panic immediately. When he came to the neighborhood in 1974, 110 of the nearly 500 parishioners in Blessed Trinity had their homes on the market. It didn't take much to frighten white homeowners in those days, urging them to sell quickly, before it was too late, to take whatever price they could get before the neighborhood changed completely and their homes were worth even less. Nor was it much of a trick to run around and sell the same house at a vastly higher price to incoming blacks. After all, they were told, Fillmore-Leroy is a fine, integrated neighborhood, a great improvement over the all-black neighborhoods of the old East Side. Its wooden homes, mostly two-family, were well-preserved and well-maintained, in move-in condition, particularly since people were abandoning the area so quickly. What's more, the neighborhood was well-situated, close to the Chevrolet plant on Delavan Avenue were many African-American men worked, and to the Meyer Memorial Hospital, the workplace of a great many African-American women. The block-busting was working only too well and Kerns was appalled by the change.

A month after he arrived in Fillmore-Leroy, hoping to bring some kind of stability to his parish, Kerns met with the district's councilman, William Price.

Born and raised in the University District in the northeast part of Buffalo, Price went to School 82 on Easton Street, Bennett High School, and the University of Buffalo, graduating in 1968. He then moved to New York City and enrolled in Columbia Law School. Price was stimulated and inspired by the people he met in New York. As a summer intern in the office of Mayor John Lindsay, Price met some of the country's most talented people in "the urban biz." It was from them, he says, that he learned what New York City teaches best: "guile" and "chutzpah." Lindsay had the best administrators in the nation, able to quickly cut through the horrific New York City bureaucracy. Assigned to work with community groups in neighborhoods throughout the city, Price was exposed to neighborhood community leaders whose names he still remembers easily, fifteen years later, people from Sheepshead Bay and Brownsville, Harlem and the South Bronx, leaders who knew how to fight for their neighborhoods. Price says his education was completed as a volunteer in the 1968 and 1972 campaigns to elect Allard Lowenstein to Congress. Working with the "best political operatives in the country," Price learned how to organize and mobilize a community's energy and support.

Price learned his lessons well. Following a stint in the Marines he returned to Buffalo and in 1974 ran for councilman from the University District. Elected by an enormous margin, he set to community organizing immediately, using federal funds from the Community Development Act of 1974. With the enthusiastic support of Walter Kerns, Price formed the Fillmore-Leroy Community Development Corporation, known as FLARE. Together they identified leaders of existing community groups—the PTA at School 61, the Fillmore–Central Park Businessmen's Association, the Kensington–Leroy Community Association, and the Jewett Avenue Block Club. By the end of 1975 a community development corporation with a board of directors of ten blacks and ten whites was formed. Price understood the workings of the block grant program better than any of the other councilman and it was he that some of the others—Higgins from South Buffalo, Masiello from North Buffalo—called on for help in channeling funds to their neighborhoods.

Things improved dramatically in 1977. President Carter was eager to help stabilize the transitional neighborhoods in the cities of the Northeast and there was plenty of money for those who knew how to get it. This was even more true following the passage of the Comprehensive Emergency Training Act in 1977.

To a city on the brink of economic and fiscal disaster, the CETA bill was a gift from God. As municipal public revenues shrank and cities were forced to lay off police and firemen, elevator operators and librarians, technocrats and bureaucrats, CETA funds became available to hire them back, keeping some people on their old jobs, hiring others for new ones, waiting for the economic and fiscal crisis of the 1970s to pass. Everyone, it seemed, was on a CETA budget line. Coming on top of block grant funds, CETA money was a boon for neighborhood and community groups. Many of them used the money to hire housing inspectors and building-code enforcers. In a thirty-thousand-square-foot building leased from the diocese, FLARE ran a senior citizens center and a youth services program and employed seven people full time as housing counselor, older adult coordinator, program director, recreation director, public-relations director, block manager, and maintenance man. All were on CETA lines. No one got money like Councilman Price. He secured $60,000 from the state for housing rehabilitation and $90,000 in block grant money to establish a high-risk loan program for home improvements for nonbankable residents. In 1979, Price's last year as councilman, FLARE received $476,000 in block grant money to implement what was called a "Neighborhood Strategy Area Program," a balanced approach to the problems of residential blight and commercial improvement.

Integrated neighborhoods have never lasted long in American cities. They are usually more transitional than integrated, white neighborhoods in the process of becoming black neighborhoods. Only when white mobility has been temporarily interrupted—during the Depression and then during World War II, for instance—has there been any significant neighborhood integration. And even then the ghetto has always remainded. It happened in the late 1940s and early 1950s on Buffalo's East Side, in the mid-1950s around Humboldt Park, and it was happening again in Bill Price's University District. Working through FLARE, Price tried to reverse the seemingly irreversible changes, to undo local bank policies that denied loans to people in the district, to stop the scare tactics of real estate brokers who profited from the panic selling they encouraged among the area's white homeowners, to stop the city's Municipal Housing Authority from steering blacks into the neighborhood's public housing project, and to preserve the community's schools as truly integrated learning environments.

Price and Kerns knew that nothing frightened whites more than the "tipping" of neighborhood schools. Whites would tolerate blacks in their schools as long as they were in the minority. They could tolerate 25 percent, 30 percent, even 35 percent minority enrollment. But once it went past a third or so, whites fled. In some cases the transition occurred frighteningly quickly. School 23 on East Delevan Avenue, around the corner from Kerns's Blessed Trinity, was 85 percent white in 1966. Ten years later all of its seven hundred students were black. School 82, Price's old neighborhood school on Easton Street was nearly all white in 1966, but its proximity to the Kenfield-Langfield low-income housing projects killed it. As the Buffalo Municipal Housing Authority concentrated blacks in that project during the late 1960s and early 1970s, the school changed too. The same was true of Kensington High, an all-white neighborhood high school in the University District. Because of the projects, it too became increasingly black, and the whites left. For a short time in the mid-1970s Kensington High was racially balanced, divided equaly between blacks and whites. By the end of the decade, however, only 30 percent of the nearly one thousand pupils there were white.

In the middle of the 1970s Price believed there was a long-shot possibility of maintaining a racial balance in the schools in his district. So, with the same intensity he and Kerns had devoted to trying to stabilize the streets of the community, Price now tried to stabilize its schools. The people who were leaving the neighborhood in the mid-1970s were part of "a second-stage exodus," not racists, Price insisted, but rather people who had lost confidence in their neighborhood. What these people wanted, Price thought, was not segregation but rather racial balance. If that could be assured, he was convinced, whites would stay. It would not be a simple task. Not only was the housing authority dumping blacks into the Kenfield-Langfield projects (4 percent black in 1960, 57 percent in 1975), but the Board of Education, through what it called the QIE program, was busing a disproportionate number of black children into the University District's schools. After all, the Board must have reasoned, there were already blacks in the University District. Surely adding a few more to the schools and to the low-income housing project there would be much simpler than introducing blacks to South Buffalo, Black Rock, Riverside, and other all-white neighborhoods of the city.

It was a tide Price tried valiantly to stem and again he turned to the residents of the neighborhood, the parents, teachers, and principals in the district's schools. Arguing that transitional neighborhoods are particularly sensitive, with special needs requiring special treatment, Price in 1976 developed an alternative plan. He was optimistic about getting a favorable hearing for it. The Board of Education was changing dramatically that year, under the leadership of a new superintendent, guided by the policies of newly elected members, and under the jurisdiction of U.S. District Judge John T. Curtin. After months of community meetings throughout 1975 and 1976, Price hammered out an agreement within his district—the parents of children in School 83, an all-white school in the northernmost section of his district, and the parents of children in School 23, the virtually all-black school on Delevan Avenue, agreed to be paired with one another. The Northeast Alternative, as the community called the plan, was a democratically arrived-at strategy to deal with one of the most volatile and complicated issues of the day.

There was more. As part of its initial plans to comply with Judge Curtin's ruling of April 30, 1976, the Board of Education planned to close ten of the city's most racially isolated schools. Slated for closing was School 85, near Bailey Avenue in a predominantly white enclave of Price's district. Price objected passionately to school closings, arguing that it was a form of "neighborhood disinvestment."

"To base a school-closing decision on economics is no more justifiable than a banker's decision to redline the area," he said, particularly in a transitional neighborhood. If it could not be used as a school, School 85 should serve the community. The Northeast Alternative proposed that it be converted into an "Integration Resources Center," where children, parents, and teachers throughout the University District would spend at least a week every year learning about "human relations." The goal of the center was to "foster a better community understanding of integration, its problems and benefits, and thereby become a public model of how well integration can function."

Price's argument was persuasive and Judge Curtin allowed him to enter the school desegregation case as an intervenor. Here, as always, Price argued relentlessly for citizen participation and in the process advanced a vision of urban participatory democracy whose message was not lost on the people of Buffalo. "Our parents must be presented with a clean slate, with a process that is not tainted by decisions accomplished prior to a full presentation of available alternatives. We cannot trade their freedom to opt out of the planning process. If we did, we would lose the trust which is the key to sustained success," Price said.

The Board of Education opposed the Northeast Alternative. So did Judge Curtin, notwithstanding his sympathetic ear. Price philosophically accepted their verdict, understanding that it would have set too dangerous a precedent, leading to the fragmentation and decentralization of the city's school system at a time when, given Curtin's desegration orders, it could least afford it. Price no longer believes that the plan would have worked anyway. Perhaps the rate of racial change was too strong, the pace too swift for even the most enlightened public policy to alter. Given the numbers, the odds were certainly overwhelming. In 1970, 4,620 white people lived in the Genesee–Moselle–Meyer Memorial Hospital area. Ten years later there were 707. More than 4,000 of 7,600 whites moved out of the Kenfield and Langfield neighborhoods, 3,000 out of the Kensington section, and 3,000 more out of Fillmore–Leroy. The efforts of Price, FLARE, and the parent and teacher groups who created the Northeast Alternative could do little to stem the tide. By 1980 Fillmore–Leroy had become an almost completely African–American neighborhood. The parish churches, St. Bartholomew's on Grider, St. Matthew's on Wyoming, and Father Kerns's magnificent Blessed Trinity on Leroy, were increasingly empty, lonely reminders of the vital role they had played in these once active and dynamic communities. As the old families moved out and no new ones moved in, the number of Catholic children in the neighborhood dropped and soon the diocese closed their schools: Blessed Trinity's became the site of FLARE's Head Start program, St. Bartholomew's now houses the African–American Family Center, and the imposing, classical structure that housed the parish school of St. Matthew's for more than sixty years is now boarded up. Only a few stragglers remained, isolated, frightened and alone in a neighborhood that was no longer theirs. By the early 1980s, close to 20 percent of the people in Fillmore–Leroy lived below the poverty level and 30 percent were unemployed. Fillmore–Leroy was struggling to stay alive.

In 1979, with a year left of his third term as councilman, Bill Price left Buffalo too. (He returned in 1981 and today practices law in the city.) Price went to Washington to serve as a member of President Carter's National Commission on Neighborhoods. Father Kerns stayed behind. He still works in Blessed Trinity, helping his changed community to survive.

Though just across Main Street, the Parkside neighborhood was different. This is because Main Street is more than just a street. Indeed, it is more like a vast canyon, a kind of no man's land that for years had separated the East Side from the rest of Buffalo. Since the late nineteenth century, when the East Side was where the immigrants lived, Main Street had been the great divide, keeping first the immigrants and then the blacks in their part of town. Main Street was also one of the only places in Buffalo that blacks and whites met, in the clubs and restaurants that lined it: at the snazzy Town Casino, where they went to hear Mel Tormé, Sammy Davis Jr., Nat King Cole, and the other jazz greats of the 1950s; at the Zanzibar Lounge for rock 'n' roll; at the Anchor Bar, an Italian restaurant owned by Frank and Teresa Bellissimo, to hear jazz and eat chicken wings, a spicy blend of Italian and African-American food traditions that by the mid-1980s had turned "Buffalo wings" into a national food craze.

They met in Parkside, too, where middle-class African-Americans had been living in small numbers since the early 1950s. Throughout most of the nineteenth century Parkside had been farmland and some of the streets—Jewett Parkway, Russell Avenue, and Elam Place—are named for the families who lived in large, expansive farmhouses here. One such house, known as "Willowlawn," was owned by a businessman named Elam R. Jewett. Located on a section of Main Street that is still lined with early-twentieth-century homes adapted over the years to business and commercial uses, Jewett's mansion was surrounded by 450 acres of land stretching from Main Street to Delaware Park. Still standing a block up Main is one of the area's old farm homesteads, built by a man named Washington Russell in 1841. Like many of the old homes on this section of Main Street, it has been converted, and now it houses the McKendry-Dengler Funeral Home. Built on a slight elevation well before the other homes in the neighborhood, the view of Delaware Park from the kitchen must have been stunning.

It was the construction of Delaware Park, laid out and designed by Fredrick Law Olmsted in the late 1860s, that led to the development of the Parkside area as a popular residential neighborhood. Olmsted's park design for Buffalo was unique, a whole system that, unlike any he had previously designed, linked the whole city, coursing through it from Cazenovia Park in the south of Buffalo to Delaware Park in the north. Delaware Park was particularly beautiful, with a man-made lake and 120-acre meadow; Olmsted scholar Charles Beveridge says that it is still "one of Olmstead's finest open spaces." By the 1880s the land northeast of the park had been acquired by the Parkside Land Improvement Company, a large development firm, which hired Olmsted, the great designer of public spaces, to lay out and design the streets for its private development. Consciously seeking to create an alternative to the formal, rigorous, dense gridiron pattern that characterized the streets south of Delaware Park, Olmsted opted for a sweeping, curvilinear street pattern that soon became standard for suburban developments in cities throughout the country. Thus, just as Buffalo was becoming more industrialized, more ethnic, and more urban, Olmsted was creating in the northern reaches of the city a refuge for the city's middle classes that was removed from the new realities of the industrial downtown.

People liked Parkside's gently curving streets and its spectacular views of Olmsted's meadow. By the early twentieth century the area was eagerly sought out by young businessmen, entrepreneurs, and professionals. One of them was Darwin D. Martin, a dynamic executive with the Larkin Company and the inventor of a card-file system that revolutionized accounting. Martin commissioned Frank Lloyd Wright to design his home on Jewett Parkway. With a virtually unlimited budget, the "Darwin D. Martin House," as it is known on the National Register of Historic Places, is the largest and one of the finest Wright homes built in his stunning "Prairie Style." At Martin's urging, Wright was hired by the Larkin Company to design its administrative building, an internationally recognized masterpiece now lost to the wrecking ball.

Although beautiful and new, Parkside was never an exclusive neighborhood, but rather a place where a variety of middle-class people lived. Because of its proximity to Main Street, where both the University of Buffalo and Canisius College were located, Parkside always attracted teachers and academics who, like everyone else here, liked the large, reasonably priced turn-of-the century homes. Parkside also attracted upwardly mobile second- and third-generation ethnics, particularly Irish-Americans. It was here, in St. Mark's Parish on Woodward Avenue, amidst the Presbyterians of Central Presbyterian Church and the Episcopalians of the Episcopal Church of the Good Shepard, that Buffalo's most successful, most assimilated Irish-Americans had by the mid-twentieth century made their home.

One of them was Richard F. Griffin, born and raised in Parkside and graduated from St. Mark's before attending Canisius High School and Canisius College. Following his graduation from the law school at the University of Buffalo, Griffin became an associate at one of the city's largest and most prestigious law firms. On his own time he did legal work for the Buffalo chapter of the NAACP, advising them on segregation in the city's public schools. Jack C. Anthony, a school teacher in the Buffalo public schools, lived down the street. Griffin and Anthony knew each other from the neighborhood and from the neighborhood elementary school, School 54, at Main and Woodward. Like others in Parkside, they had become concerned about the school's changing racial balance. By the early 1960s, as the number of African-Americans in the Fillmore-Leroy area just across Main Street grew, so too did their presence at School 54. As it did, rumors spread by realtors—poisonous, insidious, racist rumors that have undermined the health and stability of neighborhoods throughout urban America—began to be heard throughout the Parkside community. It was time, the rumors were saying, to sell, now, before it was too late.

Appalled at the prospect of block-busting in their cherished community, Griffin and Anthony formed the Parkside Community Association in the summer of 1963. Dedicated to the "maintenance and stability of the Parkside community," the association hoped to defeat block-busting and to preserve Parkside as an integrated community. Sensing the importance to the community of the neighborhood public school, the PCA focused on School 54. The organization dedicated itself to improving the school, thereby creating an incentive for people to stay in the neighborhood, maintaining its racial balance. Furthermore, the members of the PCA realized that racial balance could be maintained at their neighborhood school only if there was racial balance in all of the city's schools. The Parkside Community Association announced its support for a general plan for the integration of the Buffalo public schools. The PCA's goal was not, as some African-Americans suggested, to keep blacks out of the neighborhood, but rather to prevent the panicked flight of whites that was undermining neighborhoods throughout the city.

The people of Parkside were receptive to the messge and soon Griffin and Anthony had signed up more than two hundred members. They were diligent in their marketing efforts, sponsoring extensive door-to-door campaigns and leaflet distributions. One leaflet asked, "Who needs suburbia? Stay in Parkside and enjoy the best of both worlds." Dozens of meetings were held, alternating among the three neighborhood churches.

Gradually the pair's efforts were rewarded. In the spring of 1967, several months before that summer's riots undermined the confidence of white people throughout the city, Matthew Duggan, the principal at School 54, announced that the state Eduction Department had awarded his school a $100,000 grant to "develop a superior program at the school to encourage families not to move out of the district."

Still, the neighborhood remained unstable. When Ruth and David Lampe moved to the neighborhood from Nebraska in 1970 they saw signs of decay all around them. Their house, bought at a Federal Housing Administration foreclosure, was a large Victorian on Crescent Avenue. A beautiful structure with magnificent oak woodwork throughout, the house was cheap, but like many on the street, badly run-down and in need of major repairs. By the mid-1970s, however, the Parkside Community Association had become the community group through which Federal Urban Renewal block grant funds were being funneled into the neighborhood. By the late 1970s, with Ruth Lampe as president, the PCA was spending hundreds of thousands of dollars on code inspection, painting, and repair programs. In the spring of 1981 the PCA published an historical and architectural tour of the neighborhood and neighborhood docents led weekly walking tours of Parkside throughout the summer. Parkside, for now anyway, seems to have survived the trauma that ruined so many other neighborhoods during the 1970s. The battle had been won against blight, against the absentee landlords and the block-busting real estate agents who caused it. The efforts of the Parkside Community Association had borne fruit. By the beginning of the 1980s the Parkside neighborhood became something of a model, where people knew about integration because they lived in a neighborhood that was integrated. Indeed, it was this neighborhood that so many of the principals of Buffalo's pivotal school desegregation case lived—Richard Griffin, the lawyer for the plaintiffs in the case; Frank Mesiah, Griffin's Crescent Avenue neighbor and founder of the civil rights group that initiated the suit; and Florence Baugh, from around the corner on Woodward Avenue, who, as president of the Board of Education, was for years one of the leaders in the struggle for integrated schools. Unique in the city of Buffalo, Parkside had a very special lesson to teach. So too did Buffalo's Polonia, a different kind of neighborhood in a different part of the city.

Far across Main Street, at the intersection of Broadway and Fillmore in the heart Buffalo's Polonia, changes of another sort were taking place. By the late 1970s Buffalo's Polish community was more than a hundred years old, and like similar neighborhoods in Detroit, Pittsburgh, and

Chicago, it was a skeletal remnant of what it once had been, struggling to survive. While most people were abandoning the neighborhood in droves, moving east out Broadway to the Polish suburbs of Cheektowaga and Depew, Bill Falkowski had fallen in love with the place. He came to Buffalo in 1979 to earn a master's degree in American Studies at the University of Buffalo. He was raised in East Brunswick, New Jersey, and both his parents were first-generation Poles. His old neighborhood was a working-class community where the parish church was Irish and his best friend, Willie Long, was black. Falkowski took his Polishness for granted. His mother cooked kielbasa and listened to the Sunday evening Polish radio show. Falkowski was self-conscious about his Polish background once or twice, like when his high-school Protestant friends came over and declined to eat his mother's kielbasa, but most of the time his ethnicity was simply not an issue.

By the time he was a junior in high school, Falkowski and Long had both become vehemently opposed to the war in Vietnam. Together, the two young men pledged that they would apply for conscientious objector status. The boys began to organize student protests. After the shootings at Kent State in the spring of 1970, Falkowski and Long successfully convinced their principal to close their school in mourning.

Passed over by the draft, Falkowski spent the year between high school and college (he would be the first, and despite his forty-odd cousins remains the only, member of his family to graduate from college) as a volunteer working with children at a Puerto Rican community center in New Brunswick. Among the ethnically proud and somewhat separatist Puerto Ricans, Falkowski became interested for the first time in his own origins and ethnicity. The next summer, after his freshman year at Ryder College in Trenton, Falkowski again volunteered to work with Puerto Rican children, this time among migrant farm workers in southern New Jersey. The Puerto Ricans called the lanky blonde "Polako," and Falkowski was inspired by their deep attachment to their native island and language and the strength of their extended families. Suddenly Falkowski found himself exploring his own roots, for the first time seeking out his Polish-speaking grandmother in an effort to learn more about his past. In 1976 he went to Poland, spending six weeks at the Kosczieko Foundation in Krakow, where he studied the Polish language, history, and culture along with Polish-Americans from cities across the country. It was in Krakow that Falkowski discovered the Poland of his grandmother—not the Poland of the cities, not the writings of Miskiewicz nor the music of Chopin, but rather the Poland of the farm and the peasants. That was the Poland he had heard about growing up and that was the Poland he identified with. Falkowski went back to Poland the next year and traveled all over the country, eager to learn as much as he could about the Polish peasantry, his background.

In 1979 Falkowski came to Buffalo. He had heard about the Broadway-Fillmore neighborhood on the Polish East Side, and knew that it was one of the oldest and largest Polish-American communities in the country. Poles had been in Buffalo since the 1870s and by the early twentieth century they were far and away the largest immigrant group in the city. They settled on the East Side, near the railroads and factories, creating a large urban enclave with its center at the intersection of Broadway and Fillmore. After downtown, it was the largest and busiest commercial strip in Buffalo. On the ground floors of the blocks that lined Broadway were jewelers and bakeries, soda shops and beauty shops, clothing stores and cigar stores, candy stores, branch banks, and delicatessens. On the second and third floors were doctors, lawyers, dentists, and accountants. There were two- and three-story furniture and department stores, too: Neisner's, Zolte's, and Sattler's—the biggest store in the area by far, housed in a sleek Art Moderne building at 998 Broadway and known to every Buffalonian over forty as once the most wonderful place to shop in Buffalo, a special world of its own. Across the street was the Broadway Market, a cavernous structure owned by the city where butchers and bakers, produce merchants and candy manufacturers with long, hard-to-pronounce Polish names marketed their wares to the people of the neighborhood.

The neighborhood had begun to decline years before Falkowski got here in 1979. The decay started in the early 1960s. As African-Americans pushed further out Broadway, Poles who had been living near the long, broad boulevard for years now followed it out further east to Cheektowaga, a suburban transplant of the old Polish neighborhood. Lured by the spread of shopping malls and alienated by the growing black population, whites stopped coming to the area and soon Broadway-Fillmore's stores went out of business. Finally even Sattler's closed and in 1988 the gorgeous building was razed. Today the massive square block on Broadway between Gibson and Beck is strewn with rubble, a gaping hole waiting to be filled.

By the time Falkowski arrived on the East Side the landscape of Broadway up to Fillmore had become the landscape of the American black ghetto: men languished on street corners; solid old brick commercial buildings were boarded up; nineteenth-century churches, the names of their old German congregations carved in relief on their cornerstones, were crumbling; and everywhere there were hand-painted signs, many of them misspelled, advertising hand car washes, storefront churches, grocery stores, and bars.

However faded it became, from Fillmore Avenue to the city line the neighborhood remained distinctly Polish. Fillmore Avenue was named for the Buffalonian who, after his accidental presidency in the early 1850s, became the country's best-known advocate of immigration restriction. Nonetheless, the street was known for years as the "Polish Delaware Avenue." Designed by Fredrick Law Olmsted as an approach to Humboldt Park, Fillmore, like Olmsted's other Buffalo parkways, is a broad, richly landscaped avenue that for years was the home of the neighborhood's more affluent businesses and professionals. Since the mid-1950s, as Buffalo's African-Americans pushed east from the direction of downtown, Fillmore had been the tacit dividing line that separated the East Side's blacks and Poles. Into the late 1960s early 1970s the avenue managed to retain some of its gentility. But when Falkowski arrived in the late 1970s, even Fillmore Avenue had begun to change.

The intersection of Broadway and Fillmore, however, was still heavily Polish, still lined with Polish neighborhood institutions: the large, brick, turn-of-the-century, classically designed Unia Polski building, the St. Casimir Polski VFW Post, the Polish Cooperative Savings and Loan, and the Adam Mickiewicz Library and Dramatic Circle. Polish churches surrounded the neighborhood: Transfiguration on Sycamore Street, where the parish school's separate entrances are carved clearly in stone: *Dsiewczeta* for the girls, *Cholopcy* for the boys; Corpus Christi on Broadway; St. Adalbert's on Stanislaus Street; and St. Stanislaus, the "Mother Church of Polonia," the largest of them all, on Peckham Street.

The three greenish, tin-covered domes of St. Stanislaus, topped with crosses covered in gold leaf, can be seen throughout the neighborhood. Like a cathedral in a medieval town, St. Stan's emerges suddenly out of the fabric of the neighborhood, overpowering and dominating the wood-frame homes and shops that surround it. Built in the late nineteenth century, the church stands on what has become the border of the African-American and the Polish East Side. Peckham leads out from downtown and on most of its route it consists of run-down, ramshackle structures— decaying wooden cottages, several storefront churches, and a few tiny cafes, one called "Mrs. Tennessee Bar-b-que House." The side streets here—Smith, Coit, Townsend, and Detroit Streets—the heart of the original parish of St. Stanislaus, have become slums, and the homes, many owned by absentee landlords, are now occupied by families on welfare. The streets, like the homes, are decayed, strewn with garbage and the detritus of the urban slum. Then, at Peckham and Detroit, within sight of St. Stanislaus, the streetscape suddenly changes. On the right is Kazmierczak's Funeral Home, on the left the offices of War-dynski's, Buffalo's oldest and largest manufacturer of Polish sausage. The church itself is tall and proud, a monument to the faith of the first-generation Polish immigrants who built it.

Everything about the area, it seemed to Falkowski, was Polish, particularly the Broadway Market, the huge, public marketplace where, in dozens of stalls rented from the city, Polish merchants—butchers in blood-stained frocks, women in flower-patterned aprons—sold meat, sausage, baked goods, candy, and every household notion imaginable to the people in the neighborhood, many of them Poles, many of them blacks, and, increasingly after December 1981, many of them young Poles seeking refuge from martial law in Poland. To Bill Falkowski, recently back from Poland, politically radical and increasingly proud of his working-class, Polish-American heritage, Buffalo's Polonia was a romantic dream world. Walking around the neighborhood, where even the streets had Polish names—Sobieski, Stanislaus, Woltz, Kosciuszko, Paderewski—he felt that he had to live here. Falkowski rented a small wood-frame cottge behind an old two-family house on Krupp Street, and he knew he was going to like it.

For years Bufflao had been a great polka center with some of the best-known polka bands in the country. Polka was dying in the neigh-borhood, but there was still a handful of bands playing in the local bars. Most of them—the Dyna-Tones, the G-Notes, the Am-Pol Tones and the Buffalo Brass—played at Henry Mazurek's Broadway Grill. Every afternoon people from the neighborhood came to dance. The Grill was celebrated in a song recorded by the Dyna-Tones called "Down at the Friendly Tavern":

> *Music is playing*
> *Dancers are swaying,*
> *Happiness in the air*
> *Down at the friendly tavern,*
> *Everyone's happy there.*
> *Lights are all twinkling*
> *Glasses are tinkling*
> *Romance is in the air*
> *Down at the friendly tavern*
> *Nothing else can compare.*

That's where we'll find the cheer
Meet the friends we hold so dear
Round up the polka band
And sing a song together.

Time to get started,
Gay and light hearted,
No need to ask us where,
Down at the friendly tavern
Everyone's happy there.

If for the people in the neighborhood polka dancing was fun, for the class- and ethnicity-conscious Falkowski and his mentor at the university, an ethnomusicologist named Charlie Keil, dancing the polka was a "historio-cultural process . . . [that] unites generations in a living celebration of ethnicity." Keil had been studying the polka as a cultural expression since the mid-1970s and viewed it as an "ethnic working class phenomenon," an expression of Polish working class culture that, like the people themselves, had been suppressed by the Polish middle class. Falkowski and Keil called them *shlakta,* the Polish term for landed gentry, and interpreted their marked disdain for the polka as a desperate desire to gain social respectability by assimilating into mainstream American culture. The *shlakta* preferred to consider only the refined polonaise as legitimate Polish music. Falkowski and Keil preferred the polka because it was performed in neighborhood bars and community centers and was a cheap, popular art form free of the pretense they felt typified the Polish-American middle class.

Hoping to use the polka as a building block of community identity, Falkowski applied for and received a grant from the New York State Council on the Humanities for a historical investigation of the polka. He called it the "Polka Project." Intent on teaching the people of the community that the polka, like jazz or blues for African-Americans, was a "living celebration of ethnicity," Falkowski proposed a program for the spring of 1980 that combined lectures, polka lessons, and, as a finale, a huge community-wide polka party.

Initially there was some resistance to Falkowski's proposal by the Council on the Humanities. It was too performance-oriented, some members said, not scholarly enough. The topic of investigation, some said, did not have a "traditional historical theme," and the methods employed were not "traditional methodologies." Besides, the site Falkowski had selected for the lectures—Mazurek's Broadway Grill—was hardly the kind of "public history agency" the council usually required for this kind of proposal. The populists on the council prevailed, however, and Falkowski's project was approved. First came four Sunday afteroon lectures—"The Polka in World Perspective," "The Polka in America," "Polka History 101," and "The Polka in Buffalo: the Twenties and Thirties." Then the project staged its public polka demonstrations. Finally the Polka Project held its culminating dance. It was advertised throughout the community for weeks, and on May 18, 1980, three hundred people came to listen and to dance to the music of Marion Lush and his White Eagles, the New Yorkers, and the famous Krew Brothers. Writing about the Polka Project later, an examiner from the council said it was "the most unusual, innovative proposal and one of the most successful projects" in the history of the organization.

The project tied Falkowski more closely to his adopted neighborhood. Three years later he and his wife, Justyna, a Solidarity refugee from Krakow, bought a house on Gibson Street, around the corner from Transfiguration Church, across the street from the Kazimerek Senior Citizens Center, down the block from the Broadway Market. They thought they were there to stay.

South Buffalo was a different kind of neighborhood. Separated from the city by the meandering, moat-like Cazenovia Creek that few people from other areas of Buffalo ever crossed, South Buffalo developed as (and remains) a distinct community. While so many of Buffalo's neighborhoods began to unravel in the 1960s, overcome by the combined forces of urban renewal and racial transition, South Buffalo—mostly Irish, mostly Catholic, mostly working class—remained strong and virtually unchanged, seemingly invulnerable to the larger forces undermining neighborhoods throughout the city. With solid parish churches and schools, and neither urban renewal nor black migration to worry about (while blacks had worked at nearby Republic Steel for years, rarely if ever did they venture to settle in the area), South Buffalo remained safe, secure, and nourishing. There were jobs too, good ones and a lot of them, in the factories, at Bethlehem Steel and Republic, at the grain elevators that lined the Buffalo River, in City Hall, and in the police and fire departments, where Buffalo's Irish, like their compatriots in other cities, dominated. By the mid-1970s, however, the national decline of heavy industry shook the foundations of South Buffalo. The grain elevators and the steel mills were closing and local commercial strips—South Park Avenue, Seneca Street, and Abbott Road—were battered by the construction of shopping malls in adjacent suburbs. By the late

1970s South Buffalo's population began to drop, its Catholic schools began to close, and its public schools had come under a court order issued by one of their own, U.S. District Judge John T. Curtin, to desegregate. The people of South Buffalo began to wonder if their neighborhood could survive.

The Skyway is a high, arching "City of Tomorrow"–like elevated highway right out of the 1939 World's Fair. Built by New York State in the late 1950s to connect Buffalo with the rapidly growing suburban "South Towns," the Skyway is also the best and fastest way to get to South Buffalo—unless it is winter. Located at the eastern end of Lake Erie, where the gathering forces of wind and snow have their heaviest and most dramatic impact, in the winter the Skyway, rising high above the lakefront, is windswept, icy, and treacherous, closed as often as not. For this reason, the Skyway is another one of those projects the people of Buffalo argue about: it should never have been built, say some; it should have been underground, say others; it should at least have been built at grade level, say still others.

But for those who don't have to worry about using it everyday the Skyway is one of the most exciting and dramatic routes in Buffalo, a thrilling roller-coaster ride with breathtaking views of all that has made Buffalo great. On one side is Lake Erie, sparkling and bright on sunny days, the Canadian shore sharp and clear in the background. The lake's winter skies change rapidly. Sometimes they are just a ponderous, heavy, battleship kind of grey. More often they are fluid, with great marble-like swirls in multiple shadows of grey whirling through the sky. Such skies can be suddenly penetrated by piercing shafts of sunlight. More common is the appearance of "lake-effect snow." Created when the irrepressible, cold Canadian winds encounter the warmer temperatures of the lake, "lake-effect snow" is an almost daily phenomenon during Buffalo's long, hard winters.

On the other side of the Skyway is a fascinating and unique bird's-eye view of the grain elevators that for years were the lifeblood of Buffalo's economy. Massive, yet still elegant, some are abandoned, some are still being fed by the long shafts that join them to hulking grain freighters of the Great Lakes. Sprinkled throughout this landscape are truckyards and railroad depots filled with freight cars and locomotives. Just a few miles south of the Skyway is another glimpse into Buffalo's industrial past—the hulking remains of Bethlehem Steel's Lackawanna plant. Although the bar mill is busier than ever, the bulk of the plant, endless rows of soot-encrusted, reddish-brown buildings that housed one of the largest steel plants in the world, is being demolished. Seen from the

Skyway, the site is littered with tons of rubble, a silent, eerie, haunted industrial landscape.

But the Skyway is not the only, nor, some would argue, even the most interesting way to get to South Buffalo. Another is through the streets of the city, by way of what people in the area call the "old First Ward," or even just "the Ward." It is the original Irish district in Buffalo. At St. Brigid's Catholic School in the Ward one of the students forty-five years ago was "Jimmy" Griffin, Buffalo's quintessential "fightin' Irish" politician and the city's mayor of thirteen years and counting.

The area is one of the oldest neighborhoods in Buffalo. Settled by Irish immigrants in the 1840s and 1850s, it still contains all of the visible landmarks of its early history as a nineteenth-century, working-class Irish neighborhood. The Irish settled the area because it was close to the terminus of the Erie Canal and to the grain elevators that still tower over the one- and two-family wood-frame homes that fill the neighborhood's tiny, quiet, tree-lined streets. Their names—Vandalia, Indiana, Illinois, Ohio—refer to the great American grain belt in the Midwest, reflecting its importance to the history of this community. Only one street—O'Connell—suggests anything Irish. To visit the ward is to make a wonderful journey into the city's nineteenth-century commercial roots, past the great grain elevators that the author Rayner Banham, in his book *The Concrete Atlantis,* said represented "the triumph of what is American in American building art." These grain elevators were landmarks in the development of modern architecture, significant influences on such great twentieth-century European architects as Le Corbusier, Walter Gropius, and Walter Mendelsohn. Writing to his wife in Berlin following a 1924 visit to the Ohio Street grain elevators, Mendelsohn wrote,

> Mountainous silos, incredibly space-conscious, but creating space. A random confusion amidst the chaos of loading and unloading of corn ships, of railways and bridges, crane monster with live gestures, hordes of silo cells in concrete, stone, and glazed brick. Then suddenly a silo with administrative buildings, closed horizontal fronts against the stupendous verticals of fifty to one hundred cylinders, and all this in the sharp evening light. I took photographs like mad. Everything else, so far now, seemed to have been shaped interim to my silo dreams. Everything else was merely a beginning.

The men who worked the elevators still can be found all over the neighborhood, in nicer weather sitting on their front porches, taking walks around the ninety-year-old brownstone parish church, Our Lady of Perpetual Help on O'Connell Street—"Pet's" to the locals—or simply hanging out in the tiny Grain Scooper's union hall, a hundred-year-old wood-frame building on Louisiana Street, or at Gene McCarthy's tavern, as Irish an Irish bar as there ever was. A county map of Ireland hangs on the back-room wall at McCarthy's, and the view from the window—railroad tracks, empty grain elevators, and the shimmering waters of Lake Erie—is a glance into the past. The bar is a meeting place for generations of Irish-Americans, a place where politicians and lawyers, businessmen and retired scoopers meet to eat, talk, and reminisce.

The Ward, within a stone's throw of the Erie Canal's outlet to the lake, had been home to Buffalo's Irish since the mid-nineteenth century. Work was plentiful in the factories, on the docks, and in the grain elevators that lined the waterfront by the middle of the century, and the Irish community in the Ward grew. St. Brigid's church was founded in 1853 under the leadership of John Timon, who was appointed the first bishop of the Diocese of Western New York in 1848. The Ward became a center of Irish Catholicism and a hotbed of Irish nationalism. Hatred of England ran deep in the Ward, as it did in Irish communities throughout the country. In the mid-1860s the Ward was a center of the Fenian Movement, whose goal was the invasion of Canada, followed by bargaining with England for the independence of Ireland. Because of Buffalo's location and the strength of its Fenian Brotherhood, it was from Buffalo that the invasion was launched. Arms were stored secretly in the basement of St. Brigid's. For weeks before the invasion, planned for June 2, 1866, Fenians from cities all over the Eastern seaboard came to Buffalo, hiding in the homes and rooming houses of secret sympathizers throughout the neighborhood.

The invasion, of course, failed, but Irish nationalism lived on in the Ward. Guns are no longer stored in the neighborhood church and Fenians no longer congregate on neighborhood streets, but thousands of people, Irish and otherwise, still descend on the area for the annual Shamrock Run, a five-mile road race through the streets of the neighborhood where the promoters, the Old First Ward Community Association, promise "special prizes will be awarded to runners in Irish costume."

The Ward remained a strong and thriving Irish neighborhood through the early years of the twentieth century. In the early 1950s a man named Roger Dooley, born and raised in the neighborhood, wrote several novels set in the Ward. One, *The House of Shanahan,* traces three generations of a prototypical Irish-American family. The novel's heroine, Rose Shanahan, regularly feels an ineffable attachment to her neighborhood: "As Rose paused tentatively outside St. Brigid's, looking up at the old brick church where she had received all the important sacraments from baptism to matrimony, as her mother had before her, she wondered. How could she explain an attitude she could herself not fully understand? She only knew that to all who ever lived here, the First Ward was not a political division or even a neighborhood, but a way of life, a state of mind."

Unfortunately, it was a state of mind that second- and third-generation Irish-Americans from the Ward were willing to abandon. They began to move to South Buffalo. In Dooley's *Days Beyond Recall,* the Shanahans arrive there in the mid-1920s, moving onto McKinley Parkway, "The Delaware Avenue of South Buffalo," a broad, richly landscaped boulevard lined with large, comfortable, one-and two-family homes. "Even now Rose could hardly believe that this very parkway, where elms and maples had just begun to foreshadow an arch over the central strip, would soon be her home. . . . After Fulton Street the ample lawns, dotted with bridal wreath or snowball bushes, gave the street all the charm that Rose could have wished."

McKinley is still a beautiful street, the showplace of South Buffalo. There are many other stately and magnificent monuments in South Buffalo, beautiful buildings like the fabulous Our Lady of Victory Church on Ridge Road, the border between South Buffalo and Lackawanna, and the 1898 glass-and-steel, Art Nouveau South Park Conservatory. There are neighborhood landmarks too, schools and hospitals that have been area institutions for years: Mercy Hospital, Mt. St. Mercy School, and Trocaire College, run by the Sisters of Mercy. John Curtin was raised by Mercy nuns at St. Theresa's on Seneca Street in South Buffalo. All over are lovely, quiet residential streets, like Pawnee Place, Judge Curtin's childhood street, where a low, rough-hewn stone wall surrounds a grassy knoll and gives the impression of an English village. Many of South Buffalo's streets are named for Indian tribes—Tuscarora, Pawnee, Peconic, Niantic, Minnetonka, Seneca, Indian Orchard, and Indian Church—for it was south of the Buffalo Creek that the great Seneca Nation lived in the last years of the eighteenth century. By the mid-1800s, however, Seneca land had been sold and cleared for development. All that remains is a bronze plaque affixed to a large boulder in the middle of a small, shady park. Its fading letters tell the sad and haunting story:

"In this vicinity from 1780–1842 dwelt the larger portion of the Seneca nation of the Iroquois League. In this enclosure were buried Red Jacket, Mary Jemison, and many of the noted chiefs and leaders of the nation."

Much of the history of South Buffalo, as of neighborhoods through-out the city, is rooted in parish churches and schools. Buffalo's paro-chial school system was booming in the late 1940s and early 1950s. More than 50,000 children were enrolled in the city's diocesan schools, versus slightly over 70,000 for the public schools. Every Buffalo neigh-borhood had parish schools but none had as many as South Buffalo. There was St. Agatha's, St. John the Evangelist, St. Martin's, St. Monica's, St. Thomas Aquinas, and St. Ambrose. The largest parish school, with more than a thousand children in 1950, was attached to Holy Family, a stately church replete with Celtic motifs and decorations built in 1906 on the corner of South Park Avenue and Tifft Street. The oldest parish school was St. Theresa's on Seneca Street, where John Curtin and Eugene Reville, the superintendent of schools during the cataclysmic mid-1970s and 1980s, went until high school.

But there were no diocesan high schools. Financially strapped dur-ing the Depression, then hampered by wartime limitations on the avail-ability of building materials, no new elementary schools, let alone high schools, had been built for years. Besides, in a city three-quarters Cath-olic, where public education was controlled by a largely Catholic Board of Education appointed by a Catholic mayor, people seemed to accept and expect that their public high schools should reflect and reinforce the values and beliefs of their primarily Catholic neighborhoods. No-body, for example, questioned the common practice at the predominantly Italian School 1 on the West Side, where classes were interrupted every Friday so that the children could cross Busti Avenue to attend mass at Holy Cross. The line between church and state was finer still at South Park High School, which had been run by Catholics since it opened in 1916. The first principal was Robert Bapst, who had a reputation as a classicist. He hired teachers from Catholic colleges like Canisius and D'Youville, and ran the school like a Catholic academy. Bapst eventually became superintendent of the schools system, a post he held until 1949, when he retired to study for the priesthood. A year later he was ordained.

But after the war the diocese was intent on building a host of Cath-olic high schools and to do so it recruited John O'Hara as bishop of Western New York in 1947. As president of Notre Dame University, O'Hara had earned a reputation as a great fundraiser and builder. He was asked to do the same for Buffalo. O'Hara began immediately and two years later he presided at the opening of the first diocesan high school in the city. Named for Western New York's first bishop, Timon High School opened in 1949 with eight hundred boys in a brand-new building overlooking McKinley Parkway in South Buffalo. Timon was but the first in a high-school-building boom that continued into the early 1960s. By then there were close to a dozen named in honor of a cardinal—Daugherty—and the former bishops of the diocese—Mc-Mahon, Ryan, Colton, Fallon, O'Hara, Carroll, and Turner.

For years South Buffalo's economic foundation was the steel industry. Steel brought the Curtin family, like so many others, to South Buffalo. John A. Curtin, Judge Curtin's father, moved to Pawnee Place shortly before World War I, when he went to work at Bethlehem as an engineer. By the late 1930s he had become superintendent of mills at Bethlehem, in charge, Judge Curtin recalls proudly, of the steel rolling mills, the rail mills, the structural steel mills, but not of the strip mills. Having lived with a "steel man" and worked at Bethlehem himself during summer vacations, Curtin knows the industry and speaks knowledgeably and fondly of it: how steel is made, the layout of the mills, the nature of the work, and the economic problems of the industry in general. Like a lot of people in Buffalo, Curtin is saddened by the fate of the industry and wonders how a country that produces so little steel can long remain great.

Not only did the people of South Buffalo work in the steel plants, they built them too, particularly the iron workers, who fabricated the blast furnaces and coke ovens. One of those iron workers was Mike Fitzpatrick. First as a member, then as business agent, of Iron Workers Local 6, he helped build the new, never-used blast furnace at Republic Steel. Now president of the local and also a member of the Erie County Legislature, Fitzpatrick is a second-generation Irishman, born on O'Connell Street in the Ward and raised in South Buffalo. His father was a Buffalo cop, his younger brother a priest and he, after graduating from Bishop Timon and attending Boston University on a football scholarship, became a Buffalo iron worker. For a while things were great. It was the heyday of downtown urban renewal and Fitzpatrick and his men were busy building the new buildings in downtown Buffalo: the Rath County Hall building, the Marine Midland towers, and Republic's new blast furnace. Throughout the late 1960s and early 1970s the men in Fitzpatrick's local were working a million and a half manhours a year.

Many of those who didn't build or work in the plants, or on the South Buffalo Railroad that served them, worked in the uniformed services, particularly the fire department, which had for decades been a virtual South Buffalo fraternity. It was not unusual for whole families, like the Keanes, to join the fire department. Jim Keane, former councilman from South Buffalo and now commissioner of emergency services for Erie County, had fifteen siblings. He and his brothers Dick and Mike are firefighters. Brother Neal is a battalion chief. Another brother, Bill "Puff" Keane, was killed in the line of duty. Jim's wife, Margaret, is a firefighter too, working out of Station 3, on the Buffalo's Lower West Side. Her whole family, which encompasses the Whalens and the Healys, is filled with firefighters: Uncle "Whipper" Whalen; brother R. J. Whalen, like "Puff," killed in action; and cousins Ray and Dennis Sullivan and Danny and Jack Corcoran.

Though the pay was low, the job was steady, the hours were flexible, and the most of the firefighters and police officers in the city could easily hold second jobs. What's more, the Fire Department in general and the firehouses in particular were warm and friendly, like fraternity houses but more so. In the sometimes yawning, sometimes fatal world of the firefighter, the ties formed in parish and neighborhood were bound still tighter. In the firehouses, as in the neighborhood, the world was safe, secure, and predictable. And, like work in the steel plants, it was always there.

Until the 1970s, that is, when tremors shook the neighborhood. Like kids in neighborhoods througout urban America, hundreds of South Buffalo boys had been drafted and many killed and wounded in Vietnam. They'd gone in after high school, after graduating from Bishop Timon or from Baker-Victory (a merged Catholic high school on the Lackawanna side of Ridge Road) or from South Park High School. Some had worked in the plants before they'd gone to war, killing time until they were called. They served and when they came home they found that South Buffalo's safety and security were no longer certain. Their jobs went first. Employment at the grain elevators had been shrinking for years, and then, in 1970, Bethlehem Steel started laying people off. Everything began to crumble. The South Buffalo Railroad went next and soon Fitzpatrick's Iron Workers began to hurt too. By the end of the 1970s his men were working less than a third as much as they had just a few years before. Many, like their brothers and fathers before them, gravitated in even greater numbers to the police and fire departments. But soon that line of work was increasingly hard to come by as well. In 1977, while presiding over the Buffalo school desegregation case, South Buffalo's own, U.S. District Judge John T. Curtin, of Pawnee Place, of St. Theresa's parish, ruled against the police and fire departments. Both, he said, were guilty of long-term discrimination against African-Americans, Hispanics, and women. In a ruling that rocked these bastions of privilege, Judge Curtin ordered the remedy: for every white male hired, a black, a Hispanic, or a female would have to be hired too. For South Buffalo, the rules were suddenly changing.

The hardship of the plant closings and the pain of Judge Curtin's ruling were somewhat mitigated by the political rise of yet another son of South Buffalo, James D. Griffin, elected mayor of the city in 1977, just in the nick of time. Irish and solidly Democratic South Buffalo had always had strong political connections, but Griffin was the first from South Buffalo to be elected mayor. South Buffalo Irish politicians had dominated the Erie County Democratic Party since the early 1950s. Following the election of Griffin, they would now dominate City Hall as well.

Griffin, like so many people from South Buffalo, was born and raised in the old First Ward. The family lived on Hamburg, Fulton, Louisiana, and Katherine Streets, he remembers. "We moved around a lot," Griffin says. "I guess we couldn't pay the rent." Griffin graduated from St. Brigid's, then married his wife, Margaret, a "Pet's" girl, and then moved to Dorrance Street in St. Martin's parish in South Buffalo. The Griffins have lived there ever since.

Griffin's election could not have come at a better time for South Buffalo. As jobs in local industry began to dry up when the police and fire departments came under court order, Mayor Griffin opened up City Hall to his constituents, filling as many jobs as possible with people—mostly men—from South Buffalo. Today the halls and offices of City Hall, which has yet to come under an affirmative action ruling, are filled with South Buffalonians in their late thirties and early forties, who, after high school and the service, were unable to find work in any of the traditional places of neighborhood employment. Thanks to the mayor, they are now working in local government. In a style that has characterized urban political machines since the late nineteenth century, Griffin traded jobs for loyalty and in the process strengthened himself and his neighborhood.

South Buffalo needed all the help it could get. As the economy sagged and the population dropped, the community's cherished neighborhood Catholic schools suffered too. This was happening throughout urban Catholic America and Buffalo was no exception. The first consolidation of Catholic schools in Buffalo came in 1968 when St. Francis Xavier and St. John the Baptist, two schools in Black Rock, one of Buffalo's oldest Catholic neighborhoods, merged to become Our Lady of Black Rock. In 1970, five inner-city Catholic schools and three high schools, with a combined total of more than 1,400 students, were shut down. The trends—a declining birth rate, the relentless move to the suburbs, the growth of paid lay faculty that forced increases in tuition, and, since the early 1980s, a public school system that offered quality education for free—were too strong for even South Buffalo, where the tradition of Catholic education had been so solid, to survive unscathed. In the twenty years between 1966 and 1986 the eight Catholic schools in South Buffalo lost 70 percent of their enrollment. In 1987, St. John the Evangelist, one of the biggest, closed. Increasingly desperate, in 1988 the diocese hired a local advertising agency to promote Catholic schools. Ads appeared in print, on radio, on billboards, and on Metro buses and trolleys. "Our track record is right up there," "Personal attention works miracles," "Where God and discipline are still welcome," they said.

"We have a good product," the president of the Board of Catholic Education said, "It's time to sell it." The diocese, like people in neighborhoods throughout the city, was praying for a miracle.

While some may have accepted the destruction of their neighborhoods, others fought back. And as they did an intense flow of energy coursed through the city, raising its level of citizen participation and the spirit of democracy higher than it had ever been before.

5

THE CHALLENGE OF PEOPLE POWER

For years America's black communities had been exerting pressure for community empowerment as a logical extension of the civil rights movement. By the mid-1970s similar pressure was being generated in white neighborhoods as well. In New York and Boston, Milwaukee and Baltimore, Chicago and Detroit, long quiet and contented residents in white ethnic neighborhoods suddenly joined the voices of black militants and student radicals demanding greater participation and control in the affairs of their lives.

Their opportunity came in 1974, with the arrival of the federal government's "block grant" form of community assistance. This idea, nurtured by the Nixon administration in the Community Development Act of 1974, was a strange, Machiavellian mix of cynicism and idealism. Different people viewed it differently. Since the New Deal, government funds had been awarded to cities as "categorical grants," specific amounts of money targeted to specific housing and community development projects. These programs benefited the poorest communities, those with the most pressing community development needs. The Community Development Act replaced these categorical grants with "block grants," lump-sum monies the city would decide for itself how to spend.

President Nixon liked the bill. It fit in with the anti-Washington, anti–big government rhetoric he so cherished. More significantly, the act was yet another ploy in his never-ending effort to woo white, blue-collar ethnics away from their traditional Democratic loyalties. According to the terms of the new act, the people in the cities themselves would decide how the millions of community development dollars would be spent. And because they were well-wired and politically well-leveraged, it was the old white ethnics who stood to benefit most from the block grants.

For blacks and other minorities the 1974 bill threatened disaster. During the mid-1960s, the halcyon years of the Great Society, categorical grant programs like the "Model Cities" effort had poured millions of dollars directly into black neighborhoods in cities throughout the country. In the process it spawned countless grassroots community organizations and created a generation of black leaders. Suddenly adept at the tortuous gamesmanship of budgeting, programming, and administration, young blacks for the first time had begun to move into positions of political prominence. But big-city blacks were not part of Nixon's constituency and soon after his election in 1968 the Model Cities program was undermined. The Community Development Act of 1974 killed it completely.

The Community Development Act was a challenge to mayors, particularly to old-school, machine-style politicians like Frank Sedita. Elected first in 1957 and re-elected in 1965 and 1969, Sedita had been a strong mayor allied with, but independent of, Buffalo's powerful Democratic organization. He was a cautious and pragmatic liberal, popular and well-liked by all of the city's traditional voting blocs. Sedita had surrounded himself with old-line ethnic pols who operated the entrenched departments in City Hall. There was Carl Perla, Sr., who treated the street departments as his fiefdom. Streets was the "Italian Department" "Most of the men on the trucks had the map all over their faces," one employee remembers. "If they didn't you could be sure that Perla was paying debts"—putting the son or nephew of a crony on the trucks as a "temporary" appeared to have been a typical method of circumventing civil service requirements. Perla was indicted in 1974. He'd been using streets employees as labor on his West Side properties.

Another of the ethnic regulars around Sedita was Stanley Stachowski, the commissioner of the Parks Department. Because of Buffalo's heavy winter weather, Parks had the greatest number of seasonal and temporary jobs, which "Staschu" guarded with an iron fist. The sheer numbers kept him a party power.

But Sedita attracted other kinds of people too, idealistic, hardworking, and energetic, young men and women who had come of age in the 1960s and believed in the promises of their generation. One was Joe Ryan. Unlike most of the Irish-Americans in Buffalo politics, Ryan hailed neither from the old First Ward nor from South Buffalo, but rather from St. Mark's parish in Parkside. His family had moved there years before with a handful of upwardly mobile "lace curtain" neighbors. After granduating from St. Joseph's Collegiate Institute and Cornell University, Ryan joined the U.S. Navy and served for eighteen months in Vietnam as a lieutenant in an underwater reconnaissance unit. Eager to enter politics and government, Ryan went to work in Mayor Sedita's 1969 re-election campaign immediately upon his return to Buffalo. In early 1971 Sedita appointed him director of the Citizen's Advisory Committee. Aggressive, intelligent, and ambitious, Ryan quickly became impatient with City Hall's department heads and commissioners, many of them political hacks, old hands at the tribal back-scratching that characterized Buffalo's ethnic politics. They loved elections, Ryan knew, and were great at winning them, but they seemed to him to know nothing and care less about governing. Ryan was passionate about politics and had a keen sense of where power lay, and how, as he said, to "access" it. He loved Buffalo, and having been to Baltimore, New York, San Francisco, and Toronto, he had a vision of what a great city could be. Good looking, athletic, well-educated, superb at thinking on his feet, idealistic but with a useful bit of "old boy" in him, Ryan was "so likeable," remembers a colleague from Ryan's days on the Citizen's Advisory Committee, "that even people who had reason to resent him couldn't quite manage it." He was confident and capable, bright and hardworking, keenly aware that if given the opportunity he could run the city from his CAC offices on the fourth floor of City Hall. In 1974, when Sedita retired because of illness, Ryan almost began to.

Sedita was succeeded by Stanley Makowski. For years a councilman from the Polish Broadway-Fillmore district, then a councilman-at-large, Makowski was well-liked and respected as a "nice man," a person with more confidence in his goodness than in his intelligence. He often extolled his own humbleness. "I am," he once said, "a simple guy. I never went to college. I'm just a grain scooper at heart." (In Buffalo you didn't *have* to be Irish to scoop grain.) Unlike Sedita, people say in retrospect, Makowski was weak—afraid of power and reluctant to use it.

Joe Ryan was not. The Community Development Act of 1974 offered Ryan unprecedented opportunity to redistribute political power in Buffalo. According to the terms of the new law, Buffalo was going to receive more than $11 million dollars a year over the first three years of the program. Sensing that control of the block grant funds would be essential to the exercise of power and control in the Makowski administration, Ryan sought to establish a mechanism for the distribution of the block grant millions through the Citizen's Advisory Committee. The process he advanced, based on a proposal written by his aide, Louise Granelli McMillan, was an approach to citizen participation that was as innovative as any in the country.

Ryan and McMillan wanted to create a system that would allow block grant funds to pass as directly as possible into the communities involved. The pair could count on the support of Bill Price, recently elected council member from the University District. Like Ryan, Price was a Vietnam veteran. Like Ryan too, Price was passionate about Buffalo and, after law school and his internship with Mayor Lindsay, Price was back in Buffalo and recognized the opportunity for change offered by the Community Development Act. Price says he was "jumping at the chance to try out our notions about how a city is rebuilt and preserved." Like Ryan and McMillan, Price wanted to open the process so that departmental heads couldn't "get together in a back room and divide the money up for their pet projects." Ryan and Price knew they could bypass the existing leadership only by building a power base of their own, rooted as much as possible in the neighborhoods themselves.

McMillan's document pointed the way. Polemical but convincing, it was a long dissertation on what makes a good community and how it can be achieved. McMillan's ideas were rooted in her childhood on Buffalo's West Side. She was raised at 16th and York Streets, in Our Lady of Loretto Parish, a very close and tight-knit community where growing up, she says, was like being in nineteenth-century Italy. McMillan was taught good citizenship by her grandfather, Luigi Panichi, born, unlike most of Buffalo's first-generation Italians, on the Adriatic Coast. He taught her to do good for her family and her neighborhood, but also to do good for the world. The lessons came off-handedly, while she helped him to weed the garden or clean the pigeon coop in the backyard (which supplied the family's meat during World War II), or while sitting in front of the basement fireplace, roasting sausages.

McMillan went to School 38 on Vermont Street, in the heart of the Italian West Side, and then to Grover Cleveland, her neighborhood high school. By then she'd become a "West Side beatnik"—there weren't too many Italian girls on Buffalo's West Side, she says, who wore black tights, a black skirt, and turtleneck. In college—first at Rosary Hill, a local Catholic College, and then at UB—McMillan became increasingly active in the civil rights movement and later against the Vietnam War. She left UB after the school administration called police on campus during protests in 1970, and devoted the next several years to the movement. "It wasn't a scene," she remembers proudly. "For our little set of rock-hard American beliefs we were threatened, harassed, busted, jailed, terrorized, beaten, and in a few cases extinguished." Through it all McMillan never left the West Side, and in 1971 she was there working hard in Mayor Sedita's campaign for Erie County executive. By the end of the year she was working for Joe Ryan at the Citizen's Advisory Committee.

McMillan's CAC document breathed her upbringing on the Italian West Side. A city was "a process," she argued, an interconnected "continuum of relationships from family members to family members, from house to house, from house to block, from block to neighborhood, from neighborhood to community, and from community to city." Policies for the improvement and development of the community could work only if they reflected the "sense of community" and the way people lived in the city. Therefore, McMillan wrote, community development block grant money should be given directly to the communities involved. The mechanism she advocated was the division of the city into twelve planning districts based not on the existing council districts but rather on lines that were generally understood to reflect traditional neighborhood boundaries. Each district would elect people to run a neighborhood development corporation that, working with a community coordinator appointed by the CAC, would plan and develop housing and neighborhood development projects. If approved by the Common Council, the projects would be funded with block grant funds and implemented by the neighborhood corporation.

Mayor Makowski liked McMillan's proposal, and he prided himself on his responsiveness to emerging political ideas and groups. Prodded by Price and Ryan, he implemented the program in late 1974 with few changes. Unlike mayors in most cities, who opted for the minimum amount of citizen participation required by law, Makowski, born and raised on Buffalo's Polish East Side, encouraged the creation of a grassroots community planning program, which was soon recognized nationally for the extent of its citizen involvement. (In May 1975 the *Wall Street Journal* dispatched a reporter to Buffalo to cover the story.) Makowski had to deal with stubborn opposition to the program's openness—from the old-line commissioners and council members; from the black community, afraid that the better organized and more powerful white ethnic neighborhoods would take advantage of the program; and from the Democratic organization, afraid that too many jobs were being handed out without their say. Despite his alleged "weakness," Makowski prevailed and in late 1974 and early 1975 four public meetings were held in each of the city's twelve planning districts. The meetings were forums for people to express their hopes and aspirations for their neighborhoods. "Give us the lumber, the hammer, and the nails," said Norm Bakos, a neighborhood leader from the East Lovejoy district, "and we'll rebuild our own barns." Now, for the first time ever, grassroots community groups from all over the city were becoming intimately involved in the development of plans and programs regarding housing and community services within their neighborhoods.

By 1978–79, the fourth year of the Community Development Block Grant program, there was over $25 million to be divided up in Buffalo. In neighborhoods throughout the city, residents, community leaders, priests, and politicians engaged in heated, confusing and seemingly end-less struggles over who would spend the money, and how, and where. The final decision, generated by a degree of citizen participation un-precedented in the life of this or any other city in the country, reflects clearly the issues and problems that concerned people in the city's different neighborhoods—housing rehabilitation and paint programs, street and park repairs, commercial revitalization and façade improvements, demo-litions, housing inspections, lighted schoolhouses, recreation for young people and the elderly, van service for senior citizens. There was, Mc-Millan told the *Wall Street Journal*, one message that came through from these varied requests: "Every single neighborhood said 'Don't give us new communities, give us our own communities back!' " Not everyone liked the program, and many criticized its results, but it was clear that, in Buffalo anyway, more than any city in the United States, the people had been given unprecedented power to decide how to spend federal funds for their city's renewal. Now, said Bill Price, "It's up to us to make it work."

Voices from the grassroots were heard again in May 1974, when the people of Buffalo elected the members of the Board of Education. For years the board had consisted of seven people appointed by the mayor. Made up of failed politicians, successful social businessmen, an occasional banker or lawyer, and always at least one physician, the board was an ethnically balanced old-boys club with Irish, Polish, and Italian ethnics; one or two Jews; a white, Anglo-Saxon Protestant; and, since 1963, one African-American.

Since the 1920s, educational reformers had talked about an elected school board with its own political constituency, believing this would end the constant bickering over school funds between the board and the Common Council. But it was not until the late 1960s, when whites in cities throughout the country became increasingly troubled by the prospect of forced integration, that the movement for elected school boards gathered momentum. By 1970 all but ten of the largest cities in the nation had replaced appointed boards with elected ones.

In Buffalo, as in most cities, the drive for an elected school board originated in the city's white ethnic neighborhoods, where local politicians, sensing the depth of their constituents' concern, moved to the front of what many thought was the euphemistically named "Neighborhood School Movement." Using "busing" as a fear-filled code word, politicians from President Nixon on down exploited the easily aroused fears of urban whites. In February 1972, as State Education Commissioner Ewald Nyquist prepared for a trip to Buffalo, Jack Kemp, the area's most influential congressman, proposed an anti-busing amendment to the U.S. Constitution. Only with an amendment, Kemp said, would "the survival of local control of neighborhood public schools be safeguarded." State Senator James Griffin, Democratic South Buffalo's home boy, supported Kemp's proposal. Convinced that elected officials would never impose busing, Griffin favored an elected school board as the safest and surest protection against a unpopular policy of school integration. He introduced a bill calling for a November 1973 referendum on the question.

The reaction to Griffin's bill was mixed. While blacks had never felt that their schools and neighborhoods were truly represented on the apppointed board, they were afraid that school-board elections would give vent to and legitimize a frightening and dangerous brand of racist white urban populism. Many in the white community were worried too. They feared that an elected school board would bring to the surface generations of ethnic, racial, and geographic antagonism, making it even more difficult to deal with Buffalo's increasingly serious economic and social problems. Mayor Sedita, himself a product of one of Buffalo's oldest, most tribelike neighborhoods, the Italian Lower West Side, opposed the change for this reason. In a plea for city-wide harmony, he said, "The city has enough dissent as it is without the additional sectionalism that would develop with an elected board." Norman Goldfarb, speaking for the plaintiffs in the pending school desegregation case, agreed, saying an elected board would "aggravate the already acute racial and ethnic tensions in Buffalo." Most of the weekly neighborhood papers, like the *West Side Times* and the *North Buffalo Rocket,* favored the change, but Buffalo's two daily newspapers insisted that an elected board, as the *Courier Express* put it, would "fragment the community, putting an undue emphasis on sectional, religious and ethnic interests."

But support for Griffin's bill quickly mounted. While critics tended to depict the neighborhood school movement as racially motivated, supporters viewed an elected school board as a fair and just return of power to the people who actually sent their children to the city's public schools. As anti-busing pressure mounted during the spring of 1972, Sedita began to change his position. So did some key black local political leaders, who sensed that their constituents could well benefit from an elected school board if members were elected by districts. The State Legislature passed the bill and in November 1973 a referendum was held to decide the question.

Despite the intensity and emotion of the debate, barely 10 percent of Buffalo's eligible voters bothered to come out. Turnout was high on the black East Side and in the white silk-stocking Delaware District, where people tended to oppose an elected board. Among the city's white ethnics, where victory was perhaps a forgone conclusion, turnout was low, but enough of them voted to effect the change: the referendum passed and school-board elections were scheduled for May 1974.

While the people of Buffalo had decided in favor of an elected board, the State Legislature had not yet determined whether members should be elected at large or by district. For Arthur Eve, the Democratic deputy majority leader in the State Assembly, leader of the legislature's Black Caucus and the most powerful black politician in Buffalo, this was a critical question. In nearby Rochester, Eve knew, where blacks made up 40 percent of the public school population, an at-large system had effectively kept blacks off the elected board of education. A system of district representation could reflect the concentration of blacks on Buffalo's East Side and guarantee blacks a far more influential role on the elected board than they'd ever had on the appointed one. Using his considerable leverage, Eve was instrumental in creating a school board made up of three people elected citywide and six people voted in by geographic district. Two of those, the Central and the East districts, had a majority black population.

Eve was happy that blacks would be well-represented on the Board of Education, but he had few illusions about the effect the new board would have on Buffalo's black children. In a shocking statement that revealed his own, if not his whole community's, cynicism, Eve said, "Blacks know that they're going to have to deal with segregated schools. Their main concern is to make them the best segregated schools in the country."

The members of the new board were duly elected in May 1974. A diverse group of nine men and women, three blacks and six whites, most were public-school teachers and parents in their twenties and thirties and active in school and community affairs. The few white ethnic rabble-rousers who had run for seats on the board were defeated. The winners were moderate, serious, and responsible, a group who's diversity reflected the city.

Representing the North District was Mike Ryan, not related to the CAC's Joe Ryan. Ryan was 31, born and raised on the Upper West Side when there was still a small pocket of Irish-Americans in that neighborhood. He'd gone to Ascension Church School at Lafayette Avenue and Grant Street and then to Canisius High and Canisius College, those great Jesuit melting pots located on two of Buffalo's ethnically neutral arteries, Delaware Avenue and Main Street. Ryan went to Harvard Law School and after a wartime stint in Vietnam settled in Buffalo. He had followed the school desegregation case since its inception in 1972 and was eager to be a part of what he sensed was going to be a critcial time in the city's history.

Mozella Richardson was the board's Ellicott district representative. She had come to Buffalo as a teenager in 1943 when her mother moved here to work at the Curtiss-Wright plant. They settled in the Ellicott District after the war and Richardson graduated from Fosdick-Masten High School (now City Honors School). When her home was taken as part of the Ellicott District Urban Renewal Project, Richardson was moved into the Ellicott Projects, where she raised her ten children. Richardson's neighborhood school was School 6 on Hickory Street, a mixed school of blacks and Italians from St. Lucy's Parish. But when urban renewal hit that section of Ellicott District and St. Lucy's was torn down, the Italians left, and School 6, like the neighborhood itself, became all black. Neighborhood parents cared desparately about their school—by the end of the 1960s School 6's PTA was the largest in the city. Richardson was its president. By the time she was elected to the new Board of Education she had become skilled as a leader in the seemingly endless fight to improve her neighborhood school.

Florence Baugh was the new board's first president. She had been active in school affairs since her children started going to School 4 on South Park Avenue in South Buffalo. Following the death of her husband Baugh moved into the area's Perry Projects, across the street from School 4, and remained active in the school system after she moved to the Parkside area years later.

Meanwhile, the changes were too much for Superintendent of Schools Joe Manch. He had been a distant, some thought imperious, superintendent. Through his political ties to a succession of mayors he had long been able to hand-pick and control the members of the appointed board. He could not work with the new board, nor did they want him to, and in early 1975 Manch announced that he would resign that summer. The search for his replacement began immediately.

Quite a few people on the board's search committee wanted new blood, someone from the outside. They were suspicious of the high-ranking administrators in the superintendent's office, concerned that they, like Manch, were bureaucrats afraid and unwilling to change. Some, particularly Peter Crotty, chairman of the citizen-based search committee, felt otherwise. A legendary, long-time Democratic leader from South Buffalo, Crotty was convinced from the beginning that only a local person, someone like himself, a person with strong connections to Buffalo's white ethnic neighborhoods, would have the leverage and the credibility to push the integration orders that everyone knew were inevitable. Outside candidates were invited to apply, but, much to the consternation of those eager to bring a new perspective to the superintendent's office, Crotty seemed to have the ability to control the selection process. One candidate, an assistant superintendent from New York City, complained that he was not met at the airport nor even taken out to lunch—just told that there was a cafeteria in the basement of City Hall. The man withdrew his name from consideration the following day.

Although not an announced candidate for the job, Crotty's man was Eugene T. Reville, a former teacher who had risen through the ranks under Manch to become a principal and then associate superintendent for instructional services. Affable, outgoing, energetic, and optimistic, Reville was a natural politician. Most significantly for Crotty, Reville was raised on South Buffalo's Armin Street, around the corner from the Curtins on Pawnee. Like Judge Curtin, Reville had attended St. Theresa's on Seneca Street. Unlike many of the other significant players in Buffalo's school desegregation case, however, Reville had not climbed the parish school–Canisius College education ladder. Instead he went to public school, graduating from South Park High School in 1949. He got his degree at Buffalo State Teacher's College four years later. His wife, Joan, was from the neighborhood too, a graduate of Holy Family on South Park Avenue and of South Buffalo's Mt. Mercy Academy, "the Mount." Although she was of German origin, Reville told his mother, Agnes Murphy, when he introduced them, that Joan was an "Irish girl from Holy Family."

Crotty thought Reville was a natural for the job, but the board's three black members had other ideas. They favored the selection of Claude Clapp, the associate superintendent for finance and the highest ranking black in the school system. Clapp had been the first black principal in the city, appointed by Superintendent Manch in 1959. But a majority of the board shared Crotty's thinking. They knew they would need someone with strong South Buffalo connections, someone able to persuade the residents of this tough, proud neighborhood that their interests were protected despite the segregation orders that everyone anticipated. As it was, South Buffalo was already well represented on the new board. One of the at-large members, Joseph Murphy, was a graduate and former teacher at South Park High and a well-known businessman in the community. There was also the district representative Joe Hillary, a graduate of South Park High and Canisius, and a history teacher at Seneca Vocational School. A member of the Blackhorn Irish Club and a self-described "fifth generation South Buffalonian," Hillary had great prestige and leverage in the neighborhood. He was not worried about how South Buffalo would react to a court order from Curtin. They were, after all, South Buffalo family. Hillary had known Curtin and his whole family for years, from the neighborhood and from Canisius College and from South Buffalo's Mercy Hospital, where Curtin's brother Dan was an orthopedic surgeon. "Don't worry about Jack Curtin," he told his colleagues on the board in early 1975. "Jack'll be all right." Other board members were not so sure, and in an effort to cement still further the board's ties to both South Buffalo and Buffalo's other white ethnic neighborhoods, in July 1975 the board chose Eugene Reville to be superintendent of schools.

The election of the school board, like the overall outpouring of citizen participation that so marked the early 1970s, was a critical development in the life of the city. It democratized the making of public policy in the area of public education. Real representatives of the people themselves had the power and the responsibility to develop and implement education policy. People in Buffalo were now saying that public education, like community development, was too important to be left to the politicians and the professionals. It was time for the people to try to run things.

6

"WHO PRACTICES JUSTICE WALKS IN THE PRESENCE OF THE LORD"

Late in the afternoon on Saturday, August 21, 1971, three men and two women walked into an enormous, magnificant, late-Victorian Post Office, on Ellicott Street in downtown Buffalo. They went up the stairs to an empty room on the fourth floor and waited calmly until the building closed. Then, sometime after ten o'clock that night, the five—Charles Darst, Jeremiah Horrigan, James Martin, Maureen Considine, and Ann Marie Masters—dressed in shorts and tee shirts, their faces, arms, and legs blackened with charcoal, made their way downstairs to the draft-board offices on the second floor. Breaking in, they strewed drawers of records over the desks, chairs, and floors, quickly loading three laundry bags with the records they thought contained the names of local draftees classified 1-A, eligible to be sent to war. Their plan, the five said later, was to write to these young men, telling them that they didn't have to worry—the government no longer had their names and now they were "free."

But the bold operation was doomed from the start. An FBI agent who had infiltrated an anti-war group in Camden, New Jersey, had tipped off the Buffalo FBI. Draft boards in both cities were told they were going to be trashed the night of August 21. The five never had a chance. Testifying later, FBI agent Donald Adams said he was walking

along a corridor when he "saw a shadow duck down suddenly." Shouting
"FBI, halt!" he ran down one of the broad corridors that forms the
perimeter of the building, turned a corner with his gun drawn, and
saw four figures dashing down a stairway. He arrested two, a man
and a woman, and later discoverd a third, another woman, crouching
behind a file cabinet in the draft office. Shortly after, two men were
arrested by the Buffalo police. Strewn among the scattered papers and
records the FBI discovered a typewritten document entitled "Statement
of The Buffalo."

> Today we destroy the records of the Selective Service System in Buffalo,
> local boards 82 and 89. Likewise we confiscate records of the Office
> of Military Intelligence, records that likewise exist in the service of
> the machine of death. We do this as an attempt to expose the myth
> that the military machine really protects us from anything. We feel
> it is our right as men and women of responsibility, our duty—before
> God and men—to take this action against these records that help
> make the Vietnam War possible—a violence of extraordinary arro-
> gance and cruelty. . . . Our moral outrage and our sober rationality
> both say to us, as others have said before, "Some property has no
> right to exist." Absolutely, we say that.

Four of the five young men and women were raised in Buffalo's ethnic,
Catholic neighborhoods, and while their ideals and actions were proudly
a part of the nationwide anti-war movement, they were also rooted
in the festering synergy that had come to characterize Buffalo's Catholic
community. By the mid-1960s there had begun to emerge within these
neighborhoods, as in similar neighborhoods in cities throughout the
country, a growing number of young diocesan priests who had assumed
an increasingly active and important role in the lives of their communities.

One of them was Bill Stanton from St. Theresa's Parish on Seneca
Street in South Buffalo. Stanton's father, a Buffalo police officer and
later chief of the department's narcotics squad, had moved the family
to South Buffalo from the Ward in the early 1920s. Bill was born on
Seneca Street in 1924. Soon they moved around the corner to a street
called Roanoke Park in the same beautiful, tree-filled Mineral Springs
neighborhood where the Curtins lived and that was the burying ground
of Red Jacket. It was a short walk to St. Theresa's, a turn-of-the-century
brownstone, and at its school Stanton formed friendships that have
lasted a lifetime. Closest among them were the Curtin brothers, Jack
and Dan from Pawnee Place, and the Revilles, Gene and Bob from
Armin Place. Stanton liked the neighborhood, and following his ordi-

nation came back to teach history at Mercy Academy, the hundred-year-old school where generations of South Buffalo's Irish Catholic girls have come of age. In 1959 Stanton moved out of the neighborhood, taking a job as vice-principal of Bishop Turner High School in the Schiller Park neighborhood on the far East Side. Dominated by Poles from Queen of Peace Parish and Germans from Holy Redeemer, Schiller Park remains to this day a strong bastion of Central European Catholic ethnicity. The heart of the neighborhood, where the streets bear names like Floss, Hagen, Sprenger, Freund, and Lang, is Schiller Park. For a hundred years, until a supermarket was built there in the mid-1960s, the park had been the site for the neighborhood's annual Oktoberfest celebration.

When Stanton arrived there were few blacks in the area. There were fewer still at Bishop Turner. Stanton wanted to change all that right away. So did two of the school's teachers, priests named Joe Bissonette and Jack Weimer. Everybody in Buffalo, it seemed, knew the Weimers, owners of Weimer's Grove, a large and popular picnic grounds in suburban Lancaster, site of school reunions and Fourth of July and Labor Day picnics popular with Buffalonians since the early 1920s. "I can't begin to tell you," many of them say, "how many beers and sausages I downed at Weimer's Grove." Weimer's grandfather on his mother's side, Karl Meyer, was the proprietor of Meyer's Hof, for years a popular bar and grill on Court Street in downtown Buffalo. Like Stanton, Bissonette and Weimer were products of Buffalo's Catholic neighborhood tradition, graduates of parish schools—Bissonette from St. Joseph's on Main Street, Weimer from St. Francis de Sales on the old Humboldt Parkway. Both went to Canisius High and Canisius College, Jesuit schools that had educated young, upwardly mobile Catholic boys since 1870.

Dick Griffin and Vincent Doyle, both from Parkside, were also in Bissonette and Weimer's Canisius class of '54. After graduation both (like John Curtin, Canisius, '43) went to law school at UB. By the early 1960s they were both working with Father Stanton at Bishop Turner. Bissonette had the idea to form the Turner Interracial Club in 1961. Joined by the handful of the school's blacks and more than a few of the whites (who often told their parents they were going to a meeting of the Catholic Youth Organization), the club began to grow. Under the charismatic leadership of Bissonette, Weimer, and Stanton, the group organized discussion groups and arranged evening socials and visits to one another's homes. At a time when few schools of any kind— let alone Catholic ones—even thought about it, the club arranged for special programs on African-American history.

Throughout the mid-1960s these priests, joined by a growing number of their like-minded brethren from parishes throughout Buffalo, became increasingly involved in social-justice ministries. Walter Kerns was fighting for open housing in Clarence. Jim Mang was working with Puerto Rican migrants in nearby Silver Creek. Bissonette left Turner to work with Father Bob Sweeney among the black families at St. Brigid's, the old Irish parish in the Ward. Weimer moved to a pulpit at Buffalo State College's Newman Center, where he became increasingly involved in the anti-war movement and increasingly friendly with two Newman Center members, Eugene Reville and John Curtin.

Opposition to the war in Vietnam led this small cadre of local priests to increasingly radical community organization. Bristling under the reactionary leadership of Bishop Joseph P. McNulty, who was quick to discipline politically active priests, in 1968 Stanton, Bissonette, Mang, and Weimer organized the Priests Association of Buffalo. Hoping that such an organization would provide them with strength through unity, the priests became bold in their criticism of the war. In a full-page ad signed by close to a hundred diocesan priests in the *Courier Express,* Buffalo's morning daily, the PAB denounced the war in Vietnam and urged other Catholics to join them in civil disobediance against it. McNulty responded with a full-page ad of his own. Communism was Godless, it read, and the war was a "Crusade against communism."

In 1971 Mang led a delegation of Buffalo Catholics to an anti-war sit-in in Washington. Upon his return he was summoned to McNulty's office. The bishop told him to "cease and desist any and all activities contrary to the interests of the United States government." Mang, Bissonnette, and a priest from Lackwanna named Joe Shuster escalated their protest by announcing that they were withholding that portion of their income tax dedicated to defense. This time McNulty retaliated. Mang was fired from his teaching job and sent to a church in Lancaster, a conservative, blue-collar suburb. Shuster was sent to Niagara Falls, and Bissonette languished without an assignment of any kind.

Given the ferment of political activity in Buffalo's Catholic priesthood and the frustrating response of Buffalo's bishop, it should have come as no surprise when in August 1971 the five Catholic anti-war activists (soon to be known as the "Buffalo Five") were caught breaking into the offices of the local draft board. Most of the "The Five" and the people involved with them were Buffalo born and bred, products of the city's ethnic neighborhoods, particularly the German East Side and Irish South Buffalo. Their fathers had been cops and firefighters and first-generation neighborhood businessmen. Like many other American Catholics, by the mid-1960s they had begun to respond to calls for change that came as much from their own consciences as from the teachings of Vatican II.

The five defendants were arraigned before Magistrate Edmund Maxwell the morning after their arrest. Their pictures appeared on the front page of the Sunday newspaper—they looked tired, but were smiling after a night in the Erie County Holding Center. On Monday the Five were released on bail. They were charged with third-degree burglary and conspiracy to hinder or interfere with federal draft law. The trial was set for April.

At a pre-trial hearing in October 1971 the five defendants met U.S. District Judge John T. Curtin. They told him that they were reluctant to plead innocent to the charge of conspiring to hinder federal draft law because theirs was no criminal act. Rather, "It is a moral outcry aimed at those who, in the name of law and order, perpetuate such evils as war and poverty. . . . We want to say with our lives that we want to promote and preserve life, not death. When one is trying to stop a crime, how does one enter a plea of guilty or not guilty?" Instead, they said, attempting to engage Curtin in the passions that had motivated them, "Our plea is to you, to help us to stop the madness of the war." For this reason the defendants took for themselves the name "the Buffalo," not "The Buffalo Five," as they had been tagged by the press. "We take the name," they said "because the Buffalo, a once-powerful beast of freedom nearly exterminated under the advance of Western civilization, is returning today in even greater numbers, perhaps symbolic of nature's resiliant resistance. We are the children of nature. We stand for life, love, laughter, music, good food, friends, air, sunshine—all things green and living and beautiful. We are The Buffalo." The five didn't want to be "just five," but rather an evolving and organic conspiracy of many. They encouraged everyone to join them.

And many did. One of the group's first and most ardent supporters was Ed Powell, a sociology professor at UB. Powell had met the defendants during the summer of 1971, when "Meaux" Considine and Chuck Darst were enrolled in his course on "The Sociology of Non-Violence." Powell had come to UB from Texas in the late 1950s. He was active in campus civil rights activities during the early 1960s, but it was the escalation of the war in Vietnam that turned Powell into one of the most vocal faculty radicals at UB. A tall, husky man with a full beard and a deep Texas drawl, Powell wore only dashikis and never drove a car, riding his bicycle even during the depths of Buffalo's winters.

Powell was an ardent disciple of communalism, and by the end of the 1960s his house on Jewett Parkway had become something of a crash pad for Buffalo's counterculture. Jewett Parkway, named for the wealthy nineteenth-century founder of a stove-manufacturing company, is one of many lovely, curving, tree-lined residential streets adjacent to Delaware Park. Like most of the streets in the area, Jewett was designed by Fredrick Law Olmstead, who also designed the park. Powell's house sits directly across the street from the Darwin D. Martin House. Powell's house, though, is nothing like the one Frank Lloyd Wright designed for Martin—instead, it is a large, ramshackle, comfortable home built in the Charles Addams, late-Victorian style that, on the cold, grey days of Buffalo's winters, takes on a particularly eerie mien. Following the Five's arrest, Powell's house became the unofficial headquarters of "The Buffalo." Powell loved these five young people, and he was excited by their desire to create a "New Community" based on the communalistic values and ideals he tried to live by. During the months before the trial he mothered them, cooking their meals, serving them more as house-husband than as intellectual guru.

By early fall of 1971 the Buffalo had become celebrities throughout the city's radical and counterculture community. Powell said the Buffalo recognized, as Lenin did, that "the first duty of a revolutionary was to patiently explain." So the Buffalo carried on an active dialogue with people throughout the metropolitan area, hoping to turn their arrest and trial into a public event, a communitywide teach-in about the war and the values they felt had led to it. The five conducted coffee-klätsches in suburban homes, appeared on television and radio talk shows, spoke at churches and synagogues, in high school assemblies, and at all of the colleges around Buffalo. With money raised by their defense committee—one woman, Sally Hamlin, raised hundreds of dollars operating a Christmas store in the Unitarian Church on Elmwood Avenue—they even traveled, particularly to Chicago, to counsel draft resisters.

As the date of their April trial approached, the group's defense committee distributed leaflets throughout the community urging people to attend. In one they quoted the French writer St. Exupéry: "Nothing can match the treasures of common memories, of trials endured together, of quarrels and reconciliations, and general emotional happiness." In another they proclaimed that, "All events are free and the public is needed to make the trial a joyous time." Whether or not it would be, of course, depended on the judge, John T. Curtin.

In February 1969 Judge Curtin had presided at the stirring and highly publized trial of Bruce Beyer and the Buffalo Nine. Beyer was a draft resister who in August 1968 took sanctuary from the police in the Unitarian Universalist Church on Elmwood Avenue. It was the church of his parents. There he was joined by eight supporters. For several days FBI agents waited outside. Finally they stormed the church and, following a violent encounter with Beyer and the others, arrested them all.

The trial of the Buffalo Nine was the city's first draft-resistance case, and it captured the attention of Western New York, dominating local news from the time of the confrontation at the church to the end of the trial.

The actions of the Buffalo Nine were searing reminders that the city could not escape the upheavals that traumatized the nation during the tumultous years of the late 1960s. A first for Buffalo, the case was also a first for Curtin—he was not used to the fierce pride and defiance that characterized Beyer and the other defendents. Throughout the trial, the courtroom was filled and the hall outside lined with the defendants' fervent supporters. Curtin was nervous about the proceedings. The armed court marshals who patrolled the crowd were nervous too. Eager to establish their authority, they summoned the aid of Buffalo Police Department plainclothesmen, as well as twelve members of the department's uniformed Tactical Patrol Unit.

Curtin's anxiety led him to overreact. At one point, according to a report sent to J. Edgar Hoover from an FBI agent monitoring the trial, "Judge Curtin directed that all spectators remain in the courtroom, which was, thereupon, locked while the jurors were escorted from the building and sent home without fear of harm. After fifteen minutes, the courtroom doors were unlocked and the spectators were permitted to leave . . . the jury was taken home by members of the Tactical Patrol Force." Curtin was tough and legalistic throughout the trial, unwilling to entertain the defense's request to make the "larger crime," the war in Vietnam, rather than the defendants' resistance to it, the focus of the trial.

Beyer was found guilty of assault, but before Curtin had the chance to sentence him he left the country.

In the months after Beyer's conviction, the horrors of Vietnam escalated. The American invasion of Cambodia in April 1970, followed by the killings at Kent State in May, galvanized the nation, the Congress, and the press. In December 1970 Congress repealed the Gulf of Tonkin Resolution, the act that had long served as the legal basis of the war. In June 1971 the *New York Times* began publishing the so-called Pentagon Papers, which confirmed what many had long suspected—the government dishonesty in reporting progress about the war. In January 1972, four months before the trial of the Buffalo Five began, polls showed that nearly two-thirds of those interviewed favored American withdrawal from Vietnam. Opposition to the war grew stronger still in early spring as the United States began bombing Hanoi and Haiphong. The trial of the Five began on Monday, April 17, 1972. That day American fighter bombers flew five hundred attack missions over North and South Vietnam. There were five hundred more on Tuesday, April 18.

In the growing atmosphere of disgust with the war, few were prepared to question the moral integrity of the defendants—not the public, not even the prosecution. Much had changed since Bruce Beyer and the Buffalo Nine had appeared before Judge Curtin three years earlier. Now, people throughout the community seemed to agree with Jack Horrigan, the father of one of the defendants, who said, "I wish I had my son's courage."

One the first day of the trial the five defendants, in confident yet gentle voices, introduced themselves to the jury. Maureen Considine, age twenty-one, grew up in Williamsville and graduated from Mt. St. Joseph's Academy in Buffalo and St. Mary's College in South Bend, Indiana. Considine first became aware of the horrors of the war at South Bend, at a procession of Notre Dame students with crosses bearing the names of Notre Dame students killed in Vietnam.

Charles Darst, twenty-two, had been raised in Kentucky and Tennessee and come to Buffalo to be with his fiancée, "Meaux" Considine, whom he'd met while studying architecture at Notre Dame. Darst's brother, the late David Darst, was a priest who had been arrested with the Berrigans when they destroyed draft-board records in Cantonsville, Maryland, in 1968.

Jeremiah Horrigan, twenty-one, the oldest of nine children, was born and raised in South Buffalo. His father was a vice president of the Buffalo Bills in charge of public relations. "Tall, thin, longish, slightly flaring black hair," Ed Powell described Horrigan in a journal he kept during the trial, "dressed in faded blue jeans, black shirt with tail out." Horrigan graduated from Canisius High School, then spent two years at UB before transferring to Fordham. Horrigan said his occupation was "draft resister."

James Martin, twenty-five, was from Michigan. Martin spent eight years as a seminarian, preparing to become a missionary. He had worked with juvenile delinquents in Detroit and then joined the Peace Corps, serving in Gambia. Martin said that in Gambia he realized that the same forces dropping bombs on Vietnam could just as easily be bombing the village he was working in.

Ann Marie Masters, twenty-six, was raised in the suburbs of Buffalo and knew Considine from "the Mount" (Mt. St. Mary's). She had attended UB and then gone on to teach grade school in the South Bronx. In soft, confident tones Masters told the jury that the charges against them should be dropped. "The indictment has no merit in that what we did was the legitmate response of concerned citizens to a continuing crime, the war and the U.S. government's policies in Southeast Asia."

Judge Curtin, it was clear, liked the defendants. In upbringing, background, and education they reminded him of himself and of his own children. Deeply Catholic, products like him of Catholic schools, people for whom faith was as much an ethical system as it was a religion, the five defendants, so young, so earnest, struck a responsive chord in Curtin. He was moved by their idealism, their courage, their passion, their sense of social justice, and what he perceived as their heightened sense of patriotism.

Believing deeply in the righteousness of their cause, convinced that it was the horrors of the greater crime of the war that led them to commit their "crime," the defendants pleaded with Curtin to allow them to make the war in Vietnam the central issue of the trial. Considine said, "The legal process cannot be an autopsy. We will not allow ourselves to be dismembered by cold, hard facts. We have souls and that is what brought us here."

Curtin seemed to agree. His consciousness had been raised as much by the horror of the war as by the bravery of the dozens of young people who appeared before him in draft-resistance cases. His views on the war and on those who opposed it had changed considerably since the trial of the Buffalo Nine. Though he had rejected a similar request from Beyer and the Nine, now, three years later, to the consternation of the prosecution, Curtin permitted the Buffalo Five to conduct the trial much as they wished. Though aided throughout by their court-appointed attorney, Vincent E. Doyle, Jr., the tenor and tone of their defense they set themselves. Curtin was extremely permissive, allowing them to call him "Mr." instead of "Judge" and not requiring that they stand when he entered and left the court room. The five were buoyed by Curtin's attitude and took heart from his questions to the jury: Did they feel comfortable with the defendants or afraid of them? Did they think that whenever a person breaks a law he or she is necessarily a criminal? Did they to agree with the Nuremberg principle that every citizen has the duty to decide if his or her government is committing a war crime? When the jury was finally chosen, ten of its members said they agreed that it was time for the United States to pull out of Vietnam. Curtin cautioned them that "the defendants feel that they acted out of good motives. These arguments should certainly not be rejected out of hand." On the second day of the trial, as Curtin walked from his chambers into the large, high-ceilinged, wood-paneled courtroom, the five defendants and the more than one hundred spectators, friends, and family who had come to follow the proceedings, rose quietly to their feet. They did so every day for the duration of the trial.

Despite the continued objections of U.S. Attorney James W. Grable, Curtin permitted the defense to enter evidence into the record dealing with Vietnam War itself. The Five showed a ten-minute film showing forests defoliated by napalm and the bombing and burning of villages. They called to the stand a Vietnamese woman who testified that she had seen her village destroyed by Americans. When a former Marine testified that after one battle American troops "lined the wounded civilians up against trees and used them as targets," Grable objected to the comments as irrelevant. Curtin overruled. Grable again objected. When another vet referred to "American war crimes," Grable again objected. "The government is not on trial," he said. This time Curtin agreed that "the objection is well taken." Several days later, when Grable asked Masters to identify who was in the draft board offices with her, several spectators stood up and said, "I was there." When Curtin ordered them removed, Darst stood up and said, "If they leave you must ask me to leave too. What they're saying is that they are not just spectators but defendants too." Curtin asked the jury to leave and then patiently explained to the Five that if he allowed their supporters to voice their opinions he would not be able to stop others from coming in and "shouting that you should be sent to jail." The defendants brought a variety of witnesses to court. There was a UB history professor who talked about the origins of American involvement in Southeast Asia. There was a former FBI agent, a Buffalonian who had studied for the priesthood before he joined the agency, who told the court how the FBI infiltrated the peace movement. Father Dave Toolan, a tall, ascetic-looking, charismatic instructor from Canisius College, testified that in an unjust war, "Catholics not only have an obligation to make a judgment, but an obligation to bring about the war's end." U.S. Attorney Grable, reminding Toolan that he had been his student at Canisius (both defense attorney Doyle and Curtin were also graduates of Canisius), asked Toolan if a Catholic therefore had the right to destroy Selective Service records. Toolan said, "He could." "Would you condone it?" Grable asked. "Yes," Toolan answered.

Meanwhile, the defendants continued to treat the trial in the celebratory manner of a great happening, a week-long, joyful teach-in about the war. Every night, at St. Peter's United Church of Christ on Genesee Street on Buffalo's East Side, there was a potluck dinner. Dozens of friends and family came to share the experience of the trial, to support and encourage the five defendants, to give strength to the new community they all felt they were creating. Then, on Saturday, April 22, at the end of the trial's first week, Meaux Considine and Chuck Darst were married in the church. They had invited everybody—the jurors, Grable, even Judge Curtin—to come and celebrate with them. On Monday they were back in court, Considine tearful at the defense table as her husband, in an impassioned outburst to Curtin, cried, "People are dying this very minute by our hands. We have to stop this."

At the trial's end the defendants gave closing statements. Considine the implored the jury to understand their motives, to move beyond the limits of the law and accept what they had done as an act of patriotism. "Because of the war we acted last August out of hope, not despair. . . . We came here out of respect for life, respect for the sacredness of life." She closed, as she had opened, urging the jury to share with her and her co-defendants the spirit and the joy of their actions. "You can join us," she said.

Finally Vincent Doyle, the court-appointed defense lawyer who had remained on the sidelines throughout the trial, asked the jury for an acquittal. Like so many of the trial's participants, Doyle was an Irish Catholic. He had been raised in St. Mark's parish in Parkside. He had gone to Canisius High School, Canisius College, and then, like a many of Buffalo's Irish-Americans, to UB law school. Doyle said the trial had caused him to re-examine the whole purpose of the law. "Law is man's hunger for justice," he said. "When law gets in the way of truth, interferes with justice, then law is not something that can never be broken."

Throughout the trial Grable had been frustrated by Curtin's relaxation of the rules of evidence. In his closing remarks, he stuck to a strict interpretation of the law. Grable agreed that the defendants' motives were good, that "the war is hell." But, confident that the law was on his side, he said that, "the war is not an issue in this case."

Curtin's position on this pivotal question was not at all clear. While he had been exceedingly generous with the defendants, bending the rules of evidence so that they could get their message across, Curtin now gave clear signals that he could not overlook the fact that their actions had broken the law. Curtin's sentence in a recent counterfeiting case suggested that he would not be lenient with a crime that was premeditated. The counterfeiter was expecting his sixth child, and his attorney argued that he had not committed a violent act. Curtin imposed the maximum sentence anyway. "A violent act is brought on by a moment's loss of control," he said at the sentencing, "but this crime is the result of careful, deliberate, willful scheming and planning."

Curtin's charge to the jury confirmed the defendants' fears. He gave them little choice. "If you feel the defendants committed the acts as charged and if you further find they had good motives, or the acts were acts of conscience, or done to protest the laws and politics of the government, the acts committed would still not be justified under the law. In that case you must find them guilty of those acts. You are not to be concerned with the wisdom of the law." It took the jury seven hours to determine that the Five, the Buffalo, were guilty of burglary and conspiracy. The prosecution requested that the defendants be allowed to remain free on bail and Curtin, setting the sentencing for May 18, 1972, agreed.

The courtroom was packed on the morning of the sentencing, and as Judge Curtin entered, the defendants, now frightened by the prospect of a certain jail term, and the hundred-odd courtroom spectators, most of them family and friends, rose in a shuffle of chairs. After reviewing the facts of the case and the highlights of the trial, Curtin addressed the defendants. "A strong argument can be made," he said, that "because of your efforts, your love of country is above that of most citizens because you had the moral outrage to put into action what you believed. If others had the same moral outrage the war would have been over by now." Still, he reminded them sternly, they had broken the law. He suggested that perhaps they could have better accomplished their goals had they stayed within its boundaries. The lecture finished, Curtin sentenced the Buffalo to a year's probation. Refering to the many letters he had received urging leniency, Curtin said, "I don't speak for myself. I speak for all of the people in this community." Curtin assured the defendants they could travel to meet with their friends and to continue their activities. It almost sounded like he was encouraging them to do so. Given the aura of communality that resonated throughout the trial, it is inconceivable that Curtin could have given the Five any serious punishment. They were joined by their ethnicity (of all the principals in the trial only two—defendant Martin and prosecutor Grable—were not Irish), their pride in the ancient Irish tradition of resistance, and their connection to Buffalo's hundred-year-old Jesuit college, Canisius. Similarly, Judge Curtin and the five young defendants were connected, not by an insidious old-boy network, but rather by Lincolnesque "mystical chords of memory" that create respect and understanding, that nurture and sustain a sense of community. As Curtin rose to leave the courtroom the defendants and spectators burst into a rousing peal of applause.

While popular with anti-war movement in general (Curtin's sentence was printed on the op-ed page of the *New York Times* several days later), Curtin was bitterly and nastily criticized in a score of letters by local and national veteran's groups. But he was quietly proud of the defendants and convinced that he had done the right thing. Later in May Curtin addressed the graduating class of Trocaire, a Catholic college run by Mercy nuns that specialized in the education of nurses. Trocaire, which means "mercy" in Gaelic, overlooks Cazenovia Park in South Buffalo and is filled with Irish Catholic girls from the neighborhood, graduates of Mt. Mercy High School, destined for nursing jobs in adjacent Mercy Hospital. Curtin's brother Dan was an orthopedic surgeon at Mercy and the judge cared deeply about the hospital and the college. In an emotional address before the more than 150 graduating nurses, Curtin said, "We must end the war in Vietnam before it ends us. This war has turned all our best ideals to dust. . . . Let us think less of losing a war and more about human life. Let us think less about national honor and more about the death and devastation we have caused."

Later that summer, Jim Mang offered a course on the theology of civil disobediance at the Western New York Peace Center. One of his students was John T. Curtin, the first federal judge in the United States to allow peace activists against the war in Vietnam to freely and completely present their case that the real crime was not any that they were accused of, but rather the war in Vietnam itself.

As the war in Vietnam came to an end, activist priests turned their attention closer to home, to their declining neighborhoods and shrinking parish churches. The area had a new bishop, Edward Head, an Irish-American from New York (McNulty had died in 1973) who encouraged their community-organizing activities. David Gallivan, who came from a family of priests (his uncle, Joseph Herlihy, was a monsignor) was at Holy Cross on the Lower West Side, helping that area to survive the pains of ethnic and racial transition as it changed from Italian to Hispanic. Walter Kerns's FLARE was struggling to stabilize the rapidly changing parish of Blessed Trinity on the northeast side of the city. With Head's approval, Stanton and Bissonette went to Chicago to study community-organizing strategies and techniques at Saul Alinsky's Industrial Areas Foundation. Upon their return they harnessed their

inate sense of social justice to their newly acquired community-organizing skills. Stanton had become the pastor at St. Ambrose in South
Buffalo, and he was encouraging and reassuring his Irish-American
parishioners as they passed through the trauma of the shutdown of
the industrial base that had provided their livelihood for so long. Father Dennis Woods, as head of the Urban Studies Program at Canisius,
and Father Dan Mulvey, of Catholic Charities, following up on a study
they had conducted documenting widespread redlining by local banks,
launched a grassroots, citywide campaign against the practice.

Bissonette went to St. Bartholomew's Church on Grider Street where,
with barely a hundred parishioners left in the once-thriving Fillmore-
Leroy neighborhood, he began to build a multicultural ministry. Bissonette lived in the church rectory for years. Extraordinarily charismatic
and a brilliant speaker, he was extremely popular throughout the community and drew hundreds of people when invited to say mass and
to speak at churches throughout the diocese. His brother Ray urged
him to move on, to accept an assignment at a larger, more prestigious
parish where he would reach the decision-makers in the community,
encouraging them to create the kinds of political and social changes
Bissonette wanted for the well-being of his parish. But Bissonette refused
to leave St. Bartholomew's and continued to minister to his dwindling
congregation, saying mass before a handful of old people who huddled
in their coats in the underheated church, often dozing off before he
even got to the sermon. Bissonette rarely left the community (except,
Ray remembers with a smile, to fly all over the country marrying his
friends, former priests), and never accepted his friend Jack Weimer's
invitations to take a vacation in Florida. It wouldn't be appropriate,
he politely said, to take a vacation that his parishioners could not afford.

Bissonette's concerns extended beyond the boundaries of his parish.
In 1979, while working as an intern in Washington, D.C., for John
LaFalce, a Buffalo-area congressman (and another Canisius alumnus)
Bissonette told an interviewer that he'd "never stayed within the narrow
concept of church and religion." He said he'd always been interested
in the "larger issues." In the early 1980s, Bissonette became increasingly
distressed by U.S. intervention in Central America. As president of the
board of the Center for Justice in Buffalo, he soon became outspoken
in his criticism of American policy in El Salvador and turned his church
into a haven for illegal immigrants, political refugees from El Salvador,
Nicaragua, and Honduras seeking sanctuary in the United States and
Canada.

One night in February 1987 Bissonette opened his rectory door to two young men from the neighborhood. Bissonette knew one of them, Ted Simmons, a nineteen-year-old kid who'd been to see Father Joe several times, to talk with him about the trouble he'd been having at school and at home. His mother had thrown him out of his house, he said, and he wondered if he and his friend, Milton Jones, a seventeen-year-old from down the street, could come in. Bissonette let them in and showed them to a table in the kitchen. They sat down and waited while he made them sandwiches. Suddenly one of the boys produced a long hunting knife, cornered the priest and demanded that he lead them to the rectory's safe. Pocketing barely two hundred dollars, Simmons and Jones led Bissonette back into the kitchen, bound him to a chair, and gagged him with a pair of his own socks. Grabbing a large can of Chinese food from the kitchen cabinet, Jones smashed Bissonette on the head, knocking him unconscious. Simmons and Jones then passed the hunting knife back and forth between them, stabbing the priest repeatedly in his chest and heart. With Bissonette lying dead on the floor, the two teenagers left without a trace.

The murder of Father Bissonette was announced in bold headlines in the *Buffalo News* the following morning. A well-known and extremely popular priest, Bissonette's death was greeted with shock and horror. Bill Stanton, his old friend and close colleague since their days at Bishop Turner, told the press that Bissonette "was about the best we had." He was, said another, "a priest's priest." To Jack Weimer he was "the most courageous priest I know on any issue." Jim Mang, who had left the priesthood to become director of the Western New York Peace Center, said, "We've lost the most consistently principled priest on peace and justice issues in the diocese of Buffalo."

The police were baffled by the murder, unable to produce a suspect. Two illegal immigrants from Central America who had been staying in Bissonette's church were released after being briefly detained. Then, ten days later, Simmons and Jones knocked on the rectory door at St. Matthew's Church on Wyoming, just a few blocks away from St. Bartholomew's. Msgr. David Herlihy came to the door. Simmons knew Herlihy too, and told the semi-retired priest that his mother had thrown him out of the house. He was wondering, he asked, if he and his friend from the neighborhood could come in. Shortly after, Herlihy was found by another priest, lying dead on the rectory floor, stabbed seventeen times in his chest and heart.

Early the next morning Jones and Simmons were stopped trying to cross the Peace Bridge to Canada. Returned to Buffalo, they were tried in 1988 and both received sentences of fifty years to life.

Thousands of words were issued in the wake of the murders of the two priests. Bishop Head prayed for "forgiveness for those who have caused the great sorrow in our lives." A local psychiatrist explained that there was one common denominator in the murderers' backgrounds—"Neither of the youths has had a forceful father figure to guide him." A City Court judge wearily concluded that the killers were "very ordinary, run-of-the-mill cases . . . probably no different than thousands of others." Father Dave Gallivan, citing the commitment of the murdered priests, asked, "What is the sense of saying you love your neighbor if you don't want to be near him? Didn't Father Herlihy and Father Bissonette live by those words?" Stanton reminded people that Bissonette had once said, "I'm interested in whatever affects the people in the neighborhoods." It was his commitment and his extraordinary rapport with the African-Americans of his parish that just months before his murder had made Bissonette city vicar of Buffalo, lauded for bringing blacks into the church.

But nothing could comfort the people who lived in these neighborhoods. Few any longer believed that things were going to be all right. In the end, Bissonette and Herlihy were no safer than the children playing unawares on the street, the frightened young couples, or the aging widows who were innocent and helpless victims of the increasingly horrific crime and violence that haunted the streets of the city. Lives dedicated to community-building and to love had come to mean very little on the East Side of Buffalo.

John Curtin was part and parcel of Buffalo's liberal Catholic tradition. He had responded to The Buffalo Five with warmth and sympathy. He had known Bissonette and was moved by his life and work. So was Gene Reville, who had met Bissonette through Stanton. Reville and Curtin both worshiped at Father Weimer's Newman Center. Curtin was often there when Bissonette and other progressive priests came by for one of Weimer's special dinners. He remembers Bissonette once asking a young priest, "Do you want to be a bishop, or do you want to help people?" Curtin and Reville shared Bissonette's vision of social justice and his hope for interracial harmony. His life and ideals influenced both of them as they wrestled with the problems posed by the Buffalo school desegregration case.

7

THE RECORD SPEAKS

On April 30, 1976, U.S. District Judge John T. Curtin announced his decision in the case of *Arthur* v. *Nyquist,* a lawsuit that would change forever the character and quality of life in the city of Buffalo. The suit, brought by intrepid civil rights advocate Norman Goldfarb, Buffalo civil-rights organizations, and a number of black parents, had taken years to come to fruition. Filed in 1972, it was not tried until the fall of 1974. It was a difficult and extraordinarily complicated matter, the kind that Curtin said he'd "have to sit down and spend a long time thinking about." He did. While the community waited and wondered, Curtin deliberated. Finally, almost a year and a half after the trial had concluded, he announced his verdict. Huge headlines flashed across papers throughout the city. Judge Curtin announced, in a litany of verbs that left no doubt about where he stood, that the Board of Education was guilty of "creating, maintaining, permitting, condoning, and perpetuating racially segregated public schools in the City of Buffalo."

While many people expected that Curtin would find the Board of Education guilty, few were prepared for the sweeping magnitude of his decision. What Curtin had found was a broad and deep-seated complicity that involved many of the most significant public officials and institutions in the city. Curtin ruled that the mayor, the Common Council, the New York State Board of Regents, and the state commissioner of education had all taken actions and implemented policies that had fostered the creation of a Jim Crow school system. The black community of Buffalo had its justice, and the faith of the committed plaintiffs in the rightness of their case was vindicated. It had taken four years.

Some said it had taken a hundred and nine. In 1832 a fugitive slave from Virginia, a man named Henry Moxley, bound for Canada on the Underground Railroad, settled instead in Buffalo. Like the few dozen other blacks in the city, Moxley lived on Vine Alley, a small side-street on the East Side, across from the Vine Street African School. At first he worked as a waiter in the American Hotel, then as a barber there. By the end of the decade he had left the hotel and worked in his own barber shop around the corner at William Street and Michigan Avenue. Moxley prospered and with the money he earned he bought several lots, and built homes on them for the small but growing community of blacks living on William. By the early 1840s Moxley had become a leader in his community, a deacon in the African Methodist Episcopal Church, and an organizer of the National Convention of Colored Men, held in Buffalo in the summer of 1842.

Moxley spent the Civil War years in Buffalo, witnessing in fear and horror the draft riots of the summer of 1863. The riots were rooted in the conflict and tension that existed between the Irish dock workers and the blacks on Buffalo's East Side. It had been building for years, caused as much by economic competition as by feelings of racial hatred. Because they were allowed to work on the docks only as strikebreakers, black workers were loathed by the Irish workers, whose life-blood was dock work. Insult was added to injury when, following the issuance of the Emancipation Proclamation in 1863, the Irish dock workers of Buffalo were told they would now be drafted not only to restore the Union but to free the slaves as well. Enraged, they erupted. In late July 1863 dozens stormed to the east side of Main Street and violently invaded the small, terrified community of blacks on Vine Alley. Several hours after their rampage began, the rioters were finally dispersed. When Moxley and his neighbors emerged cautiously from their hideouts, they found one black man lying in the street, dead.

Heartened by the war, Moxley was emboldened by the peace. He followed the events of the Reconstruction closely and took the Radical Republicans at their word when they promised in the Fourteenth Amendment that from that time forward "no state could deny to any person within its jurisdiction the equal protection of the laws." In June 1867 Moxley and several other black parents, in an action that anticipated by more than a hundred years that of the plaintiffs in the school case, appeared before the School Committee of the Buffalo Common Council to argue that the segregated Vine Street African School violated their rights under the Fourteenth Amendment. Moxley demanded that blacks be allowed to send their children to the district schools on the city's East Side. When the council ignored their plea, Moxley and the others ignored the Council and enrolled their children in two East Side neighborhood schools.

The School Committee was furious and immediately directed the superintendent of schools to refuse to admit any black child into any public school other than the African School. On September 24, 1867, Superintendent John S. Fosdick personally expelled the black students from the schools. Fosdick, who had come to Buffalo from Vermont in the 1830s and had once been a volunteer "conductor" on the Underground Railroad, said that Moxley was misleading his own people while alienating those whites who believed in integration. In the interests of racial harmony, he maintained, Moxley had to be stopped. On October 8, 1867, overcoming the resistance of "a burly Negro and his colored troops," Fosdick reported to the council, "I found the number of colored children attending the public schools to be eighteen. . . . These pupils have been directed to attend School 9 [the African School] and have not attended any of the other schools since they were sent away from them."

Disappointed but not dismayed, Moxley decided to pursue his case in the courts. Following the advice of Albert J. Stevens, a white lawyer who agreed to manage the test case without fee, Moxley decided to bring charges against Fosdick in order, he said, "to test the law of the city as to the admissibility of colored children into the public schools." Their suit charged the School Committee of the Common Council with violation of the Civil Rights Act of 1866. Fosdick himself was charged with assault and battery.

On January 10, 1868, the case was heard before State Supreme Court Justice Charles Daniels (later the first dean of the Law School of the University of Buffalo). Fosdick's lawyer, City Attorney George S. Wardwell, argued that Fosdick could not be found guilty because his actions were done at the behest of the Common Council and because the city charter gave the Common Council authority in school matters. Daniels wasted little time on the decision and on the same day found in favor of Fosdick. Moxley was assessed court costs of $192. He instructed Stevens to appeal immediately. In his appeal before the State Supreme Court in May 1868, Stevens argued that "If construed to exclude colored children, the provisions of the city charter are inconsistent with the Civil Rights Act and therefore inoperative." In words that anticipated Judge Curtin's decision of 1976, Stevens argued that New York State, which had enabled the city of Buffalo to write its charter in the first place, was as responsible as the city for the maintenance and perpetuation of the racially segregated school system. The court, with Daniels again presiding, was not convinced, and reaffirmed the earlier judgment. "But one question is presented for the consideration of this court," the judges wrote, "whether a colored child is lawfully entitled to attend a school provided by the city authorities for the education of white children." The answer, they told Moxley, was no.

Decades later, Leland Jones, Buffalo's first African-American elected official, had better luck. He managed to win a seat on the Erie County Board of Supervisors from the Ellicott District in 1949. He soon learned that the Board of Education was drawing new district lines for School 32, his alma mater on Clinton Street. Beginning in September 1950, he was told, 125 black children would be taken out of nearby schools and sent to School 32. Jones was convinced that the board was deliberately trying to contain Ellicott District blacks in one school. He vowed to fight the plan. Working with African-American parents in the school and the community, Jones coordinated a letter-writing and telephone campaign designed to force the board to back down. The protest culminated in mid-June with a dramatic "March of Mothers." Fifty black women and more than a dozen fathers carried signs protesting the new school boundaries. They marched down William Street, past Steinhardt's New York–Style Deli, Teibel's Butcher Shop, and Saltzman's Fish Market, past Baker's Drug store, across Michigan, past the old Baptist church and the Little Harlem Hotel and Nightclub, under a brightly painted mural advertising the Club Moon-Glo, "Buffalo's Only All-Sepia Review," past the Soldier's and Sailor's Monument in Lafayette Square, down Court Street, to City Hall. Later that summer Jones learned that he and his parents' group had been successful. The board had backed down.

Since the days of Henry Moxley, race had not been an issue in the Buffalo public schools. Although blacks rarely received permanent teaching positions, public education policies were racially neutral and the behavior of the Board of Education was no more or less segregationist than any other branch or agency of city government. The board didn't pay much attention to the question. They didn't have to. As long as the black population was small and black children were a minority in a handful of East Side schools, nobody, let alone the Board of Education, cared. There were other questions to deal with.

The Board of Education consisted of five members carefully appointed by the mayor to represent the city's ethnic groups. There was always one Irish-American, one Italian, one Pole, one Protestant, and at least one Jew. (Although they made up only 2 percent of Buffalo's population in 1950, Jews were thought to be especially concerned about education.) The board was a mixed group of businesspeople, professionals, and would-be politicians who served for no pay. In 1950 the members of the board were Lester Gross, who owned a hat-manufacturing company; Mary Kazmierczak, a neighborhood doctor who lived over her office on the Polish East Side; Pasquale Rubino, an occasional candidate for political office and the proprietor of a well-known West Side funeral parlor; Sam Markel, a dentist; and Peter Gust Economu, maitre d' at the Park Lane Hotel, a favorite haunt of the city's business and political power brokers. The superintendent of schools was Robert T. Bapst, born on the German East Side in the 1880s, a graduate of local parochial secondary and high schools, a respected Latin scholar, and a deeply religious Catholic—"the most prominent Catholic layman in Buffalo," the *Buffalo News* wrote at the time of his appointment in 1935. In fact, many thought Bapst cared far more about the parochial schools than he did about the city's public schools.

Buffalo's Catholic schools are on their last legs now, some closing, some consolidating in a desperate effort to survive. But for years parochial schools were the lifeblood of the city's Catholic immigrant communities, the places where, until the late 1950s, at least half of the school-age children in Buffalo were educated. The parochial schools were scattered everywhere, attached to churches in neighborhoods throughout the city. There were more than 210 of them in Buffalo in 1950. Anyone who is anyone in Buffalo today went to them: Curtin and Reville to St. Theresa's in Irish South Buffalo; Mayor Jimmy Griffin to St. Brigid's in the Irish First Ward; Associate Superintendent of Schools Joe Murray, "the godfather of Buffalo's school integration plan," to All Saints in Riverside.

Robert Bapst was a product of the parochial school tradition and believed in it deeply. The first principal at South Park High School, Bapst without shame or apology inbued the school with parochial school traditions. His teachers—the men from Canisius, the local Jesuit College, and the women from D'Youville College, run by the Grey Nuns of the Sacred Heart—were Catholic, and his curriculum was the classical and religious curriculum that had long characterized the Catholic education.

Bapst's reputation at South Park led to his appointment as superintendent in 1935, but he was afflicted with a divided loyalty. Throughout his tenure as superintendent Bapst was charged with favoritism toward the Catholic schools. Because so many people in the city were already

paying for Catholic education, Bapst was reluctant to ask the Common
Council for additional funds for the public schools. He was proud of
his frugal operation and boasted that Buffalo spent less per pupil on
public education than any of the "Big Six" cities in New York State.
Convinced that if given a choice the people of Buffalo would spend
still less on public education, in 1949 Bapst argued unsuccessfully for
the creation of a fiscally independent elected school board.

Because of Bapst's Catholicism, the Board of Education was particularly sensitive about keeping religion out of the public schools. In
January 1949 the Kiwanis Club sought the permission of the board
to advertise and sell tickets for a traveling performance of the world-
famous Passion Play put on every Easter in Oberammergau, West Ger-
many. The Board refused. Board members were even more adamant
when the club asked to have students released from school to see the
play. Over Bapst's objection the board denied the request, telling the
Kiwanis Club to schedule the performance on a Saturday.

Sometimes the separation of religion and public education was a
ruse to hide other fears. In March 1949 a Jewish philanthropist offered
to place a copy of the Jewish Encyclopedia in each of the schools'
libraries. Samuel Markel, the Jewish member on the board, advised
against it, saying that the book was "religious in character." Most of
the board members, however, wanted to accept the books. Chairman
Michael Montessano thought Markel's position was excessive. He said
the board was "leaning over backwards for fear that someone may
construe it as an action bordering on the religious." When it began
to appear that Montessano would prevail, Markel revealed his real
motive—he was opposed to the gift because it was an open invitiation
to anti-Semitic vandalism. Revealing just how raw was this particular
wound, Markel said, "Somebody may go in there and take those books
and deface them, and may use it as a means of poking fun at a group."
The board reversed itself, acceding to a tacit ethnic prerogative and
rejecting the generous offer. Ethnic prerogative was again recognized
in 1950, when Mary Kazmierczak received permission from her fellow
board members to collect funds and clothing in the schools for the
Polish Relief Fund.

The board was proud of its vocational schools. The mural on the
entrance walls at Burgard High School, painted in the heroic, romantic
style of all the murals created in the 1930s by the federal Works Progress
Administration, reflect this pride. The picture, on two huge walls, is
of the city's skyline. The sky is bright blue and the buildings in the
background, with factories and the airport prominently displayed (for

years Burgard has offered courses in automobile and aviation mechanics) are gleaming and colorful. In the foreground are handsome, Nordic-looking young men, white work coats covering their suits and ties, diligently repairing cars, trucks, and planes.

The growth of wartime industries had increased the demand for vocational education and by 1950 more than half of the boys of high-school age in Buffalo were enrolled in the city's six vocational schools (there was only one vocational school for girls). Each of the schools specialized in the skills needed by one of Buffalo's dominant industries. McKinley offered courses in pattern-making and moulding; Burgard in car and airplane tool and die making; and Buffalo Technical, a highly competitive technical rather than a vocational school, in engineering. The State Education Department was pleased with the condition of vocational education in Buffalo, but concerned that there was an over-emphasis on industrial training. Compared with students in Rochester, Pittsburgh, Boston, and Chicago, the department said in one report, not enough of Buffalo's youngsters were being prepared for careers in the business world. The report implied that Buffalo was failing to pro-vide its children with the skills necessary for the modern age. The depart-ment's analysts thought that "the relative stability of the economic life of the area is assured," but they wanted to take no chances and, in a prescient reminder, urged the Board of Education to think about the future by adapting vocational schools to the needs of the changing economy. "Specialized education in the vocational fields must be broad enough to condition trainees in other areas as jobs shift as a result of labor-saving equipment and the like."

The State Education Department was also concerned about "inter-group relations" in Buffalo's public schools. Noting that "it appears that the relative concentration of certain ethnic groups in particular sections of the city will persist for several generations," the department urged school officials to "concentrate . . . on interschool activities as a way of teaching better intergroup relations."

The department was also worried about a group of high-school students who were neither college-bound nor in vocational programs. These youngsters, 60 percent of all the students in Buffalo's high schools, were destined to work in jobs the department called "operational," clearly manual jobs that required few skills. These students needed "pre-employ-ment preparation, including some business and management skills and certain social skills involved in dealing with the public." Buffalo had a high dropout rate (20 percent in the academic high schools and an incredible 50 percent for students in vocational programs), and the department proposed a program to allow dropouts to re-enter school on a part-time or full-time basis, "as their experience after leaving school reveals the need for further education."

While Buffalo's dropout rate was high, the number of students going on to college—15 percent—was low, the department said. Not everyone agreed. Welles Moot, for example, scion of one of Buffalo's oldest WASP families and the author of a 1949 Board of Regents report on vocational education, saw nothing wrong with the situation. "I don't believe in pushing them," Moot told the *Buffalo Evening News* in 1949. "If they don't want to go to college they shouldn't be forced to. If they want to go to work after they finish high school, let them go to work." The Board of Education seemed to agree.

When Superintendent Bapst resigned in 1950 he was replaced by Benjamin Willis from Yonkers, known nationally for his expertise in vocational education. By this time the Board of Education had begun to devote more attention to the growing numbers of black children in the city's public schools. And, like the Buffalo Municipal Housing Authority, it began to take steps that would result in the isolation of blacks in a handful of schools on Buffalo's East Side. While the West Side had its share of immigrants, particularly Irish and Italians near the Niagara River, and even a few blacks, the tone, character, and reputation of the West Side had always been determined by the more affluent families who lived in the large and oppulent single-family homes lining the broad and magnificent streets that ran between Elmwood and Delaware Avenues. Even in the 1950s, when many of the old mansions on Delaware were being either torn down or converted to offices, and as Dutch elm disease killed thousands of the tall, arching trees that had graced the city's streets so beautifully for so many years, the Delaware District retained its cachet. Linwood Avenue, however, parallel to Delaware one block to the east, had by the mid-1950s begun to "go," in the minds of some white people. A magnificent street lined with immense and imaginatively designed turn-of-the-century wood-frame homes, Linwood, people began to say, was "too close to Main." Some blacks, in fact, had already begun to cross from the east side of Main to the west, renting apartments and buying homes on Harvard and Oxford Streets, small side streets between Linwood and Main. Main Street, it seemed, was no longer an impenetrable barrier to black settlement. In 1954 the Board of Education, in a sweeping change of high-school districts, did what it could to reinforce Main Street as a dividing line between black and white Buffalo.

Since the turn of the century, the high school for the Ellicott District had been Hutchinson Central, at Elmwood and Chippewa on the West Side. For the most part the kids from the Ellicott District took public buses to school, getting off at Main and then walking west down Chippewa, a busy street lined with clothing stores, jewelry shops, cleaners, coffee shops, and drug stores. The merchants liked the kids. They catered to them, welcomed them into their stores, and bought ads in the Hutch-Central yearbook. But the Ellicott District was changing and gradually more and more of the kids who passed by on their way to "Hutch" were black. That, the merchants didn't like. Nor did the members of the Board of Education. Beginning in September, they announced in April 1954, all youngsters living east of Main Street would go to East High. Meanwhile, the board made sure that Hutch would become a predominantly white school.

For years the flagship of Buffalo's vocational schools had been Buffalo Technical on Cedar Street on the East Side. A degree from "Tech" was a ticket to success in the engineering field, and admission was prized by the first- and second-generation immigrant fmailies who sent their kids there.

Though Tech's neighborhood had become completely black, very few African-Americans were admitted to the school. The Board of Education, under intense pressure from parents as well as the skilled unions that the school fed, had no intention of allowing the school's admission policies to change. The solution: as part of the sweeping district changes of 1954, the school was combined with Hutch Central and moved into its building on Elmwood—"a better geographical location on the West Side." The school was renamed "Hutch-Tech."

The purpose of the 1954 plan was to keep blacks in their neighborhoods and whites in theirs. While blacks were spreading throughout the East Side, small pockets of white settlement, sometimes protected by railroads or broad avenues, remained. Lovejoy, part Italian, part German, part Polish, was one. While most of the kids in the neighborhood went to parish schools—Precious Blood, St. Agnes, and Visitation— many went to the old neighborhood school, School 43, on Benzinger Street. For years 43 had fed into East High. But now that East had been designated as Buffalo's "Negro high school," Lovejoy parents wanted out. In 1955 the board drew district lines that sent Lovejoy's kids to Kensington High, in the all-white Kensington section east of Lovejoy.

The board did the same on the West Side, allowing white parents to take their kids out of schools when the number of blacks increased. As the population of the Masten District swelled in the mid-1950s and schools got overcrowded there, the board allowed blacks to cross Main

Street and send their kids to School 16 on Delaware Avenue. White parents who didn't like that could send their kids to School 30, an all-white school a few blocks west on Elmwood Avenue. The city's schools, like its neighborhoods, were fast becoming racially isolated. All it took was the stroke of a pen.

Still, some blacks were optimistic. Interviews with five black ministers in a 1958 *Courier Express* story headlined "Our Negro Neighbors" revealed a sense of hope and an eagerness to be liked. Decrying white exodus from central city neighborhoods, the clergymen urged whites to stay in their homes, churches and neighborhoods. "We are sure they will find Negroes very good and helpful neighbors," they said. One of the ministers, Kenneth Curry, wasn't convinced that their pleas would be heeded. He urged Buffalo's whites to "become a Negro for a day," to see what it was like. "No matter how talented or diligent my son or daughter turn out to be they must face their future in Buffalo with one handicap—they are Negroes," Curry said.

Later that year rumblings of a debate that would linger for years were first heard by the Board of Education. The upheaval caused by population changes and urban renewal had led to a desperate shortage of housing and schools on the East Side. Finally, in 1958, after years of politicking by Cora Maloney, the African-American woman who represented the Masten District on the Common Council, the board agreed to build a new school for the neighborhood. Known as Woodlawn Junior High, it was to be built on the site of Offerman Field, an old baseball stadium in the heart of the emerging African-American neighborhood at the corner of Masten and Ferry. Convinced that the board chose the site knowing that as a result of its boundaries the school would become segregated, a group of African-Americans from the Masten District argued against the location.

Pasquale Rubino, the chairman of the board, was unconcerned. "Build schools for the children," he said, "wherever the children find themselves, whatever ethnic group they represent or whatever nationality they happen to be." The board could not be responsible for residential patterns, he argued. Was it any fault of the board's, he asked, that schools on Buffalo's West Side were Italian, those in South Buffalo were Irish, or those on the East Side Polish? Frank Caldwell, a black opponent of the Offerman site, warned the board to "commence right now to accept the fact that residential segregation creates an educational problem that must be faced by the board."

Most blacks in the neighborhood supported Maloney's drive to have Woodlawn built, and seemed reassured when Superintendent Joseph

Manch told them that "any thought of segregation is one thing I won't stand for." The racial question, he said, would be dealt with later, when district boundaries for the new school were drawn. When Caldwell reminded Manch that just four years earlier the Supreme Court had found that segregated education was inferior education, Manch proferred reassuringly that "the court was concerned with schools in the South, Mr. Caldwell, they were not concerned with schools in Buffalo . . . We just don't operate that way."

The NAACP didn't agree. In 1962 the local chapter of the NAACP reported that there were twenty-eight schools with black majorities and seventeen, all on the East Side, that were close to 100 percent black. Saying that Buffalo "has taken a back seat among cities in the fight for integration," chapter president Raphael DuBard demanded that the Board of Education, using a variety of strategies including site-selection and redistricting, "fulfill its educational and legal responsibilities by entirely desegregating the school system." In June 1963 New York State Commissioner of Education James Allen corroborated DuBard's data. Reporting "clear and overwhelming evidence of racial imbalance" in the Buffalo public schools, Commissioner Allen ordered the board to produce a remedy to be implemented in January 1964.

It might have appeared that time had begun to run out for the board, but Allen didn't seem to have his heart in forcing it to desegregate. The board seemed to sense this and responded half-heartedly to the order. At the suggestion of Superintendent Manch it considered a voluntary transfer plan that would permit any child in any school in the city to transfer to any other school, if space permitted. Space, not race, Manch said, would be the determining factor. It would take time, however, even to achieve this concession to the segregation of Buffalo's schools.

Joe Manch was born and raised on the old Jewish East Side where his father, a rabbi, owned a Judaica shop considered one of the best west of the Hudson. Manch had been an English teacher at South Park High School before joining the downtown staff as associate superintendent for community relations in 1954. In that post Manch was known less for his views on civil rights than for his public statements on discipline and conduct. One of his pet projects had been the creation of a student dress code. For boys, Manch's code prohibited dungarees, motorcycle jackets, and hobnail boots, and required ties and jackets or sweaters except when in shop. For girls, pants, tee shirts, "tight sweaters," "clinking jewelry," and big earrings were prohibited. In 1958, one year after being appointed superintendent, Manch addressed the forty-first annual convention of the National Association of Retail Clothiers in Chicago. "The boy who learns that it is smart to dress in good taste for school will grow up to be the man who will practice the art of appropriate dress," he said. Manch had a keen eye for publicity. A seemingly permanent fixture at virtually every civic function in Buffalo, his name and face were known throughout the city. In 1960, with more than three more years left on his six-year contract, Manch renegotiated his salary, managing to make himself the highest paid public official in Buffalo.

By the early 1960s Manch had become a favorite of the city's small but articulate liberal establishment. He was a vice president of the Urban League and the recipient of man-of-the-year awards from churches and community and civic groups throughout Buffalo. Manch said he welcomed Allen's support in the matter of desegregation, and that he hoped it would strengthen his hand with the recalcitrant board. Both of the city's newspapers, neither of which had previously taken a strong stand on the question, also supported Allen's intervention. The board, wrote the *Evening News,* "has not been sufficiently aggressive and determined in seeking a feasible plan of action."

For the next twelve years, Joseph Manch was the man in the middle, caught between the pressure of a handful of civil rights activists on one side and the racial hardliners, in the community and on the board, who were opposed to virtually any plan designed to overcome the isolation of blacks in the city's schools. Manch's plan—the simple edict that children could attend any school they chose—came under immediate fire from the racial demogogues on the board.

Lydia Wright, a doctor and the sole African-American on the Board, didn't like it either. Her reasons, of course, were considerably different from those of Parlato and Slominski. By 1962 Wright and her husband, Dr. Frank Evans, had in the ten years since they'd been in Buffalo built a successful and highly regarded pediatric practice. Working out of a second-floor office in a turn-of-the-century brick business block at the corner of Jefferson and Ferry, a major node on the Black East Side since the mid-1950s, Wright and Evans were well-respected in their own community as well as in the world of Buffalo medicine at large. They did well, too, in maintaining a beautiful home on Humboldt Parkway, despite the highway that had been built in their front yard.

While Wright turned her back on the expressway, she was always involved in her community, particularly in the affairs of School 74, the neighborhood school on Donaldson Road. By the late 1950s and early 1960s, the school, once filled with the Jewish kids who lived on

Brunswick Boulevard, Hamlin Road, and Goulding and Butler Streets, had a growing minority student body. It was one of the first schools in the city to sponsor a program commemorating Negro History Week. Wright came to one of those programs in 1960 but was appalled by what she felt was the vapid and insulting tone of the presentation. She wrote a letter to Manch suggesting more substantial and significant ways to honor the occasion. Two years later, under increasing pressure to appoint a black to the board, Mayor Sedita followed Manch's advice and appointed Lydia Wright. For the next five years she was always the leading and often the only board member committed to equal rights for Buffalo's African-American schoolchildren.

In opposition to Manch's plan Wright argued that whites had been running away from inner-city schools for the better part of a decade and to think that they would choose to go to them now was foolish. She wanted a program that would integrate all of the schools in the city, leaving none with more than 30 percent of its pupils black. To accomplish this sweeping goal she proposed a combination of voluntary and mandatory strategies. Wright proposed the creation of a series of specialty schools whose academic excellence would, she was convinced, attract black and white students from all over the city. "Magnet schools," she called them. Other students would simply be bused to schools outside their neighborhoods in order to achieve racial balance.

The board refused to support Wright's plan and she refused to support Manch's. Angry and eager to force the issue, she introduced a motion to postpone indefinitely the implementation of Manch's proposal. The board, hoping to avoid the controversy that even Manch's mild integration would create, unanimously and happily approved. In January 1964, one month later, the U.S. Commission on Civil Rights entered the picture, reporting that Buffalo "had the largest problem of school segregation in New York State." The commission blamed the state rather than the city for the problem. It seemed to sympathize with, if not actually exonerate, local authorities, and criticized the state for its failure to provide leadership and direction in the cause of public school desegregation. As a result of the state's dereliction of its duty, it said, "Buffalo has had to grope for solutions." There was little groping, however, when in March 1964 the board drew the district lines for its new school, Woodlawn Junior High.

The Woodlawn redistricting case became the most rancorous and emotional civil-rights question the people of Buffalo had ever confronted. In the racially charged atmosphere of the mid-1960s, "Woodlawn" was a buzz-word. Where a person stood on the Woodlawn issue revealed where he or she stood on the whole burning question of Negro rights. For Buffalo's civil-rights groups Woodlawn had become something of a crusade.

The civil-rights movement in Buffalo was weak, less a movement than a group of scattered individuals, primarily black and Jewish. In other cities an alliance of black and Jewish as groups had created and maintained the civil rights struggle ever since World War II. But in Buffalo, where blacks, like other ethnic groups, tended to be quiet and conservative, and Jews, in the absence of a large Jewish working class and a Jewish labor movement, were equally so, the civil rights movement lacked the drive and leadership that it had elsewhere. Thus, it was up to individuals. Among them the most dynamic, committed, and energetic was Norman Goldfarb.

Goldfarb was born and raised on Madison Street on Buffalo's East Side. The son of Jewish immigrants, Goldfarb's father was a rag peddler, and the boy spoke only Yiddish until he was five years old. Like many Buffalo Jews in the mid-1920s, in Goldfarb's early teens the family moved to Humboldt Parkway. They lived in a two-family home on Brunswick Boulevard, a street filled with Jewish families. Goldfarb graduated from Fosdick-Masten, the local high school located on a hill overlooking the old Fruit Belt. Then, on a football scholarship, he continued at the University of Buffalo, where he played alongside Leland Jones, one of the great quarterbacks in that school's history. Goldfarb was drafted into the army during World War II, where he became aware of discrimination against both Negroes and Jews. Goldfarb returning to UB after the war and became involved in the university's small but vocal "Jim Crow Must Go" movement.

Growing up on the East Side Goldfarb had always mixed easily with blacks. "Blacks were in my house and I was in theirs," he remembered shortly before he died in 1982. Goldfarb thought blacks and Jews were fighting the same struggle, and during the 1950s and early 1960s he almost singlehandedly fought against racial and religious discrimination in Buffalo's town clubs and golf clubs. As director of personnel for a local department store during the 1950s, Goldfarb argued relentlessly for the hiring and promotion of blacks.

Given his attitudes and his ideas, it was no wonder that Goldfarb became a leader of the struggle to make Woodlawn an integrated school. For Goldfarb, the Woodlawn redistricting case was a critical test for Buffalo, a barometer of the character of the community. In speeches to community groups during the tension-filled winter days of 1964, Goldfarb said that Buffalo was at a "moral crossroads." It was time, he said, for Buffalonians to accept their "responsibility as citizens of the "City of Good Neighbors" by supporting the creation of an integrated district for the new school. Goldfarb, Dubard, and Frank Mesiah, a black school teacher, all of whom had gone to the August 1963 March on Washington, organized a citywide campaign to generate support for an integrated school. At community meetings and in newspaper ads, letters to the editor and television talk shows throughout January and February 1964, they carried the fight to neighborhoods and community groups all over the city, engaging the people of Buffalo in a dramatic and intense debate. But their efforts, hampered by a tiny budget and hostile public opinion, could not match those of the opposition.

The campaign to make Woodlawn an all-black school was led by board members Carmelo Parlato, from the Italian West Side, and Alfreda Slominski, from the Polish East Side. Banking their political future on the easily aroused fears of Buffalo's ethnic voters, they talked up Parlato's plan to restrict Woodlawn's students to the children east of Main Street. By late January the grassroots movement in favor of Parlato's Wood-lawn plan had spread to white neighborhoods throughout the city. Just a few months before Manch had assured the public that Woodlawn would be integrated. "The zone will cross Main Street if I have anything to say about it," he had said. But white pressure on him began to mount, and he seemed to waver. By the end of January, Manch said, he had received more than ten thousand signatures from parents west of Main Street as well as thousands from people in other neighborhoods not affected by the plan, all opposed to the drawing of Woodlawn's boundaries west of Main. Manch called the feeling among these parents "akin to panic."

While Manch claimed to want to integrate Woodlawn, he was unwilling to exert the leadership necessary to leverage the support in the community that could counter the powerful and virulent anti-inte-gration forces roused so effectively by Parlato and Slominski. In March Parlato introduced a resolution creating an all-black district east of Main Street for the new school, and all the other members of the board, except Wright, went along. Anthony Nitkowski, a leader of the International Association of Machinists and considered a liberal, joined the majority in favor of Parlato's all–East Side boundaries. "I came here to vote against this motion," he said. Suddenly reversing his position, however, he added, "Of course, in the interests of unity I vote 'yes.' " Manch was the last to capitulate. "It is not now feasible," he said, "to draw the district lines for Woodlawn in such a way as to achieve a racial balance that would be meaningful or stable." Goldfarb was furious with Manch. Both men were products of the old integrated East Side, and Goldfarb expected Manch to support integration, to fight the board, and to resign in protest if it failed to do the right thing.

In his order of June 1963 Commissioner James Allen had expressed his "fervent hope that local authorities will deal with the elimination of *de facto* segregation, that the responsibility will be accepted at the local level." Woodlawn, which opened in September 1964 as an all-black junior high school, was the board's response.

The historical record regarding East High School offered the plaintiffs in the school case still more damning evidence.

By the early 1970s East High, located just east of Main on Northampton Street, had become a symbol of the ghettoization of Buffalo's African-American community. Until the mid-1960s, the school, like the neighborhood, had been white, filled with German, Polish, and a sprinkling of Jewish kids. But suddenly East changed, faster even than the neighborhood. Board policy, the plaintiffs argued, not demographics, was responsible.

Because so many Poles lived in the district, the Polish language had been offered as an elective at East High School since the school opened in 1927. In 1960, however, the board took the Polish program out of East and moved it to Kensington High School, in the all-white Kensington-Bailey neighborhood, and to South Park High School, in all-white South Buffalo. This strategy, according to the plaintiffs, encouraged hundreds of white parents who lived in the East High district to take their kids out of East and send them instead to predominantly white schools in outlying white neighborhoods. As a result, the isolation of blacks at East High School was reinforced.

Meanwhile, after constant pressure from Commissioner Allen, who insisted that they "do everything within their power consistent with sound educational principles to achieve racial balance," the Board of Education produced Manch's previously postponed voluntary pupil-transfer program. It was implemented in September 1964, but without any plan for enforcement and with all of the transportation burden borne by black children.

The plan was a sham and everybody, Manch included, knew it. So did the citizens Council on Human Relations, a group of black parents represented by Norman Goldfarb. In December 1964 Goldfarb petitioned Commissioner Allen, warning him of the inadequacy of the soon-to-be-enacted plan and demanding that he intervene in the case. In February 1965 Allen did intervene, rejecting Manch's voluntary transfer plan and issuing his most sweeping and comprehensive order to date. He gave the board three months to submit a plan "for the progressive elimination of racial imbalance" in the public schools of Buffalo by September 1965.

But when the time came, Manch offered little more than he had a year earlier: a voluntary transfer plan for blacks into white schools when space permitted, new district lines for several of the city's high schools, and compensatory educational programs for the growing number of all-black schools. There were fourteen such schools in 1965 (an increase of five in five years) and twenty-one more that were more than half black.

Opposition to the plan was immediate. Parlato and Slominski were predictably furious. So was Goldfarb's Citizen's Council. The group's lawyer, Herman Schwartz, a UB Law School professor with a reputation as a radical, charged that the Manch plan merely "tinkered" with the segregated school system. Schwartz further charged that Manch and the board were not capable of desegregating the schools of Buffalo. A local plan drawn up by local people would not do the trick. Schwartz argued that Buffalo needed a plan drawn up by a group of "human relations experts who are also educational experts," and he urged Allen to appoint one.

Schwartz's suggestion that the Buffalo school board was not up to the task touched a sensitive chord. Slominski particularly took offense. In a speech before the Daughters of the American Revolution, a group that obviously accepted as members no people of her ethnic heritage, Slominski said that the last thing Buffalo needed was more experts. The Board of Education had already "entrusted matters to professional educators and they have failed that trust," she charged. It was time, she said in a cry that became more persistent over the years, for the people of Buffalo to elect their own school board.

Despite the opposition of civil-rights groups on one side and the neighborhood school movement on the other, the mainstream—both newspapers, the Council of Churches, the Board of Rabbis—supported Manch's lackluster plan and in April 1965 the Board of Education passed it. Commissioner Allen, however, like Herman Schwartz, had little confidence in this watered-down, home-grown attempt to desegregate the city's public school system of more than seventy thousand pupils. Buffalo needed help, Allen decided, and in June 1965 he dispatched to Buffalo a triumverate of "experts" from New York City—Kenneth Clark, a black psychologist, John Fischer, president of Columbia Teacher's College, and Rabbi Judah Cohn. Like so much of the good intentions of 1960s liberalism, Allen's move was foolish and arrogant, hardly likely to win the support of Buffalo's proud white ethnics. Without that support, Allen must surely have known, no integration plan could ever work.

Allen's commission of inquiry was not all that worried Manch and the members of the Board of Education. By the mid-1960s Buffalo's public schools were experiencing a steady decline in academic achievement. In 1965, 38 percent of the city's public school students failed to pass the Regent's exam. Only Schenectady did worse. Among the state's Big Six cities—New York, Buffalo, Yonkers, Rochester, Syracuse, and Albany—none paid its teachers less, none had fewer teachers with baccalaureates, and none spent less per student per year than did Buffalo—$496, compared to a state average of $740. According to the National Educational Association, the problems of the Buffalo public schools were far more than academic or budgetary. The primary problem was citizen apathy. "One of Buffalo's most distinctive features," the NEA reported, "is its lack of interested, vocal, effective individuals with a commitment to public education." Change of any kind, the report suggested, would be long in coming.

Over the years Manch had done what he could about the budget. He thought the creation of a school board fiscally independent of the mayor and the Common Council would be able to raise more funds, so he lobbied every year in Buffalo and Albany for legislation to that effect. It was easy for Manch, critics said. After all, he was Jewish. He didn't pay Catholic school tuition. Most of the city's politicians agreed. This was certainly true of the mayors elected since World War II— Mruc, Kowal, Pankow, Sedita—all Catholics, all rooted in the city's parochial-school tradition. Separate school taxes, they argued, would be unfair. Given the perennial budget crises, Allen's rejection of Manch's desegregation plan for the second time, and the impending report of Allen's commission, people in Buffalo concerned with public education did not know what to expect.

The next two and a half years were a series of tense and seemingly endless negotiations between the constantly prodding commissioner and an increasingly recalcitrant board. For Manch it was a particularly difficult time. He very carefully calculated his moves, sometimes leading, at other times dragging his feet. As a result he often alienated everyone. Convinced that the Board of Education would never accept an integration program that required the busing of white children into schools in black neighborhoods, Manch encouraged board member Lydia Wright in September 1966 to introduce a resolution promising "no transportation of white children into nonwhite residential areas except by their own choice." Since it had been introduced by the sole black member of the board, Manch hoped the resolution would assuage the fears of the city's whites and thereby provide him the cover to pursue less controversial and divisive programs for the desegregation of Buffalo's schools.

The ploy seemed to work. Immediately upon approving the resolution the board passed another of Manch's desegregation plans. Considerably stronger than the others, this plan required the creation of a middle school for children in grades five through eight with district lines that crossed into both black and white neighborhoods, and the busing of some 750 inner-city black children to schools in white neighborhoods. It was the first time busing had been proposed. Nonetheless, the plan pleased none of the concerned community organizations, and both civil rights and neighborhood school groups called for Manch's resignation. Commissioner Allen didn't like the plan either. Finding it "disappointing and unsatisfactory," he rejected it in June 1967. He gave Manch and the board yet another deadline, this time until November, to submit a timetable for the development and implementation of what he called "a total integration plan."

The timing of Allen's new order could not have been worse. During several days in late June, Buffalo experienced its first riots, though they were limited to a handful of streets on the city's East Side. The destruction shocked and frightened whites and blacks throughout the city. The trouble started late in the afternoon on Tuesday, June 27. Small groups of black teenage boys (some of the newspaper accounts referred to them as "gangs") cruised the streets around William Street and Jefferson Avenue smashing car and store windows. By nightfall more than 150 riot-equipped policemen had been dispatched to the area. Following a melee during which three policemen (all of whom happened to live in the suburbs) and one fireman were injured, crowds were quickly dispersed by a flying wedge of forty police officers who marched down the middle of Sycamore Street firing tear gas.

Floyd Edwards was a black desk lieutenant at Precinct 3 on South Division Street the night the riots broke out. He had joined the department in 1950, when there were only six other blacks on the force. In 1960 he became Buffalo's first black lieutenant, and five years later the city's first black desk lieutenant. He had no illusions about his position, he says, snidely referring to himself as "Mayor Sedita's spook at the desk," promoted because he was black. Edwards had been in the Marines during World War II, stationed first at Guam and then at Guadalcanal, thousands of miles away from his father, who was fighting in Europe as a member of the 99th Fighter Squad, the first black fighter battalion in the country's history. Unlike his father, Edwards never fought. Black marines were laborers, not soldiers, and they were not allowed to fight. They weren't even permitted, Edwards subsequently found out, to shoot their rifles. He was once severely punished for doing so. Following his discharge from the service Edwards worked at Westinghouse as an engine lathe operator. It was a good job, his father said, but it didn't have the security of civil service. So, in 1950 Edwards took and passed the police exam and joined the force as a patrolman. He was assigned to Precinct 3, and his beat took him up and down the streets of St. Lucy's parish, the old Italian neighborhood on the East Side. It was still a nice neighborhood, he says, before they cleared it for the Ellicott Projects. The houses were old and the people were poor but it had the character of a real Italian village. You could smell it in the air, he says. It was on his beat that Edwards met his wife, a baker at Christiano's Bakery on Swan Street.

Edwards had been on the East Side his whole life and had seen all the changes, from the mixed neighborhood that it once was to the black ghetto it had become. Edwards knew it inside and out and wasn't surprised by the outbreak of violence that June. The morning after the riots Edwards was put back in uniform. With a battalion of police officers under his command, he went back onto the streets. The ghetto was still smouldering. Fires still burned at William and Jefferson, Maple and Carlton, and Peckham and Monroe Streets. Plate glass windows all along Broadway and Sycamore had been smashed, and the streets were sprinkled with glass, empty cartons of shotgun shells, tear-gas cannisters, broken eyeglasses, and bricks. Many of the store windows were boarded up, covered with large pieces of plywood bearing the glowing red and white lettering of the Macaluso Emergency Enclosure Company. Small groups of black teenage boys clustered on the corners, taunting the passing police cars from a distance.

As the day wore on the situation grew worse. Beginning at about 4:30 P.M. buses passing through the neighborhood were stoned. As night fell the gangs grew larger and more menacing, and still more windows were broken (even those store owners, some white, others black, who had written "Soul Brother" on their windows were not always spared). Fires were started, cars overturned, and stores looted. Taking no chances, Police Commissioner Frank Felicetta, an Italian-American from the old West Side, dispatched more than four hundred policemen to the neighborhood on Wednesday night. By early morning the crowds had been dispersed. Forty people were treated for injuries, fourteen for gunshot wounds. Forty-six teenage boys were arrested. Superintendent Manch, checking for damage to School 41 at Jefferson and Sycamore, had to be escorted out of the area under police protection.

The response to the riots of 1967 was predictable. Mayor Sedita and Police Commissioner Felicetta sounded like officials in some Southern town—they blamed "outside agitators." Civil-rights leaders blamed the system and "Buffalo's broken promises." Lieutenant Edwards, sympathetic to the voices of discontent within his own community, was nevertheless convinced that the riots were criminal as much political actions. "It was very apparent," he told the *Evening News*, "that the troublemakers were shiftless, irresponsible people who wanted trouble and had nothing to lose." Black minister Milton Williams agreed. "It was neither a riot nor a race disturbance. It was rather a group of highway robbers and burglars seeking to take whatever they could get their hands on in the guise of a racial disturbance." Something, however, had to be done. During the next several days the mayor convened and presided over a series of highly publicized meetings with black and white civil-rights leaders, black community leaders, white ministers and rabbis, labor leaders, and others eager to "do something" for "the Negro community." Sedita promised more summer jobs and more low-cost housing. Local banks pledged more mortgage money. Felicetta urged his officers to attend human-relations courses. The board of directors of the Chamber of Commerce, gathering at the all-white Buffalo Country Club in suburban Williamsville, pledged at a pool-side meeting to press their members to hire more blacks. Gov. Nelson Rockefeller dispatched baseball great Jackie Robinson to Buffalo.

The riots of 1967 ended the lingering white presence on the near East Side. The last Jewish stores still on William Street—a few dry good shops, a tailor, a grocer, and a fish market—closed. The handful of Germans still in the Fruit Belt left. Poles, secure for so long in their neighborhood bastion at Broadway and Fillmore, joined the quickening exodus from that neighborhood to the nearby suburb of Cheektowaga.

Racial divisions were growing sharper and the tension they generated grew ever more ripe for exploitation. No one sensed this better than Alfreda Slominski of the Buffalo Board of Education. In the wake of the riots whites quickly lost confidence in the school system. By 1970 there were four thousand fewer white students in the Buffalo schools. In the fall of 1967 Slominski ran for councilman-at-large, campaigning vigorously as a champion of "neighborhood schools." In a raw, rhetorically charged campaign aimed particularly at the city's East Side Poles, Slominski won the election with the largest majority of any candidate in the city, 85,000 votes.

On that same day, voters in Cleveland, Ohio, and Gary, Indiana, elected black men, Carl Stokes and Richard Hatcher, to be their mayors. Two days after Slominski's victory, Martin Luther King addressed a largely white crowd of 2,500 people at Buffalo's Kleinhan's Music Hall. "Revolts" grow out of revolting conditions," he said. "These are dark nights of social disruption, but it is the policymakers of white society who have created the darkness."

John T. Curtin was unfazed by Slominski's crushing victory. At the time Curtin was U.S. Attorney. Convinced that the Bethlehem Steel Co. was guilty of racial discrimination in the hiring and promotion of African-Americans, Curtin filed a civil suit against the company in federal court in December 1967. Bethlehem was the largest company to be sued to date under the Civil Rights Act of 1964. Curtin outlined the charges against the giant corporation: preferential hiring of whites, particularly for the skilled jobs in the mechanical and electrical departments; assignment of blacks to "hot and dirty" jobs in the coke ovens and blast furnaces and to menial work in the outdoor yards; failure to provide equal opportunity for advancement and to offer supervisory jobs to blacks on an equal basis with whites.

Superintendent Manch seemed equally unfazed by the Slominski landslide and the increasing evidence of white backlash in Buffalo. Indeed, he appeared suddenly challenged and inspired by it. In a series of speeches throughout the city, he began to sound far more like a crusading liberal than the cautious administrator he had always been. He urged a group of Methodist ministers to do their part to "effect a change in the hearts and minds of people about one another." To a luncheon at a local synagogue he insisted that he wanted to "demolish the walls of racial separation that exist in our city." Manch vowed that he would press for integrated schools.

Indeed, in late 1967 Manch made the most progressive suggestion of his career. Convinced that only a metropolitan solution would solve the problem of school segregation, he proposed that, following UB's imminent move to a new campus in the suburbs, a unified city-suburban public school system be created on the grounds of the Main Street campus, which at the time the university had planned to vacate. Lacking the political leverage and the personal energy to implement such a visionary scheme, Manch soon saw his bold and provocative notion die a sudden death. He fell back on his old strategies.

In early 1968, Manch appointed a white man named Donald Laing director of school integration. Laing unveiled a strategy to desegregate the schools based on the middle schools. Like many people, Manch believed that integration was too controversial, too frightening, too upsetting to be tried on the young. It was best delayed until at least fifth grade, he thought, when the children, at about the age of ten, could more easily deal with it. Thus, from kindergarten through fourth grade, all children would go to schools in their own neighborhoods. Beginning in fifth grade, they would go to middle schools (fifth through ninth grades) located in white neighborhoods. These schools would have a mix of white neighborhood kids (two-thirds) and blacks kids bused in (one-third)—whites, after all, had been promised that their children would never be bused into black neighborhoods. These integrated middle schools, the thinking went, would feed high schools, which in turn would also become integrated. If the plan was implemented in 1969, Manch promised, the entire school system from grade five through twelve would be integrated by 1975.

Manch's latest plan quickly came under fire, once again criticized by activists in both white and black communities. The neighborhood schools groups again demanded Manch's resignation. It was bad enough, they argued, that black students (about seven hundred in September 1967) were already being sent into white elementary schools. Civil rights activists hounded Manch from the other side, accusing him of stalling. Integration, they said, must not be postponed until the fifth grade. According to Norman Goldfarb, the plan was "a slap in the face to the Negro community." William Gaitor, the leader of a new civil rights group called BUILD, was more critical still. "Dr. Manch's 'pray now and wait till 1975' plan is unacceptable to Buffalo's black community," he said. The Board of Education was no more fond of Manch's proposal and in December 1967 voted to table it. Meanwhile, Commissioner Allen seemed to have lost some of his ardor. In a continuation of what seemed to be a well-choreographed ballet, he again postponed his deadline for action, this time until May 1968.

Meanwhile, conditions in the schools continue to deteriorate. In December 1967 the State Education Department issued a report bitterly critical of virtually every aspect of public education in Buffalo. In a nine-part series starkly entitled "Our Starving Schools," the *Evening News* ran excerpts of the report. Racial isolation was getting worse, it said. Citing a February 1967 U.S. Civil Rights Commission Report, the report noted that 77 percent of the twenty-five thousand black children in Buffalo's public education system were in racially isolated schools. Only Cleveland, with 82 percent, and Chicago, with 90 percent of black children in segregated schools, presented worse pictures of racial isolation. Data from other cities showed New Haven with 37 percent, Indianapolis with 70 percent, Detroit with 70 percent, Newark with 51 percent, Cincinnati with 49 percent, Pittsburgh with 50 percent, and Milwaukee with 72 percent. The report concluded that Buffalo's Board of Education was not completely to blame for the problem. So great was the decline of the white population in Buffalo that there was little that the board, even had it been so inclined, could have done to desegregate the schools.

There were other problems too, according to the state report. Buffalo was still the lowest of the Big Six cities in per-pupil spending. School buildings were overcrowded and old—seventy-five of the one hundred schools in the city were in need of "extensive renovation." Indeed, after the local papers uncovered unsafe and unsanitary conditions in some of the school buildings in the fall of 1967, the assistant superintendent for plant services resigned. Teachers were older and "inadequately prepared," since the system was losing its best and youngest teachers to the suburbs. The report said that many of the departing teachers simply wanted to avoid assignment to the East Side. As for the continued high number of students in vocational programs and the low number taking Regents exams, the report writers were troubled by what they called the "low level of student aspiration." Barring a doubling of the school budget to $80 million, the future of Buffalo's public schools was "bleak," the report concluded.

Manch paid little attention to the report, concentrating instead on Allen's desegregation order. In the early spring of 1968 he adopted one of Allen's experts' suggestions to desegregate Buffalo's schools—the construction of portable classrooms at thirteen schools in white neighborhoods. While Manch was not willing to alter his basic integration strategy—the busing of black children into white neighborhoods—he was willing to increase the numbers involved. Portable classrooms, he said, would add more than seven hundred black students to the over seven hundred already attending schools in white neighborhoods. The Board of Education, by a slim one-vote majority, voted to implement the portable-classroom plan beginning in the fall of 1968. Commissioner Allen also approved and in May 1968 announced that he was satisfied that the portable classrooms, the newly created Office of Integration, and the board's committment to create three integrated middle schools were clear signs that Buffalo was finally taking serious steps toward the elimination of racial imbalance in its public schools.

Rioting and looting on the streets of the East Side following the assassination of Martin Luther King in April 1968 exacerbated racial tensions. The Common Council suddenly balked at the idea of portable classrooms, particularly when it became apparent that the opposition of anti-integrationists within the white community was intense and passionate. In early June it passed a resolution to place the question before the voters in a November referendum. Mayor Sedita, a sixty-year-old organization Democrat popular with blacks as well as with the city's white ethnics, was eager to keep this increasingly volatile issue off the ballot. He vetoed the measure. Undaunted, the council passed a resolution introduced by Councilwoman-at-large Slominski that required that any additions to existing school buildings be made of the same material as the original building. This would have effectively prevented the construction of the portable classrooms. "Kiddie coffins," one council member called the proposed portable classrooms. The city should not build "plywood outhouses," said another. Several of the city's craft unions agreed, because the plywood additions would be built in Syracuse, costing local jobs.

That day the Common Council was debating another issue of critical importance to the city's black community, a fair-housing bill introduced by Councilman Horace Johnson of the Masten District. Unlike the state Fair Housing Law, which exempted the one- and two-family homes that comprised the great bulk of housing stock in the city, Johnson's bill would have made discrimination illegal in all kinds of housing. The bill was defeated on July 10, 1968, the day the council overrode the mayor's veto of its portable classroom ordinance. Indeed, more than twenty years later, Buffalo still has no fair-housing law on its books.

The council was determined to prevent the construction of Manch's three integrated middle schools, too. It refused to pass the bond issues needed just to plan for the schools. Superintendent Manch was outraged. He had had high hopes for the middle schools, believing that they would move the city cautiously and reasonably in the direction of integration while at the same getting Commissioner Allen off his back. Indignant, Manch called for a "convocation of city leaders" to help him deal with the "divisive recalcitrance" of the council. Manch was not alone in his feeling. Respectable opinion throughout Buffalo, including that of both newspapers and of the Chamber of Commerce, was embarrassed and angered by the council's behavior. They were concerned that it would only reinforce the city's image as blue-collar, rednecked, and ethnic. The opposition of the council members, people with names like Slominski, Lewandowski, Franczyk, Whalen, and Perla, had perhaps as much to do with considerations of class and ethnicity as with questions of race. Councilman Lewandowski captured the poignancy of the historic resentment and frustration long felt by his Polish, working-class constituents.

Referring to the composition of the three-member panel of experts who had first recommended the construction of middle schools, Lewandowski said, "There were no Perlas, Mattinas, or Seditas, no Lewandowskis, Gorskis, Makowskis, or Slominskis, no Whalens or Buyers, either." Nor were there "any representatives of the working people who send their children to the public schools of this city," he said. Insisting that the Board of Education, under the influence of Joseph Manch, was "force-feeding integration" and "thumbing its nose" at public opinion, Lewandowski urged the Common Council to continue to oppose both the middle schools and the portable classrooms.

There was an apathetic element of grandstanding in the council's position, for it quickly became a losing cause. In August 1968 the New York State Supreme Court, in a suit brought by the Board of Education against the Common Council, ruled that its oppositon was unconstitutional. One of the middle schools, West Hertel, located in an all-white neighborhood adjacent to the Black Rock–Riverside area, finally opened in September. Of its 420 students, 30 percent were blacks bused in from the East Side.

Meanwhile, somehow, despite the escalating racial rhetoric, despite the violence in the streets following the King assassination, despite the racial tension and conflict in the schools that led Superintendent Manch to cancel all high-school track meets that spring, life in the schools continued.

Racial imbalance, however, was growing, and in 1971 a report on public education in New York State said that in Buffalo the problems were "grave." The middle schools, the portable classrooms, and the Quality Integrated Education program notwithstanding, the report, issued by a commission headed by prominent Buffalo attorney Manly Fleischmann, concluded that, "Almost nothing has been done to overcome" the system's segregation. "Given the current community attitudes and lack of leadership, there is very little reason to believe that anything will be done voluntarily." Even Superintendent Manch began to despair. In April 1971 he admitted sadly, "There is no such thing as equality of educational opportunity in this city at this time."

Racial polarization threatened to increase during the mayoral election of 1969. Following her sweeping victory in the council election in 1967, Slominski had become the embodiment of white ethnic urban backlash, like Louise Day Hicks in Boston. She was a female Archie Bunker, the woman liberals loved to hate, and a woman many white ethnics loved to vote for. (In 1967 Slominski carried every district in the city except the black Ellicott and Masten districts and the "silk stockings" Delaware District. "The blue bloods and I," she had said during the campaign, "don't speak the same lingo.") Slominski was smart and ambitious and following her election made it no secret that she would run against Mayor Sedita in 1969. With the conservative endorsement safely in hand she announced during the spring of that year that she would seek the Republican endorsement as well.

The Republican Party in Buffalo was virtually nonexistent. Although the party won the mayoralty in 1961, it was only because two Democrats split the ballot. Whatever Republican organization there was, was controlled by the city's Protestant old money, moderates who traditionally had looked to the likes of Thomas Dewey, Dwight Eisenhower, and Nelson Rockefeller as leaders of their party. They were appalled by Slominski's demagoguery, her rhetoric barely clothed in the racist euphemisms of the time: "neighborhood schools," an "elected school board," "law and order," and "safe streets." Richard E. Moot was one of the "blue bloods" Slominski had mentioned—a descendant of one of the city's oldest families, a graduate of Harvard College and the University of Virginia Law School and a partner in Moot, Sprague, Marcy, Landy, Fernbach and Smythe, one of the city's oldest law firms. In February 1969 he urged the people of Buffalo to reject Slominski's "politics of hate." He announced that he would challenge her for the Republican mayoral endorsement. The effort was hopeless from the beginning and in the June primary Moot was trounced. He carried only the Delaware District and the black neighborhoods, with their handfuls of Republican voters. Slominski had expected to lose the Delaware District, a neighborhood of old homes, some large and magnificent, but all genteel, one of the few neighborhoods in Buffalo that had held its own during the onslaught of postwar suburbanization, the place where, since the early twentieth century, Buffalo's most affluent and best-educated citizens had always lived.

Slominski was confident about the general election and her campaign against Mayor Sedita, the two-term Democratic mayor. The city's Democratic newspaper, the *Courier Express,* was concerned. In an editorial following Slominski's win over Moot, the paper said, "Political attitudes this year will transcend political affiliation."

Already concerned by the likely defection of usually Democratic ethnic voters, particularly Polish-Americans on the city's East Side, the Democratic organization was further threatened when Ambrose Lane announced that he too was running for mayor. Lane was a black social worker and lawyer; executive director of the Community Action Organization, the city's largest public agency serving the black community; a founder of the *Challenger,* a black community newspaper; and a bright and articulate racial moderate who believed that the "overriding issue is to bring the community together." He called for programs that would unite whites and blacks. Relying on the recently published findings of the Kerner Commission, Lane's campaign consisted of pleas for fair housing, economic justice, better schools, and racial integration. But it was not his platform that concerned the Democratic Party, it was the threat his candidacy posed to the traditional Democratic coalition that had long dominated local politics.

Suddenly faced with the desertion of both blacks and white ethnics, the party did what it could to keep its coalition intact. The Democratic organization thrived on loyalty and quickly and harshly punished those who strayed. Sometimes whole communities suffered as a result. In 1961, following two two-year terms as the Democratic councilman from the Black Rock–Riverside area, Victor Manz became disenchanted with what he felt was Sedita's boss-controlled administration and challenged the incumbent in that year's Democratic primary. Relying on enormous support within his own council district, Manz defeated Sedita. Denied the Democratic endorsement, Sedita, with the backing of Erie County Democratic chairman Joseph Crangle, promptly entered the mayoral race as an independent. Manz and Sedita divided the votes between them, thereby allowing the election of Chester Kowal, the Republican candidate. Better a Republican victory, Crangle felt, than one by dissident Democrats.

Unfortunately, it was the neighborhood that paid for Manz's disloyalty. Soon after the election, the Common Council, controlled by Democrats loyal to Crangle and Sedita, separated Black Rock from Riverside by placing them in separate council districts. That ended not only Manz's power base, but also the power of that once politically strong community.

Black challenger Lane and his Unity Party had been far easier prey. Timing its actions perfectly to cause the greatest damage, the county Democratic Party brought suit against Lane, challenging his nominating petitions. The legal system seemed to cooperate with Crangle and it was not until one week before the election that the state Court of Appeals threw out the suit, allowing Ambrose Lane, the first black candidate to run for mayor of the city, to run. By then it was too late. Even without Crangle's shenanigans, Lane never had a chance. His candidacy turned out to be futile, far more visible among "limousine liberals" in the Delaware District and sympathetic university types than in the black community, where Lane made virtually no effort to register and organize voters. That the Democrats went to such lengths to hinder his campaign indicates that they believed far more in the threat and the power of a black challenge than did blacks themselves—and feared it.

Dealing with Slominski was not as easy in these halcyon years of President Nixon's "silent Americans." White backlash, encouraged by Nixon's "Southern strategy" (it was obvious even then that this was as much a strategy to win disgruntled Northern white Democrats to the Republican Party as it was to win Southern white Democrats) was at its peak. Anger about anti-war activism, which would reach a crest of violence in Buffalo when students returned to UB in the fall of 1969, was peaking too. (In October campus ROTC offices were firebombed and destroyed by rampaging students.) Crangle wasted no efforts dealing with the Slominski insurgency, and throughout the fall a host of national party figures—former vice president Hubert Humphrey, Sen. Ted Kennedy, and Sen. Edmund Muskie—all came to Buffalo, campaigning for Mayor Sedita. In the end Sedita won handily. Even with Lane in the election, blacks voted overwhelmingly for the mayor (approximately 30 percent of eligible blacks voted), while many of the city's white ethnics, particularly Italian-Americans on the West Side and Irish-Americans in South Buffalo, remained loyal to the party. This, plus the support, both financial and otherwise, of Buffalo's Republican establishment (Moot and his following gave their enthusiastic support to Mayor Sedita) ensured a Democratic victory. Perhaps "white backlash" was not as strong in the City of Good Neighbors as many people seemed to think. A year earlier George Wallace's third-party campaign for president had collapsed in Buffalo. Now Slominski's campaign for mayor had failed. Perhaps the time had finally come for healing.

The numbers seemed to prove otherwise. At the end of the year, as he began to prepare his decennial report, the associate director of the U.S. Census Bureau reported preliminary figures indicating that the cities of America were experiencing an annual increase of 300,000 blacks, a third of whom actually migrated to the cities, the rest resulting from birth rates. In the meantime, 900,000 whites, three for every one arriving black, were leaving. The numbers were threatening. So were the events, particularly the uprising at the correctional facility in Attica, New York, in 1971.

On Thursday morning, September 9, 1971, more than 1,200 black and Hispanic inmates, as well as one Native American named John Hill, took control of all five cell blocks of the maximum-security state prison in Attica, a small, rural town thirty miles southeast of Buffalo.

The inmates seized forty-three white guards as hostages. Within hours the media descended on the town, and focused the eyes of the nation on the frightening confrontation. All three Buffalo television stations had reporters on the scene around the clock, examining in minute detail the unfolding drama: the comings and goings of Corrections Commissioner Russell Oswald; the status of William Quinn of Buffalo, a guard hurled from a second-story cell-block window; the arrrival of black militant Bobby Seale and radical attorney William Kuntsler, whose presence at the scene had been requested by the prisoners; and the efforts of Herman Schwartz, the UB law professor chosen by the prisoners to negotiate their case with state authorities.

For a while it seemed that Schwartz, tireless in his efforts, might be able to negotiate an end to the uprising. On Thursday night, September 10, one day after the takeover began, he flew off in a state plane at midnight to Manchester, New Hampshire, where Judge Curtin, attending a conference, signed a federal injunction barring administrative reprisals against the prisoners.

But it soon became apparent that neither the state nor the prisoners were in any mood to negotiate, particularly after the prisoners, rejecting an ultimatum from Commissioner Oswald, paraded eight blindfolded hostages around the prison's D Yard holding knives at their throats. Meanwhile, Gov. Rockefeller, who throughout had refused to come to Attica, had already decided on a forceable retaking of the prison. At 9:50 on Monday morning, September 13, 1971, four hundred state troopers entered the prison. An official report issued a year later by the New York State Special Commission on Attica recounted the ensuing events: "Forty-three citizens of New York State died at Attica Correctional Facility between September 9 and 13, 1971. Thirty-nine of that number were killed and more than 80 others wounded by gunfire during the fifteen minutes it took the State Police to retake the prison on September 13." The Commission concluded somberly, "With the exception of the Indian massacres in the late 19th century, the State Police assault which ended the four-day prison uprising was the bloodiest one-day encounter between Americans since the Civil War." The Commission was sympathetic to the inmates, who they said were "demanding recognition as humans," and for whom confrontation was the only language that could "call attention to the system." Thus, the report concluded, "the possibility that the Attica townspeople will again hear the dread sound of the powerhouse whistle is very real."

Like the riots on the Crystal Beach boat twenty-one years earlier, the uprising at nearby Attica shocked and terrified the people of Buffalo.

Whites particularly were repelled by the images relayed relentlessly on their television screens, pictures of hooded black prisoners wearing bandanas strutting arrogantly and angrily, bare chested and sweating in the heat of the prison yard. Never had the images of black power been more graphically displayed and for the whites of Buffalo. "Attica" became a buzzword for terror. Meanwhile, for the younger, more militant members of the black community and the activists on the university campus, Attica quickly became a symbol of the violence and perversion of racism. In the wake of the uprising, the struggle for integration seemed more insurmountable than ever.

Norman Goldfarb was not about to give up the fight he had been leading for so long. In December 1971, he again brought his concerns to the attention of the State Education Department. In a letter to State Commissioner of Education Ewald Nyquist (President Nixon had recently made James Allen the secretary of education), Goldfarb denied that segregation in the city's schools was, as Manch had said, a result of segregated housing patterns. As he had for years, Goldfarb argued that the Board of Education had deliberately created and maintained a system of segregated schools.

Goldfarb admitted that the demographic patterns of Buffalo—the rapidly dropping white population, the rapidly growing black population, the maintenance of racially segregated neighborhoods—made it difficult to integrate the schools. But, Goldfarb wrote, that was only part of the problem. Goldfarb was bitterly critical of Commissioner Nyquist himself. "You have left the battle to a Board of Education that refuses to lead the community in this matter, and quite likely cannot, because of the political and economic ties as well as the social outlook of its members." Goldfarb accused Nyquist of "timidity" in dealing with the board, in effect encouraging it to "cling to a bankrupt desegregation program and to continue an educational system that is not relevant for over thirty thousand black children." In a vein that revealed his lifelong concern with the more subtle impact of racism, Goldfarb added, "At the same time, thousands of white children have been warped by their parents' stereotypes by the time they come in contact with black children, if they ever do. The situation has not been an accident and its perpetuation, permitted by you, is no accident." Goldfarb demanded that Nyquist order the Board of Education to submit a plan for the "complete desegregation of the Buffalo Public Schools," to become effective in September 1972. He further insisted that the plan include the surrounding suburban districts, which he called more than 90 percent "segregated white."

Three weeks later Nyquist issued a brand new order. In language far stronger than any ever used by Allen, he demanded that the city's integration plan be ready by April, and that it guarantee that every school in the city (Nyquist made no mention of suburban school districts) reflect the racial composition of the entire school district. Given that blacks constituted close to 30 percent of Buffalo's population, Nyquist's order was far and away the most sweeping the city had ever received.

Toward the end of February 1972 Nyquist came to Buffalo to explain his order. By then the local climate of opinion had become more heated than at any time since the districting of Woodlawn Junior High and the debate over "cross-busing." In addition to the busing of blacks into white neighborhood schools, whites might now be bused into black neighborhood schools. The Board of Education was now under the presidency of Arnold Gardner, a lawyer actively in favor of aggressive desegregation measures. Slominski and others felt Gardner could afford to be liberal. He was a wealthy member of the city's legal establishment and his children all attended private schools. Slominski's two daughters attended Archbishop Carroll High School, and at one point during the debate surrounding Nyquist's order she chided him, "As long as Mr. Gardner keeps his own daughter sheltered in a private school he doesn't really believe what he is saying he believes."

Gardner took Nyquist at his word, and in January 1972 had James Heck, the black integration coordinator for the Board of Education, prepare a plan that would involve the cross-busing of black and white children. Though he often fudged on the more visible desegregation issues, since the late 1960s Manch had quietly appointed a handful of blacks as high-level administrators in the school system. Heck was one of them.

Most of the members of the board clearly opposed the plan—one of them, Joseph Murphy from South Buffalo, asked in February 1972, "Who in their right mind can see people from North Buffalo and Kensington [at the time, both were white neighborhoods in outlying sections of the city] putting their kids on a bus in the morning and sending them to schools in the inner city?" But, under the watchful eye of Nyquist and the prodding of Gardner, the board had no choice but to at least examine the subject.

Gardner knew that. Throughout 1971 federal courts all over the United States had begun to put the force of law behind the busing of both black and white school children as a means of desegregating the nation's schools. The trend began in April 1971, when, in the North Carolina case of *Swann* v. *Mecklenburg County,* the Supreme Court unanimously affirmed the ruling of a circuit-court judge approving the use of cross-busing if it led to desegregation of Mecklenburg County's schools. Chief Justice Warren Burger's opinion was clear and to the point: "All things being equal, with no history of discrimination, it might well be desirable to assign pupils to schools near their homes. But all things are not equal in a system that has been deliberately constructed and maintained to enforce racial segregation." Based on this unambiguous message from the Supreme Court, federal judges in Richmond, San Francisco, and Detroit began to rule that segregated schools were segregated not because of housing patterns but because of specific efforts by local officials to deliberaely create segregated school systems. The remedy, these judges agreed, was cross-busing.

Despite the direction of these decisions, the climate of public opinion did not support busing. In early 1970 the *Courier Express* ran a front-page story under the headline "National Push for School Integration Losing Momentum." Quoting white liberals like Yale law professor Alexander Bickel, and black civil-rights activists like Roy Innes of the Congress of Racial Equality, the story, reprinted from the *Los Angeles Times,* concluded that "the integration kick is a dead issue. It is time to make schools good where they are." Some drew other conclusions, like the sociologist James Coleman, who in 1970 reported that integration, far more than compensatory education, led to the educational improvement of black children. But it was the negative voices that were heard most strongly in Buffalo and other cities throughout the country. Opposition took different forms in different places. In August 1971 firebombs destroyed ten school buses in Pontiac, Michigan. In September, when six thousand Chinese-American children in San Francisco were scheduled to be bused as part of a citywide integration program, their parents protested. Saying that the integration plan would undermine the "cultural integrity" of their community, the parents of more than a thousand of the children withdrew them from the public schools and enrolled them in private schools.

President Nixon made the most of these growing doubts. According to a September 1970 Gallup Poll, 75 percent of all Americans felt that school integration had gone too far, too fast. Nixon began to undermine the Supreme Court's recent rulings and began to reassert the distinction that used to be accepted between segregation created by law, *de jure* segregation, and segregation that emerged from changes in housing and neighborhood patterns, *de facto* segregation. There was nothing, the president said, that the federal government could or should do about the latter. To underscore his position, Nixon made inflammatory speeches throughout the country during the election of 1972, and supported the growing movement for a constitutional amendment that would bar the use of busing to achieve racial balance in the nation's public schools. Gov. Rockefeller agreed with Nixon and in March 1972 proposed a two-year moratorium on busing in New York State. Two months later the U.S. Senate passed a bill imposing a one-year moratorium on all federal district court busing orders. It is little wonder that amid these increasingly mixed signals, in an atmosphere of growing indecision and ambivalence about what could and should be done to achieve integration, authorities in Buffalo, notwithstanding the January 1972 order from Commissioner Nyquist, wavered.

Mayor Sedita, however, seemed to be caving in. Two weeks after Nyquist's order Sedita appointed Carol Williams, a housewife from Riverside and a staunch and outspoken opponent of busing, to a vacancy on the Board of Education. The mayor said he selected her because "she is a woman, a mother and I am sure that she'll represent the feelings of thousands of others like her in the city."

The majority of five board members opposed to busing was then joined by the Common Council. In mid-February, a week before Nyquist was going to be in Buffalo to meet with the board, it passed a resolution approved by all but the three black council members demanding that Nyquist "rescind the mass busing order" (there had in fact been no mention of any specific remedies in his order) and reiterating the board's committment to "neighborhood schools."

On the day that Nyquist arrived in Buffalo, the *Courier Express,* in what appeared to be a blatant attempt at sabotage, ran a long front-page story describing in detail what it called the "Heck Plan" for the integration of the public schools. Intended only as a proposal for consideration by the board and never as a final plan, Heck had suggested the possible creation of five pie-shaped wedges extending outward from the black inner city. By busing both black and white students within these districts (the plan required the busing of at least twenty-four thousand children), Heck thought a large measure of integration could be achieved. Despite efforts by Manch, Gardner, and Heck to clarify that this was merely a working document, opposition to it was instant, passionate, and strong. When Nyquist came to Buffalo later that morning to meet with the board, he was stopped by several hundred anti-busing demonstrators representing such groups as "The Silent Majority of the West Side," "Citizens for Neighborhood Schools," "The National Traditionalist Caucus," "Concerned Citizens of the East Side," and "The Broadway-Bailey Beltline Businessmen's Association." The demonstrators were successful in temporarily denying Nyquist entrance into City Hall.

At a press conference after a hurried meeting with the board, Nyquist seemed to stick to his guns. The board "had no realistic options," he said, and their continued opposition could lead to a loss of state funds as well as dismissal from their seats on the board. Nyquist did say that he would demonstrate flexibility about his April 1 deadline if the Board acted with "good will." Things never got that far. On March 23, 1972, the Board of Education, with Carol Williams voting in the majority, tabled the Heck proposal without discussion. Five days later, the board, with Parlato writing for the majority, sent a letter to Nyquist. "We regret to advise you," it said, "that we are unable, consistent with our responsibilities as we see them, to submit any plan to you within the period of time you have in mind." When asked later if more time would help, Parlato replied, "We could come up with a plan in forty years."

Never before had a school board in the State of New York refused to comply with a desegregation order, and Gardner was outraged. Manch was more philosophical. "My conscience tells me that judging from what has been done here today we have far to go before we can claim title as 'The City of Good Neighbors.' "

Goldfarb and his friends and colleagues in the Citizen's Council on Human Rights had already decided to act. On June 28, 1972, they filed a suit in U.S. District Court charging that the state commissioner of education, the State Board of Regents, the superintendent of the Buffalo schools, the members of the Board of Education, the mayor, and the Common Council had, "while acting under the color of state law, deprived the plaintiffs and their class of rights guaranteed in the Fourteenth Amendment of the United States Constitution by creating, maintaining, permitting, condoning, and perpetuating racially segregated public schools."

On that morning, on a day that began a long and difficult process that would alter forever the tone and tenor of community life in the city of Buffalo, Norman Goldfarb, Buffalo's relentless crusader for racial justice, lay in a hospital bed undergoing heart bypass surgery. Uncertain about the outcome of his surgery, he made some calls the night before to his friends in the movement seeking assurance that they would continue the fight without him. Assured that they would, Goldfarb rested easier. For now anyway, the case, which would judge the past as well as determine the future of race relations in the city of Buffalo, was out of Goldfarb's hands.

8

AND THE VERDICT IS . . .

Summers are beautiful in Buffalo, soft and gentle, cooled by breezes blowing steadily off Lake Erie. Trees abound—lindens, Norway maples, flowering pears, hackberries, cherries, and hornbeams. Mornings are quiet and billowy. At the Juicery in Delaware Park, the greenhouse in Martin Luther King Park, the Tosh Collins Community Center in Cazenovia Park, and along the walkway at LaSalle Park on the Lower West Side, people gather in the slowly rising mist, some alone, some in groups, to walk, jog, meet, and talk. In summer evenings, in the neighborhoods, people still walk, stopping to chat with their neighbors, many of them still rocking away the evening on old-fashioned, vine-covered porches.

The winters are long and cold, the spring slow in coming. When the sun shines on the city, which it does consistently only in the summer, Buffalonians seek it out, pouring into the streets of downtown during breaks and at lunch, crowding into the Hatch, an outdoor restaurant on the waterfront; lining up at Ted's, a wonderful hot dog stand on the Lower West Side, known for its charcoal-grilled hot dogs and deep-fried onion rings. Elmwood Avenue, popular with pedestrians even during the winter, fills up and it is hard to find a table on the patio at Rigoletto's, the Acropolis, or Ambrosia. Just across the Peace Bridge in Canada, small, still-pristine beaches—Waverly, Crescent, and Hidden—are dotted with people. Many stay until the sun sets—in the twilight, the gleam of the sun's last rays on the Buffalo skyline just across the lake is stunning.

In the summer of 1974, as Judge John Curtin pondered the school case, Jesse Kregal was thinking about the Skylon Marathon. Kregal had moved to Buffalo in 1970 from Portland, Oregon, to become the principal timpanist in the Buffalo Philharmonic Orchestra. He lived on Auburn Avenue in Buffalo's Delaware District. Kregal is a great outdoorsman, a hiker who has backpacked throughout the world. And he loves to run. Kregal began running up and down the streets of his neighborhood—Lancaster, Highland, Lexington, Elmwood, Ashland, Norwood, and Richmond Avenues. These are lovely, peaceful, tree-lined streets that resonate of a slower and quieter era in the city's history. Shabbily genteel, these streets, with their large but unpretentious frame homes set near the front of relatively small lots and built in the wide spectrum of styles that is "Victorian," are among the nicest and most desirable in the city. They resonate "community," too, tradition and a strong sense of place. Kregal, like many people in the neighborhood, loved the area and loved running through it. Soon after he arrived in Buffalo he heard about the Niagara Parkway, across the Peace Bridge on the Canadian shore. It is a magnificent, beautifully landscaped, gently rolling two-lane road set down gently in the landscape like a carpet. The parkway borders the Niagara River, following its fast-moving journey from a benign beginning at Lake Erie to the crashing drop at Niagara Falls. In the spring of 1973 Kregal and a few of his friends began to run there. Gradually, they began to hatch the idea of a race, an international marathon that would start in Buffalo, cross the Peace Bridge, and continue up the Niagara Parkway to the Falls.

What started as a lark quickly became a tradition that by 1984 was celebrating its tenth anniversary—the Skylon International Marathon. It began modestly with a group of energetic and sincere runners— a few musicians from the orchestra, a dentist, a businessman, and a couple of school teachers—in what turned out to be an extremely successful volunteer effort. None of them had ever done anything like it before. Money had to be raised, goods and services arranged for, authorities and bureaucrats—customs, immigration, and police officials on both sides of the border—dealt with. Volunteers, hundreds of them, were desperately needed to serve the runners at the pre-race banquet, to check bags at the start of the race and make sure they were returned at its end, to dispense water along the course, and to guide the runners along the route. By the spring of 1974 a huge organization of volunteers, drawn from communities throughout the city, was in place. Throughout the year they worked and by race-day—October 26, 1974—they were ready.

On that cool, color-filled fall morning, on a small bridge overlooking the Delaware Park Lake, waiting tensely in the shadows of the austerely magnificent Greek Revival portico at the back of the Albright Knox Art Gallery, more than five hundred runners stood ready to begin their long and arduous run through the streets of Buffalo, over the soaring Peace Bridge with the fast-moving waters of the Niagara River below, up the breathtaking Niagara Parkway to the crashing, monumental beauty of the falls and the finish line. It was a glorious, spectacular event. Word of the race—the beauty of the course, the excellence of its organization—spread, and soon the Skylon Marathon (named for the company that helped support the race) became one of the most popular marathons in the country.

For many, however, it was the spirit of the race that made it special. For, like the Blizzard of '77 three years later, the Skylon Marathon offered the people of Buffalo a positive model of community life. Because the marathon was created, developed, and implemented by volunteers from the grassroots it strengthened the fabric of community life, creating confidence among people that they could, if they cared and if they tried, affect and improve the quality of life in their city.

Judge Curtin loves to run and though he was too busy with the school case to train for the first Skylon race, he ran it in subsequent years. Five feet eight inches tall, Curtin is handsome, with a ruddy complexion, grey hair, and strong, bright, Paul Newman-like blue eyes. Lean and athletic, Curtin is an avid runner, a good competitor, and a regular participant in Buffalo's active racing scene. In 1988 he was third in his age group in Buffalo's Runner of the Year competition. For years he ran indoors at the track at the old downtown YMCA, but since the 1970s Curtin has been running marathons and now he trains only outside. He tries to run every day, sometimes in Delaware Park, near his home in North Buffalo, more often downtown, during his lunch break. From the Buffalo Athletic Club just around the corner from his chambers on Niagara Square, he takes off with a bunch of running buddies on a four- or five-mile run down to the Erie Basin Marina; through LaSalle Park; up the Riverwalk, a long and winding path that hugs the banks of the Niagara River; and then back downtown to the club. Sometimes, on nice days when there isn't much wind out of the south, the group does what Curtin calls his "grain elavator run," through the streets of the old First Ward, over the Ohio Street bridge that spans the Buffalo Creek, around the hulking, lofty, strangely graceful grain elevators that for more than 125 years were a mainstay in the economic life of Buffalo. An hour later, Curtin is walking back to his chambers, his sweat-drenched running clothes stuffed into the crushed gym bag that dangles in his hand.

Curtin had wanted to run in the first Skylon Marathon, but around that time he had other things on his mind—on October 1, 1974, the Buffalo school desegregation case, *Arthur* v. *Nyquist,* began.

The day the trial began racial fears and tensions throughout the country were reaching a peak. Throughout the nation people watched the "agony in the cradle of liberty," the desegregation confrontation in the streets of Boston. Just three months before, in June 1974, U.S. District Judge Arthur Garrity ruled that the city's School Committee had deliberately created and maintained a segregated public school system. Garrity ordered a two-phase remedy. The first phase, to take place that September, would implement a state-created desegregation plan. The second phase, to be fashioned by the School Committee, would become operative in September 1975. As lawyers in Judge Curtin's courtroom argued the merits of their positions, the Buffalo press covered closely the gruesome events unfolding in Boston: five thousand white demonstrators marching through the streets of South Boston protesting Judge Garrity's order; the stoning of blacks as they made their way to South Boston High School, of whites as they went to Roxbury; the stabbing of a black bystander with an upended flagpole bearing the American flag; the harassment of Sen. Edward Kennedy, jeered and pelted with rocks and tomatoes as he addressed and anti-busing rally in front of Boston's City Hall. Calm returned soon, though temporarily, to the streets of Boston, but the seriousness of the passion and violence aroused among the people of Boston by Judge Garrity's decision was lost on none of the participants in the Buffalo case. The shadow of Boston would haunt the people of Buffalo for the next several years as they attempted to deal with segregation in their city.

The plaintiffs were confident—particularly Norman Goldfarb and Frank Mesiah, the team who founded the Citizen's Council on Human Rights in 1963, and Raphael DuBard, the president of the Buffalo chapter of NAACP, a man who had been active in the local civil-rights movement since the early 1950s. They were no strangers in federal court. In 1969, when the New York State Legislature passed a law that prohibited appointed school boards (Buffalo was the only large city in the state that still had one) from "assigning or compelling" a student to attend any school on account of race, Goldfarb, Mesiah, DuBard, and a group of parents challenged it. They had won that case and were confident that they could win this one too, for Goldfarb and DuBard had worked together for years, fighting a lonely struggle for racial justice in a city that often seemed not to care.

Goldfarb's commitment to social justice was deep and long-standing. Without him, says everyone involved, the school desegregation case would not have happened. A passionate and persuasive crusader for racial justice, Goldfarb, who earned his living as an arbitrator for the Buffalo branch of the National Labor Relations Board, devoted all of his spare time (except, his friends say, when playing golf) to civil rights. From the mid-1950s until his death in 1982, "Norm," often working alone, politicked, advocated, argued, convinced, and wrote passionate and angry letters to state and local officials protesting segregation in the schools; to officers of private clubs that discriminated against blacks, Jews, and women (Goldfarb resigned from the Erie Downs Country Club in 1968 when it denied membership to a black family); and to individuals in cities throughout the nation who, like him, were, in his words, "fighting to foster better intergroup relations." In June 1967 Goldfarb wrote to Superintendent Manch suggesting that the Board of Education sponsor an essay contest on "The Injustice and Harm Done by Racial Prejudice." There had been essay contests in the public schools for years and the subjects were always uplifting. Angered by the hypocrisy of the subjects—Thomas Jefferson and the Declaration of Independence (don't mention mulatto children), Patrick Henry and freedom (don't mention slavery)—Goldfarb felt that malleable minds might be better served by trying to sort out in their own heads what racial prejudice was all about rather than discussing whether or not George Washington ever told a lie. But mostly Goldfarb organized, leading the struggle not only for integrated public schools but for integrated work forces too. During the late 1960s and early 1970s, as construction proceeded on the half-billion-dollar suburban campus of the State University of New York at Buffalo, it was Goldfarb, along with Assemblyman Arthur Eve, who led the movement to demand that the state hire a representative number of black construction workers. Late in 1970 Gov. Rockefeller came to Buffalo and Goldfarb mustered his troops for the community meeting the governor had convened. Among the nearly one thousand people there were more than a dozen nuns and priests, led by Father Joe Bissonnette, who, after the meeting, told a friend, "I would do anything that God and Goldfarb asked me to do."

Goldfarb lived in the city and believed deeply in the promise of pluralism that he felt was possible here. While hundreds of his Jewish neighbors from the East Side and Humboldt Parkway moved to the suburbs, Goldfarb stayed on, sensing that it was here, on the streets and pavements of the city, that one of the great dramas of this century's history was being played out. In 1970 he took the struggle into hostile suburban territory, addressing a meeting of the Board of Education in the gilded, nouveau-riche town of Williamsville, about three miles east of northern Buffalo. Goldfarb urged his incredulous audience to join him in a metropolitan-wide solution to the problems of segregation in Buffalo's public schools. When the suit against the Board of Education and the city was filed two years later, in June 1972, Goldfarb was forced to monitor the case from his hospital bed, where he was recovering from open heart surgery. Even with tubes protruding from all over his body, Goldfarb was organizing, trying to convince the nurses that, like their aides, they should unionize. Following his release from the hospital, he immediately rejoined the team working on the case. When attorneys for the plaintiffs were taking pretrial testimony from a key witness, Goldfarb sat taking notes, not about the testimony, he told his colleagues later over lunch at the Mocha Java, a popular downtown luncheonette on Delaware, but for ideas in the suit he was going to file against the Buffalo Yacht Club, charging them, he said with an excited grin, with racial discrimination.

As the date of the trial approached Goldfarb was confident. Despite the terrible press from Boston and the "fierce opposition" to integration he knew existed within his own community, he and the other plaintiffs were optimistic. So was their trial lawyer, Richard F. Griffin. While much of the pretrial work had been handled by Herman Schwartz, Goldfarb had picked Griffin, a founder of the Parkside Community Association, to be the litigator in the case. Griffin had spent his whole life in Parkside, home to many of Buffalo's "lace curtain" Irish Americans. He went to school at St. Mark's, a lovely turn-of-the-century, English-style village church, and then to Canisius High School on the other side of the park. It was at Canisius, Griffin says, that he first made friends with Polish and Italian kids and even a small number of blacks. He graduated in 1950, a classmate and close friend of Joe Bissonette and Jack Weimer. Griffin stayed on the path trod by so many members of Buffalo's professional classes: from Canisius High School to Canisius College and, like a majority of the members of the local bar, to the law school at UB. Hired by Moot-Sprague, one of the city's largest and most prestigious corporate law firms, Griffin, handsome and articulate, soon became one of the firm's most successful litigators, specializing in railroad cases. He argued many of them in federal court and in 1962 U.S. District Judge John Henderson asked him if he wanted to try something different.

Thirty-odd black Muslim inmates at Attica, Henderson told him, had filed a suit against the state. They charged that prison authorities had denied them their religious freedom by refusing to recognize the special dietary and ritual requirements of their religion. Henderson asked if Griffin would take the case. He did. Griffin had never had a civil-rights case before, and he plunged into it with vigor. He went to New York City, where he met with Malcolm X, who agreed to come to Buffalo to testify. In a courtroom packed with the then strange and exotic-looking followers of Elijah Muhammad, Griffin spent four days examining his star witness. At the trial's end, victory in hand, Griffin invited Malcolm X to his home for dinner. Malcolm X accepted and, as he ate, two of his bodyguards, Messengers of Islam, sat waiting in a car outside.

It was Griffin's reputation as a litigator as well as his commitment to racial justice that recommended him to Goldfarb, and in June 1972 he agreed to represent the plaintiffs in the school desegregation case.

Like Goldfarb; Frank Mesiah; Marilyn Hochfield, another lawyer from Moot-Sprague who was extremely active in the case; and all the others who had worked so long for desegregation, Griffin was optimistic, confident that Judge Curtin would rule in their favor. Given the Supreme Court's recent verdict in a 1973 case known as *Keyes* v. *School District Number One* involving Denver, Colorado, they were convinced Curtin would have little choice. What *Brown* did for schools in the South, *Keyes* did for the cities of the North, where the schools were segregated by demographic trends and neighborhood development rather than law. Not until *Keyes* did the court rule that school segregation violated the Fourteenth Amendment's guarantee of "equal protection of the laws" whether it came about by law or by historical patterns of development. Writing one of the majority opinions, Justice William O. Douglas said, "It is time to state that there is no constitutional difference between *de jure* and *de facto* segregation, for each is the product of state actions and policies." Justice Powell of Virginia, known for his conservative views on the question of school integration, agreed. In a barbed separate opinion he stripped away the façade that had allowed Northern school systems to avoid the burdens of school integration that had been borne exclusively by schools in the South for close to twenty years. The distinction between *de jure* and *de facto,* he wrote, "has been nurtured by the courts and accepted complacently by many of the same voices which discovered the evils of segregated schools in the South." Quoting Sen. Abraham Ribicoff of Connecticut, Powell wrote, "Somehow residential segregation in the North was accidental or *de facto* and that made it better than the legally supported *de jure* segregation of the South. It was a hard distinction for black children in totally segregated schools in the North to accept." Because of that false distinction, Powell said, "No comparable progress has been made in many non-Southern cities with large majority populations." But their time had finally come. "In my view," he concluded, "we should abandon a distinction which long since has outlived its time, and formulate consitutional principles of national rather than merely regional application."

The plaintiffs in the Buffalo case reduced the significance of *Keyes* to two questions: (1) Could they show that a meaningful or substantial portion of the district was segregated? and (2) Could they show that any of the segregation that did exist was brought about or maintained by the purposeful or intentional segregative acts of the defendant? There was little doubt about the first. Indeed, in a broad pretrial stipulation urged on them by Curtin, plaintiffs and defendants agreed that both students and staff were segregated by race in schools throughout the system. Since it was agreed before the trial even began that racial imbalance existed in the Buffalo public schools, the critical question for the court to determine was whether the defendants intended to segregate the school system. In order for the plaintiffs to establish this, Justice Brennan said in writing for the majority that it would be sufficient to demonstrate that "the probable and foreseeable result of a defendant's act was segregation." Thus the plaintiffs set out to prove that the Board of Education, the mayor, and the Common Council of the City of Buffalo, the New York State Board of Regents, and the commissioner of education, in combination with the segregative policies of federal and municipal housing authorities, had intentionally created, perpetuated, and maintained a segregated school system. A similar argument, the plaintiffs knew, had convinced Judge Garrity in Boston.

The defendants, meanwhile, relied on the argument used by Superintendent Manch for years—despite the fact that it was an argument decisively rejected in *Keyes*. City Corporation Counsel Leslie G. Foschio, an attorney for the defendants, simply asserted that the school segregation was never mandated under law and its mere existence could not be ruled unconstitutional. In a brief Foschio maintained that the 1965 finding by State Education Commissioner Allen of racial imbalance existing in the Buffalo public schools, and his subsequent order to desegregate them, was issued not on constitutional grounds but rather for reasons of educational policy. Foschio agreed that twenty-one of the city's seventy-seven elementary schools were predominantly black in 1973.

But, he asked, "does the evidence establish that these schools were caused to be predominantly black due to intentional segregative actions of the Buffalo Board of Education?" He thought not, of course. "Nothing in the testimony proves that the school board created the racial imbalance in the schools. Rather, what evolves is that the board failed to integrate these racially imbalanced schools. We submit that in the absence of any segregative intent such an affirmative duty does not arise." Foschio was indignant that the defendants should be held liable for the racial imbalance that had occurred in inner city elementary schools, arguing that it was "purely the dramatic population shift of blacks" in those areas that had created and caused the problem.

The city defendants were helpless, Foschio claimed. Not "segregative intent" but demographics, the staggering racial turnover in the neighborhoods and schools of the East Side, created racial imbalance in the schools. Even in the case of Woodlawn, Foschio told Curtin, "segregative intent" was not the board's motive. Foschio said that, had the boundaries of that school been drawn to create racial balance, many African-American kids in the neighborhood would not have been able to attend the school. The defendants' admitted failure to integrate Woodlawn was, therefore, a far cry from the plaintiffs' charge that the Board of Education had purposefully created a segregated school there.

Foschio insisted that the evidence not only refuted the plaintiffs' charges of intentional segregation, but also showed that "racial balance by any standard" had been achieved at eleven of the city's thirteen high schools. Foschio admitted that racial isolation and imbalance in Buffalo's elementary schools had worsened, but he maintained that the plaintiffs had failed to show a causal relationship between the defendants' conduct and racial imbalance. Foschio told Curtin that the plaintiffs complaint should be dismissed.

The plaintiffs made no effort to refute Foschio's general defense, accepting without challenge the causal relationship between segregated neighborhoods and segregated schools. What they did not accept, however, was that these trends and patterns were, as the defendants argued, inevitable, historical, and racially neutral—developments beyond the power of policymakers to affect. In a two-pronged argument, the plaintiffs insisted that Buffalo's neighborhoods, just like its schools, were segregated not by accident but rather because public officials intended it.

The first witnesses for the plaintiffs testified that for over twenty years the Board of Education had acted to create, maintain, and perpetuate school segregation in Buffalo. In exhaustive detail, one witness after another recounted the examples: the redistricting of high schools in the 1950s, the Woodlawn case, the East High School language transfers, the discriminatory admissions procedures in vocational high schools, and the segregation of staff. Then came witnesses who testified that the Common Council, by its opposition to portable classrooms, its refusal to fund the middle schools, and its anti-busing regulations, had "willfully blocked whatever efforts the board did make to reduce school segregation." These were followed by witnesses who swore that the New York State Board of Regents and the state commissioner of education had "wrongly and unconstitutionally failed to reduce school segregation in Buffalo." Further, their "unjustified inaction has aggravated the situation." One of the star witnesses for the plaintiffs was Kenneth Clark, a black social psychologist and member of the New York State Board of Regents. Clark's testimony about the psychologically harmful effects of segregation on the victims as well as the perpetrators had been persuasive in 1954 in *Brown*. He made many of the same points during his testimony in the Buffalo case.

Finally, the plaintiffs summoned witnesses who testified that discrimination in housing, and the segregated neighborhoods that resulted from it, were a direct result of city, state, and federal actions. Victor Einach, an inspector for the Buffalo Municipal Housing Authority during the 1930s and 1940s and former director of the wartime Buffalo Committee on Discrimination, testified that MHA policies and actions had fostered and maintained the isolation of blacks in segregated housing projects. Martin Sloan, a Federal Housing Administration official, testified that federal housing policies during the 1930s and 1940s expressly directed housing developers to discriminate against blacks. Sloan read into the record from the Federal Housing Administration Underwriting Manual, section 310, which said, "The infiltration of inharmonious racial or national groups" was "an adverse influence on home values"; and from section 315: "The appeal of a residential neighborhood results from . . . the kind and social status of the inhabitants."

Other witnesses offered testimony about other aspects of Buffalo's legacy of segregated housing. Cleon Service, a black realtor in business since before the war, testified about racial steering and the discriminatory policies of the Greater Buffalo Board of Realtors. Anthony Dutton, a long-time officer of a local fair housing group with the acronym HOME, provided evidence of countless instances of discrimination in owner-occupied rental housing and in surrounding suburbs—both of which, Dutton maintained, contributed to the containment of blacks in inner-city neighborhoods.

After two weeks, the plaintiffs rested their case. Their contentions,

supported by thousands of pages of documents, the testimony of dozens
of witnesses, and boxes of exhibits stacked high in Judge Curtin's courtroom, made them confident that their arguments were convincing. Like
people thoughout the community, they waited while the judge deliberated.

Meanwhile, as chief judge of the district of Western New York, John
Curtin had other cases to think about. His was one of the busiest of
the country's ninety-four federal court districts. Its seventeen counties
generated more than sixteen hundred civil cases, three hundred criminal
cases, and five thousand bankruptcy cases each year. No case Curtin had
tried had taken as long as the school case, even with one of his two
clerks working on it full-time for more than a year. Anyway, Curtin was
in no rush. He had wanted, he said after the trial, "to take my time."

Nearly a year and a half after the trial, Curtin was ready, and
on April 30, 1976, he delivered his opinion. Over a photograph of a
relaxed Curtin, large headlines in the *Evening News* announced the judge's
decision. Most people thought he would find against the Board of Education, but few were prepared for the sweep of his judgment. The ruling
was unequivocal. "It is the finding of this court that the defendants
have violated the plaintiffs' Fourteenth Amendment rights to equal protection under the law by intentionally causing and maintaining a segregated school system." In a 156-page opinion reprinted by the *Evening
News* in its entirety, Curtin said, "A thorough study of the board's action
since the 1950s convinces the court that the already proven allegations
of segregative actions and omissions are unfortunately not isolated
incidents. The board's course of action for the last two decades, and
more specifically since 1965, has been consistently dilatory, evasive, and
at times obstructionist." Such board actions as the districting of Woodlawn Junior High and the use of language transfers to encourage whites
to leave the segregated East High School district, Curtin found, had
a "racial impact" that was "clearly forseeable." Curtin was strong and
pointed in his criticism. "Like a clever photographer who uses an airbrush
to eliminate what he does not want in a picture, the defendants try
to haze over what the evidence clearly shows. But we are not dealing
with art here and the Constitution does not permit this court to avoid
the evidence, however unsightly."

Curtin found equally reprehensible the actions of the Common
Council. "Whenever the Board of Education was forced to implement
integration plans, even if quite modest, the Council quickly shut off
the money supply or enacted an ordinance that would effectively negate
the board's actions. And, like the board, if it was forced to act, it would
always find the route of least possible integrative consequences, hoping

to stall until another day any meaningful integration."

New York State, Curtin ruled, was also at fault. "However much the Board of Education or the Common Council procrastinated or wavered," he said, "an equal share of the blame for the segregation in the Buffalo public school system must be attributed to the state defendants." The Board of Regents and the commissioner of education "have the central responsibility for education in New York State," he said. It was a responsibility they "shirked," and in so doing, "encouraged the city defendants to continue their own segregative actions. They . . . must be held accountable."

Eager to add his voice to that of his federal judicial colleagues throughout the country who found the distinction between *de jure* and *de facto* segregation untenable, Curtin was particularly clear about the relationship between segregated housing and segregated schools. In some cases, Curtin noted, the courts did not rely on testimony dealing with segregation in neighborhood housing. But the Buffalo case was different, he said, because the defendants relied so heavily on housing and neighborhood patterns as a defense. "The city defendants," he wrote, "cannot use residential segregation as a defense because as the evidence demonstrates they helped to create it." Curtin noted particularly the Ellicott Urban Renewal Project. He thought the evidence proved that residential segregation in Buffalo was caused in substantial part by the policies and practices of the federal government, the Buffalo Municipal Housing Authority, the private real estate industry, and the Common Council. "The citizens of Buffalo, both black and white," the judge intoned in conclusion, "have been affected by the legacies of these actions stretching back over many generations."

For the *Evening News* Curtin was "The Man in the News." The writer profiling him noted briefly his educational background and his record as a fighter pilot for the Marines in both World War II and the Korean War, but was particularly impressed by Curtin's relaxed demeanor. "He strolls casually from the bench as if walking through a park, unfazed by the heavy burden of court business. In chambers he sheds his robe unceremoniously, bursting into a few bars of 'When Irish Eyes Are Smiling'; coffee mug in hand, glasses pushed above his forehead, he walks to the outer office to check the day's agenda with his law clerk. In mid-conversation he bends over to touch his scuffed brown shoes, not quite succeeding. Later, after the hearings, he walks the block from the federal court building to the YMCA and chugs two and a half miles around the indoor track."

For others, though, particularly the recently elected Board of Education and Superintendent of Schools Eugene T. Reville, now was not the time to burst into song. The burden of developing a remedy, Curtin told them, was not his. "The court is not nor does not want to be a school administrator. It does not have the specialized training, the knowledge or the experience that belongs to the defendants. It is therefore the responsibility of the defendants to come forward with a plan that comports with the Constitution. The problems presented are difficult and will require rigorous effort to overcome. But overcome them the defendants must." They had less than three weeks, Curtin said, to offer their remedy. Superintendent Reville and his closest colleague, Associate Superintendent Joe Murray, had been ready for months. They said they had a plan: "The Buffalo Plan."

9

THE BUFFALO PLAN, I

The Buffalo Plan was passed by the recently elected Board of Education
in April 1976, two weeks before Judge Curtin's decision. Reville and
Murray called it "homegrown" and "voluntary," terms they hoped would
assuage the fears of Buffalo's white ethnics. But when they submitted
the plan to Curtin in May the two men who would preside over the
desegregation of Buffalo's public schools were uncertain about his reaction.

The new plan called for the closing of ten schools in white and
black neighborhoods, the expansion of voluntary busing of black children,
and the creation of two racially balanced "magnet" schools. With no
forced busing, no racial quotas, no minority hiring plan, the plan, while
not popular with parents whose schools were closed, quickly earned
the general support of the community. The newspapers liked it. It was
"moderate and homegrown," said one; "mild and restrained" said the
other. While admitting that the plan would leave at least seventeen all-
black schools untouched, the *Evening News* applauded the fact that
it guaranteed that "every pupil in Buffalo will have at some point in
their school career an integrated learning experience."

The plaintiffs, on the other hand, scoffed at the plan, dismissing
it out of hand because, as their attorney Richard Griffin said, it "hardly
scratches the surface of racial isolation in the Buffalo public schools."
Griffin called it a "school closing plan hidden in the rhetoric of desegregation." Neither Goldfarb, the most dynamic force behind the plain-

tiffs, nor William Gaitor of the civil-rights organization BUILD had any faith that whites would ever attend schools, no matter what their academic quality, that were located in the inner city. Gaitor denounced "the whole hypocrisy of magnet schools and all that jazz." Goldfarb called it "sheer fantasy" and said the plaintiffs would present their own desegregation plan—one that involved a substantial amount of cross-busing.

The hearing before Curtin in late May 1976 had the atmosphere of a showdown between two vastly different approaches to the problem of school desegregation. The plaintiffs would settle for nothing less than immediate, system-wide desegregation. To strengthen their case they hired a professor of education from Rhode Island named John Finger as an outside expert. Goldfarb said Finger was picked because he had developed plans for Denver that had not tolerated even one segregated school. Finger had also been appointed the court desegregation monitor in Dayton, Ohio, after his predecessor was assassinated by an angry mother. As a result of that unfortunate incident, when eating in Buffalo restaurants Finger always sat with his back against a wall.

When he testified before Curtin, Finger outlined a proposal he said would desegregate all of Buffalo's schools, leaving none more than 55 percent black. His plan required the busing of 56,000 students, more than 80 percent of those enrolled in the Buffalo school system. Magnet schools and other voluntary programs would not work, Finger said. Only by pairing white and black schools through a citywide busing program, he argued, would white participation be guaranteed.

Reville and Murray thought Finger was wrong. They had faith in the willingness of Buffalo's whites to participate in a voluntary de-segregation program. The Buffalo Plan lacked guarantees, they said, because it didn't need them. The magnet schools, one an honors school on Main Street, the other an open-classroom elementary school on the waterfront, were the crux of the plan. When questioned by the attorney for the plaintiffs Murray admitted that similar programs established since 1974 in Boston, Philadelphia, and New York had failed to attract significant numbers of whites to schools in black neighborhoods. But he remained convinced that they would work, "barring outside inter-ference or people stirring up parents against the program." He had "faith in the people of Buffalo," he said. Reville and Murray admitted that the Buffalo Plan would leave thirty-five of the city's ninety-six elementary schools still segregated, but, they argued, they were not constitutionally required to desegregate the whole school system anyway.

Judge Curtin wasn't so sure. On July 10, 1976, before a crowded courtroom, he slowly and carefully read a seventy-seven page opinion. For an hour and a half the several hundred people in the packed courtroom sat listening quietly as he read. He began casually, conversationally, almost rambling. "I want to thank all of you for coming here and doing it this way. It seemed to me that the quickest and best way would be to meet like this. That means that you have to sit and listen to me for a while. I hope not too long . . . but I'd appreciate it if when we start here that you stay, that you don't walk in and out. After the meeting . . . I will be glad to meet with anyone in chambers. As you know, we have a ban on any cameras in the courtroom. Sometimes people think it is a good idea to have a picture along with a story so I will be glad to meet in chambers and answer any questions."

This wasn't a criminal case, Curtin said. He wanted to "make it clear that I am not in this instance criticizing any particular individuals." After all, "some of this history came about a long time before any of us had anything to do with the schools of the City of Buffalo." But now, he said, "we are at a particular point in our journey. In some ways we can go forward and in some ways we ought to wait a little." Given the shortness of time before schools opened in September, Curtin had rejected a plaintiff's motion in May seeking an order restraining the defendants from implementing the Buffalo Plan. They would be allowed to go ahead with it, he said, but, he reminded them, "the court is not approving in whole or in part the Buffalo Plan."

If the Buffalo Plan fell "short of a true integration effort," Curtin said, and the Finger Plan, while setting forth a comprehensive and theoretically ideal arithmetic solution for the complete integration of almost all of the schools, failed "to take into account some important practical considerations." The most significant, he said sternly, were the "opinions of the community." Curtin seemed politely contemptuous of Finger. While he may have been an expert "at the technical aspects of drawing up such plans . . . he knows little or nothing about the Buffalo public school system in particular." Curtin knew the city's schools. "This court toured some of the schools involved in the Buffalo Plan and it is evident from that experience alone that mere paper knowledge of the school system will not suffice." Curtin said it would be "foolhardy" to endorse Finger's plan. Yet, barely finished excoriating Finger, Curtin told the defendants that his plan showed the possibility of integrating all the schools in Buffalo, and highlighted "the failure of the board to integrate its system as fully as it can." Curtin told the defendants they had three months to submit a new plan.

"The opinions of the community" were important to Curtin. In his ruling he spoke extensively about the importance of involving the people of the city in the development of a desegregation plan. He said any plan had to have as much community input as possible if it was to have any chance of being successful. Curtin's call for citizen involvement went beyond the concerns of the school desegregation case and reflected his deeper understanding of what constitutes a strong and healthy community. He said in his concluding comments:

> We should keep in mind that our nation is a nation of laws and we must follow the law, but it is also, and this, I believe, is most important in a problem such as this, a democracy where the best decisions are those in which individual members of the community have the ability to be heard and have their views listened to and considered and considered seriously. We have the duty as far as possible to integrate the schools in this district, I believe the board and the commissioner and the court have a responsibility to listen to the common-sense, practical views of the parents and the teachers and other people who are involved in this very complicated process. It is one thing to make decisions and it is another to be a parent of a small youngster or a teenager going off to school. They have insights which we cannot know until we listen to the views of all individuals in the community.

In a rambling tone that suggests he was speaking spontaneously or at best from notes, Curtain continued:

> Too often, I think we all have had this experience or something happens, there are many complaints in the bars and beauty parlors and other places of converse and activity but no one takes the time to meet with the people who are making decisions and this, I believe, is imperative.

Like Reville and Murray, Curtin had confidence in the willingness of the people of his community to deal with integration. While he believed that the surrounding suburbs had a responsibility to share the burden and appealed to them to do so, Curtin sensed that even if they didn't, the people of Buffalo could do it on their own. "Medieval Florence, a miserable hovel of a city compared to modern Buffalo, gave the world the Renaissance but it did it only because its leaders and its people believed that it could be done and willed that it should be done." In closing, Judge Curtin exhorted the citizens of the city to rise to the occasion, quoting Tennyson's Ulysses: "Come my friends, 'tis not too late to seek a newer world."

The defendants were satisfied with Curtin's decision. Reville and Murray welcomed the challenge of desegregation, seeing it as an opportunity to improve the quality of education in the city, and were pleased that the judge was willing, at least for now, to let them proceed at their own pace. They liked his moderation, and what they saw as his willingness to put educational questions ahead of the strict numerical guidelines favored by the plaintiffs. For example, Curtin had allowed the board to proceed with its plans for School 17. Located on Main Street in the Parkside neighborhood, 17 was an all-black school the board wanted to convert into a highly academic school called City Honors. The plaintiffs were opposed—whites would not attend, they said. Moreover, the plaintiffs argued, the board's plan for School 17 sent three quarters of its 175 black students to all-black schools on the East Side, leaving them, Griffin argued, "in the same segregated conditions." Curtin liked the idea of an integrated honors school, however, and approved it. As for Griffin's concern, he told the board to make sure that the displaced black students attended an integrated school beginning in 1977.

Despite his ruling on School 17, the plaintiffs were generally pleased with Curtin's July decision, confident that the Judge would eventually impose a system-wide solution. They were willing to wait until Curtin's October deadline for a more comprehensive plan. Some fretted. The *Courier Express* was critical of Curtin's insistence that the board go beyond the Buffalo Plan. It snidely advised the judge to pay more attention to his docket of criminal cases. Representatives of more than a dozen community groups and several members of the Board of Education also publicly expressed their fear of the judge's insistence that more be done. Throughout the summer of 1976 they urged the board to appeal his decision.

Suburbanites were concerned about Curtin's plea (given Millken, all he could do was plead) that they join the city in bringing an end to school segregation. School boards in all of the surrounding suburban communities quickly and flatly refused. The superintendent of schools in Williamsville, the wealthiest of Buffalo's suburbs, was fired for simply agreeing to discuss the matter with Reville. Community groups in the city, however, were far more cooperative and by the summer of 1976 an ad hoc Coalition of Community Leaders—people from business, labor, and government—and a religious group active in social justice issues called the Buffalo-Area Metropolitan Ministries, pledged to support Curtin's decision. Most significantly, the decision was supported by the bishop of Buffalo, Edward Head, an Irish-American who had come to Buffalo from Brooklyn. In a December 1975 conference on "Positive Approaches to School Integration" sponsored by a group called the

Buffalo Committee For Quality Integrated Education, Head had committed the diocese to the principle of "basic quality education and equal
educational opportunity for every child in public as well as nonpublic
schools." Hoping to involve Head in the desegregation process from
the beginning, Judge Curtin wrote him a letter in August 1976 in which
he explained his recent ruling and urged Head's participation in the
development of the remedy. The bishop's response was immediate. In
a letter to his "Brothers and Sisters in Christ" in parishes throughout
Buffalo, Head outlined "diocesan policy and guidelines to support quality
integrated education in the Buffalo public schools." The bishop made
himself perfectly clear. "Catholic schools," he said, "will not become
havens for those seeking to avoid public school integration." Students
seeking admission into a Catholic school would be admitted only if
"the receiving officer is morally certain that the request for admission
is consistent with the above stated diocesan policy."

Reville, Murray, and the Board of Education needed all the help
they could get. In September 1976, just as they were scheduled to implement the most sweeping changes in the history of the Buffalo school
system, the city was confronted with a fiscal crisis and drastically reduced
the school budget. According to Reville, it was "the worst year fiscally
in memory." Spending per pupil had been $1,890 per year, well below
the statewide average of $2,300. In the city's new budget the figure was
reduced to $1,670. Programs were cut, teachers dismissed. In response,
Buffalo's public-school teachers went on strike the day the schools were
scheduled to open.

When the strike was finally settled and school finally opened three
weeks late, school officials reported that more than three thousand more
pupils had left the school system than had left the year before. It was
the second greatest loss in ten years. Despite the optimism of Reville
and Murray, the people of Buffalo, it seemed, had lost confidence in
their schools. Perhaps James Coleman, the highly respected sociologist
who years before had touted the educational advantages of racial integration, was right. At a conference in New York toward the end of
September he reported the findings of his latest studies. Court-ordered
integration, he said in a story that made the front page of both newspapers
in Buffalo, leads to "massive white flight." Other strategies had better
be tried, he advised.

But it was too late. Judge Curtin had already ordered the implementation of what was called "Phase I" of the Buffalo Plan and finally,
at the end of September 1976, it began. The community mobilized for
the occasion. A liberal coalition of ministers, the Buffalo Area Metro-

politan Ministries, had arranged to have adult volunteers ride the school buses during the first several weeks of school. So did the Council of Churches. The director of the Justice Department's New England regional office came to Buffalo to monitor events. He was pleased with what he saw. The three-week delay caused by the teacher's strike had proved to be a blessing. Everyone, it seemed, was eager to get their kids back to school, and when school did finally open in late September the atmosphere was calm and enthusiastic.

Phase II would not be so easy. In his July ruling Curtin had given the board until October to present the second, and presumably final, phase of its desegregation plan. However, preoccupied with the teacher's strike, Reville and Murray requested an extension until January 1977. The plaintiffs objected. So did the U.S. Commission on Civil Rights, whose chairman wrote Curtin a letter in late September urging that he hold the defendants to the October deadline. Curtin, however, granted the request with little hesitation. Soon after, the plaintiffs, again joined by the civil-rights commission, urged the judge to appoint a monitor to supervise the desegregation process. Reville argued that a court-appointed monitor would give the community the impression that the board was not making progress. Again, Curtin agreed.

Although they now had until January, Reville and Murray had been working on Phase II of the plan since the summer. Taking seriously Curtin's mandate to involve the community, Reville and Murray orchestrated an elaborate public-relations campaign. Beginning in September 1976 and continuing through that school year and the next, the Board of Education, under orders from Judge Curtin, conducted regular meetings in the neighborhoods throughout the city, hoping that a dialogue between community residents and the board would produce a desegregation program that was both meaningful and well-received. In October and November Reville, Murray, and Ken Echols, the black director of the Board of Education's Office of Integration, visited schools throughout the city, reminding their audiences, as Echols told one group at an all-white elementary school in Black Rock, that he was there "not to discuss whether schools should be integrated—that's the law." Rather, "We are here to see how it can be done." The members of the various audiences had a choice, the three said. Unless they volunteered to send their children to the new inner-city magnet schools that Reville and Murray were planning for the second phase of the desegregation plan, the court would impose a plan of its own.

Curtin wanted to know how the people in the neighborhoods were responding. In September he contacted the Erie County Bar Association, requesting that one lawyer volunteer to be assigned to each school in the city, acting as a court-appointed monitor of board-community relations. They soon reported back to the judge. At School 67 on Abbott Road in South Buffalo, one lawyer reported that "Most of the comments were directed against the concept of school integration and that neighborhood integrity is a higher value than school desegregation." He complained that both South Buffalo Councilman Daniel Higgins and Joe Hillary, South Buffalo's representative on the Board of Education, were acting in an "inflammatory manner," and said that "the situation in School 67 [was] potentially volatile. From nearby School 72 on Lorraine Avenue, another monitor wrote of the parents: "Vehemently oppose any kind of busing. Against pairing and the expanded neighborhood school. In favor of magnets and will consider busing if it is voluntary. Feel strongly that there is no educational value to desegregation. Parents indicated that they would move if there was forced busing." At School 28 on South Park Avenue, "Seventy-five people attended the meeting. Their pervasive mood was one of anger and frustration. Most people came to vent their anger rather than to offer comments or ask questions."

At School 12, an all-black elementary school on Ash Street on the East Side, parents felt somewhat different. Like many black neighborhood schools, over the years School 12 had been the beneficiary of a variety of federal compensatory education programs. Most people in the community, the volunteers from the bar reported, were happy with the school. They liked its white principal and predominantly white staff. They were afraid that the school, like other older schools in the black community, would be closed and the children bused to schools in white neighborhoods. Above all, the residents did not want their children sent to schools where they would not be welcome. Feelings were similar at another East Side all-black elementary school, School 31 on Stanton Street, where parents were strongly opposed to their school being paired with a school in South Buffalo, "which they perceive," Curtin was told, "to be a hostile environment." Area parents were also concerned about rumored plans to turn the school into a performing arts magnet school. It was more important, a group of parents insisted, that there be "strict discipline in the schools and that their children should be thoroughly schooled in the traditional subjects." At School 37, an all-black elementary school on Carlton Street in the Fruit Belt, "The people are almost unanimously opposed to busing their children if the busing is going to be one way, that is, busing them out of their community into white schools."

Anti-busing sentiments at School 19 on Delavan Avenue, on the

largely Italian West Side, were of great concern to the lawyer who monitored the meeting. "The attitudes in this regard I dare say were unanimous
and there were members of the audience who voiced the sentiment that
if they were ordered they would either move away or ignore the order."
Down the street at School 38, "busing was vehemently opposed." It
was obvious, the lawyer reported to Curtin, "that this is a close community
with much concern over the fate of 'their school.' " Parents at School
38 on Vermont Street "could not accept the possibility that the choice
of the school which their children could attend could be left to a potentially
unresponsive and uncaring administrator who would make assignments
on the basis of quota." Similar fears were echoed by parents at School
57, on Sears Street, in the heart of the Polish East Side. "The fear
of all present was that their children would be assigned to a school
by a faceless, unapproachable bureaucrat." Curtin read these letters,
carefully digesting their contents. He heard what they were saying. People
wondered if he would listen.

Meanwhile, as the board prepared to announce its plan for Phase
II, the Supreme Court, in a school desegregation case out of Austin,
Texas, seemed to narrow the grounds for finding school boards liable
for racial imbalance. On December 7, 1976, the court ruled in *Washington*
v. *Davis* that it was not enough for plaintiffs to show that a school
board's actions would have the "foreseeable result" of causing segregation.
Rather, they had to show that the board actually intended to cause
segregation. Assistant Corporation Counsel Anthony Gregory, who had
handled much of the oral argument for Buffalo's Board of Education,
immediately urged Judge Curtin to reconsider his original ruling in light
of *Davis*.

Curtin was not easily swayed. He responded that since the Supreme
Court's ruling remanded the Austin case to the U.S. Court of Appeals,
it would have no immediate impact on Buffalo. The board was to proceed.
"The board can't simply go ahead with the idea that Austin has changed
everything," he said. "It can't sit on its oars." Curtin promised to decide
on the impact of Austin "when the dust settles there."

Meanwhile, on December 20, 1976, accompanied by an flurry of
publicity—"School Plan Avoids Forced Busing," proclaimed the *Evening
News* in a banner headline—Superintendent Reville announced the
board's latest plan. Phase II would be completely voluntary and would
rely on the creation of nine new magnet schools, all located on the
African-American East Side and each with an academic identity of its
own. These new magnets, plus expanded use of the voluntary busing
of black students through the Quality Integrated Education (QIE) pro-

gram, would guarantee that at least 20 percent of the students at every school in the city would be minority, Reville promised. He also pledged a policy of racial balance among the teaching and nonteaching staff, promising that no racially identifiable minority schools would have more than 12.5 percent minority staff and that no majority school would have less than 7.5 percent minority staff. Reville admitted that thirteen of the city's sixty-eight elementary schools would remain all black, but said that since they were far from other schools with which they could merge, it was not possible to integrate them. Board President Florence Baugh agreed. When asked how she thought Judge Curtin would react to the plan's failure to desegregate the remaining all-black schools and the voluntary nature of the magnet schools, Baugh was confident. "Just wait until he sees it. Just wait."

The rest of the board, which had passed Phase I unanimously, was less enthusiastic about Phase II, passing it by a margin of only one. Opposition in South Buffalo was particularly strong. Joseph Hillary was worried about the plan's "guarantee" that all schools in the city would have at least 20 percent minority students. Hillary said parents in South Buffalo were worried that if not enough white students from the area chose to attend the magnet schools they would be forced to leave their neighborhood schools in order to make room for incoming black children. He couldn't see it, he said—couldn't picture all those fair-haired Irish kids standing on Seneca, Abbott, or South Park waiting for buses to take them to schools on the East Side. Neither could Joe Murphy, the at-large representative on the board from South Buffalo. Not appeased by cheery optimism of that other South Buffalonian, Gene Reville, Hillary voted against Phase II. Despite his concern about the narrow vote, in early January 1977 Reville submitted the plan to Curtin.

The plaintiffs wanted Curtin to reject the plan. It integrated schools in white neighborhoods by busing nearly eight thousand black students into them. The burden of integration, the plaintiffs argued in hearings before the judge in March and April, fell exclusively on black students. There was nothing "voluntary," Richard Griffin argued, for the black kids whose neighborhood schools were going to be converted into magnet schools. Where were they supposed to go? Worse, Griffin said, the program would not touch the ten thousand black children left behind in the thirteen inner-city elementary schools still segregated. Finally, there was no guarantee whatsoever that the magnet schools would work. Indeed, the plaintiffs were convinced they would not. Finger argued that whites simply would not attend schools, no matter how good, that were located in black neighborhoods. Another expert witness for the plaintiffs, Forbes Bottomley, a professor of education from Georgia State University, ridiculed the magnet schools as a desegregation tool. Arguing for a stronger, compulsory program, Professor Bottomley said, "We've found no voluntary program that has brought about desegregation."

Reville and Murray, however, had faith in their plan, and were convinced they would be able to sell it to the white people of Buffalo. The plaintiffs had correctly argued that blacks had little choice but to go along once their neighborhood schools closed. For them it was either voluntary busing to white schools or transfer to other segregated elementary schools.

Judge Curtin's opinion on the matter took time. As he explained in a memo written later that spring, there was "a delay of the remedy hearing caused by the disastrous weather conditions which plagued the Buffalo area for the last several weeks of January and the first week of February." The judge, as was his wont, had somewhat understated the case, for the Blizzard of '77, as it quickly became known, was a cataclysmic milestone in the history of the city that became deeply etched in the collective consciousness of the community.

As with the assassination of President Kennedy and the attack on Pearl Harbor, everyone in Buffalo remembers where they were on the Friday morning in January 1977 when the vicious, awesome, swirling torrent of snow and wind called the Blizzard of '77 struck the metropolitan area. People cherish their memories of the blizzard, commemorating it with an annual "Blizzard Ball" now in its thirteenth year, relishing the details, sharing them with a new generation of Buffalonians too young to remember and with those who have moved here since.

"Brutal" is the word that most aptly describes the weather of January 1977. It was bad all over the East: snow in Florida, temperatures in the teens throughout Georgia, Virginia, and the Carolinas. It was particularly bad in the midwest, where since Christmas the entire area had been wrestling with the meanest, coldest winter in memory. Buffalo had had a foot of snow in October. November's low temperatures broke an 1880 record, and on the twenty-eighth and twenty-ninth another two feet of snow fell. There were storms throughout December, though Christmas Day was mild and pleasant. The next day was even nicer and by noon the temperature had climbed into the mid-thirties. Then, suddenly, the weather changed. It happens that way all the time in Buffalo. The wind roars off Lake Erie, the powerful gales forcing their way up Court Street, whipping around Niagara Square into the heart of the city. Like kites, traffic lights strung helplessly across the city's streets dance in the wind and pedestrians clutch desperately to street lamps. Then the sky starts to darken and the temperature starts to drop. It was thirty-six degrees at noon on December 26, 1976. By early evening it had dropped to ten degrees. The cold and snow continued into January: two inches on the first of the month, three on the second, four and a half on the seventh, and thirteen on the tenth. Four inches more followed on the fifteenth, and seven on the seventeenth. Meanwhile, with temperatures averaging fourteen degrees, the snow would not melt and snow removal was impossible, despite a much-heralded "snow blitz" and endless pleas to motorists to get their cars off the streets. On January 18 it was six degrees below zero. On the nineteenth the temperature rose to the low teens but dropped down into single digits overnight. It hovered there—lows near zero, highs near twenty—through the weekend of the twenty-second and twenty-third. Meanwhile, the snow was mounting: thirty-four inches had already accumulated. Snowplowing proceeded at a snail's pace, hampered by scores of abandoned cars strewn throughout the streets and an exhausted crew that was, in the words of Streets Commissioner James Lindner, "shell-shocked." The weather had become front-page news, and in daily headlines the local press told of a frustrated people wrestling with the relentless wind, cold, and snow of the winter of 1977.

The forecast on Wednesday, January 26, was a bit more encouraging. There had been a letup in the snow, and the snowplow crews had finally begun to make some progress. Within a week, Lindner said, "we'll have it back to normal." The National Weather Service predicted temperatures in the mid-thirties. It warned, however, that should the warming trend continue, flooding was likely. But the next day, winds accompanied by heavy snow squalls returned and the temperatures dropped once again to near zero. Fuel supplies dwindled and Buffalo's schools and many businesses and factories closed for the balance of the week. Everyone lowered thermostats and on Thursday night Gov. Hugh Carey declared a "fuel emergency." The weather deteriorated overnight and by early Friday morning officials at the office of the National Weather Service at the Buffalo airport were very concerned about reports out of Ohio. The weather had worsened throughout the Midwest and a storm was moving quickly across the twelve-hundred-mile expanse of Lake Erie. By seven o'clock in the morning a vicious storm had struck Cleveland, Toledo, and Erie. Officials at the National Weather Service considered issuing a "blizzard warning." The service described "blizzardlike" storms and "near-blizzard conditions in Buffalo"—it had never in its history predicted an actual blizzard. But this was different.

The Blizzard of '77 had arrived, and the people of Western New York had to be warned.

Weather reports were far from encouraging: "Blizzard warning later this afternoon and tonight. Winds becoming westerly, increasing to twenty to forty miles per hour with higher gusts during the afternoon and tonight producing blizzard conditions and blowing and drifting snow. Occasional snow this afternoon accumulating up to three inches by evening. Bitter cold, with temperatures five degrees above zero or colder by evening. Occasional snow likely tonight. Lows five to fifteen below zero, colder in some valleys."

On Friday the twenty-eighth, between eleven o'clock in the morning and one o'clock in the afternoon, the savage storm finally arrived. It dwarfed all that had come before, devastating all of Western New York. The *Evening News* reported that the area "lay prostrate, flattened by the most destructive and disruptive storm in memory." With winds up to sixty miles an hour, thick and heavy falling snow, and temperatures close to zero, the storm was classified as a "severe blizzard." Thirteen thousand people were stranded downtown. At AM&A's department store, where three hundred were stuck, blankets and mattresses were distributed and the cafeteria stayed open throughout the night. It was the same story in department stores and offices everywhere. Six hundred people spent the night at City Hall, many of them gathered around the one color television set in the building watching "Roots," the mini-series about one black family's history that had gripped the nation that last week of January 1977.

The next day President Jimmy Carter, sworn into office less than a week before, declared a state of emergency in the area. A week later he declared Western New York a "national disaster area." Two hundred and fifty National Guardsmen—by the end of the week there were more than five hundred—were mobilized and placed under the control of Thomas Casey, the Northeast regional administrator for the Federal Disaster Assistance Administration. Working out of a "Buffalo Command Zone" established at the State Office Building downtown, Casey mapped out his strategies. All vehicular traffic was immediately banned and streets leading to area hospitals were cleared. A convoy of milk trucks was arranged with the Upstate Dairy Cooperative and eight half-block-long tankers crawled along the New York State Thruway from Batavia to Buffalo. Meanwhile, the Red Cross organized a convoy to transport food from a supermarket warehouse in South Buffalo to Red Cross headquarters on Delaware Avenue. There the food was packed up by tireless Red Cross workers and distributed to community centers throughout the city by dozens of volunteers: owners of snowmobiles and four-wheel drive vehicles, citizens-band radio operators and volunteer firemen, workers at the public service agencies, the Salvation Army, the Red Cross, and the staffs of hospitals and community centers. They worked without relief, as if at war.

The storm continued over the weekend. The sky cleared for a few hours on Sunday afternoon but by three o'clock whirling black clouds again covered the city. On Monday and Tuesday the snow and wind increased again and on Thursday still more snow fell. On Friday, one week after the blizzard first struck, squalls and heavy drifting combined with near-zero visibility produced conditions that some weather officials felt were similar to the blizzard's of the Friday before. At dusk on Saturday, however, as the sun slid down behind Lake Erie and the sky cleared. The night was bitter cold, but the wind died down, the clouds finally disappeared, and the rich, deep blue winter sky was filled with stars. The next day, everyone knew, would be beautiful.

Some people tried to explore the snow-covered city on foot. They awoke that morning looking out at the sparkling, glistening, powdery-white streets. The snow was piled high everywhere, and the sidewalks and driveways were buried under thick blankets of white. People dressed in layers of their warmest clothing. Then, pushing against masses of snow they forced their doors open and stood outside, silently looking and listening. As much as by the shimmering beauty of the snow-filled streetscape, they were struck by the quiet. All but emergency vehicles had been banned from the streets and now the whole city was plunged deep into an eerie, awesome silence.

For some it was a time of fantasy. "It makes me think of poetry," one person remembered. "The quiet, the white city, the city in the clouds. It was so bright that there was little difference between day and night . . . streets and sidewalks went away. A city without streets, a city without going to work, a city on vacation, and all the kids were home. They piled the snow in the park . . . there were snow mountains everywhere. Next time I think we should pour food-coloring on the mountains and make them even more wonderful."

People couldn't travel very far that first day, but the sun stayed out for the next several days and gradually they were able to get around to different parts of the city. With schools and offices closed and automobiles banned, the streets were filled with people, some digging out, others pulling sleds stacked with grocery-filled bags, others just walking, gazing in wonderment at how the snow had transformed their city. People were friendly and concerned. They seemed to care about one another.

Gradually, over the next several weeks, Buffalo returned to normal and people went back to their routines. Slowly the snow was cleared. Some was removed by a half dozen machines, Rube Goldberg–like contraptions borrowed from Toronto. These thirty-foot-long vehicles managed somehow to scoop, store, and then melt tons of snow while lumbering noisily up and down the side streets of the city's neighborhoods. Much of the snow was dumped in Delaware and La Salle Parks, creating huge, packed, filthy mountains that did not melt till June.

Spring was unusually beautiful that year and the summer of 1977 turned out to be one of the most pleasant in memory. Soon people stopped talking about the blizzard. No one, though, would ever forget it. These were hard times for Buffalo, years when the economic foundations of America's industrial cities were irreparably weakened by changes in the world economy. But, like the blizzard, the battering of Buffalo's industry was a phenomenon over which the people of the city had little control. There was somehow a poignant connection between these two disasters, one natural, the other economic, and as the people of Buffalo struggled through them, the ties that bound them to their community were strengthened. To some it seemed that Buffalo was in its finest hour.

10

THE BUFFALO PLAN, II

In mid-February 1977, as the city lay under a still-enormous blanket of snow, Judge Curtin strongly affirmed his original ruling in which he found the Board of Education guilty of maintaining segregated schools. He now went out of his way to establish the connection between discrimination in housing and public education, a subject that many thought the narrow guidelines of *Davis* v. *Washington* might have made moot. For Curtin the relationship was essential to understanding the Buffalo case. Not only, he wrote, did it "provide a more complete historical perspective to the school situation here, it punctures the popular conception that all minorities either desire to live apart or are forced to by economic circumstances." Curtin's conclusion was equally clear and unambiguous. "I am convinced beyond a shadow of a doubt that there can be no other answer than the one that we reached."

The defendants were disappointed. In an argument echoed by both daily newspapers, the lawyer for the Board of Education, a black attorney from Detroit named Aubrey McCutcheon, said that the Supreme Court's finding in *Davis* meant that a desegregation remedy could affect only those schools that were intentionally segregated, not the whole system. The defendants said they would appeal Curtin's original ruling.

Richard Griffin meanwhile argued forcefully against what the plaintiffs felt were the double standards implicit in Phase II: one for blacks, many of whose neighborhood schools had been closed and who were now offered no choice but to be bused; the other for whites, who could choose to go or not to go to magnet schools. Besides, Griffin insisted, whites simply would choose not to attend schools located in the inner city, regardless of how "magnetic" they were. The plaintiffs again summoned the redoubtable John Finger, who once again proposed carving the city into five pie-shaped attendance zones, pairing the black schools in the narrow, inner-city segment of each zone with white schools in the broader, outlying segment.

Judge Curtin appeared as skeptical about the voluntary nature of Phase II as the plaintiffs, notwithstanding the reassurances of a parade of defense witnesses that the magnets would attract enough white students. He questioned James Williams, the black principal of Woodlawn Junior High School, which, under Phase II, was to become the Buffalo Traditional High School. "You'll have to convince white parents it's to their advantage. Explain to me as if I were a parent why I should volunteer to send my children to your school." Williams's response was evasive and hardly convincing. Guarantees, he said, were not necessary. "If I didn't believe in the program I wouldn't be on the stand."

Though he seemed impressed with the educational programs that Murray and Reville proposed for the magnet schools, Curtin reminded the defendants that "it is equal opportunity, not the quality of education, which is germane to the constitutional issue." He remained skeptical that the magnets would work in this regard. The defendants, he complained, offered no timetable, no back-up plans. Curtin was frustrated by Reville and Murray's faith in an untested program. "There is nothing in this plan," he said, "to suggest how things will be accomplished."

In the meantime, Curtin had been doing homework of his own. Having spent his whole life in the city, he was already very familiar with the contours of the physical as well as social geography of Buffalo. He could follow perfectly the often minutely detailed descriptions of the different locations of the city's schools, often adding comments of his own about the neighborhoods under discussion. During the hearings on Phase II, Curtin made several trips, sometimes on his own, sometimes with his law clerk, Michael Brady, sometimes with Reville and Murray, to the schools and neighborhoods affected by the board's proposed changes. After one such tour, the judge made notes upon returning to his office: "We drove to a number of schools on the lower East Side. In almost every instance the means of access to the school is difficult. Schools 75 and 31 are on side streets, one way and very narrow, some distance from the nearest thoroughfare. It is obvious that there will be some difficulty moving buses up and down the streets. . . . The surroundings in each instance are very bad with a number of burned out and tumble-down houses and a very depressing air in the neighborhood. . . . At the end of the day we went to the Waterfront School, which is certainly a beautiful place."

Curtin was eager for a resolution of the impasse over Phase II and at the end of April, arguing that "each plan has its advantages and disadvantages," he urged plaintiffs and defendants to reach a compromise. Everyone, it seems, was in a compromising mood. The plaintiffs, in what the *Evening News* announced in banner headlines was a "stunning shift," accepted the board's Phase II plan virtually intact. Rejecting Finger's plan for paired schools as a "mistake," they accepted all of the board's proposal for magnet schools, although they did insist on a back-up pupil-assignment plan if not enough whites participated. Defendants compromised too, accepting without complaint Curtin's warning that this was not a final but an interim plan. They also agreed to a court-appointed "desegregation master" to oversee the process, and at Curtin's request they and the plaintiffs submitted names for consideration. Curtin compromised, too, and did not push the parties farther than they were willing to go, promising that his order—an "interim ruling," he called it—would encompass only those areas agreed to by plaintiffs and defendants.

Important grievances—an expanded voluntary busing program and the fact that Phase II left untouched thirteen all-minority elementary schools—remained. Michael Brady wrote a memo to Curtin saying it was "intolerable that ten thousand to sixteen thousand black children were left in all-minority schools." Curtin, pleased that the parties were making progress, did not, at least for now, agree with his clerk. The judge also accepted much of the board's proposals for dealing with racial imbalance in staffing patterns. Not only did he postpone action on the plaintiffs' request to eliminate the teacher-eligibility examination, which they argued discriminated against black candidates, but he accepted at face value the defendants' promise that between 7.5 percent and 12.5 percent of the faculty at each of the city's schools would be minority.

In his decision of May 9, 1977, Curtin also seemed to limit his skepticism toward the magnet schools—as long as they ended up desegregated, he warned. He gave Reville and Murray a month to report back to him on this matter and would then rule on both the magnet schools and the thirteen still-segregated elementary schools. When Reville asked for two months, though, Curtin agreed, apparently eager to give him the benefit of doubt.

By mid-July Curtin was becoming concerned over the defendants' progress. He decided he would permit no magnet school to open unless at least one-third of its students were white. That was easy with the highly touted City Honors School and the new open-classroom elementary school known as the Waterfront School, but now white applicants for the other magnet schools were becoming fewer. As Finger and Bottomley had predicted, whites appeared to be reluctant to apply to, let alone attend, schools in the inner city. Only at the one magnet did more whites than blacks apply, and it was not located in the inner city but was an elementary school on the campus of Buffalo State College.

With less than a month remaining until Curtin's deadline, Reville and Murray launched a last-ditch public-relations campaign designed to attract whites to the schools. A glossy, elaborately designed twelve-page brochure with pictures of black and white children and teachers, studying and playing together, was printed and distributed throughout the city. Still more information sessions were held at dozens of schools and neighborhood community centers. The newspapers helped too, with both the *Evening News* and the *Courier Express* running highly favorable series on the new magnet schools. Curtin himself touted the program before a Chamber of Commerce breakfast in early July. Two weeks later, with the number of applications from whites still insufficient, he extended the deadline for his decision on the magnet schools until August. Others now joined the effort.

The Chamber of Commerce announced that it would fund an annual college scholarship for graduates of the Buffalo Traditional School. The National Hockey League's Buffalo Sabres promised to fund a hockey team at the school. Even local disc jockeys got into the act. One of them, a popular iconoclast named Shane, had contacted Murray in the spring, asking if there was anything he could do to help. Soon a handful of DJs were plugging the new magnet schools on several of Buffalo's radio stations. After a song had played Shane would croak in his trademark throaty voice, "You want to play like that, boys and girls, check out the High School of Performing Arts. If it's tradition you want, dress codes and rules and regs, call Traditional. For more information call. . . ."

The publicity campaign began to pay off. On August 2, 1977, after studying the projected enrollments at the proposed inner-city magnets, Curtin approved six: the Academic Challenge School, emphasizing an individual approach to elementary education with 70 percent minority, 30 percent white enrollment; a Montessori elementary school and a Performing Arts high school, each balanced equally between blacks and whites; the BUILD Academy, a community-based elementary school whose primary goal was parent and community participation, 57 percent black, 43 percent white; and Campus West, an elementary school operated jointly by Buffalo State College and the Board of Education, 55 percent white, 45 percent black.

When it became clear that the Traditional High School and a school called the Follow Through Center, which emphasized basic learning skills, generated far fewer white applications than the 30 percent required by Curtin, the judge gave the board still more time. Two weeks later, white applications to Traditional rose to 50 percent in response to a frenzied publicity drive by the board, and Curtin approved the opening of the school. Curtin finally accepted the Follow Through Center as well, although whites would comprise only a quarter of the first year's enrollment. The defendants had much to be pleased about. McCutcheon said that it was "something we've been looking for for a long time." The compromise gave Buffalo the chance to be "the first city in the nation to formulate a successful yet voluntary desegregation plan."

Patient with the defendants, Curtin was less sympathetic to the demands of the plaintiffs. Although they were still segregated, Curtin said that the thirteen all-black elementary schools could open again in September 1977. The board, he said, would have another year to desegregate them.

To all but the plaintiffs, Curtin was the man of the hour. The *Evening News* applauded his "stern wisdom, moderation, and balance." By "holding the defendants' feet to the fire," it wrote, he had "caused them to move with more alacrity." The *Courier Express* added that "the instructions that have emanated from the court of Judge Curtin have had a dramatic effect on the school system. Everything seems to have moved along in a smooth and efficient fashion." All this praise was delivered despite the dramatic change of "the greatest reorganization in the history of the Buffalo schools," as Superintendent Reville called the implementation of Phase II. "Nothing else even approaches it."

On the opening day of school in September 1977, ten thousand children, compared with only a thousand two years before, rode buses to schools outside their neighborhoods. Six thousand children, up from eight hundred the year before, were enrolled in magnet schools. Eighteen thousand of a total of fifty-three thousand students went to new schools. Three high schools located in racially isolated working-class ethnic neighborhoods saw their black enrollment double. Somehow, it all seemed to work. A Justice Department official who was in Buffalo to monitor the opening of the schools and who had had similar assignments in Louisville, Boston, and Chicago, said, "This is the best school opening that I have ever seen. . . . Never in my entire experience have I been more gratified than I have been in Buffalo." Florence Baugh seemed not at all surprised. She expected "nothing less," she said.

A parent, Carol Holtz, was not as optimistic. Some say Holtz once threatened to lie down in front of the buses. Holtz and her husband, Richard, a steelworker at Bethlehem, had lived in South Buffalo all their lives. Like many of their neighbors, they would live nowhere else. To this day Holtz has passionate feelings about the neighborhood and, with only a trace of humor, says that she likes everything about her daughter-in-law except that she's not from South Buffalo.

Today Carol Holtz works at the Parent-Child Center, one of many programs run by the Board of Education that are aimed at some of the more intractable social problems that afflict the public schools. The Parent-Child Center deals with teenage pregnancy. It is located in a building, on Hamburg and Louisiana, that for more than a hundred years was the schoolhouse of St. Brigid's parish across from the Perry Projects in the old First Ward.

While most of the people in the neighborhood lived in the Ward's tiny frame homes—cottages really, most of them without basements— many also lived in the Perry Projects. Built in the early days of World War II to accommodate Buffalo's rapidly growing wartime population, the projects, red-brick garden apartments surrounding a pleasantly land-scaped interior court, were Irish to a family. The Irish left years ago, moving onward and outward to South Buffalo and beyond, and the Perry Projects have since been inhabited mainly by blacks. St. Brigid's, whose congregation had shrunk almost beyond recognition, burned down in the late 1960s. The parish school stayed open, however, and under the leadership of several community-minded priests (Joe Bissonette worked there for a while during the early 1970s), St. Brigid's welcomed the African-American children, Catholic and non-Catholic alike, from the Perry Projects. The school finally closed in 1982, and when it did, among the priests in South Buffalo only William Stanton, from St. Ambrose, attempted to persuade his congregation to accept the black children now bused into the community.

As has happened with many of Buffalo's abandoned Catholic schools, St. Brigid's was taken over by the expanding public-school system. In the fall of 1988 it became the site of the Parent-Child Center. Responding to the problem of a growing number of pregnant school-age girls, the Board of Education created the center because so many young women were dropping out and so few of them returned after their babies were born. Every day thirty-odd young mothers and their babies are picked up at their homes and brought to the center. Since September 1989 the girls take all their classes at the center and then, in their senior year, transfer to South Park High School in South Buffalo, where they graduate. The infants spend the day in the beautifully renovated facility, cared for by a gentle and hovering staff, while their mothers are bused to South Park. At the end of the day the young mothers are brought back to pick up their babies and then get back on the bus for the ride home.

Carol Holtz has been in charge of recruitment at the center since it opened. She believes deeply in the program and argues persuasively that the girls should not be denied an education "because they made a mistake." The center is the only way, she says, to get these girls "back on track," to help them not have any more children until they are ready. Holtz likes working in the Ward because it is close to South Buffalo. She considers the neighborhood's public schools "family." Holtz's neighborhood school is School 70 on Buffum Street, across from an old Indian burial ground. The Holtzes are very attached to the school and they talk fondly and with nostalgia even about long-lost teachers and principals they never knew. Carol and Richard Holtz went to School 70 in the 1950s, and their kids were going there when Curtin announced his desegregation ruling in 1976. There was no way, Carol and Richard vowed, magnet schools or no, that their kids, or the kids of any of their neighbors, would ever go to schools outside of South Buffalo.

Reville, Murray, and Curtin understood this attitude. The board had worried about South Buffalo ever since it had hired Reville as superintendent in 1975. Sensing that if South Buffalo could be won over the rest of the city could too, the board proceeded cautiously. Reville and Murray soon found that if they could win over Carol Holtz, they would have a real chance with South Buffalo as a whole. But they knew that Holtz, like her South Buffalo neighbors, would have to be won over gently. They could not be forced.

It was with this in mind that in the spring of 1977 Murray dispatched Evelyn Cooper to South Buffalo to talk about Phase II of "deseg" and about the new magnet schools the board was planning to open in September. Cooper was born and raised on the East Side, when Watson and North Division Streets, where she lived, were populated by a mixture of Jewish, Italian, and black families. She remembers the neighborhood fondly, recalling curbside potato roasts on chilly fall evenings and Italian funeral parades that wound, snakelike and sombre, through area streets. Cooper went to School 75 on Monroe and Howard Streets and then, like many of the black women who became successful teachers and principals, to Hutchinson Central and Buffalo State Teachers' College where she graduated in 1953, one of only three African-Americans in the class. Cooper taught for a while and then became a principal at all-black School 12 on Ash Street before she was called by the board in 1977 to help implement Phase II.

Cooper had never been to South Buffalo before and had never heard of Buffum Street, let alone of the Indian burial ground there. Several times she came speaking, quietly and directly, to white parents gathered in the auditorium of School 70. She told them about the conversion of old schools on the African-American East Side; about how the infamous Woodlawn Junior High, which had opened in 1964 as an intentionally segregated school, was becoming Buffalo Traditional High; about how old School 32 on Clinton Street, once the object of Leland Jones's ire, would become a Montessori school. Across Clinton, in the old Buffalo Tech building, would be the School of Performing Arts, while around the corner on Hickory Street old School 6 was to become the Academic Challenge Center, where students with learning problems would receive special attention.

Holtz was interested in what Cooper had to say, particularly about Performing Arts and the Academic Challenge Center. School 70 couldn't compare with what these new schools had to offer her children. For one Holtz child, consumed by television and radio, Performing Arts offered courses in electronic communications; for another, who was having difficulty with his basic subjects, the small classes and low student-teacher ratio promised by the ACC seemed perfect. Holtz and her husband made several trips to the East Side during the summer of 1977, visiting the ACC and the School of Performing Arts. In the heart of the Ellicott Urban Renewal District, these two imposing old brick buildings stand alone. Both were built in the 1920s, when the neighborhood teemed with Italian and Jewish children. Now they hover monumentally over the modern, strangely skeletal buildings that punctuate the cold, anonymous-looking streets of the area. As part of the desegregation program the schools had been renovated (far more successfully than the neighborhoods), and the Holtzes liked what they saw.

Carol Holtz was willing, she finally decided, to try these new magnet schools, even if it meant that her children would have to be bused across the Buffalo Creek and into the East Side. But Holtz didn't simply put her kids on the bus that cold and sunny day in early September 1977. For several weeks she and some of the other mothers drove behind the bus as it weaved through the streets of South Buffalo, down South

Park Avenue past Holy Family, South Park High, and the Club Como, for so long a hangout for South Buffalo's Irish-American politicians, past the old Republic Steel plant, making its way to Hickory and then to Clinton. For weeks Holtz stayed the day in the neighborhood, spending the mornings at the Challenge Center, the afternoons around the corner at Performing Arts. The more time she spent at the schools the more she liked what she saw. Holtz talked to her friends in South Buffalo and the word began to spread. Soon South Buffalonians began to follow Holtz's example and send their kids to the inner-city magnet schools. Curtin heard about what Holtz was doing, and in the spring of 1978 sent her a certified letter asking her to serve on a court-appointed desegregation monitoring committee.

The caution Curtin demonstrated in his rulings during the spring and summer of 1977 seemed justified, given the Supreme Court's ruling in *Dayton Board of Education* v. *Brinkman* at the end of June. In a decision that rendered unlikely the Buffalo plaintiffs' hope that all of the schools in the Buffalo public-school system would be desegregated by federal court order, the court ruled that an Ohio district court had gone too far in ordering the busing of eighteen thousand children to achieve systemwide desegregation. Writing for the majority, Justice William Rehnquist said that unless the defendants' actions had a segregative effect on a "meaningful portion" of the local school system, the remedy would have to be specific to the violations. It would be up to Judge Curtin to determine just how "meaningful" was the portion of the Buffalo public-school system that had been segregated.

Curtin had his own ideas about the remaining all-black elementary schools, and in a memo to clerk Michael Brady in September 1977, he expressed doubts about the board's constitutional responsibility to desegregate them. "I think it would be most difficult in most cases to find anything in the history of the board's actions or other defendants' actions to show that as far as these particular elementary schools are concerned the board intended that they be all black. In most cases it's simply a question of neighborhood." Besides, Curtin said, he was worried about "the practical problems"—the narrow streets that he noted after his visit to School 31, the long bus rides if those schools were to be paired with schools in white neighborhoods. These problems were "very, very difficult to overcome." Curtin worried about local politics, too. He was concerned that if South Buffalo's Jimmy Griffin were elected mayor in November 1977, he would make the job of desegregating the schools harder still.

With the exception of four short Republican years in the early

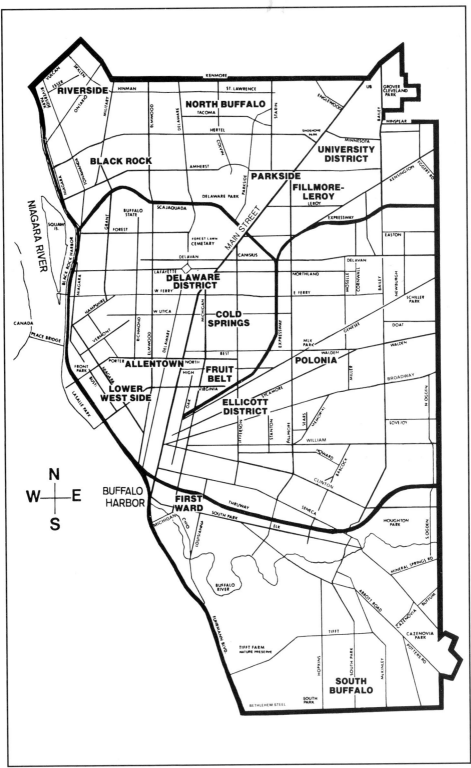

Buffalo and its neighborhoods.

A view of the Buffalo Skyline from Lake Erie. (Photo by Joe Trauer)

Bird Island Pier going underneath the Peace Bridge. (Photo by Lauren Tent)

Humboldt Parkway before the Kensington Expressway was built. (Photo courtesy of the Buffalo and Erie County Historical Society)

Today: the Kensington Expressway. (Photo by Mark Goldman)

Top left: St. Stanislaus Roman Catholic Church seen from Peckham St. (Photo by Mark Goldman)
Bottom left: A house in the Old First Ward. (Photo by Lauren Tent)
Right: Gethsemane Baptist Church in the Fruit Belt. (Photo by Mark Goldman)

Left: Judge John T. Curtin in downtown Buffalo; the City Hall is in the background. (Photo by Joe Trauer)
Top right: Riots on the East Side, 1967. (Photo courtesy of the *Buffalo News*)
Bottom right: Sign seen in Buffalo, 1982. (Photo by Mark Goldman)

The lighthouse at Erie Basin Marina seen from Stanley Swisher's rose garden. (Photo by Lauren Tent)

Grainscoopers c. 1952. (Photo courtesy of the Buffalo and Erie County Historical Society)

Bethlehem Steel plant. (Photo by Patricia Layman Bazelon) **Inset:** Black Rock graffiti. (Photo by Mark Goldman)

City Honors School observes the birthday of Martin Luther King, Jr., January 1990. (Photo by Lauren Tent)

1960s, the Erie County Democratic party, under the leadership of Peter Crotty and then Joe Crangle, two classic Irish-American political "bosses," had for years dominated local politics and controlled City Hall. Crotty was born, raised, and continues to live in that great Irish-American nesting ground in South Buffalo. Crangle was born there, but like many of his compatriots, came of age in St. Mark's parish in Parkside. Since the mid-1960s Crangle, like many of his compeers in Buffalo a graduate of Canisius College and UB law school, had been a dominant figure in the national as well as the local Democratic party. Allied to the Kennedys, Hubert Humphrey, Pat Moynihan, and other politicians whose pictures lined his office at Democratic headquarters in the old Genesee Building, Crangle, despite his comparative youth, was in style and substance very much a politician of the old school. A framed copy of "Loyalty," a homily by Buffalo's own Elbert Hubbard, hung on the wall outside his office door: "If you work for a man, in Heaven's name work for him; speak well of him and stand by the institutions he represents." By the 1970s, however, complacency within the Democratic Party and demographics—a shrinking white population that produced proportionately more black voters—had led to the decline of the party's influence. Finally in 1977 the party lost control of City Hall. The primary was the beginning of the end.

Crangle's man was Les Foschio, the highly intelligent lawyer who, as Buffalo's Corporation counsel, had argued the city's case in the school desegregation trial. A lackluster candidate, Foschio was trounced in the primary by two Democrats who ran in opposition to the party. One was Arthur Eve, the city's preeminent black politician who, as deputy majority leader in the state assembly, had played a key role in virtually every aspect of Buffalo's relations with the state. The other was Jimmy Griffin, a state senator the *Evening News* described as "the dukes-up Irish Democratic independent from South Buffalo."

Acting as a spoiler, Foschio drained enough white votes away from Griffin to hand the primary to Eve, who garnered virtually unanimous support from the black community. The primary was a disaster for Crangle, who knew that a victory by either Eve or Griffin in the general election would deny him access to the patronage his political machine needed to survive. He sat out the general election. "Imagining an election without Crangle dominating the scene," wrote one local commentator, "is a little like watching the Bills without O.J., the Stanley Cup without the Canadiens, or the World Series without the Yankees." For Crangle the election of 1977 was the beginning of the end.

Griffin, meanwhile, fell back on his Conservative Party ballet slot and in a three-way election between him, Eve, and a liberal Republican, a blue-stocking lawyer named John Phelan, Griffin won handily. Depicted as something of a redneck during the campaign by both Eve and Phelan, Griffin seemed to wear the tag proudly, boasting of his lack of education, his rise from private to lieutenant in the army, and his rough-and-tumble childhood in the Ward, where he worked in the grain elevators and railroads before being elected councilman from the Ellicott District in 1963. To the city's white ethnics, Griffin was a hero, and he was triumphantly elected mayor with more than a 40 percent plurality. He still holds the majority today—Buffalo had entered the Grifin Era.

Some people, Judge Curtin among them, had misgivings. Curtin was worried too about Buffalo's economy, concerned that the people had had enough. "I think it is appropriate in this kind of case," he wrote his clerk in September 1977, "to include the fact—in a footnote if not in the actual text—of the further decline of the Buffalo economy, the dropping of another thirty-five hundred jobs at Bethlehem."

11

THE VANISHING
INDUSTRIAL ECONOMY

Deep blues and purples, rich pastels, a bright sun shimmering on the lake, dark furnaces and factories in the background—these were the colors and images that appeared on the cover of *Fortune* magazine in July 1951, announcing the story "Made in Buffalo," twelve pages of stunning photographs "portraying the industrial diversity of a great city." The text was detailed and read like copy from the Buffalo Chamber of Commerce. As recorded in *Fortune,* Buffalo was the eleventh largest industrial center in the country in 1951, the third largest producer of steel, the largest inland water port, the second largest railroad center, and the "first city in the world" in flour milling—Buffalo produced enough flour to supply every family in the country with half a loaf of bread every day. The city had twelve railroad freight terminals that served forty-five thousand trains a year, and five passenger terminals serving fifty thousand trains a year. And with more than half a million people living in the city itself and a million and a half in the metropolitan area, Buffalo was the fifteenth largest city in the country.

Its five iron and steel plants employed close to thirty thousand workers, one-eighth of the city's total labor force according to *Fortune.* Buffalo's American Brass was the "number-one fabricator of copper and brass sheet, strip, and tubing"; Chevrolet's Tonawanda plant produced a third of all Chevy engines. The city hosted heavy industries like Lake Erie Engineering, Eastman Machine, Buffalo Forge, and Worthington Pump, manufacturers of cloth-cutting machines, presses, and machine tools. There were electrical-equipment manufacturers—Sylvania, Westinghouse, and Western Electric; electro-chemical companies—Carborundum, Hooker, and Vanadium; brewers—Magnus Beck, Iroquois, Phoenix, and William Simon; and a number of renowned specialty companies, including Kittinger Furniture, "known the world over" for the furniture it made for the recreated colonial village in Williamsburg, Virginia; and Birge Wallpaper, famous for its "unusual twelve-color presses." While to the casual visitor, *Fortune* wrote, "the city may seem as conventional, unassuming and unexciting as a businessman in a blue-serge suit," Buffalo, "behind its unexceptional façade, reveals a fascinating industrial kaleidoscope." What stands out about the article above all are the power and magnitude of industrial strength and dominance conveyed by the photographs, shot by Victor Jorgensen. They depict the city as an awesome, powerful, even overwhelming industrial giant that is also sleek, modern, and successful. Such was the image of Buffalo in the middle of the twentieth century. The people of Buffalo, at least its business leaders, liked what they saw, and believed the city's industrial base to be indestructible. Speaking to his organization in 1958, Chamber of Commerce President Dexter Rumsey, the owner of a large and prestigious real-estate firm, said, "there has never been a time when we could look forward to a more brilliant future. We are favored by three tremendous projects which will greatly help our industrial progress: the [New York State] Thruway, the St. Lawrence Seaway, and the Niagara Power Project. These offer unlimited potential for dynamic economic growth."

Ever since it was first proposed in the early 1920s, however, most Buffalonians had felt differently about the St. Lawrence Seaway. By extending the St. Lawrence River from Montreal down into Lake Ontario, the project would provide a direct inland water-route between the Great Lakes and the Atlantic Ocean, completely bypassing Buffalo. The results, as anybody who knew anything about the city's history should have known, would be disastrous. Since the 1820s and 1830s Buffalo's *raison d'etre* had been its location at the mouth of the Great Lakes and its link, via the Erie Canal, with the Atlantic Ocean. By the middle of the nineteenth century Buffalo had become the world's largest inland port, the flour-milling center of the world by virtue of the fact that it linked the American Midwest with the Eastern seaboard and even Europe. Lake boats stuffed tightly with grain and feed made the long, slow voyage from Duluth, Minnesota, down Lake Superior, through the narrows of Sault Ste. Marie into Lake Huron, through Port Huron into Lake Erie, then east to Buffalo. Here it was unloaded, manually in the early years, shoveled out of the deep holds of the hulking lake freighters and into elevators, then, beginning in the 1840s, by steam, in a contraption invented by Joseph Dart, a local merchant restless with the pace of unloading grain by hand. Dart built a mechanized grain "elevator" that revolutionized the business, vastly increasing the capacity and the potential of the city's port. Others soon followed in Dart's footsteps and Buffalo's grain elevators became a world curiosity. People came from miles around and from abroad to see the new machines. One wrote, "the huge elevator, by the use of steam, funnels its trunk into the holds of vessels, swallows up the grain without stopping to take a breath and discharges it in one continuous process into large storage bins or canal boats without effort except trifling puffs of steam." Anthony Trollope was ecstatic when he saw the machines in the 1860s. "I went down to the granaries and climbed into the elevator and saw the wheat running in rivers from one vessel to another," he wrote in his diary. "I saw the men bathed in corn as they distributed it on its flow. I saw bins by the score laden with wheat . . . I breathed the flour, drank the flour, and let myself be enveloped in a world of breadstuff . . . I began to know what it was for a country to overflow with milk and honey, to burst with its own fruits and be smothered with its own riches."

Some of the grain was milled into flour in Buffalo, the rest was loaded onto canal boats for the next leg of its voyage east. Other products—iron, lumber, livestock—followed the same route across the country, through the Great Lakes to the Erie Canal and the East, creating in Buffalo a broad and diverse manufacturing economy. The list of things made from the products that were shipped through the city was astonishingly diverse.

The St. Lawrence Seaway, a direct water link between the Atlantic Ocean and the Lake Erie built jointly by the United States and Canada, threatened that long-standing dominance. In the early 1950s, as passage of the legislation to effect the project seemed imminent, several delegations of Buffalo businessmen traveled to Washington to lobby against the seaway. The Common Council approved funds for a special lobbying effort that claimed the seaway should not be built because it would be vulnerable to Soviet air attacks. Other Buffalonians tried to be more optimistic. Certainly most outsiders were. In an extremely bullish article on the seaway in 1955, *Newsweek* referred to Buffalo as the "Inland Empire of the Sea," whose economic growth would be increased by the seaway. But the article, like the local people who supported the seaway, was long on bluster and short on economic reality. Frank Sedita, elected mayor in 1958, said the seaway made Buffalo "the most accessible city on the North American continent," while an editorial in the *Evening News* crowed, "Seaway Bolsters City's Stature as Great Center of Commerce." One business executive said, "The Seaway means push and purpose for this community." Another claimed, "Smart men will see the potential here and ten years from now Buffalo will enter a period of great growth. I don't know anything that can stop it."

Despite the apparent conviction of the rhetoric it is hard to believe there was anybody in Buffalo unaware that a water route that diverted shipping from the city could only undermine the city's economy. They must have been pretending, trying to make the most of it, hoping for the best despite what reality and the lessons of history must certainly have taught them. Perhaps something like a collective urban death-wish led the Western Savings Bank (now Goldome) to have an enormous mural of the seaway painted around the walls of a branch office it opened on Delaware Avenue in 1960. Whatever motivated these local boosters, it became apparent that they were dead wrong soon after the seaway opened in an elaborate ceremony at the mouth of the St. Lawrence during the summer of 1959 presided over by President Dwight D. Eisenhower and Queen Elizabeth.

For a while Buffalo's grain industry was able to hang on. In 1960 the city's six milling companies—General Mills, Pillsbury, Peavey, Standard Milling, International Milling, and George Urban—were so productive that more than a third of the population of the United States used flour or flour products milled in Buffalo. But by the mid-1960s Buffalo's grain business began to hurt. In 1966 alone five flour mills were shut, and in 1981 Standard Milling, a Kansas City-based company, closed the largest mill in the city. Such was the legacy of the St. Lawrence Seaway.

Industry, however, was booming in the mid-1960s, spurred on by an economy overheated by spending on the Vietnam war. Other factors also played a role. Beginning in 1962 the federal government offered industry generous incentives ("investment tax credits") for the purchase of modern equipment. By 1964 Bethlehem Steel and Republic Steel, the two largest steel companies in Buffalo, had installed state-of-the-art basic oxygen furnaces able to produce as much steel in one hour as the old open-hearth furnaces produced in six. Bethlehem's nearly twenty thousand employees and annual capacity of six million tons (Republic produced about one million tons a year) made it the third largest steel company in the country. Never had Buffalo's steel industry been more prosperous; never did the future seem brighter.

The local auto industry, too, was at its peak. With more than twenty-two thousand people working in the seven General Motors and one Ford plant in the area, production and payrolls broke all previous records in 1964. Each year another payroll record was set. As a regional officer of the United Auto Workers said in 1964, "As far as the economy is concerned the greatest effect of all this boom and expanison is the fat paycheck that auto-plant workers are pocketing." Naturally the manufacturers of auto parts also did well; Buffalo Tool and Die, American Radiator, American Brass, Dunlop Tire, and Trico, the windshield-wiper company, all had record years during the 1960s.

Though it was heavily dependent on the steel and automobile industry (a bit more than half of the approximately seventy-five thousand people in Buffalo's private sector workforce in 1960 were employed in one or the other), Buffalo's manufacturing economy was nevertheless quite diversified. The list of manufacturing activities is long and fascinating: twelve hundred people worked in fifteen sausage and hot dog factories, thirteen hundred in twelve beverage companies, including nine hundred in four breweries; four hundred people, primarily women, worked in six knitting mills, eleven hundred in eight factories that made mens' and boys' clothes. There were twenty-three hundred people working in twenty paper-products companies, three thousand in thirteen printing companies, thirteen hundred in thirty newspapers, seven hundred at thirteen companies producing drugs and medicine, four hundred in twelve soap companies; and twelve hundred people in fourteen toy factories. At an average pay of $108 a week, Buffalo's factory worker was the highest paid in New York State.

Despite this seemingly sound bill of health, some, like Paul Willax, an economist with the Chamber of Commerce, detected hints of weakness in the Buffalo economy. In a 1962 report entitled "Economic Analysis of Buffalo Area Industry," Willax offered some "qualifications" to his generally bullish prognosis. There were, he suggested ominously, without offering any specifics, "economic trends that could produce unfavorable occurences in the Buffalo area." One was foreign competition.

Though not yet a factor in the steel and automobile industry, foreign competition had begun to have an effect on local industry. Some companies responded to the challenge by modernizing and cutting costs. Reporting that "every single product we make is suffering from foreign competition," American Brass, whose thousand-plus workers made copper and brass tubing for the auto industry, spent more than $15 million during the late 1950s to introduce cost-cutting machinery. Other companies simply quit. In 1954 DuPont discontinued rayon production in

Buffalo, laying off more than half of its nearly two thousand employees, blaming "the lower-priced synthethics imported from abroad." Imported synthetics led George Laub, proprietor of the last leather tanning company in Buffalo, to close down his plant two years later.

A steady reduction in local ownership was another bad sign—at least on the surface. As the national and even the international economy became increasingly integrated, as markets became larger and more closely linked, the loss of local ownership, particularly in cities like Buffalo that were not home to many corporate headquarters, was inevitable. The trend that began in the 1920s accelerated during the 1950s as larger national companies extended their reach into smaller markets like Buffalo. Sometimes locally owned manufacturers were preyed upon by national companies eager to penetrate local markets and destroy the competition; at other times the national companies made local firms offers they simply couldn't refuse.

But while locally owned companies are a justifiable source of local pride and the tendency to romanticize them is understandable, they are not always a source of economic strength. Indeed, locally owned companies, particularly when family owned, as they usually are, are often a source of economic weakness. Inbred, plagued by personal problems and family struggles, undercapitalized, and unable or unwilling to attract new, outside management, it is possible for only the most exceptional family-owned local businesses to survive the changes like those that occurred in the national economy during the postwar years. Throughout the 1950s and 1960s these Buffalo companies, many of them owned and operated by the same family for close to a century, began to fail in every sector of the economy.

As the center of the nation's population moved further west and manufacturers and producers in the older cities of the East began to worry about access to markets, Buffalo-based companies began to look elsewhere for centers of operations. Companies large and small began to move. In 1958 Ford closed its assembly plant in Buffalo and moved it to Lorraine, Ohio, where it would be "more advantageously located in relation to rapidly growing markets." Buffalo lost 1,250 workers and an annual payroll of $8 million. Stanley Aviation, a small locally owned manufacturer of aircraft equipment, moved to Denver that same year.

The loss of Ford, the biggest since Curtiss-Wright moved out of Buffalo in 1947, shocked the business community. Gov. Harriman was asked to intervene. Combined with the shocks to the local economy administered by the deep recession of 1958–59 (a downturn that left close to 11 percent of the local workforce unemployed), the Ford shutdown led to a period of reflection. A series in the *Courier Express* examined the development strategies and incentives some Southern cities were using to lure industry. In early 1961 the Chamber of Commerce sponsored an all-day conference on "Industrial Modernization," with panel discussions of such topics as "How Obsolete is Western New York Industry?" and "Business and Government Partnerships for Profits and Growth." Some of the speakers called for more funds for research and development. Franklin D. Roosevelt, Jr., the federal undersecretary of commerce, said the problem was deeper and required remedies more drastic. Noting that the number of people in the area employed in manufacturing had dropped from 217,000 in 1953 to 165,000 in 1960, he said that Western New York was "rapidly becoming a depressed area." Roosevelt urged the creation of a regional agency that would plan and initiate economic development. But by then the recession had bottomed out and with the country on the eve of an unprecendented economic boom few people—least of all those in the steel industry—heard what Roosevelt said or read what economist Willax wrote.

On Monday, December 27, 1982, the *News* reported that the Bethlehem Steel Company was going to shut down almost all of its steelmaking operations permanently over the next six months. Thirty-nine hundred workers would be let go. Thirty-four hundred more already on temporary lay-off would not be recalled. The company promised that thirteen hundred would remain employed in steel finishing operations—the bar mill and the galvanizing line. The *News* and the three local television stations covered the story as a tragedy. Feature writers and reporters descended on the bars and union halls in Lackawanna, a municipality just south of Buffalo that was virtually a Bethlehem company town. They interviewed workers and with sentimentality told the "human side" of the drama, the story of laid-off workers, their families, and a town about to lose 70 percent of its tax base. The rhetoric of community leaders was predictable. Mayor Griffin was "in a state of shock." Sen. Daniel Patrick Moynihan was angry. "You cannot simply close down a plant and say 'sorry,' " he said. Gov. Mario Cuomo announced the formation of a task force to deal with the problem.

None of the surprised rhetoric was convincing. Bethlehem's decision to close should not have shocked anyone with even the slightest understanding of the economic upheaval that was shaking the industrialized world in the late 1970s and early 1980s. Least surprised should have been the steel workers themselves. Steel production at Bethlehem had been declining steadily since the mid-1960s. Following a visit to the plant in November 1970, James Walker, Bethlehem's vice-president in charge of finance, had told the *Courier Express*, "The Lackawanna plant has been weighed in the balance and found wanting." The plant was simply not profitable, he said, and costs would have to be cut. Although Walker complained about low labor productivity, the high cost of federally mandated pollution-control machinery, and high tax assessments by the city of Lackawanna, it was clear that larger questions dealing with the economics of the steel industry were undermining the ability of Bethlehem to survive. Saying that "we must manage to live in today's reality," Bethlehem President Walter Williams announced that the company was cutting back, reducing plant output by a third. Four thousand of the plant's 18,500 workers were permanently laid off.

Conditions worsened throughout the 1970s as the whole American steel industry began to suffer from competition from European and Third World countries. There were other problems too, like the decline in world demand for steel following price increases triggered by the Arab oil embargo. This didn't hurt too much, however, since the American steel industry had never been particularly export-minded. There were cutbacks all over the East: in Cleveland, half of Republic's workforce; in Pittsburgh, a quarter of the 112,000 local steel workers; in Youngstown, Ohio, half of the 40,000 employed by steel plants.

In September 1971 Bethlehem reduced capacity at Lackawanna still further, laying off over five thousand people. "The future of the steel industry in this country," said Bethlehem's director of community relations, "is subject to a great deal of uncertainty." For a while, it looked as though 1977 would be the year Bethlehem finally went under. The *Evening News* called it "a blockbuster cutback"—half of the plant, three ironmaking blast furnaces, and five coke ovens were being mothballed. Capacity was to be reduced 40 percent and the workforce cut from 11,500 to 5,000.

By 1981 Bethlehem's Lackawanna plant had virtually become history. Although five thousand workers still produced two and a half million tons of steel a year, Bethlehem, the company made perfectly clear, had no future in Lackawanna. In Buffalo in May 1981, President Williams said that while the plant was not "a shut-down target," he could not justify capital expenditures to modernize it. Bethlehem's problems at Lackawanna, he indicated, although aggravated by high local taxes, were deeply structural, caused by the plant's "unfavorable location" and a product mix too heavily dependent on the automobile industry. The company had already spent more than $500 million at the Lackawanna plant since 1970, he said, and now there was little that either the company or the community could do. Williams said

Bethlehem was committed to its new plants in Burns Harbor, Indiana, and at Sparrows Point, outside of Baltimore, Maryland, where it was investing $750 million.

A year later, in June 1982, still six months before its December announcement, the *News* announced, "Strength of Buffalo Steel Industry Melting Away." The paper asked rhetorically, "Will fresh hot steel soon join Wildroot Cream Oil and the Pierce Arrow automobile on the list of things they don't make around here anymore?" Citing Bethlehem plant closings earlier in the year—a steel plant in Los Angeles, shipyards in Seattle—the *News* warned, "Don't bet against it."

So there should have been nothing surprising about Bethlehem's announcement in December 1982 that it was ending its steelmaking operations in Lackawanna forever. For years the people of Buffalo had been aware of the critical problems in the local steel industry. Community leaders, businesspeople, politicians, educators, and union representatives should have known and should have been working on plans and programs to save the plant.

The story of Republic Steel is somewhat different. Republic's mill in South Buffalo was much smaller than Bethlehem's, one of a series of small, integrated mills that the company had in Chicago, Birmingham, Troy, and Cleveland, which was Republic's headquarters. It had been "a good little plant," remembers Frank Palumbero, president of Steelworkers Local 1743, compact, highly integrated, capable of producing high-quality, low-priced steel. The South Buffalo plant could make and ship ingots to Republic's plant in Gadsden, Alabama, more cheaply than the Gadsden plant could make them. "It was like making soup," Palumbero says. "The smaller the kettle the better the soup." With only twenty-five hundred workers at its peak in the mid-1970s, Republic was a good place to work, a plant where almost everyone knew one another. People liked it there and the plant employed a number of families—fathers and sons, uncles, nephews, cousins. As at Bethlehem, the workforce was integrated. It had been in the steel plants that many of the workers in white South Buffalo first encountered blacks.

Republic specialized in bar products for the automobile industry—crankshaft steel, spring and coil steel—and as cars went, so did Republic. Business was good during the Vietnam era, the swan-song years of American industry, and in 1970 the company spent $40 million dollars at the South Buffalo plant, replacing the open hearth with the basic oxygen furnace, raising the plant's capacity and increasing its work force. Bethlehem, of course, was moving in the opposite direciton. The major cutback at its Lackawanna plant, followed by the opening of the gigantic Burns Harbor plant where a far smaller work force could produce far more steel, indicated that it would be increasingly difficult for the company's older plants to survive. Republic experienced the same kind of pressures. In 1970 the company closed its two oldest and smallest plants, in Birmingham and Troy.

Nevertheless, Republic's Buffalo plant continued to do well throughout the 1970s. Profits were good and wages and benefits increased while capacity and employment levels remained steady. A decline in the domestic automobile industry in late 1980 and early 1981 and a cutback in bar business gave the company some breathing room, a chance to shut down temporarily and modernize. On August 15, 1981, the plant closed for six months and the company embarked on a massive modernization and improvement program, spending $46 million on a state-of-the-art blast furnace, a new basic oxygen furnace, and a new blooming mill. The shutdown was temporary, employees were told, and the plant would reopen in December. By late November the work was done and Alan Marquardt, the superintendent of the blast furnace, was ready to go "pedal to the metal." He heard nothing from headquarters in Cleveland, however, and began to worry that moisture would settle in the new blast furnace as the temperature dropped. Marquardt arranged to have enormous heaters installed in the furnace. Winter came and went and still the South Buffalo plant stayed closed. While some continued to hope that it was just a question of time before the plant reopened, Marquardt, for one, was not surprised when, on June 1, 1982, he was told that the plant was going to stay closed for good. Despite its difficulties, the company behaved in good faith, purposefully delaying the final shutdown to allow workers close to retirement to qualify for pensions. When the plant finally shut down in January 1984, well over half of the workforce received full pensions.

The 1970s were devastating years for the American steel industry and there was little anybody could have done to save its Buffalo components. The rise of steel and automobile imports, an oil embargo that drastically changed the way cars were made, a rising dollar that undermined the ability of American producers to compete—these were developments far too strong for the industry as a whole to resist, let alone the plants in any one city. Location, too, Buffalo's glory just forty years earlier, now worked against the city. By the early 1980s "location" didn't simply mean place. "Buffalo" said "Lake Erie," but it also said unions, taxes, "northern-ness," age, and dispirit. Even had people been willing to settle for less—the companies for a lower return on their investments, the workers for lower wages, the city for lower taxes—it is unlikely that the steel mills in Buffalo, given their age, size, and location, could have survived as profitable operations.

Nineteen eighty-two ended gloomily in Buffalo. It was the year, *News* reporter Ray Hill wrote, that "Western New York took it on the chin . . . the year the bottom fell out . . . the year we found a new subculture, the chronically unemployed." The shutdowns at Bethlehem and Republic and deep cuts at GM and Ford badly weakened the rest of the economy. The whole city shook as the list of closings, like school-closings on a stormy winter day, mounted. Whole chains of retail and wholesale department stores, restaurants, shops, and service organizations were going out of business, while venerable institutions like the Buffalo Philharmonic Orchestra, the Albright-Knox Art Gallery, the Buffalo Museum of Science, and the Buffalo Historical Society teetered on the brink of bankruptcy.

In April 1983 ten thousand men and women lined up outside American Brass on Military Road when the company announced that it was hiring forty people. A month later, on its last day of operation, Bethlehem's seventy-nine-inch bar mill produced a record 275 slabs of steel. "We wanted to go out in a blaze of glory," one of the workers said. In the middle of the night of August 16, 1983, a group of workers at Bethlehem's Lackawanna plant hoisted the international distress signal—an American flag flying upside down—on top of blast Furnace C. The gigantic flag, twelve by twenty-four feet, was illuminated for all to see by two glaring one-thousand-watt mercury vapor lamps.

12

NEW SCHOOLS FOR THE OLD CITY

John Curtin is unabashed in his love for Buffalo and he knows the city inside and out. His knowledge of its history, the nooks and crannies of its neighborhoods, the location of its churches and schools, the complexities of its various ethnic groups, is detailed and intimate. This, as much as his relaxed, unpretentious manner, helped earn him credibility in the school desegregation case—a case whose successful disposition was vitally dependent on the trust of the community. Caring deeply about the city and keenly aware of the power he had over the lives of the people who lived in it, Curtin sought from the beginning of the case to dispel the notion that he was a judicial ogre like Boston's Garrity, insensitive to the impact of his rulings on the people in the neighborhoods. Curtin identified strongly with the city and shared in experiences common to many Buffalonians. He had lived in the city all his life, first in South Buffalo, in the house his father built on Pawnee Parkway, and since the late 1940s on a modest street of single-family homes in North Buffalo. A graduate of St. Theresa's, Canisius High School, and Canisius College, he joined the Marines following his graduation in 1941, serving for three years as a dive-bomber pilot in a single-engine Grumman torpedo plane, involved, he says modestly, in "rear island action in the Guadalcanal area." For a while Curtin considered becoming an engineer, following in the footsteps of his father and grandfather, but decided instead to go to law school at UB. He graduated in 1949 and entered general practice in downtown Buffalo.

It was particularly important during the long duration of the school case, Curtin felt, that he remain close and available to the people of Buffalo. Immediately following his first ruling in April 1976, he began accepting invitations to speak—to the Chamber of Commerce, to high-school and college classes, and to the North Buffalo Jaycees, the South Buffalo Businessman's Association, and numerous other community groups. This came easily to Curtin, who is as relaxed and naturally comfortable with his colleagues of the bar as he is with his friends in his running club, the Bell Watling. Friendly and warm, Curtin encouraged contact and communication with people throughout the city, kept his phone number listed, and personally answered much of his own mail. He wanted to hear, he said in his July 1976 ruling on Phase I, from the "parents and the teachers who are involved in this very complicated process." His court, he made it clear, would not be imperious, distant and removed from the feelings of the people who had to live with his decisions. "It is one thing to make decisions," he wrote, "It is another to be a parent of a small youngster or a teenage youngster going off to school. They have insights which we cannot know about until we listen. It is not only within the spirit of the law but it is in the spirit of the United States as a democracy to listen to the views of all individuals in the community."

The people heard from Curtin and he, amidst a growing pile of letters, heard from them. Most of the letters were predictable, angry communications from white parents. Many were filled with threats. "Think it over, John Curtin," went one of them. "I hope you know the moral code. The good Lord reminded us that whoever hangs a millstone around the necks of little children shall be punished." Some were nasty, one suggesting that he had been paid off by "the Goldfarbs and the Schwartzes." Some were poignant efforts to apply the lessons of the past to a very different present. One implored, "You must recall that for many years the Poles lived on the East Side, the Italians on the West Side, and the Irish on the South Side. We lived in segregation and managed okay. We enjoyed our neighborhood schools. But you are determined to destroy them." Some were thoughtful efforts to come to terms with the problem of black and white relations. One man, a "grandfather concerned about his grandchildren" and hoping they would grow up free of racial prejudice, claimed that "tolerance is best learned in the privacy of one's own home and not in a polarized bus or classroom." The man was afraid that the "spontaneous friendships" his grandchildren had with black children would be "terminated by court interference."

Many letters contained specific requests not to close this or that school—
"I know you are a busy man," wrote Dolores Landsman of Riverside,
eager to keep her neighborhood School 79 open, "but we just cannot
get anybody to listen. . . . Please, I'm begging you to really take a look
into these things. We need your help." Some asked him to intervene
in areas totally unrelated to the case, to "do something" about the bands
of teenagers roaming around Black Rock, the potholes on the streets
of the West Side, high city taxes, and even the growing rate of inflation.
To many people in Buffalo, Judge Curtin had become an omnipotent
authority figure, a man with the power to bless the community with
his benevolence or harm it with his malevolence.

But in the fall of 1977 it seemed that Curtin was uncertain about
which direction to take. His doubts led him on September 15, 1977,
in a thought shared only with Michael Brady, to conclude that "it is
my present judgment, at any rate, that we should file an order saying
that we do not believe that any further steps are needed either in law
or are permissable under the practical considerations of this case." Perhaps
he was referring to the outcry in the white neighborhoods, particularly
in South Buffalo where, beginning that month, Phase II of the desegregation plan had led to a large increase in the number of black
children being bused into schools in white neighborhoods. At School
27 on Curtin's family street, Pawnee, the number of blacks increased
from 11 to 140; at School 28, at the South Buffalo intersection of Abbott
Road, South Park Avenue, and McKinley Parkway, the number went
from 30 to 78. People in South Buffalo were furious and the area
councilman, Daniel Higgins, was petrified when he was told that a man
with shotgun was marching back in forth in front of the entrance to
South Park High School.

Worried about the potential for violence, Higgins called Joe Pirakas.
Higgins and Pirakas had worked together since the late 1960s, when
Pirakas, the owner of a large grocery store on South Park Avenue,
had organized the Federation of South Buffalo Community Organizations. Pirakas's plan was to bring a sense of direction and purpose
to the more than thirty community groups in South Buffalo. A Greek
whose father had come to South Buffalo in the 1920s to open an ice
cream parlor, Pirakas maintained that only an outsider, with loyalties
to no particular parish, with no roots in any particular neighborhood,
could have brought about this coalition of dozens of different community
groups representing more than fifteen thousand people. Now, in the
fall of 1977, Pirakas and Higgins worked to soothe the angry feelings,
to reassure people that Superintendent Reville and Judge Curtin were

not the neighborhood traitors the people of South Buffalo made them out to be.

While he seemed to be wavering privately, in public Curtin maintained the pressure on the defendants. Although he delayed appointing a desegregation "master," he did establish a Citizen's Committee on School Desegregation, consisting of twenty-two people selected jointly by defendants and plaintiffs. The Committee was to be, in Curtin's words, "an arm of the court." Its primary purpose was to "foster public awareness and involvement in implementation of the court's desegregation plans; to monitor desegregation at all schools affected by the court's order; to serve as a contact for community input; and to encourage cooperative efforts by all sectors of the community with the Buffalo public school system." While he looked to the committee to foster better community relations, Curtin insisted on maintaining control of the day-to-day management of the case, to remain intimately involved with all of its details and implications. Beginning in September 1977 he presided at weekly Friday meetings in his chambers at which Reville, Murray, and other members of the board's administrative team met with the plaintiffs, usually Goldfarb, Mesiah, and Griffin, trying to resolve outstanding grievances. Curtin's interest in school affairs could be quite minute.

Despite the judge's doubts about how far he could push the defendants, he was given little choice, for the plaintiffs refused to lessen the pressure. On November 5, 1977, the people of Buffalo had elected as mayor Jimmy Griffin, a man long associated with Alfreda Slominski's "neighborhood school" movement and an outspoken opponent of "forced busing"; one week later, perhaps sensing further opposition, the plaintiffs filed a motion asking the court to resolve the question of the remaining all-black schools. At hearings in April and May of 1978, the plaintiffs argued that Phase II, like Phase I before it, simply did not go far enough. Not only were there still at least thirteen all-black schools, but the burden of desegregation fell far too heavily on the shoulders of black children. "The principle of equity is absent from these plans," Richard Griffin said. What if black parents chose not to participate in the QIE program? Wouldn't they have to be assigned to attend them? Would whites, Griffin asked rhetorically, be forced to attend schools outside their neighborhoods if they chose not to participate in the magnet program? Since there was no such provision for white students, Griffin demanded that Curtin end the QIE program. "The plaintiffs do not believe that the constitutional rights of black students depend on the voluntarism of the majority." While Griffin attacked in court, Goldfarb maintained the pressure in the press. In a letter to the *Evening News,* he charged that the board was guilty of "the four Ds." They have "deceived, delayed, denied, and defined," he chided. The people of Buffalo, and Judge Curtin too, had fallen prey to a "superior advertising effort, leading Buffalonians to believe that everything has been taken care of." Goldfarb was baffled that Curtin had allowed the thirteen all-black elementary schools to remain open. Increasingly convinced that not only the board but now Curtin too lacked the will as well as the political strength to implement a more sweeping desegregation program, Goldfarb promised that the plaintiffs would "keep pressing them in the courts."

They did and it seemed to work. In his ruling of June 30, 1978, Curtin accepted many of the arguments the plaintiffs had been making since the suit began in 1972. He began with lavish praise for the efforts of Reville, Murray, and the board. "The entire Buffalo community, through its response, has enabled the board to establish a number of successful magnet schools to bring desegregation to many schools which have previously been racially isolated. Both the board and the community have shown tremendous interest and cooperation in this effort." He had been and would continue to be sensitive, Curtin promised, to the difficulties the board faced because of the "bleak financial picture which faces the city of Buffalo." But he was also mindful of the fact that, "as plaintiffs argue, financial problems cannot be used as an excuse for not implementing integration." While he was reserving his ruling for another month, Curtin indicated that far more would have to be done.

Curtin was particularly concerned about the magnet schools and the QIE program. The magnets, Curtin said, agreeing with the plaintiffs, were having a "disappointing" impact on desegregation. Some schools, like City Honors, were disproportionately white. Others—the remedial Follow Through School, for example, were disproportionately African-American. In addition to the "less than satisfactory" levels of integration, Curtin now agreed that the magnet schools did nothing at all to alter the patterns of segregation in the schools that fed the magnets. He would no longer permit the transfer of white and black children into magnets, he said, if that would have an adverse effect on the racial balance of the feeder schools. Curtin also agreed with Griffin's arguments about the QIE program and, despite extensive support for it within the black community, he threatened to dismantle it unless the burden of desegregation was more "equitably shared."

Curtin seemed suddenly stern in the ruling, adamant in giving the board just one more year to offer a final plan for school desegregation. While he praised Reville, Murray, and their staff for "their extraordinary effort—they have managed to shift a large number of students, to renovate many school facilities and to establish new programs for the magnet schools with a minimum of disruption"—Curtin suggested that maybe Goldfarb and the other plaintiffs were right, that perhaps it was impossible for Reville, Murray, and the elected board to go much further. It might become necessary, Curtin concluded, for the board to hire an outside consultant in order to "bring new ideas to old questions."

Yet, just as it appeared that he was losing faith in the moderate, homegrown strategies of Reville and the board, Curtin altered his tone. It was too late, he said in a decision issued a month later, to do anything about the thirteen segregated elementary schools. Equally disappointing to those hoping for a speedy and more forceful disposition of the case (included among these were his two clerks of the moment, Mark Hellerer and Carol Linden, who, prior to his June decision, had written Curtin strong memos urging, in Linden's words, "a final order in one fell swoop") was the judge's ruling that he would not require any changes in magnet-school admissions policies for yet another year. Curtin also delayed, yet again, the appointment of a master.

In a speech a week later to a convention of Lutheran educators meeting in Buffalo, Curtin explained his reluctance to move too quickly. "We still have schools with a large minority population and the burden of transportation is still greater on minority students," he said. The choice of pronoun suggested that from Curtin's perspective the plaintiffs, the defendants, and the court were all involved together. "I see my court's role as being sure that changes are being made in good time. . . . In some other cities the timetable of changes has been most unreasonable and the courts have interfered too much—as in Boston—with detailed educational decisions. . . . This court's only reason for being in the picture is implementing integration at a reasonable timetable and it is my philosophy to stay out of other areas." In September 1978, as school opened, Curtin reiterated this philosophy to the *Evening News*. "I don't know how they do it in other cities," he said. "It takes a long time to do the thing right and to do it carefully. . . . You can use all the orders you want but if you don't have the people involved working in a spirit of cooperation, what have you accomplished? . . . Things can be done best if they're done voluntarily."

While many cheered Curtin's stance, many were confused by what they regarded as his "mixed signals." Sometimes his opinions even seemed conflicting. An example was one of the many budget battles between the Board of Education and the mayor's office. Since his initial ruling in April 1976, school budget matters, because of their impact on the desegregation programs, had fallen within Curtin's jurisdiction. The costs

of desegregation were enormous and by the spring of 1978 the Board
of Education was faced with an $8 million deficit. Curtin believed Reville's
statement that, barring financial aid, the schools would have to close
in May. He ordered the board and the mayor to resolve the problem
together.

Reville had no place to turn. The Supreme Court had recently
ruled in a Kentucky case that the federal government did not have
to bear the costs of court-ordered desegregation. More serious was the
decision of the Second Circuit Court of Appeals in March 1978, reversing
Judge Curtin's ruling that the state bore some of the blame for the
segregation of Buffalo's schools. The plaintiffs, the court said, had failed
to prove segregative intent on the part of the Board of Regents and
the commissioner of education. The state, of course, could therefore
not be held financially responsible for the costs of desegregation. The
City of Buffalo would have to bear these costs alone. Financial problems
worsened during the summer of 1978, when the city cut $3 million from
the board's 1978–79 budget. Reville was outraged. Board President
Florence Baugh, the director of the Community Action Organization,
the largest federally funded agency in the inner city, said in an angry
statement to the press, "As the school system becomes more black, you
see a diminishing commitment on the part of the public to that school
system. It's happened in other cities. It's happening here." In early
September 1978, a week before school opened, the board laid off four
hundred teachers and nonteaching professionals. The result was the
elimination of all art, music, physical-education, and foreign-language
programs in the city's schools. Curtin demanded that the teachers be
rehired and the programs restored, arguing that it was essential to
maintain the quality of the desegregation programs and to "restore public
confidence in their continued success." While parent groups approved,
many, including Mayor Griffin and the city's two newspapers, did not.
In the wake of extensive criticism that he was insensitive to the city's
fiscal problems and not demanding enough of the bureaucracy-laden
Board of Education, Judge Curtin, without explanation, rescinded his
order. "I cannot," he said in March 1979, "ignore the financial plight
of the city."

Three months later, however, Curtin issued his most sweeping order
to date. In June 1977, in the case of *Dayton* v. *Brinkman,* the Supreme
Court had ruled that unless a school board's actions had a segregative
effect on a "meaningful portion" of the district, any remedy would have
to be specific to the violations. In June 1979 Curtin applied the *Dayton*
guidelines to Buffalo's case, ruling that the city's segregative acts had

indeed been "system-wide." The remedy, Curtin concluded, must therefore also be system-wide. The Buffalo Plan had successfully integrated the higher grades but it had failed at the lower ones. And it was in the elementary schools, Curtin insisted, before racial attitudes hardened, that integration was essential. Therefore Curtin announced that he would no longer tolerate the continued segregation of even one—let alone thirteen—of Buffalo's elementary schools.

Even more controversial was the judge's decision to end the QIE program. Since the mid-1960s the board had relied on the busing of blacks into schools in white neighborhoods as its primary desegregation strategy. While the plaintiffs had been arguing for years that the burden of the program fell disproportionately on black children, many black parents, convinced that quality education was only available in white schools, fought to retain the QIE program, insisting that the plaintiffs did not properly represent them. In testimony before Curtin, one black parent said angrily that "to suggest that the QIE program is a burden to me is an insult. If it were I would not participate in it." Curtin himself had mixed feelings about the program. On the one hand, he said, "the board, by the use of the QIE, has eliminated virtually every all-white school in the city." On the other hand, Curtin recognized the validity of the plaintiffs' arguments and concluded that the program had to go. He ordered the defendants to develop other strategies to desegregate the elementary schools of the inner city.

Curtin was tightening the screws. For the first time he issued specific guidelines for desegregation remedies, including the pairing of schools. Voluntary measures, such as magnet schools and the QIE program, could be used, he said, only if they "promise speedy and effective means of desegregation and do not place unequal burdens on any racial group." The board had until August 1979 to present a program for the complete desegregation of the schools beginning in September 1980.

But again Curtin seemed to send mixed signals. While he insisted on system-wide integration on the one hand, on the other he offered the board a loophole. He said he would consider "hard evidence explaining why full desegregation cannot be effected," and even gave the defendants an example. "If there is sufficient believable evidence in the record that resegregation will occur, it may be considered as part of the practicalities of administering the plan."

The plaintiffs greeted Curtin's latest ruling first with a jab—how could he have "stonewalled" as long as he did knowing that more than 50 percent of all black elementary school children were racially isolated schools?—and then, of course, with satisfaction: the plaintiffs were "thrilled by the judge's latest decree," Goldfarb said, and hopeful that the case was nearing an end.

Throughout the community, however, the reaction was one of shock. Reville and the members of the Board of Education were stunned, and so was the press. Curtin's ruling, the *Evening News* said, "makes it clear that the desegregation controversy is far from over . . . the board's toughest decisions still lie ahead." Debates in the Common Council had generally been quiet since Curtin's first ruling in 1976. Now, for the first time since its obstructionist role in the middle-schools-funding controversy ten years earlier, the Common Council revealed that opposition to the pairing of schools in black and white neighborhoods remained intense. Frightened by what many believed was an implicit call for cross-busing, one member was convinced that "Judge Curtin is trying to destroy our neighborhoods." The ruling, said another, "will provoke only violence and will spell disaster for the city." An ethnic, neighborhood newspaper, the *Am-Pol Eagle,* reiterated this theme, telling its Polish-American readers on the city's East Side that Curtin's decision "means the end of the East Side as we know it." A good number of blacks were disappointed as well. Despite concerns about the psychological and emotional hardships caused by having their children bused to schools in white neighborhoods, many had liked the QIE program.

Despite Curtin's apparent growing impatience with the school board, he continued to refuse to appoint a "desegregation master," or to impose a plan of his own. Rather, as he had with the development of Phase II in April 1977, he again urged defendants and plaintiffs to work together to create a plan. Several times throughout the summer Reville and Murray met with Griffin and Goldfarb, but little progress was made. Griffin accused Reville of "foot-dragging" and demanded that Curtin stop delaying and impose a plan of his own. Reville denied the charge, countering with a request for more time. He said he needed until November to develop a final plan. With the caveat that this time the plan had to be "complete and total," Curtin agreed. Reville promised the plaintiffs and the court that he would offer a plan that in five years would give Buffalo "a better integration program than any other city in the country."

Reville's optimism seemed inappropriate to some, given the problems that continued to plague the city's schools. In the fall of 1979 white enrollment was down 8 percent, compared to 5 percent the year before, while overall enrollment continued to decline at the steady, almost predictable rate of two thousand a year. The drop-out rate rose to 15 percent in 1978, and absenteeism among teachers also rose to an average of ten sick days a year. Buffalo's teachers were absent 35 percent more often than the national urban average.

With these concerns in mind, Reville, Murray, and their staffs worked throughout the fall of 1979 on a plan they hoped would meet Curtin's increasingly strict standards. Their thorniest problem was the desegregation of the thirteen inner-city elementary schools. Since Curtin had said he would no longer accept one-way busing, Reville and the board, still committed to voluntary desegregation, had to rely on their ability to convince still more white parents to send their children to these schools. Again gambling on the continued willingness of white parents to send their children to good schools—even ones located in the inner city— Reville announced what he called Phase III of the Buffalo Plan in October 1979. Curtin's June ruling notwithstanding, the heart of the program was the conversion of six more inner-city schools into magnet elementary schools. Developed by a team of educators led by Joe Murray and called "early childhood centers," these schools stressed what Reville called "early intervention strategies." They would specialize in the particular learning needs of children from pre-kindergarten through second grade. And, Reville promised, the ECCs would be racially balanced, drawing on black children from within the neighborhood and white children from without. Whites would send their children to them, Reville said, "because they will want to."

13

NEW SCHOOLS FOR A CHANGING CITY

Charlie Kam runs the computer laboratory at School 51 in Black Rock. He lives in South Buffalo. Like many of his neighbors there, he was born in the old First Ward, in the Perry Projects. He went to school at St. Brigid's, now the home of Parent-Child Center. Kam's family moved to South Buffalo in the early 1950s, to St. Theresa's, Curtin's and Reville's home parish on Seneca Street. Kam lives there today with his wife, a teacher in the Buffalo public schools, and their two daughters, Jenny and Kristen. He's been working at School 51 in Black Rock since 1987.

The principal, John Bargnese, is also from South Buffalo, and he and Kam drive to work together every day, over the Skyway, onto the Niagara Extension of the thruway, past downtown and the new, high-priced condominiums along the waterfront, under the Peace Bridge, then off the highway at Austin Street in Black Rock.

Black Rock is Buffalo's oldest neighborhood, with a strong sense of community identity and pride. Located at a bend in the river where the fast-moving waters of the Niagara are slowed, Black Rock was settled before Buffalo. Black Rock residents lobbied hard in 1820s to be named the site where the Erie Canal would terminate, but lost to Buffalo, a smaller, but more aggressive settlement just up the river.

Black Rock began to languish until it was annexed in the 1850s by its rapidly growing rival, but the people of Black Rock—"The Rock" —didn't forget the neighborhood's legacy as a separate, independent town. It is something of which everyone in Black Rock is aware. In some ways Black Rock is like South Buffalo. Both share a lost industrial heritage, both are still solidly white. But where South Buffalo is Irish, Black Rock is mainly Eastern European—Polish, Hungarian, and Ukrainian. The Irish of South Buffalo figured out long ago how to use the city's arcane political structure and civil service system to their advantage, and have developed a strong professional middle-class that has enabled the area to make a successful accommodation to the changing requirements of a post-industrial economy. The residents of Black Rock, by and large, have not managed this feat, so despite its magnificent location at the edge of the Niagara River, the area remains shabby and run-down. Unemployment is high, and even the most diligent efforts have not prevented a steady increase in the number of absentee landlords, who rent their old, dilapidated wood-frame doubles to anyone and everyone with little concern for the consequences.

School 51 on Hertel and Guernsey Avenues is in fine shape. Its main wing is a red brick building built in 1897. It is beautiful inside— arches made of yellowish brick give it a strangely Moorish, monastic look. Kam's room, with soft ceramic brick walls and a maple floor, is on the third floor of the building. Computers are arranged neatly on a row of desks in the middle of the room. On a beautiful morning in June the windows are open and the sounds from the street in this old industrial neighborhood in the heart of Buffalo—birds, electric lawn mowers, and slowly passing cars—are peaceful and nostalgic, the way cities are supposed to sound.

Before coming to 51 Kam had taught at School 37 on Carlton Street in the Fruit Belt. By the late 1960s and early 1970s the Fruit Belt had declined terribly. Since the mid-1950s the old German neighborhood had been in a state of shock, reeling from the combined blows of sweeping demographic trends and disastrous public-policy decisions. Cut crudely in half by the Kensington Expressway, devastated by the sudden departure of its hundred-year-old German community and the massive influx of blacks, the Fruit Belt was on its last legs, weakened almost beyond recognition by the ravages of poverty and decay. As the neighborhood declined, so did School 37.

While the building is magnificent, an Art Deco masterpiece decorated inside and out with fluted columns and the sculpted reliefs typical of the public buildings built in the early 1930s, by 1976, the year of Judge

Curtin's order, 37 had become an all-black school plagued by violence and high suspension and dropout rates. Like many inner-city schools, it was scheduled for closing. A handful of parents wanted it kept open, and they worked frantically with officials from the Board of Education to develop a plan to rescue their neighborhood school.

One parent was Elizabeth Burgos. Burgos had grown up on Madison Street on the far East Side. Since 1966 she has been living on Rose Street around the corner from School 37. By the end of the 1960s teacher morale at 37 was low and student behavior was worse. There was no parental involvement, Burgos says, because parents and children felt alienated from the school, which was perceived as belonging not to them but to "the board" and "the principal." As one of the original members of BUILD, the African-American community organization, Burgos believed deeply in citizen participation.

BUILD had been created in 1967 when a group of white and African-American churches and community organizations brought Saul Alinsky, Chicago's community organizer, to Buffalo to organize the black East Side. The result was BUILD—an acronym for "Build Unity, Independence, Liberty, and Dignity"—a coalition of more than a hundred civic, religious, business, labor, social, youth, and other groups. The BUILD constitution articulated the organization's purpose as "Unifying the black people of Buffalo in order that they may assume their rightful role in solving the problems and determining the course of actions that affect their lives in this city." Elizabeth Burgos joined BUILD soon after it was founded. So did William Gaitor.

Gaitor had come to Buffalo from Anniston, Georgia, in 1945 at the age of eighteen. He was fascinated by what he remembers as the "majesty" and "stateliness" of Buffalo, its incredible tree-lined streets and the Fruit Belt, "all those tiny, wooden homes, like dollhouses really, nestled in between all those trees."

Gaitor found work right away at a railroad-car repair factory. Living was easy in Buffalo then. He made close to fifty dollars a week and paid only twelve dollars a week for board. "It was fun and exciting—being young and on my own in Buffalo." For a Southerner, Gaitor says in retrospect, Buffalo seemed fine. He married and he and his wife had six children. He worked as a bus driver for Niagara Frontier Transit Authority, and the family lived comfortably on Butler Avenue in the old Humboldt-area Jewish neighborhood.

It was at his daughters' schools that he first became involved in the affairs of the black community. Two of his daughters went to Wood-lawn Junior High, the new school on Michigan that had been intentionally segregated by the Board of Education when it opened in 1964. One day Gaitor's daughters asked his permission to participate in a civil-rights demonstration at the school. He agreed and then, concerned about their safety, followed them to school. He stayed, mesmerized and inspired by the students' commitment. The black community was alive in those days with the heady talk of social activism and community involvement, and by early 1967 Gaitor was becoming increasingly active in BUILD, particularly in its efforts to improve East Side schools. Shortly after the riots of 1967, BUILD began a study of the Buffalo public schools and early in 1968 issued a report it called "Black Paper No. 1." Citing the "murderous conditions in ghetto schools," the paper called for the creation of a "ghetto academy" that would stress parent involvement, a strong program of black history and culture, better guidance counseling, and maximum integration. The report concluded. "We have got to take back the schools. We have got to make them community schools. Public schools are run by people who don't understand black people, our history, our culture. In fact, most of the people who run and teach in our schools are afraid of black people, afraid of black children."

Elizabeth Burgos believed that was certainly the case at School 37. BUILD was articulating a philosophy of community control and parent involvement that appealed to her, and she joined the organization. She was annoyed that when kids failed it was their home life that was blamed, and when they succeeded it was the schools that took the credit—she wanted the schools to take responsibility for both. With that in mind, in early 1969 BUILD proposed the creation of the BUILD Academy. Eager to rid themselves of the increasingly pesky BUILD organization and at the same time take credit for the creation of the community-based school, Superintendent Joe Manch and the old appointed Board of Education went along with the idea and in September 1969, BUILD Academy, for children from kindergarten through fourth grade, opened at old School 32 on Clinton Street. It was Buffalo's first magnet school.

What distinguished the BUILD Academy from all the other schools in Buffalo was its dedication to strong and effective parent and community participation in school affairs. The academy was governed by a board consisting of a representative from the African-American community, a representative from Buffalo State College, and, from the Board of Education, Associate Superintendent Reville. In addition to strong ties to South Buffalo, Reville for years had been principal at School 53, a racially isolated elementary school on Roeher Street on the black

East Side, and he'd earned the confidence and respect of parents there. BUILD Academy's board, with a degree of independence unique to the Buffalo public schools, had the power to create the school's curriculum and to hire its own staff. The Board of Education cooperated and so did Buffalo State, which created a special program for BUILD parents to pursue bachelor's degrees. It was at Buffalo State that Elizabeth Burgos earned her B.A.

By the end of the 1970s Burgos had begun to put organizational skills and her concern for responsive education to work at School 37, forming a parents' group. But 1976 brought Judge Curtin's court order, and as the board began to look around for inner-city schools to close, rumors spread throughout the Fruit Belt that 37 was destined to be one of them.

Burgos and her parent's group were horrified. Burgos knew the scenario by heart: another black neighborhood school would be closed, and the children, for the sake of integration, would be bused to schools in outlying white neighborhoods. The rumor was confirmed one day in late 1977 by the redoubtable Evelyn Cooper, the board's most effective "advance person," once again dispatched by the board to deal with the community. Gently but firmly Cooper challenged the neighborhood's parents: if they wanted the school to stay open, they had to create a program to integrate it. The incentive, Cooper admits, came from Curtin. His insistence that parents be involved in the development of desegregation programs, became the motivating force for "creative thinking" on the part of parents and school officials.

Burgos was concerned about the changing economy. Her husband worked at Bethlehem Steel and had barely survived the massive layoffs of 1977; he, like Carol Holtz's husband, was finally let go in 1982. Burgos knew that the days of heavy industry were numbered and was concerned about developing what she called a "real-life curriculum" at her old neighborhood school that would adequately prepare the children of the Fruit Belt for the future. Burgos, Cooper, and Lewis Sinatra, the State Education Department consultant assigned to help School 37's parents, worked throughout the spring and early summer of 1978. They drafted a proposal to convert School 37 into what they called "Futures Academy." The new school's primary objective, the group wrote in a report submitted to the Board of Education in July 1978, was to "develop and implement a futuristically oriented curriculum" that would address the need to learn basic skills within a realistic context that would prepare the students for "meaningful careers and pursuits in the future." As the program developer for the school, it was up to

Cooper to sell Future's Academy to the community.

She began with Curtin, without whose approval the school could not exist. Cooper had first met the judge a year before, when she testified before the board about her community-relations work on behalf of desegregation. Cooper was petrified of Curtin at first, she remembers, but he was so kind and friendly, "it was a piece of cake." Now, in August 1978, Cooper met with Curtin in his expansive, homey chambers: old leather armchair, a cluttered desk, an even more cluttered worktable, a couch covered with papers and the judge's half-opened briefcase, a pair of beat-up Nikes not quite hidden behind the bathroom door, walls covered with family photographs, a painting of the bomber Curtin piloted during World War II, and a pencil-drawn profile of Bobby Kennedy in shirtsleeves, intense, brooding, and pensive. Cooper sat in the armchair; Curtin listened, paced slowly in front of his desk before sitting down in a straight-backed chair next to her. He liked the proposal and encouraged Cooper to pursue it, reminding her gently but firmly, she says, that he would not be able to approve the new school unless it was racially balanced.

When Cooper left Curtin's chambers she crossed Niagara Square to the mayor's office in City Hall. Jimmy Griffin liked the idea of Futures Academy and its emphasis on voluntary integration. He was particularly struck by Cooper's persuasive way of equating the rebirth of School 37 with the mayor's vigorous effort to do the same for the city, and agreed to write a letter pledging his support for the project. Using Griffin's letter as leverage, Cooper scoured offices, businesses, companies, and institutions throughout the metropolitan area and by early 1980 she had secured the commitment of newspapers and television stations, banks and utility companies, colleges and the university to become "partners of Futures Academy." Cooper wanted their participation, she said, not their money, their involvement with the school as advisors to the teachers and mentors to the students. She wanted to create a "town" in one of the large empty rooms on the school's third floor, where all the functions and operations of a working community would be replicated. In the "town"—in the "bank," the "supermarket," the "civic center," the "post office" and the "movie theater"—the children, from kindergarten through eighth grade, would learn about the skills and responsibilities required by the world of work in an increasingly service-oriented economy. Working with representatives from the business community, Cooper promised, teachers would develop mini-courses that could combine theoretical and practical aspects of the world of work and the nature of life in a community managed and governed by the children themselves.

Everyone was responding well to Cooper's enthusiasm and to the breadth of her proposal, and in early 1980 the Board of Education approved her plan. In September 1980 a "Futures Academy," with Evelyn Cooper as principal, opened at School 37.

In addition to launching the new program, Cooper had to worry about recruiting white children in an area of the city that had been off-limits to them since the late 1950s. She turned to Carol Holtz, her friend from her days in South Buffalo, the charismatic Pied Piper who had enticed dozens of children from her insular, fortress-like community of South Buffalo into the magnet schools on the black East Side. Holtz's first suggestion was that Cooper hire John Bargnese as assistant principal. Yes, he was Italian. But, Holtz told her, he was from South Buffalo, a graduate of Timon High School and Canisius College, and "they really like Bargnese down there." Bargnese, like most South Buffalo Italians, was born in St. Lucy's Parish in the old Swan Street section of the Ellicott District. He lived there until the late 1940s at the corner of South Division and a street that is no longer there, Chestnut Street. The neighborhood was changing rapidly then, Bargnese says, with many blacks moving in. Like many in the neighborhood, the Bargnese family didn't wait for urban renewal to chase them out. Bargnese's mother enrolled him in Bishop Timon even before they had moved to South Buffalo.

Holtz was right about Bargnese. With Bargnese and Cooper at the school and Holtz in the streets, Futures went over big in South Buffalo. When the school opened in 1980 it had 250 children, 30 percent of them white. By 1983 the school came close to racial balance.

So too was School 31, tucked away on Stanton Street, a narrow side street off Broadway on Buffalo's East Side. For years the neighborhood contained a mix of German, Jewish, and Polish children who walked to school from the old frame singles and doubles that still mark the street. In the early 1950s the neighborhood began to change and 31 became one of the first elementary schools in the city with a predominantly African-American student body. Bypassed by the early phases of the school desegregation program, in 1979 School 31 was one of the thirteen remaining all-black elementary schools with which Judge Curtin and the plaintiffs were so concerned. But just two years later, it had become a fully integrated early childhood center sought out by white and black parents eager to enroll their children in its innovative programs.

How did it happen? School 31 had become one of the early childhood centers that had been the brainchild of Joe Murray and elementary-school teachers Marion Canedo, Joan Downey, and others working in early childhood education. Faced with the challenge of enticing the white parents of Black Rock, Riverside, and South Buffalo to send their children into schools on the black East Side, Murray's team dangled two lures before them. One was educational, a promise to create schools committed to strengthening basic academic skills through strategies of intense early intervention. The other was strategic, "pure Murray," it was said.

The son of a Buffalo cop, Murray had grown up in Riverside and graduated from All Saints, the local Catholic elementary school on Esser Street. Riverside was tough, what some may call a redneck bastion. Except for a handful in the Jaspar Parish projects, few African-Americans lived in Riverside. In 1972, as part of many half-hearted attempts to desegregate the schools in the pre-Reville era, a few dozen blacks were bused to Riverside High. They came as close to being lynched as anyone ever has in what is sometimes called the "City of Good Neighbors." Riverside was inbred, paranoid, even racist. But, as Joe Murray knew as well as anybody, it had been devastated by the demise of the factories that surrounded it: among the largest, Pratt and Letchworth and J. H. Williams, two large steel mills, and Wood and Brooks, an internationally known manufacturer of piano keys.

As Buffalo's economy crumbled throughout the late 1970s and early 1980s, as jobs were lost and incomes dropped, family structure changed drastically and women all over industrial America were suddenly forced into the workplace. To the increasingly stressed parents of Riverside and South Buffalo, Joe Murray offered an early child-care and education program that was exactly what they needed. Instead of the half-day kindergartens available to them in their neighborhood elementary schools, Murray offered an all-day program in six elementary schools on the East Side for children from two years old through second grade. All the parents of Black Rock, Riverside, and South Buffalo had to do, Murray said, was to put their children on a school bus and he'd take care of the rest. Murray needed help—persuaders—and once again he turned to South Buffalo's own Carol Holtz. This time she had a partner, an African-American named Theresa Muschat.

Unlike most Buffalo African-Americans, Muschat grew up in Gardenville, an all-white residential community just south of the city. She lived there on her father's farm until her early twenties, when, after marrying a Buffalo man, she moved onto Riley Street, off Jefferson Avenue on the East Side. Muschat's neighborhood school, however, was west of Main Street, on the white side: School 16 on Delaware Avenue. By the mid-1960s, as a result of the legerdemain of the Board of Education, School 16 had become overwhelmingly black while School 30, one block further west on Elmwood Avenue, was overwhelmingly white. Muschat, head of School 16's PTA and working with a handful of School 16 parents, met repeatedly with School 30 parents hoping to devise a strategy to blend the two schools. When she heard that the Delaware Avenue Jewish Center was planning to leave its building, following its membership out to the suburbs, Muschat tried to convince its officials and later School 30's parents to convert the building into the blended school she was working to create. The latter weren't interested and the former decided to hold on to the building after all, but Muschat's vision of an integrated elementary school was finally realized in 1976 when, as part of Phase I of its desegregation plan, the Board of Education closed both 16 and 30, blending its student body into a brand-new, fully integrated elementary school on Buffalo's waterfront.

Active as a parent at the Waterfront School, Muschat was assigned by Judge Curtin to serve on the city-wide transportation committee, where she met Holtz and Murray. In the spring of 1980 Murray called on the team of Holtz and Muschat to help him integrate the new early childhood center at School 31 on Stanton Street.

According to the Phase III plan, six all-black schools would be voluntarily integrated by attracting white parents from Black Rock, Riverside, and South Buffalo. Holtz had begun to demonstrate her mastery of arm twisting and it was her passionate advocacy first of the Academic Challenge Center and the School of the Performing Arts and then of Futures in the Fruit Belt that had filled those East Side schools with large numbers of students and teachers from South Buffalo. Now, working with Muschat, in the spring of 1980 Holtz began to do for School 31 what she had already done for the other inner-city magnet schools. Looking like Jehovah's Witnesses, they thought, Muschat and Holtz went together into each other's neighborhoods, walking streets one or the other had never been on—Muschat in lily-white, Irish South Buffalo, Holtz in the African-American East Side (though she'd been in the Fruit Belt on behalf of School 37, she'd never been this far into the East Side). The pair went door to door, talking to parents, cajoling them, hoping to convince them to send their kids to the early childhood center at School 31. One night in July 1980, at a meeting packed with white parents at the Tosh Collins Community Center on Cazenovia Park, Carol Holtz, whose Ethel Merman–like voice more than compensates for her diminutive size, loudly and proudly introduced her partner for all to hear. "This is Theresa Muschat. She's my friend. We work together. Don't anybody offend her."

In fact, they had become friends, Theresa taking Carol shopping downtown and to services at the African Methodist Episcopal Church she belonged to on Ferry and Masten, Carol taking Theresa to bingo at St. Theresa's on Seneca. Meanwhile, parents in South Buffalo began to respond to their efforts. In 1977 all of the four hundred or so children at School 31 were African-American. By 1981 the ratio of black children to white was 70 percent to 30 percent, and by 1985 it was sixty-forty, a balance that has held steady since.

Meanwhile, in Black Rock and Riverside, Gene Reville, Joe Murray, and others were at work trying to convince parents to send their children to ECCs in other sections of the African-American inner city. One was at School 61 on the corner of Leroy Avenue and Grider Street, in the Fillmore-Leroy neighborhood. School 61 was built in the 1920s, when the neighborhood contained a mixture of first- and second-generation Italians, Germans, and Poles. Just a few blocks down Leroy from the school was Walter Kerns's Blessed Trinity Church. A few blocks the other way, down Grider, across from the mammoth and labyrinthine jungle of buildings known as the Erie County Medical Center, is St. Bartholomew's Church, where Father Bissonette was slain in the rectory. Today Fillmore-Leroy clearly is fighting a tough battle for survival and School 61 is right in the middle of it. Across the street from the school is a tiny, ramshackle "convenience" store where Principal Marion Canedo says neighborhood kids can conveniently buy marijuana and crack. On a recent school outing, on a beautiful early spring morning's walk around the block, one of 61's second graders pointed out "the van man," a fellow who sells crack out of the back of his beat-up grey Chevy van. Despite the environment of decay, School 61 gradually began to attract white students eager to attend one of the early childhood centers created in response to Judge Curtin's court order.

And so they came from the city's die-hard white ethnic neighborhoods that so many were convinced would go the route of South Boston. They came even though it meant "busing" into the dread neighborhoods on the African-American East Side of Buffalo. The numbers of white children grew steadily and beginning in 1980, the year the ECC program began and Evelyn Cooper's Futures Academy opened, a degree of racial balance prevailed in Buffalo's inner-city schools that defied even the highest hopes.

But still, the plaintiffs persisted. Others, less energetic and less vigilant, might have left well enough alone. After all, so much had really been accomplished since the suit had been filed in 1972, particularly compared to other cities. In Cleveland, all desegregation matters had been in the hands of a court-appointed administrator since August 1980, when a federal judge there found Cleveland school officials in contempt of court. In Boston, wracked by a horrendous fiscal squeeze and hemorrhaging white flight, the public schools were in a state of virtual ruin. Buffalo, meanwhile, had enjoyed a peaceful transition to an increasingly and largely integrated school system.

Superintendent Reville, many Buffalonians thought, had reason to be proud. By 1980, for the first time in years, the decline in the number of students in the Buffalo system was closer to one thousand than two thousand, federal funding for the racial balance of the magnets was improving, and so was white participation in them. Finally, after nearly twenty years of ranting and raving about busing, white parents in neighborhoods all over the city were sending their children to schools on Buffalo's black East Side. In September 1980 three thousand white children were attending inner-city magnet schools in sections of the city whites hadn't been in for years. More than eight hundred children were attending the six early childhood centers. Even suburban participation, that illusive symbol of success in urban public education, was on the increase. Indeed, there was not enough room for the 170 suburban children who applied for admission to the magnet schools in September 1980.

The plaintiffs, arguing before the U.S. Second Circuit Court of Appeals, presented a different picture of Buffalo's desegration efforts. They were not impressed, and they did not want Phase III to proceed. Looking around them the plaintiffs saw a public school system in which more than six thousand blacks—more than a third of the city's elementary-school children—still attended primarily black schools. They saw a busing program whose burden continued to fall particularly heavily on black children. White students were being actively recruited to attend magnet schools, but despite Curtin's ruling three thousand blacks were still being bused to regular neighborhood schools under the QIE program. This, when combined with the continued closing of schools in black neighborhoods, resulted in what the plaintiffs considered to be forced busing for blacks. For whites, on the other hand, participation in the desegregation program was voluntary, depending on the child's willingness to attend a magnet school. Having eighteen schools more than 65 percent black and nine more than 70 percent white did not meet Curtin's requirements for racial balance, the plaintiffs said. They further argued that there was no reason for the two-year delay of complete integration allowed by Judge Curtin. Final desegregation should be in force in September 1981, not 1983, they said. The plaintiffs pleaded that unless something happened quickly, "We or our children will be back here arguing about Phase 27 or 33."

The appeals judges seemed sympathetic to these arguments, and though they denied the appeal they did so in a way that considerably increased the pressure on Judge Curtin. The court expressed doubts about Phase III, wondering whether it did in fact "represent the maximum desegregation achievable," and was even more concerned with its time-table. In strong wording meant as much for Judge Curtin as for the defendants, the Second Circuit judges said that too many years had elapsed since the litigation had begun. The timeliness of the remedy, they concluded, was of the "utmost importance."

The weight of these words was not lost on Curtin, who immediately ordered that the parties to the case meet and prepare the next phase. Within a month Reville and Murray unveiled a plan they called "Phase IIIx."

Phase IIIx was an extremely controversial plan. Until now white participation in the school desegregation effort had been strictly voluntary. Although schools in white neighborhoods like South Buffalo, Black Rock, and Riverside were paired with schools like 31 and 61, parents in those neighborhoods could simply continue to send their children to their old neighborhood schools. Phase IIIx added an ultimatum: if enough whites didn't volunteer, there would be "forced student assignments" matching the ECCs on the East Side with schools in white neighborhoods called "Academies." These schools, for children from Grades 3 to 8, would be paired with the early childhood centers, creating a system of cross-busing similiar to that long espoused by the plaintiffs.

Reville knew he had little choice but to accept the forced-assignment back-up plan. He had seen reluctant boards in Cleveland and Boston lose control of the schools, and didn't want that to happen in Buffalo. "The board, in taking this step, maintained its position of keeping control of the desegregation process," Reville said." We did not want a master to be assigned or the plans of the plaintiffs to be put into effect. If the board hadn't done this the probability of someone else taking over the planning would have been very strong." He would have liked another year to convince white parents to voluntarily send their children to the ECCs, but he knew that time was running out. "I still believe that a voluntary effort is better and that for a successful voluntary effort you need time. But because of the pressure of the plaintiffs and the courts, the pace is being quickened." Norman Goldfarb was heartened, but though he gave the board credit "for coming to this point," he could not resist adding that the plaintiffs had had to "drag them there."

The reaction to Phase IIIx was loud and vocal. While many had serious reservations about a forced integration program, it was the timing as much as anything that disturbed several members of the Board of Education and the Common Council. David Kelly, the board president, voted against the plan, fearing that the introduction of force could jeopardize the generally good feelings that had characterized white response to all of the other desgregation programs. "We've had a viable, productive, and peaceful integration plan because it was implemented in reasonable time, not jammed down the throats of the people," he said. "We could be jeopardizing all the good things we've done to date."

Both the *News* and the *Courier* lamented the court's pressure, wishing that it had given the board until the beginning of the 1983 school year. Mayor Griffin lent his voice to the growing chorus of people now virtually begging Curtin to delay implementation of Phase IIIx. The Common Council had already done so and now, in a public appearance at School 65 in Riverside, where emotions were raw on the question of busing, Jimmy Griffin fanned the flames of resistance that had lain dormant for years. Speaking to parents in a school to be paired with an inner city elementary school, the mayor, whose own children attended parochial schools in South Buffalo, railed, 'It is that judge over there that is making the decisions. If he says 'bus' there's not a thing you or I can do about it, unfortunately." The plan, he said, "hurts the city badly." When asked if the fixed assignments called for in Phase IIIx would lead to white flight, he said, "Yes, it will, and I wouldn't blame anybody for leaving." Soon after, Griffin softened his tone, saying it was not the busing he objected to so much as the end of voluntary measures. Like most, he seemed to forget easily that busing had long been voluntary only for the city's white children; for the thousands of blacks whose neighborhood schools had been closed, involuntary busing had been the rule of thumb for more than a decade. Mozella Richardson, a black member of the board, expressed the feelings of the plaintiffs as well as many of the people in her community following the passage by the Board of Phase IIIx: "All my life I've been forced. Now I want to see someone else forced a little bit."

The key to the success of Phase IIIx was white participation. In an intense effort to assuage fears, Reville, Murray, and several board members once again "worked" the city's white neighborhoods throughout the spring of 1981. Unlike public officials in Boston and Cleveland and unlike their predecessors in Buffalo, Reville and Murray spoke directly, honestly, and often to community groups. There was no effort to mislead or deceive. To one group of Irish-American parents in South Buffalo whose two-, three-, and four-year-old children faced the prospect of being forced to attend early childhood centers in the black inner city, Murray said, "I'm going to look you in the eye and tell you what the facts are. You might not like them but I'm going to tell you: the schools have to be desegregated to the greatest extent possible and it may come down to forced assignments this September." He then asked rhetorically, "How bad is that? Call it forced busing, busing babies, whatever inflammatory rhetoric you might want to use. But our board acted in a responsible way and came up with a good program. The ECCs give you a good program at the end of the ride." Reville was equally forthright in a talk before Riverside parents at School 65. In a veiled reference to the obstructionist rhetoric of Mayor Griffin, Reville warned parents to be wary, suggesting that if they listened "to people who for political expediency tell you what you want to hear," the pain would be much greater. Referring to the Slominski-Parlato demagoguery of the late 1960s and early 1970s, Reville reminded his audience that obstructionism had been tried and had failed. "That's why we're before the courts today," he said. When asked by a parent in Riverside just how much power Curtin had, Reville responded only partly in jest, "Enough to call out the 101st Airborne." To encourage white parents to cooperate, the board sponsored a series of well-publicized tours of several inner-city early childhood centers. Reville promoted the trips to his audiences—what they saw, he told them, would be what they got. "We have no choice," he said. "Judge Curtin is under pressure from the Second Circuit Court of Appeals to accelerate the process. There's no alternative." Even for Riverside.

Riverside is perhaps the best-situated neighborhood in Buffalo. Hugging the shores of the Niagara River, the view from many of the neighborhood's streets is staggering: of the river, the Canadian shore, and, in summer, of long, slow, orange sunsets over the water. Old-timers in Riverside, people who have been around since the 1950s, talk nostalgically about the fishing clubs that used to line the river's banks, of boating and swimming off the shore, of walking along the banks of the towpath of the old Erie Canal. It is all talk and memories now, since 1958, when Riverside's access to the waterfront was obliterated by the construction of the Niagara Section of the New York State Thruway. Riverside residents fought hard against it and when they lost a mock funeral for the waterfront was held. A pedestrian bridge over the Thruway was built in the mid 1970s, and people can walk over the highway to the river's banks, but it's not the same, not even close. There is a long, concrete ledge that hugs the riverbank but it is as close to the thruway as it is to the river; it is noisy, dirty, and not a bit like the old Riverside waterfront. Riverside Park, however, designed, like parks in neighborhoods throughout Buffalo, by Olmsted, is lovely, and its long views of the Niagara River attract the area's people throughout the year.

There had been isolated pockets of settlement in Riverside since the late nineteenth century, but it was not until the 1920s that the neighborhood really grew, filling up with Germans and Poles from Black Rock and large numbers of Canadians attracted by the prospect of viewing their native land from the other side of the Niagara. There were jobs here too, good-paying factory jobs. By the 1940s and 1950s Riverside had become, like South Buffalo, a solidly Catholic, largely blue-collar neighborhood, prosperous and, thanks particularly to the magnificent Niagara River, a very pleasant place to live.

By the late 1970s, however, Riverside had lost not only its access to the Niagara River but its industrial base as well. Now, on summer evenings and on weekends, kids on baseball and soccer teams and men decked out in ill-fitting polyester uniforms bearing the names of sponsoring taverns play softball on a field named for the J. H. Williams Steel Company. Here, when the sun sets, the Williams field—"J.H." it is called in the neighborhood—is covered with the long, slender shadows cast by the abandoned plant. On the other side of the park, on Vulcan Street, the border of the Town of Tonawanda, stands another empty factory, the large, poured-concrete structure that once housed the Wood and Brooks piano-key factory.

Around the corner from the old Williams plant is School 65. Like 61 in Fillmore-Leroy, the school it was paired with under Phase IIIx, 65 is an old neighborhood school, an institution, where school loyalty was deep and passionate. Reville and Murray were worried about Riverside, afraid that the violence thus far avoided in South Buffalo could well erupt here. It had almost come to that point in September 1972, when Theresa Muschat's son was one of about a hundred black children bused from the East Side to Riverside High school. The kids had been met with bitter, ugly, and frightening demonstrations by parents and children. For two weeks Muschat and her neighbors organized a posse of cars and followed their children's buses across town to Riverside in the morning and back again in the afternoon, to make sure they were safe. Riverside remained fertile ground for racial demogoguery throughout the decade and it was not surprising that Mayor Griffin chose the area to vent his opposition to Phase IIIx.

Joanne Skorka had been elected to the Board of Education from the West District, which includes Riverside. She was afraid parents at School 65 would respond to the mayor's rabble-rousing and resist being paired with School 61, blowing the lid off the desegregation process.

Skorka had lived on Breckenridge Street on Buffalo's West Side for years, and she had earned a reputation as a vocal, active, and popular leader of the PTA at School 45 on Hoyt Street. Hoyt is part of the "real" West Side, an almost exclusively Italian neighborhood since the mid-1940s, when the prospect of the West Side Arterial drove the Italians northward. The school is on one end of Hoyt, Annunciation Church at the other. In between are homes, almost all of them doubles. While Hispanics have taken over much of the Lower West Side, large sections of the upper West Side are still bedrock Italian. Hoyt, like streets throughout the Italian West Side, overflows with the sights, sounds, and smells of an Italian neighborhood. The people seem to be outside all the time, even in cooler weather, sitting on front porches or working on their homes and in their yards. Around the corner is Grant Street, an on-the-skids commercial strip lined with Italian-owned stores: Guercio's Produce, Spasiano's Cleaners, Russ's Pastries, Licata's Sausage, and countless pizza joints.

School 45 is in this neighborhood. It has always been a crowded school and until the late 1960s it had always been white, mostly Italian-American. In the early 1970s small numbers of blacks from the East Side were bused into the school under the QIE program, but they remained a small minority until 1976 when, under Phase I of the Board of Education's school desegregation plan, close to three hundred black kids were introduced into the school. Joanne Skorka wanted to make sure the change went smoothly. A product of mixed blood herself (her father was a Mohawk Indian, her mother a Hungarian immigrant), Skorka believed in integration and wanted to make it work at 45. Area parents were worried. In 1972 many of them had had kids at Grover Cleveland, the neighborhood high school, when one spring day the Mad Dogs, the Manhattan Lovers, and the Matadors—black teen-age boys from the East Side known as the "Three M" gangs—invaded that school in a frightening hit-and-run attack, rampaging through the halls, threatening any teacher or student who stood in their way. Because of that incident, many of the Italian-Americans took their kids out of "Grover" that year and now, four years later, they worried that such an incident could be repeated.

Skorka worked throughout the summer of 1976 preparing her community, first at the school and then at the homes of several neighborhood parents, many of whose children would find themselves in integrated classrooms for the first time. The transition went smoothly and the foundation Skorka built has lasted. In a neighborhood that remains much as it was when the school desegregation plan began in 1976, there has been little white flight from School 45 and it remains a place where there are close to equal numbers of African-Americans and whites, as well as Hispanics, Asians, and a smattering of Russian Jews.

In 1981, when Skorka was confronted with the challenge of pairing Riverside's School 65 with 61, the early childhood center on Grider and Leroy, she knew that much depended on the principal. For this she enlisted the aid of Joe Murray.

There is an art to selecting the right principal for a school and Murray had already made some masterful choices. He was particularly adept at selecting them for the early childhood centers. For 31 on Stanton Street, he picked Mildred Stallings, an African-American whose deeply held traditional views about education and discipline have had a strong appeal in the school's black neighborhood as well as in South Buffalo, the area with which it was paired. Another was Marion Canedo, picked for School 61. Canedo had worked with Murray in creating the ECC program implemented in September 1980. She has lived in Buffalo all her life, graduating from local public schools and earning two masters degrees from Buffalo State College. She is extremely attentive to detail. "I can tell you where every one of my seven hundred kids is in reading and math," she says. "They don't fall through the cracks here, because there are none." During her first year as principal at 61, in 1980, Canedo developed a program called the "Inventive Thinking Curriculum." When a child is asked to invent something, Canedo says, he or she must learn by doing and thus will synthesize and apply a wide range of knowledge, experience, and skills. Her curriculum—which includes the annual city-wide "Invention Convention," at which students in the early childhood programs submit inventions for every conceivable problem of daily living—has been adopted by school systems all over the country and has made Canedo one of the nation's recognized experts in early child-hood education.

Skorka wanted someone like Stallings or Canedo for School 65, someone strong and energetic enough to lead the frightened parents, both in Riverside and Fillmore-Leroy, through the touchy first steps of Phase IIIx. Murray was from Riverside and he knew how insular and parochial the neighborhood was. His theory was that if integration was to work, if the changes that were beginning to take place in race-relations were to last, it was essential that the sheltered white folk of Riverside be exposed to a superb African-American role model.

Murray found just such a person in Erma Robinson. Robinson came to Buffalo in 1956 from Oklahoma via Virginia and moved into the Cold Springs neighborhood on the East Side. The area was changing then and most of the whites still left there were poor. Robinson had had a comfortable, middle-class upbringing and a very good education. Unlike Buffalo's other black principals, all of whom were products of Buffalo's public schools, Robinson, a Southerner, had gone to all-black schools her entire life, including for college. She had combined careers in education and social work, and was a good choice for Riverside's School 65, under Phase IIIx named the Roosevelt Academy. Somehow she managed to make the black parents feel at home in the white neighborhood without raising the easily aroused fears of white parents.

Although some white parents were shocked to learn the new principal was black, there was little racial tension that first year. At first, Robinson remembers, it was difficult to get the black parents to come to meetings at the school, a problem Canedo said she was also having with the white parents at School 61. They didn't know the way, some said. They were scared, said others, to drive to Riverside at night. Robinson insisted on their participation. Refusing to listen to their excuses, she borrowed a van from her church and brought them to the school herself. Soon the school had an integrated parent-teacher group. By the spring it had raised enough money to take the whole eighth grade for a five-day trip to Washington, D.C. Under the banner of the "Buffalo Public Schools" a black principal from South was leading two buses filled with white and black parents and children, people from neighborhoods long isolated from each other, to the nation's capital. It was a trip Robinson says she'll never forget. Nor will those who went with her. The following year Robinson took them to Boston. She wanted to take them on the "Freedom Trail," she said.

Despite the anxieties, the first day of school in September 1981 was a proud one for Buffalo. With more than half the city's forty-four thousand public school students riding buses to schools beyond the confines of their neighborhoods, the streets in every neighborhood of the city were calm and peaceful. The newspapers boasted of the achievements of the day. It was "a lesson in tranquility," said the *News*. The *Courier* reported in a banner headline that "Everyone Cooperates as Busing Commences." The integration specialist from the State Education Department reported that the implementation of Phase IIIx was exemplary. "We saw not one picket, not one so-called protective parent hanging around," he said. "I was impressed. I just finished visiting other cities undergoing desegregation—Indianapolis, Louisville, Saint Louis, Chicago, and Milwaukee—and this is not the way it usually goes." The Buffalo police commissioner concurred. "We had no incidents relating to busing, thank God."

There were other things to be thankful for on that opening day of school in 1981. While Buffalo's school population continued its decline, the loss of barely one thousand students (2 percent) was substantially less than in previous years. More significantly, the rate of decline in Buffalo was considerably lower than in school districts in the surrounding suburbs. White flight was limited to barely more than a handful of disgruntled parents who were able to finesse their way past the scrupulous admissions officers ordered by Bishop Head to deny admission to refugees from integration. Indeed, contrary to the expectation of Mayor Griffin, who sent his own children to a Catholic school in South Buffalo and who had predicted a flight to the parochial system, the Diocese of Buffalo reported a 4.5 percent decline in enrollment in September 1981. In fact, four hundred children had left diocesan schools that year to attend Buffalo's magnets schools. Within a year enrollment in the city's Catholic schools was down 30 percent.

But the problem of racial isolation in Buffalo's schools was not yet completely solved. Enrollment figures for September 1981 showed that blacks made up 54 percent of the children in the schools; there were still close to three thousand blacks in nine schools that did not meet Judge Curtin's requirements that no less than 35 percent and no more than 65 percent of every school's population consist of minorities. According to the plaintiffs, this meant that 20 percent of all black elementary school children remained in segregated schools. The board did not deny the charge and promised that within a year the situation would be remedied. At that time, Reville said, there would be only two racially isolated schools in all of Buffalo. The plaintiffs refused to accept this and began a push for what they said would be "a final order." What they wanted, they said in the spring of 1982, was the pairing of four inner-city elementary schools with seven schools in white neighborhoods. The board objected, saying that such a plan would result in the busing of over two thousand more whites while upsetting the racial balance in existing schools.

Despite its continued legal struggle and a Reagan administration cut of federal integration funds from $6 million to $600,000, the Board of Education was enjoying a great deal of success and attention. Most recent figures continued to show a marked slowdown in enrollment decline; a growing number of applicants to the magnet schools, the ECCs, and the academies; and growing national attention for a desegregation program increasingly regarded as a model for the country. In an interview in the *News* in January 1982 James Barnes, the director of the National Educational Strategy Center in Hartford, Connecticut, said, "Over the past few years we've sent about five hundred people to Buffalo from other areas to look at the system. It's got to be the best there is." Several months later the court-appointed desegregation monitor for Cleveland said, "I keep telling people here they should take a trip to Buffalo—they could learn a lot."

The apparent success of Buffalo's desegregation program was occurring at a time of increasingly reactionary tendencies in Washington. Indeed, just as Buffalo was in the process of achieving its greatest success in desegregating its schools, the U.S. Senate passed its strongest anti-busing bill ever. "Busing," said Sen. Jesse Helms of North Carolina, "just doesn't work." The view from other cities suggested that perhaps he was correct. Boston's public schools were in terrible shape. They had lost more than thirty thousand pupils since court-ordered integration began in 1974, with the portion of the student body that was white falling from 70 percent to 30 percent. There were now more whites in private and parochial schools than there were in the city's public schools. In Cleveland, too, opposition to court-ordered desegregation had been intense—"as broad and as deep as you can imagine," the court-appointed monitor reported in January 1983. White flight in Cleveland, Detroit, and other cities throughout the North and Midwest had led to the virtual resegregation of their public schools.

Not only were the board and the public in general pleased with Buffalo's progress, but Curtin was too. For the first time in the history of the case he put the burden on the plaintiffs to demonstrate that further racial balance was not only desirable but even possible. Curtin seemed to agree with the board's argument that, given the number of whites in the school system, further desegregation could not be achieved without destroying racial balance in existing schools. He hinted that, like judges in other cities, he might rule that despite the existence of two all-minority schools the system could still be considered constitutionally desegregated. Curtin's ruling in August 1982 was a double-barreled victory for Reville's school board. Because it was "financially burdensome" and "disruptive," Curtin rejected the plaintiffs' proposal for the additional pairing of black and white neighborhood schools. In addition, he insisted that the city, as a defendant in the case, make up the losses the board had suffered as a result of the Reagan budget cuts. The board had requested a minimum budget of $156 million; the city had given it $150 million. Curtin now ordered that the city give the board an additional $7.4 million in order to maintain the desegregation program. Mayor Griffin was furious and promised to appeal Curtin's rulings.

Norman Goldfarb was outraged for different reasons. "I am indignant at the judge's approach to remaining segregation in the schools," he said. He wondered if Curtin had not "forgotten his promises to the black families of this community." He was scornful of Curtin's dismissal of the plaintiff's plan to desegregate the remaining two all-black elementary schools. Yes, it is disruptive, he said, "Every change is disruptive." Seeming to flail at windmills, Goldfarb said the plaintiffs would continue their struggle. "The judge has ordered it and the board has refused. They must desegregate."

Goldfarb's appeal fell on deaf ears. Desegregation continued to go smoothly. The 1-percent decline in school enrollment in September 1982 was the smallest in twenty-five years, much smaller than in all the other large cities of the Northeast. Furthermore, Buffalo's 52 percent minority student population was far lower than almost every large city in the country, down 2 percent from a year earlier. In a ruling in May 1983 Curtin expressed satisfaction that the board had done all it could. Racial imbalance at the three remaining all-black elementary schools could not possibly be the result of segregative actions, he said. "The imposition of any new measures to desegregate the schools under the circumstances could only be viewed as counterproductive." While there were still some unanswered questions, Curtin said, the issue of desegregation was resolved. "The board has met its burden of demonstrating that further desegregation of these schools is not practical at this time."

In 1985, Curtin was interviewed for a laudatory article on school desegregation in the *New York Times*. "I am distressed by people who make statements nationally that integration doesn't work," he said. "It does work. It's plain wrong to say that it doesn't. It's working in Buffalo." No one would have bet on successful desegregation in Buffalo in 1976. Indeed, many thought the white people of Buffalo, long isolated in ethnic neighborhoods, battered by economic decline and population change, would finally draw the line and resist rather than succumb to the orders of a federal judge—or at least flee the city. That had certainly been the pattern in New York, Boston, Cleveland, Detroit, Chicago, and all the other cities that had come under the desegregation orders of federal courts.

For a while the pattern held true in Buffalo. During the 1970s, the city's white population dropped by 30 percent; the number of white children in the Buffalo public schools dropped to 46 percent. The decline only accelerated after Curtin's ruling in 1976. But things began to turn around in 1981, the very year of Phase IIIx and its dread "forced" participation of whites. White population and school-enrollment decline slowed. While the number of white children in the Buffalo school system continued to decline throughout the 1980s, the rate of decline—11 percent—reflected the decline in the number of whites in the city at large. By the end of the 1980s, there were signs that despite a continued decline in Buffalo's white population, the number of white children in the city's schools, particularly in pre-kindergarten through eighth grade, was actually increasing. Given the growing racial isolation that character- ized public schools in cities throughout the United States, Buffalo's achievement was extraordinary. Suddenly, in age-old neighborhood schools that had been bastions of racial isolation for years, an unprece- dented racial mix was occurring. Every day thousands of children— white, black, Hispanic, Asian, and Native American—were venturing out beyond the confines of their neighborhoods on school buses and metro buses, headed for magnet schools, vocational schools, early child- hood centers, academic high schools, and just plain neighborhood schools tucked away in all corners of the city. In the Fruit Belt and the Ellicott District, in Black Rock and Riverside, in South Buffalo and North Buffalo, on the West Side and the East Side, the people of Buffalo were giving meaning to the long-illusive goal of integration on which Judge Curtin and the plaintiffs in the school case had for so long insisted.

Buffalo's public schools improved as they integrated. In 1988 Buf- falo students earned 165 New York State Regents scholarships, twice the number won in 1977. Fourteen Regents Empire awards, the most generous and prestigious, were won by students at the City Honors High School. A far higher percentage of Buffalo's third- and sixth-grade students passed pupil evaluation tests in reading and math than in any city in the state. Eight of the city's schools, more than in any city in the nation, received presidential citations for excellence. At a White House ceremony 1988 honoring 287 of the nations best elementary schools, president Reagan called specific attention to the crowning achievement of Evelyn Cooper's career. "All Americans," he said, "can be proud of schools like Futures Academy in Buffalo, New York." Cooper was there to bask in the glow of that presidential praise.

People began to flock to Buffalo from all over the country and from Europe and Japan to see for themselves how this down-in-the- dumps industrial city in the heart of the Rust Belt had done what Boston, Cleveland, Detroit, Chicago, and New York had been unable to do. The principals in the case—Judge Curtin, Gene Reville, Joe Murray, Carol Holtz, Theresa Muschat, and Evelyn Cooper—had become celeb- rities and experts on the question of desegregation, traveling through- out the country sharing their skills and wisdom with educators, politi- cians, lawyers, and judges eager to learn "how Buffalo did it." Journalists wrote about this unlikely story. Curtin sent one highly laudatory piece from the *Chicago Tribune* to Reville and Murray with a note attached: "For your information and enjoyment, and with my compliments."

In fact, much of the credit for the achievement belongs to Curtin. The *Buffalo News,* selecting him as one of its "Citizens of the Year" in 1986, noted Curtin's "quiet power on the bench." Curtin's former clerk, Mike Brady, who had played a significant role during the early phases of the case, recalls Curtin's "judicial temperament." Curtin's wife, Jane Good Curtin, talks about his "patience," both in court and at home. Deeply aware of the difficult and complex changes he was requiring the people of the city to make, the judge had been patient with the Board of Education as well (far too patient, for the eager and idealistic plaintiffs). Patrick Martin, another clerk, said Curtin understood that "the carrot does better than the stick if you're willing to wait a bit longer for the results." Sometimes the judge had threatened to impose a solution or to appoint a "master"—but always he delayed, hoping to rely as long as possible on voluntary measures.

He had given the people of Buffalo power as well as time, insisting on extensive and meaningful citizen participation at every step of the desegregation process. "Curtin 'inserviced' everybody," said Evelyn Cooper, referring to the training sessions the judge required of all school personnel. Cooper led so many of the resultant participation sessions— for building superintendents, crossing guards, and bus aides, not to mention parents and teachers. Because of the careful development insisted upon by Curtin, said Florence Baugh, people "felt ownership in the process." Letting all the people affected by desegregation play a role in how it was carried out worked in Buffalo; it may well have worked in Boston too. In an interview in the *News* early in 1983 the president of Boston's School Committee said that he wished his city had done things differently. "If we had it to do over again," he said, "we would make sure, like Judge Curtin did in Buffalo, that the people of this city had some ownership of the plan." Citing the court-ordered pairing of all-white South Boston High with its all-black equivalent in Roxbury, he said, "In Boston it was just thrust on us."

The greatest gift Curtin gave the people of Buffalo was his faith in them, his belief that they—not the board, not the plaintiffs, not he himself nor a court-appointed "integration master"—could best determine the particulars of school integration. Throughout the school case Curtin remained convinced that, if given the chance, the people of Buffalo would rise to the challenge.

While Buffalo continues to have serious educational problems, they are more the result of larger, historical questions of culture, race, and class than of educational policy. While much clearly needs to be done in the area of public education, much has already been accomplished—today Buffalo has an active and vocal education constituency made up of people from all over the city empowered and bonded by the very process they had had seen as the greatest threat to their community.

14

A NEW ECONOMY FOR THE CHANGING CITY

By the mid-1980s the erosion of the industrial economy that had devastated the community and led Judge Curtin to consider softening the remedy in the school case had begun to ease. Led by a host of job-creating industrial-development agencies in the public sector and by a rapid expansion of jobs in the "service sector," Buffalo's economy began to creep back, slowly, painstakingly, attempting to create new forms of work in a new economic era.

Sometimes it seemed hopeless. So it appeared on November 8, 1985, when Trico Corporation, the world's largest manufacturer of windshield wipers, announced that it was moving the bulk of its operations from Buffalo to the border of Texas and Mexico. The windshield wiper was invented in Buffalo by a man named John Oshei, who, after driving home on a rainy afternoon in March 1917 decided a gadget was necessary that would mechanically wipe the rain from his windshield. Enterprising as well as creative, Oshei formed Trico; since the 1920s it has led its field. Housed in three aging but still grand and imposing turn-of-the-century plants scattered around the city, Trico is one of Buffalo's last large, family-controlled and locally owned companies. The Osheis still own close to 30 percent of Trico's outstanding stock.

Trico was always a good corporate citizen and the Oshei Foundation a magnanimous contributer to a broad range of community charities. But, like a growing number of American manufacturers, the company decided to open a *macquila* ("contract work") plant. Macquila operations have their origins in the mid-1960s, when changes in the tax laws encouraged American companies to take advantage of cheaper foreign, particularly Asian, labor. The new laws allowed an American company to ship manufacturing machinery and unfinished products into a foreign country, assemble the products there, and then bring them back into the U.S. market, paying duty only on the value added during the assembly process. During the 1970s this system led to the creation of assembly plants in Taiwan and in other Pacific Rim countries.

As the peso lost value during the early 1980s, Mexican businessmen and government officials became interested in the program. And the U.S. Department of Commerce became interested in Mexico as a way to stem the loss of jobs to the Pacific Rim. Beginning in 1984, the Commerce Department sponsored conferences designed to introduce American companies to the cost-cutting advantages of the program. The labor movement throughout the country as well as the political leadership in Buffalo and other industrial cities were appalled at what they saw as a government-encouraged program of deindustrialization. Others saw it differently, arguing that the jobs that were headed for Mexico were being lost anyway; better that they went to Mexico than the Orient—at least part of the product would be made in the United States. Toy manufacturer Fisher-Price, one of the most successful companies in the Buffalo area, agreed. In 1984 the company set up twin plants on the Texas-Mexico border. If it hadn't, the president of the company said, "we'd be buying completed toys from the Orient."

For Trico, the macquila program sounded too good to be true. For years the company had comfortably and lackadaisically dominated the windshield wiper industry. Unchallenged, Trico had grown lazy, making little effort to modernize, simply coasting, earning profits not from wipers but from its gigantic stock portfolio. In 1985 Trico owned nearly $62 million in common stock in General Motors, Exxon, and Ford Motor Company. Under increasing pressure from foreign producers and particularly American automakers who demanded that Trico cut its prices lest they begin buying from Japan, the company suddenly woke up. That same year, company president Richard Wolf announced the decision to build an assembly plant in Matamoros, Mexico, and a distribution center across the border in Brownsville, Texas.

Trico would equip the factory in Matamoros and stock it with windshield-wiper components, all duty free. The components would then be assembled into finished products and shipped back across the border to the company's warehouse. Trico would pay duty only on the value added in Mexico. The cost savings, Wolf said, were too hard to resist. In Mexico workers got $1.20 an hour in wages and benefits, Wolf told a stunned meeting of Trico workers; in Buffalo they got $14 an hour.

The people of Buffalo were horrified that their community and their workforce was being held hostage by what they saw as the slave labor of a pathetically underdeveloped country. Others saw it differently. By 1988 more than 250,000 Mexicans were working in macquila plants. They were pumping over $1.1 billion into the Mexican economy, behind oil but ahead of tourism in economic impact. The program, some said, would help Mexico deal with its terrible economic problems, give work to many who would otherwise slip across the border, and help the country pay its foreign debt. Small comfort, said others, to the industrial workforce of Buffalo.

Losing out to cheaper, foreign labor was nothing new to the proud unionized workers of Buffalo. But the macquila program was different, and particularly hard to swallow. In the months following the Trico announcement, Norman Harper, president of Local 2100 of the United Auto Workers of America, which represents the Trico workers, made several trips to the Brownsville-Matamoros area. He took a tape recorder and camera with him, and the words and images he brought back to Buffalo are shocking. Harper found teeming shantytowns that had sprung up on the dirt roads near plants owned by GM, Delco, and Fisher Price. These ramshackle villages, with only minimal plumbing and sanitation, housed thousands of people, many of them young women, who had come from all over Mexico looking for work in the macquila factories. Some of them had found it; most had not. The unemployment rate on the border was higher than anywhere else in Mexico. Conditions in Matamoros, Harper's slides indicate, are desperate. There are few schools and medical facilities and hardly any municipal facilities of any kind. Harper says the women and children of Matamoros line up every day to cross the border to schools and hospitals in Brownsville. Rapid, unplanned expansion has turned the town upside down as companies and developers, using generous municipal handouts, have constructed a host of jerrybuilt warehouses, homes, and shopping plazas.

There's something terribly wrong, Harper fumes, when corporations are permitted to play the vulnerable, low-paid workers of one country against the high-paid but also vulnerable workers of another. It is worse when governments encourage it, he says. But this is exactly what has happened in this cynical partnership, a compact between a desperate underdeveloped country and American corporations eager to improve their balance sheets by drastically cutting their labor costs. The only beneficiaries of the program are the corporations. Clearly the workers in places like Trico's Buffalo plants don't benefit. Nor, Harper says, do the Mexicans who have moved in droves to the border to work in the macquila plants. Despite their government's alleged desire to make Mexico economically independent of the United States, the macquila program puts Mexico's workers more at the mercy of the Americans than ever. Is Trico more committed, Harper wonders, to Matamoros than it was to Buffalo? Will it not move again when it finds another place in some other corner of the world where wages are lower still? And what about the Mexicans who work in the macquila plants, the young women who, earning so little, with so few benefits, have no job security?

Norm Harper was born and raised on the East Side of Buffalo. He went to work at Trico in 1953 when the only jobs blacks could get were janitorial. He eventually entered the skilled trades and since 1979 has been president of the Trico union local. Harper says Trico has a "moral obligation" to its employees and to the community to stay; that somehow the company "shouldn't be allowed to leave." But that is a sentiment, not an argument, and in the world of business it would garner deservedly little credibility. Only by convincing Trico that it could do as well financially by staying in Buffalo as by moving to Mexico could the company have been persuaded to stay. Harper tried and failed. He blames Trico, insisting that had he been given more time, he could have been worked out something.

Perhaps Harper is right. If Trico had been willing to share its problems and concerns over a period of years with the union, with bankers, and with public officials at all levels of government, its local production might have been saved. The company paid lip service to the efforts of a task force intent on keeping it in Buffalo, but it had waited far too long. Only with the greatest effort were Harper and the UAW able to save the few hundred jobs that remain in the city.

It is unlikely, however, that even the most sophisticated early warning system would have kept Trico in Buffalo. As long as corporations are permitted to exploit the low-paid workers of Third World countries, companies like Trico, regardless of their "commitment to Buffalo," will continue to leave. There is little more that Harper and the UAW could have done for Trico's more than six hundred laid-off workers. With combined federal and state unemployment benefits of $180 a week for two years, the workers were able to scrape by while they adjusted to their new situation. Harper knew that there was little he could have done to prevent Trico's departure, but he tried anyway. In the process he became an expert on the macquila program. The shelves in his office were filled with articles and studies about it. Harper tried to stop companies in other cities from abandoning their communities for Mexico. He spent a lot of time on the border talking with labor leaders and public officials. Many, fearing the human and environmental exploitation that has invariably followed the establishment of a macquila company, were glad Harper was there, but many had doubts about what he could do. "You should have come a year ago," one of them told him in 1988. "It's too late now."

It was also too late for the eight hundred employees working at Westinghouse Electric near the airport in suburban Depew. Westinghouse, which manufactures electric engines, had bought its plant in 1947 from Curtiss-Wright, a Buffalo-based airplane manufacturing company that moved to California. Westinghousegrew continuously and in 1970, when John Perry came to Buffalo to work for the company as strategic projects manager of motor operations, there were seventy-two hundred workers in the plant. But the engine plant had reached capacity and the company, like General Electric and the U.S. Electrical Motor Company, rather than expanding in the area, began to move its production out. Westinghouse moved its welding operations to Maryland, and its copper wire production to Virginia. The number of Buffalo employees dropped steadily throughout the 1970s and early 1980s. For a while the *Union Messenger,* the newsletter of the International Union of Electrical Workers, denied the obvious. "There are many topics of discussion circulating around the plant" the paper reported in early April 1986. "The main issue seems to be when and if it will all come to an end." For a while, in fact, the workers at Westinghouse thought perhaps it wasn't true as they passed on still more rumors that "due to an influx of orders the life of the Motor Division will be extended." But soon they could deny it no longer. In early 1987, with just under eight hundred employees left, Westinghouse announced that it was closing.

By then Perry had a new job: coordinator of the Westinghouse Placement Center. In an interview in the *Messenger* Perry promised the workers "the most humane plant close-down to ever take place." He began by coordinating a series of workshops for Westinghouse workers, on training for new jobs, personal finance (how to apply for unemployment insurance and deal with creditors), and food and health (how to apply for food stamps, Medicaid, and home energy assistance).

"The top priority now," the union paper wrote, "is to pick up the pieces and resume industrial life again, as painful as it may be. We must begin to plan for our respective futures. . . . It is said that adversity is the glue that binds together the working people. . . . Let's make sure that rings true by sharing and caring for each of our brothers and sisters."

And then there was the steel industry. When the *Courier Express,* Buffalo's morning daily with a publishing history that went back to the 1840s, folded in 1982 Joe Ritz, who had written so movingly about the impact of urban renewal on the Lower West Side, went to work for the Buffalo *News,* covering the labor scene. In the spring of 1988 he wrote an article called "Once Mighty Bethlehem Steel Slowly Being Reduced to Rubble."

> Seen from the Father Baker Bridge, the once mighty Bethlehem Steel Corporation's Lackawanna plant—where motorists once looked for the rosy glow in the sky as the open hearths poured steel—is being reduced to rubble. Demolition of the sprawling plant has been going on since late 1984, but the first phases consisted of tearing down long unused coke batteries and blast furnaces hidden from the eyes of the public by the deserted but untouched black metal buildings of the steel plant. Now, work by four demolition companies is rapidly proceeding on the 218-, 48-, and 54-inch bar mills. . . . Less visible is the No. 3 open hearth, now rapidly becoming a tortured, twisted jungle of metal halfway to destruction. . . . Ironically, the scrap from the plant mostly will go to operating steel plants, including those owned by Bethlehem, to be melted down into new steel. Demolition of the plant is half completed, according to Eliot Gordon, Bethlehem's supervisor of reclamation. "This is the largest demolition project in the country," he said. It will take at least another two years, Gordon said, before the demolition is completed. The ripping down of the largest single building, the massive basic oxygen furnace, which towers over the closed plant like a sooty metal castle, is expected to begin late this year or early in 1989. . . . When the project is completed, approximately thirteen hundred acres of waterfront property will become an empty field. . . .Even much of the railroad tracks on the property are being ripped up, although some will remain for use by a buyer of the land. In a year or so, Gordon said, motorists on the Father Baker bridge will be able to see Lake Erie when they pass the former steel mill.

No reader could avoid the conclusion that there was something irreversible about the decline of industry in Buffalo. The destruction of such a mighty edifice as the sprawling Bethlehem complex led one to wonder what Buffalo could possibly do to halt the decay. After all, the changes that undermined Buffalo's steel industry were really global, the result of the integration of the international economy that spelled a seemingly inevitable end to America's long dominance of world industry. Sections of New England, the South, and the West, where manufacturing is flourishing, have benefited from the changes in Buffalo and elsewhere in the Great Lakes cities of America's industrial heartland. Such a large proportion of the workforce in Buffalo had engaged in manufacturing for so long that it was devastated by decline of the city's industrial base. Though the average pay for so many years had been among the highest in the nation, by the mid-1980s, as a result of layoffs, pay cuts, and concessions by once-cocky workers desperate to hold on to their jobs, Buffalo had suddenly become a low-wage town. Jobs and wages were not all that were lost. As was true in industrial cities throughout the world, the decline of industry struck at the core and the fiber of the community, undermining family stability, weakening neighborhoods, and permanently altering the values and beliefs many people had long lived by.

The economy of the area had gone through a major shakedown. The shift of jobs out of manufacturing since the late 1970s was more pronounced in Buffalo than in any area in the country. By 1983 jobs in trade and services exceeded those in factories for the first time in the city's history. Between 1977 and 1987 more than forty-five thousand jobs, 31 percent of Buffalo's manufacturing positions, were lost. The average loss of manufacturing jobs nationally was just 25 percent. Manufacturing employed 28 percent of Buffalo's workers in 1977. By 1987 it was 18 percent. Meanwhile, by the end of the 1980s some distinctly bright trends had finally begun to emerge. During the last three years of the decade the Buffalo area suddenly became one of the fastest growing in the state. Fueled primarily by the rapid expansion of the service sector of the economy, thousands of new jobs were created and unemployment rates, which for years had been carefully monitored for the tiniest movement up or down, fell to under 8 percent, their lowest level in many years.

Certain indicators clearly pointed to signs of what local boosters were calling a "Buffalo Renaissance," but some suggested that its foundations might be shaky. In an industrial economy where jobs are secure and wages high, unemployment rates are a valid measure of the general health of the economy. In an increasingly service-oriented economy, however, they mean less. While plentiful, jobs in the booming business, health, and retail service sectors of the economy are often part-time, unusually unstable, and always low paying. Traditionally considered by economists a "nonbasic" part of the economy, the service sector produces no tangible good. Rather, it is residual activity dependent on other sectors. This definition is clearly borne out by a list of the fastest-growing occupations in the Buffalo area compiled by the State Department of Labor in early 1990: "Other managers, miscellaneous sales workers, food workers, waiters and waitresses, cashiers, secretaries, nursing assistant occupations, stock handlers, guards and related occupations, cooks, bookkeepers, lawyers and kindred workers, bank tellers, professional nurses, physicians, coffee-shop managers, other health technicians, typists, receptionists, and dental hygienists." At the beginning of 1990, the department reported, 85 percent of the openings in the Buffalo area were in low-paying, unskilled job categories—clearly not the kind to inspire young, ambitious, career-oriented people to stay. There are well-paid technical and professional jobs in the service sector, but they tend to be located in the large urban centers like New York, Boston, and San Francisco, not in Buffalo. It is this, more than anything, that has contributed to the steady exodus from the city of the young, educated, and ambitious workforce.

George Symentek, the chief economist at the Buffalo office of the State Department of Labor, is an expert on the regional economy regularly called on by anyone looking for an explanation of area economic trends. "There just is no upward movement in Buffalo for the skilled and educated worker," Symentek says. His personal experience bears out this data. His son is an electrical engineer who, like many young college-educated Buffalonians, has moved away. There were one or two positions in Buffalo, his father says, "but he could only have gone so far here anyway. It made more sense for him to start his career in Philly." It is just this kind of migration of educated and skilled workers, combined with the loss of blue-collar workers looking for industrial work in other areas of the country, that has left Buffalo with an uneducated, unskilled labor pool, the opposite of what it needs to prosper.

Manufacturing, however, is far from dead in Buffalo. General Motors, with more than fourteen thousand employees and an annual payroll of over $500 million, is the area's largest private employer. Ford is close behind. Both are stable, well-managed companies, with long-term commitments to the Buffalo area. At the end of 1989 Ford announced a $260 million investment in its Buffalo Stamping Plant. The investment, to be completed within a year, will make the facility one of the company's most sophisticated. Other manufacturers, though not quite as large, remain extremely significant in the local economy. Some, like Gibralter Steel and Columbus McKinnon, a manufacturer of materials-handling products, are locally owned. In fact, there remains an impressive array of large and successful locally owned manufacturers, companies like F. N. Burt, a producer of paperboard packaging; Ruslander and Sons, maker of stainless steel food service equipment; Perry's Ice Cream; Mentholatum; Marlette Plating; Niagara Envelope; Dinaire Furniture; Niagara Blower; and Curtis Screw.

And at Bethlehem Steel more than one thousand people still work in the coke-oven operations. Bethlehem's continued presence in Buffalo is a mixed blessing at best. In early April 1990 the company was ordered to pay a $1 million state environmental fine, the largest ever levied against any company in New York. Meanwhile the U.S. Environmental Protection Agency said that it found 104 hazardous-waste dumps on the 2.5 square mile plant site and was demanding that Bethlehem clean up or contain the dumps. The Buffalo *News* reported to the people—many of whom thought that the company was no longer doing business in the area—that the chemicals leaking from the dumps were fouling ground water, six creeks, and Lake Erie.

Defense spending and military work remain important to Buffalo's manufacturing economy. During World War II Buffalo was one of the great centers in the free world for the production of planes, steel armor, machine guns, ammunition, tugboats, parachutes, uniforms, TNT, and gunmounts. (One Buffalonian, Seymour Berkoff, once an infantryman in France, remembers, "Every gun mount I ever saw overseas had a little tag on it: Made in Buffalo, New York by Bell Aircraft. It made me proud. The girls in the plant put little notes in the mounts for us. It was nice.") Bell, now called Bell Aerospace and owned by Textron, still employs more than seven hundred people producing antennas, satellite equipment, and mobile aircraft-control systems. Over a thousand employees at Calspan, Comptek Research, Moog, and Sierra Research manufacture flight-inspection systems, missile components, and electronic warfare and aircraft testing systems.

Keeping industry alive and well in Buffalo has become the preoccupation of Dean Sallak of the Erie County Industrial Development Agency (ECIDA). Sallak has been living in the area since his father moved here from New York in 1948 to head the local branch of this American Tuberculosis Society. He is extremely knowledgeable about the confluence of forces that led to the decline of Buffalo's economy. "Buffalo has been killed by absentee ownership and managerialism," he says. In the early twentieth century, Sallak says, Buffalo's economy was managed by a powerful group of local owners with deep roots in the area and a deep commitment to it, captains of industry who contributed to and cared about the community, nurturing and sustaining cultural, educational, and recreational activities that enriched local life. Things changed after World War I, however, and local owners, threatened by the increasing competition of large national corporations, began to sell out and merge with larger companies headquartered in other cities. By the end of the 1950s the bulk of Buffalo's vast industrial economy had been sold to outside interests.

By 1960 Buffalo had become a "branch town" with factories in the hands of regional managers whose main concern, Sallak says, was "how to get through my three years in Buffalo and then move on." Local ownership continued to decline and by the end of the 1980s locally owned firms employed fewer than sixteen thousand workers. Fifty-five thousand people, meanwhile, were working for out-of-town companies. It is these companies, owned by outside capital, argues local economist David Perry, that were more than twice as likely to shut down or move out. Buffalo, Perry said, had fallen into a state of economic dependency.

There have been some significant efforts to reverse this trend. Sallak calls them "Buying Back Buffalo." In the mid-1980s local investors, aided by public agencies, began to regain control of the economy through a series of leveraged buyouts. One of the most successful was the buyout of the American Brass Company from Atlantic Richfield.

Early in 1985 the Western New York Economic Development Corporation (WNYEDC), a subsidiary of the state Urban Development Corporation, was approached by local businessman Randolph Marks, chairman of a recently formed company called Buffalo Brass. In the mid-1960s Marks had left IBM to create a company of his own, Computer Task Group, which became one of Buffalo's most successful locally owned public companies. Now he wanted to buy American Brass, and he wanted WNYEDC to help him. Founded by local industrialists in 1906 as Buffalo Copper and Brass, American Brass was located on one and a half acres in the Hertel-Military section of Black Rock. The company was one of the world's largest producers of high-quality, finished copper products. Over the years it had changed hands repeatedly, the ownership moving further away from Buffalo each time. In 1917 it was swallowed by American Brass, in 1924 by Anaconda, and finally in 1977 by Atlantic Richfield. Then, in 1985, with more than seven hundred employees and annual sales in excess of $300 million, Atlantic Richfield announced that it was going to sell its brass and copper division and concentrate instead on its vast petroleum businesses.

American Brass, Marks told WNYEDC, was sound, financially

stable, and, as a result of a recent $140 million modernization program, in excellent physical condition. And Atlantic Richfield was a cooperative seller, willing to provide a substantial bridge loan to local investors that would make the deal possible.

The price was $160 million—a steal, Marks thought. Some funds for the purchase, he said, would come from investment banks in Toronto and Los Angeles. He needed to strengthen his equity position, however, and for this he was turning to the public sector. In an unprecedented departure from their traditional role as mere lenders, the UDC, WNYEDC, and the ECIDA together took an equity position in the deal, which was completed by the end of 1985. As a result of this totally friendly and cooperative buyout, involving a close working partnership between Atlantic Richfield, the local investment/management group, and the public sector, one of the area's most significant companies was not only saved but transferred to owners based in Buffalo. American Brass has been extremely successful under its new management and by early 1989 profits were up 66 percent from 1987. The company exceeded its 1988 sales target by almost 30 percent and as a result, at the end of the year the company's workers received bonus checks averaging two thousand dollars. Unfortunately, in June 1990 American Brass was bought out by a Finnish holding company called Outokampo Group.

Advancing further still the role of public-sector economic development agencies, in 1988 the ECIDA was instrumental in the creation of CAPTEX, a private venture capital corporation designed to encourage risk-taking in the manufacturing area. Dominated for so long by heavy industry, Buffalo lacks the daring entrepreneurial tradition found in larger, more economically diverse communities like New York City and Toronto, which are constantly stimulated by a large immigrant population and a banking community used to risk-taking. ECIDA formed CAPTEX by combining $500,000 of its own with $5 million raised by local investors. It is one of the few venture capital companies in the country that combines public and private funds. By making loans to high-risk, start-up manufacturing ventures, CAPTEX is hoping to broaden the community's economic base while creating a new generation of locally rooted business leaders.

Some buybacks have occurred without the participation of the public sector. Such was the case with Graphic Controls, Inc., founded in the mid-1950s by George Clarkson and his two sons, who created the firm by consolidating six chart-paper and printing companies. Located in a million-square-foot office building designed between 1902 and 1904 as part of the Larkin Soap Company industrial complex, Graphic Controls prospered under the Clarksons and by the mid-1970s had become one of the world's leading manufacturers of industrial and medical chart paper (used, for example, in electrocardiogram machines). The company caught the eye of a multi-billion-dollar conglomerate, the Los Angeles *Times-Mirror* company, which bought Graphic Controls from the Clarksons in 1978 for more than $55 million. In 1986 a group of the company's senior managers bought it back and Graphic Controls, with annual sales of over $140 million and a workforce of more than six hundred, is once again owned and operated by people who live in the Buffalo area.

It was not so much local ownership as local economic strength that concerned the local economic development agencies. Sometimes, as with Freezer Queen, the deal they brokered resulted in the transfer of ownership of the company to foreign investors. Freezer Queen was founded by local entrepreneur Paul Snyder in 1958 to sell and distribute a line of frozen sandwich steaks. Changing hands several times, it was finally bought by United Foods of Tennessee in 1982. Under the new ownership, management drastically reduced costs and overhead while significantly increasing Freezer Queen's market share, sales, and cash flow. Indeed, when the parent company began to founder, Freezer Queen was its most profitable subsidiary. In an attempt to resolve its financial problems, United Foods decided that it had to either sell Freezer Queen or close it down to integrate its operations into the company's other operating units. In a "Notice to all Employees" dated January 15, 1985, United Foods announced its intention to close Freezer Queen and consolidate its operations into other distribution plants.

Meanwhile, James Crean PFC, an industrial holding company headquartered in Dublin, Ireland, with extensive holdings in the food and beverage sector, expressed interest in the Freezer Queen. Helped by a $10 million bridge loan from Marine Midland Bank as well as public-sector assistance, Crean came up with the $36.9 million purchase price. It had been a complicated deal. Crean was willing to commit substantial equity—$15 million—and Marine Midland was lending $10 million more. But there was a gap of $10.3 million. Enter a new brand of venture capitalists, leverage artists who were not wild, risk-taking bankers but public servants like Dean Sallak at ECIDA and Judith Kossey, now the president of WNYEDC. In a complex deal brokered in Albany and Buffalo, $1 million came from the federal government in the form of a no-interest loan due in twenty years; $2.5 million came from a low-interest loan from the UDC; and $7.2 million came from a combination of taxable and tax-exempt bonds from the State's Job Development Authority. Finally, the Buffalo and Erie County Regional Development Corporation provided a working capital loan of $750,000. By February 1986 the deal was complete. With more than five hundred workers and a backlog of orders, Freezer Queen, the beneficiary of a risk-taking Irish entrepreneur and a generous policy of public support for economic expansion, appears to be in Buffalo to stay.

Dunlop Tire is another case where the transfer of ownership from local to foreign owners allowed the company not only to survive, but to flourish. Within months of a 1985 leveraged buyout in which a local management team bought Dunlop "back" from the British conglomerate that owned it, the new, local owners sold the company to Sumitomo Rubber Industries, a division of the Japanese Sumitomo Group, the eighth largest industrial corporation in the world. Sumitomo immediately invested millions in Dunlop, both in operating capital and for modernization. The infusion of cash allowed a company that most certainly would have folded to succeed; Japanese ownership has also brought new energy, enthusiasm, and productivity—and resultant profit-ability—to the company. The change appears to have been accepted by management and workers alike. Hoping to dispel anxiety about the introduction of Japanese-style management, Sumitomo took a hundred Dunlop union and management people on a tour of its Japanese factories. Sumitomo's investment of over $20 million dollars in capital improvements and the introduction of a creative profit-sharing agreement persuaded the workers at Dunlop to accept a wage cut as well as dramatic, Japanese-style changes in work rules. While Dunlop's workers were content with the new owners, others were not. When the company hired non-union labor in December 1988 to work on a new building for the manufacture of a new line of radial truck tires, members of all eighteen Buffalo-area building trades unions, dressed in rented Japanese army uniforms, picketed at the site, demanding an end to foreign investment and the use of non-union labor.

The purchase of Freezer Queen and Dunlop by outsiders rejuvenated them—but the acquisiton of Pillsbury Flour by an English firm has had a questionable impact on that venerable industry in Buffalo's old First Ward. On the surface, not much has changed in Buffalo's flour business. Since the mid-1970s it has been on a steady, productive, and profitable path. For a while it had been tough. The opening of the St. Lawrence Seaway in 1959 robbed Buffalo of its international market while the deregulation of interstate freight rates in the late 1970s ate into domestic business. Since then employment and growth have been constant and today grain and flour are a strong and a stable element of the local economy. While there are not nearly as many mills as there used to be, four big ones—Pillsbury, General Mills, Cargill, and Con-Agra—with more than six hundred people working in them, mill close to a million pounds of flour a day for shipment throughout the southeastern United States. Cereal is produced here too—10 million cases annually, including Wheaties, Total, Cocoa Puffs, and Count Chocula. Business is good and steady. For years there has been little change in the number of people employed or the amount of flour milled, and little change is predicted for the future. The industry itself hasn't changed much either.

The *Henry Steinbrenner,* a mammoth grain ship built in 1909, is a floating warehouse that can hold 500,000 sixty-pound bushels of grain. It's fittings—a compass set in a highly polished bronze case mounted on a carved wooden stand, a glass-enclosed bronze chronometer—are, in the words of its captain, Robert Johnson, "just like in the movies." Its ambience, too, is out of the past, rich in the history and folklore of the American Midwest. Burly men, middle-aged and older, sit around a plastic-covered table in the ships' mess hall and are served by a beefy, bawdy, friendly, fifty-ish woman as much mother hen as waitress to the rough-cut, unshaven, coffee-drinking, cigar-smoking crewmen of the ship. From the beginning of April to the end of October the *Steinbrenner* makes twenty trips back and forth across the Great Lakes from Duluth to Buffalo. For three days, the gigantic ship, more than two football fields long, is tied up to the dock at the foot of Ganson Street in the old First Ward. There, nestled against the massive, soaring concrete grain elevators that inspired Mendelsohn, Le Corbusier, and other great architects of European modernism, tons of grain are emptied from the ship's gigantic hold in much the same way they were when the *Steinbrenner* was first put into service eighty years ago. Gradually and continuously from the time the ship docks to just before it leaves, six large aluminum shovels swing back and forth, attached to steel cables that run the long length of the hold, scooping and shoveling the grain into funnels that take it into and up the hulking elevators. It is a rhythmic, relentless, almost mesmerizing process, swishing, crunching, and sweeping in continuous motion. Then, gradually, as the grain in the hold dwindles and what remains can no longer be scooped up by machine, the men emerge and, in a ritual first performed a century and a half ago, sweep out by hand the residue until the last shred of the *Steinbrenner's* vast cargo has been emptied.

From the elevators the grain is dumped into large container trucks that are driven across the harbor to the mills. Buffalo's Pillsbury mill, at the corner of Michigan and Ganson Streets, still the largest flour mill in the world, has been in continuous use since 1898. While the plant has been increasingly modernized over the years, the milling process itself has always been highly mechanized. So little has it changed, in fact, that much of the milling equipment in the huge, labyrinthine historical structure was installed in the early 1920s, when the plant was taken over by Pillsbury in Minneapolis. But despite the quaint, unchanged activities in the daily life of the industry—the strong smell of roasting oats and cereal, the steady loading and unloading of grain—some developments, barely visible, were being set in motion.

By the mid-1980s Pillsbury had diversified. Fast-food and "family-style" restaurant chains—Burger Kings and Bennigans—had become the jewels in the company's crown. Flour products, for many years Pillsbury's staple, had dwindled in importance and by 1989 represented no more than 5 percent of the company's business. Meanwhile, the more than three hundred men and women from the old First Ward and South Buffalo who still worked there comprised the tiniest fraction of the company's hundreds of thousands of employees. In 1989, in one of the increasingly routine deals in which so many seemingly senseless economic conglomerations have been formed, Pillsbury was bought out by a British holding company, one of the largest in the world, for the staggering sum of more than $5 billion. Grand Metropolitan was the company's name. It owns hotels (the Intercontinental chain), liquor companies (Heublein, Sambucco Romano, Gilbey's Gin, and Watney's Breweries), and casinos, "gaming clubs," the company's glossy brochure calls them. "Grand Met" was attracted (barely) by the prospect of owning the old Pillsbury mill on Ganson and Michigan—it had its eyes on Burger King. The old mill and the people who worked there were just part of the package.

Dan Cunningham, the head of the Buffalo local of the International Longshoreman's Association, has spent his whole life here. Born and raised in the Ward, his family moved out only when Our Lady of Perpetual Help closed in 1969. Like many Irish-American kids of his generation, Cunningham went to Bishop Timon High School on McKinley Parkway where, he remembers, half the school was absent on those days in the early fall and late spring when the mammoth grain ships sat in the harbor and anyone could get temporary work unloading them. Cunningham stayed on with the industry after high school and soon became head of the ILA local. Working closely with his members, most of whom are friends and neighbors from the Ward and South Buffalo, as well as with the Pillsbury people in Minneapolis, Cunningham pushed through controversial work-rule changes that have led to an increase in both productivity and wages. He's proud of his role in keeping work for his local in Buffalo, but he is also concerned about what will happen to those who work on the docks and in Pillsbury's grain mills now that the company has been bought by Grand Met. In Grand Met's glossy annual report there are no heroic photographs of men working hard on the ships and docks of the Great Lakes cities of the American Midwest. Pictured instead are the glitzy, posh interiors of hotels and casinos and an artfully arranged montage of Burger King restaurants in cities all over the world.

While economist Perry's analysis of plants closed in the Buffalo area between 1965 and 1980 shows that companies with out-of-town headquarters were twice as likely as locally owned firms to move out, local ownership is obviously no guarantee against disinvestment, bad management or financial loss. Indeed, in many cases locally owned companies are undercapitalized and unable to make improvements or attract the best personnel. There are ways, in fact, that the transfer of even the best businesses to local ownership can hurt the community. Following their leveraged buy-out of American Brass and Graphic Controls, for example, the new owners were not in the same economic position to support the local community as former, outside owners had been. Both Atlantic Richfield and Times Mirror had been extremely good corporate citizens. At ARCO, for example, for every dollar contributed by an employee to the United Way, the company gave two. The local onwership now gives one. At Graphic Controls the old, outside owners offered a three-for-one match, while the new local owners make a one-for-one match. Highly leveraged local owners, regardless of their attachment to the community, simply cannot be as generous as larger, wealthier, outside-owned companies. In November 1989, management at the Tonawanda plant owned by General Motors, a particularly generous, not to mention extremely well-managed and highly profitable corporation, gave $50,000 to the City Mission to help pay for the construction of a haven for homeless women and children. (American Brass meanwhile donated the brass for a new roof on the old casino overlooking Delaware Park Lake.)

Though local ownership is often good for the community, what matters most is who the owners are, not where they live. One outside owner who has had a major impact in Buffalo is Robert G. Wilmers, an investment banker from New York City who in 1983 headed the investment group that bought M&T Bank, since the 1850s one of Buffalo's leading financial institutions. Intent on making M&T "America's best regional bank," Wilmers increased its role as a local lender and deposit-taker as well as its position in the local mortgage market. The year he bought M&T, the bank made $3.5 million and its lending limit was $20 million. By the end of 1988 it had increased its profits to $40 million and its lending limit to $60 million. From the time he arrived Wilmers was involved in the public life of his new community. So too were the many junior- and senior-level executives Wilmers had recruited to Buffalo. By the end of the decade Wilmers had become the city's dominant private sector power broker. Creative and progressive in his thinking, he had brought with him a broad and informed vision of a good community. As a result he was committed not only to improving the local economy but, as his diverse and active role within the community indicates, to its cultural life and, to a degree unusual for a business leader, to its public schools as well. Rarely had local ownership been as enlightened as Wilmers turned out to be.

Clearly, the behavior of many of Buffalo's local owners suggests that community life is strengthened and enhanced when local businesses are owned and operated by local people. Computer Task Group, founded and managed by two local men, has recently "adopted," by its generous support, the Academy of Math and Science, one of Buffalo's magnet schools. CTG's chairman, Randolph Marks, and its CEO, David Campbell, both born and raised in the Buffalo area are two of the community's most energetic and public-spirited businessmen.

Don Quinlan, the CEO at Graphic Controls, is similar. Born and raised in St. Thomas Aquinas parish on Abbott Road in South Buffalo, he attended School 72 on Lorraine Avenue, the old Buffalo Technical School on Clinton Street, and Buffalo State College, where he graduated in 1953. Quinlan married a woman from South Buffalo who had been a classmate of Gene Reville's at South Park High School; though four of Quinlan's seven children have moved out of the area, three have stayed. One of his sons recently bought a house in South Buffalo and two of his grandchildren are in the Buffalo public schools. Quinlan, like Campbell, is deeply concerned about the state of public education in Buffalo and has contributed his time and his company's resources to many projects, including the Board of Education's recent search for a new superintendent of schools.

Other local business owners have played varying roles in the public life of the community. One of the most active is Robert Rich, president of Rich Products Corporation. Starting as a small dairy company in the 1930s, Rich Products expanded rapidly in the mid-1960s, when a soybean-based coffee creamer called Coffee Rich became the company's flagship product. Rich Products now manufactures more than eight hundred frozen food items and employs more than six hundred people in Buffalo and six thousand throughout the United States and Canada. With annual sales of over $600 million, Rich Products is the fifth largest frozen food packager in the nation. The Rich family is extremely civic minded and is continuously expanding its role in community life. In 1987 the Riches acquired two local radio stations.

An earlier generation of philanthropists were involved primarily in the arts. The Goodyears and the Knoxes, for example, held bold modernist views that led to the creation of Buffalo's Albright-Knox Art Gallery, which holds one of the world's finest collections of modern art. The Rich family, however, has been more interested in sports, particularly their value as a promotional tool for the company. In 1973 the family made a deal with Erie County whereby the new football arena in Orchard Park would, for twenty-five annual contributions totalling fifty thousand dollars, be named Rich Stadium. Ten years later, Robert Rich, Jr., the oldest son of the company's founder, bought Buffalo's minor-league baseball team called the Bisons. Two years afterward he transformed them into a Triple A team. Rich became the driving force in the effort to build Pilot Field, downtown Buffalo's new baseball stadium, and is currently spearheading the effort to attract a major-league team.

By the end of the 1980s Rich had become something like a benign godfather to the city. He had a great deal of confidence in Buffalo but somehow came to the conclusion that it needed a new image—and that required a new name. In 1985 Rich suggested that Buffalo be called "New Buffalo," an idea he has since dropped. Buffalonians have always been ambivalent about the name of their city, never certain of its origins. With the exception of a handful of bison in the Buffalo Zoo, nobody could ever remember actually seeing a buffalo in or near the city. Perhaps, some thought, it was an Indian word. The consensus is, however, that the name derived from the French *beau fleuve*, "beautiful river."

While Rich has not succeeded in convincing people to change Buffalo's name, he has unquestionably been successful in creating a new and different image for the city, one based more on sports and recreation than industry and work. Baseball particularly resonates for Rich—not the haunting, sepia-toned view of baseball depicted in *The Natural,* a movie shot in Buffalo in 1982 in the city's now-demolished 1930s-era War Memorial stadium, but rather a spanking new, shiny, glossy vision of baseball, where the grass is always brilliantly green and the sky is always brilliantly blue. Rich relishes his role, and like successful businessmen in cities everywhere is convinced that if there was to be an economic revitalization in Buffalo he and other businesspeople will have to work together, doing what they can, often far more effectively than government intervention could ever hope to.

Jeremy Jacobs, who has played an important but far more private role in the life of the local economy, is the president of Delaware North Companies. With its 205 affiliates, it has annual sales in excess of a billion dollars. It is one of the largest privately owned companies in the country. The owner of the Boston Bruins and Boston Garden, Delaware North also holds the concession contracts for fourteen professional baseball, hockey, football, and basketball teams, including the Detroit Tigers, the Milwaukee Brewers, the St. Louis Cardinals, the Cincinnati Reds, the Chicago White Sox, the Boston Bruins, the Chicago Blackhawks, the Buffalo Sabres, the Boston Celtics, the Phoenix Suns, the Chicago Bulls, and the Cincinnati Bengals. Delaware North is also the nation's largest pari-mutuel company, owning two horse-racing tracks, three dog tracks, and two jai-alai frontons. Twenty-five percent of Delaware North's business is parking—it is one of the largest owners of public parking in the country—and in 1986 Jacobs bought the Dairy Farm company, a Hong Kong food service business with contracts at six airports in Asia.

Delaware North was started by Jeremy's father, Louis, a Jewish immigrant who came to Buffalo in the early 1920s. Jacobs started by selling popcorn in movie theaters but soon branched out to food concession stands in theaters and stadiums throughout the country. The company was alleged to have links to the underworld (in 1972 *Sports Illustrated* did a cover story on the company, then known as *Emprise,* in which Louis Jacobs was referred to as the "Godfather of Sports"), but under Jeremy's management the company has shed much of its questionable taint. Jacobs, meanwhile, is a good citizen—in 1983 he donated $2 million to endow two chairs at UB's School of Management, in return for which the university, over the objections of protesting students, named the school's new management building after the Jacobs family. An accomplished equestrian, Jacobs lives on a vast estate in exurban East Aurora, and maintains beautiful offices in a stately Victorian mansion on Delaware Avenue; he is one of the key players in the local economy.

Jacobs is Goldome Bank's largest single shareholder, and in early

1989 he made himself chairman of that rapidly failing savings and loan. In explaining the move Jacobs said he was guided as much by concerns over the bank's future as by its past, its "historic value," the role it has played in the community since "my father came to Buffalo as a little boy with his immigrant parents."

It had been Jacobs's concerns about economic conditions in general that had, several years earlier, led him and a handful of other business leaders to meet to discuss the situation. They began to meet informally during the early 1980s, when the news of Buffalo's decline—the closing of the steel mills, the folding of the *Courier Express*—was at its worst. Then, in 1985, eighteen members of the group began meeting on a more regular basis. Gradually word got out about what the *News* (whose publisher was a member) called the "Group of Eighteen." The group's purpose, the paper said, was to give a sense of direction to future plans for the development of the local economy. Drawn from leaders in business, banking, the press, and the service sector, the group was a blend of new outsiders (the president of UB, the publisher of the *News*, Wilmers from the M&T), a few local old boys (Jeremy Jacobs, Bob Rich, Seymour and Northrup Knox, and others), and several of Buffalo's new entrepreneurs, among them Campbell and Quinlan.

It was a dynamic, powerful, and highly influential group, and while its impact on community life was unclear, many felt threatened by what became referred to increasingly as the "Gang of Eighteen." Unions were among those most threatened. The president of the local AFL-CIO, at least, is usually included in all major gatherings of the Buffalo economic elite. But no union members participated in the meetings of the Eighteen. When asked what he would do if the Hyatt Hotel on Main Street went bankrupt, Mike Fitzpatrick, head of the Iron Workers local, one of the investors in the project, said that he would put the "Gang of Eighteen" in uniforms and have them work room service. Local politicians and university liberals alike complained, railing against the group as a kind of secret society that could make end-runs around the democratic process. While there was reason to be concerned about the concentration of power in the hands of people with no public accountability, the creation of the Group of Eighteen, despite its all-white, all-male elitist composition, was, it seemed, far more a response to a long-term vacuum in private-sector civic leadership than a threat to the existing order. Unlike other cities—smaller ones like Rochester, or larger ones like Cleveland, Pittsburgh, and Atlanta, let alone the great metropolitan giants—Buffalo had no huge locally owned companies to provide direction and purpose to the area's economic agenda. After

Houdaille Industries and National Gypsum left in the 1970s, none of the Fortune 500 companies had headquarters in Buffalo. As the center of business decision-making shifted away from Buffalo, the Group of Eighteen, like the public-sector development agencies, hoped to reverse the process, to try to return to local control some of the economic power that had been dribbling away over the years. As a result of the decline of local ownership in Buffalo and the consequent weakening of private-sector leadership, the decision-making arena had become increasingly dominated by politics and politicians.

While business leaders were trying to give more shape and direction to the local economy, Buffalo's location, which over years had worked for and against the city, once again provided glimmers of hope to a community eager for good news. In the middle of the nineteenth century, it was Buffalo's location at the end of the Great Lakes that turned a tiny lakefront settlement into the greatest trading port in the world, the place where wheat and lumber, livestock and iron, carried down the Great Lakes on huge steamers, converged and were unloaded, reloaded, and finally transported on the Erie Canal to points eastward and abroad. Being the crossroads for so many raw materials was the perfect precondition for the creation of a robust and diverse manufacturing economy. From the mines of the Mesabi Range in Minnesota came iron ore. When combined with coal railed in from Western Pennsylvania and worked by the muscles of thousands of Eastern European immigrants, the city's life-blood for the better part of a century emerged— a steel industry. But the westward movement of the market and the development of new transportation lines eventually undercut the advantages of Buffalo's location. Bypassed first by railroads and then by trucks, Buffalo's commercial stranglehold on the East gradually weakened. Then in 1959 came the construction of the St. Lawrence Seaway. Thirty years later, however, the hopes that were dashed in 1959 have been rekindled with the 1989 signing of the Canadian-American Free Trade Agreement. Located on the border of America's greatest trading partner, Buffalo could once again become a great port of transshipment, the primary point of entry for Canadian and American businesses eager to access one another's vast markets. Such a scenario is still little more than hype, but in the game of urban economic development, hype often generates action.

By the end of the 1980s the economy of the Buffalo area had achieved a degree of stability that none had thought possible at the disastrous beginning of the decade. Though the loss of more than forty thousand industrial jobs since the late 1970s devastated the community, the result has been a far more diversified and potentially healthier economy. With 18 percent of its workforce in industry in 1989 compared to over 30 percent ten years earlier, Buffalo's economy by the end of the 1980s was far more in line with state and national averages. Even with the decline in manufacturing there were still more than a hundred thousand people working in industry in the Buffalo area. Though more than twenty-five thousand of these jobs were in the highly cyclical automobile industry, the rest were in an increasingly broad and diverse range of smaller manufacturing companies.

Some of the success of the late 1980s was due to the efforts of local people, private business leaders as well as public-sector development agencies consciously struggling to shape and direct economic forces that long worked against the community. While the bold and innovative intervention of the UDC and the ECIDA saved hundreds of jobs at Freezer Queen and American Brass, there was something else at work— less tangible, far more difficult to quantify than jobs retained or created— that had by the end of the 1980s begun to infuse the community with a renewed sense of faith in and commitment to the local economy.

But for the tens of thousands of people who, as a result of background, experience, or education were not able to adapt to the changes in the Buffalo economy, the prospects of recovering from the nightmare of industrial decline seem increasingly dim. For them, all the talk of a "Buffalo Renaissance" is little more than talk.

15

CURTAIN UP: A NEW DOWNTOWN

"Curtain Up," the seasonal opening of Buffalo's theaters, has been celebrated every September since the early 1980s, when downtown's "Theater
District" was created. Buffalo had a long and envied theatrical tradition;
it once known, with Philadelphia and Boston, as one of the great
try-out towns in the country. All that died during the 1950s and 1960s
but things have been changing for the better since the early 1980s, when
Mayor Griffin made the Theater District a priority for development;
the cultural life of this struggling city of barely 325,000 soon focused
around it, and was rich, diverse, and very impressive in 1989. The Studio
Arena Theater, a nationally known institution located in a converted
burlesque house on Main at Tupper Street, featured Kaufman and Hart's
You Can't Take it With You. In small, black, box–type theaters—the
Cabaret in an old factory on Franklin Street, the Buffalo Ensemble
Theater in an old office building on Delaware and Chippewa—talented
actors offered exciting low-budget productions of offbeat plays, sometimes featuring the original work of local playwrights. At the intimate
Franklin Street Theater, the Theater of Youth staged a one-woman
musical about Billie Holiday called *Lady Day at Emerson's Bar and
Grill;* it played before sell-out crowds for weeks. A restored nineteenth-
century theater called the Kavinoky offered a revival of *The Glass Mena-
gerie.* The Pfeiffer Theater on Main Street played Sophocles' *Antigone*
while Hallwalls, an avant garde art gallery and entertainment center

offered what it called "The Twenty-Five Hour Show," featuring a day-long extravaganza of videos, music, performance art, and readings. Around the corner, the tiny Alleyway Theater premiered a brand-new Canadian play called *The Melville Boys* while down the street the cavernous Shea's Buffalo hosted the Greater Buffalo Opera Company's production of *Carousel.*

These nights in the Theater District were exciting and the Main Street area was packed with people enjoying downtown Buffalo in a way they hadn't for years.

If it bustles during Curtain Up, at Christmas Main Street is bright and cheerful. Throughout the early 1980s the area was a shambles, torn up during the more than five years it took to build the mile-long pedestrian mall that now joins the Theater District with the Marine Midland Tower. It is in the Theater District that the city's subway system emerges from its five-mile underground route and it is here that Buffalo's "new" downtown begins. Tubes of neon light in sculptural arrangements are bright and funky, making even some of the drab and desolate spaces look interesting from a distance. The subway helps too. The large stanchions that support its overhead power lines are lit brightly with red, white, and purple dangling lights, and the train cars clang by, casting flickering light on the dignified and powerful-looking early-twentieth-century office blocks that line Main Street. Occasionally, usually on weekends, Main Street is busy—when there is a play at Studio Arena, or a touring Broadway company performs at the Shea's Buffalo Theater, a glorious 1920s movie palace. But even then, with several thousand people in the theater or across the street at the new Market Arcade cineplex, the streets themselves—even in the heart of the Theater District—are strangely quiet. People come and go but nobody lingers. Main Street, interesting and attractive, well-lit and well-designed, resembles a stage set more than a city street, waiting for the actors to appear.

On the wall of Estelle and Bernie Siegel's drive-in car wash on Main Street in downtown Buffalo there is a large black-and-white photograph. Taken in 1960, it is a view of what is now the Theater District. Although downtown's share of the area's retail and commercial business had been dropping since the mid-1950s, Main Street was still busy then, lined with theaters, restaurants, stores, shops, nightclubs, and bars. A lively entertainment district, it was crowded with buses, cars, and above all, people—walking, huddling against the cold, smiling. Main Street was a street then, before it was allowed to die, before almost a billion dollars was spent trying to revive it—to little avail.

The Siegels have owned and opeated their car wash since the photo was taken. Estelle Siegel always called herself "the hostess, not the cashier." To Estelle, "My customers are individuals. I talk to them. They're not just dollar signs." For years she sat behind a glass-enclosed booth where she took the money and displayed colorful costume jewelry she made for decoration, not for sale. She sat there all day—"This is my cocoon, my little island, my inner sanctum"—while her husband hand-dried the cars as they rolled off the line. Estelle loved her job and enjoyed her cheerful and animated exchanges with her customers. Then, one day in late winter 1987, a young man held her up. He took out a gun and shot her through the lungs. For more than a year she stayed at home recuperating; when she came back, the glass around her booth was bulletproof. Estelle Siegel's story tells a lot about Main Street. So does the photo on the car-wash wall.

It could have been different—it would have been—if only they had put the new UB campus downtown, on the waterfront. It's not that they didn't try. For several years during the mid-1960s a coalition of downtown businesspeople, civic leaders, representatives of the African-American community, do-gooders, and general meddlers fought to convince Gov. Rockefeller that the new campus, housing one of the nation's best state universities, was just what Buffalo needed, that a half-billion-dollar campus with more than thirty thousand students, faculty, and staff, would turn the city around, ending forever the hemorrhaging that had been weakening downtown since the rise of the suburbs and the proliferation of the automobile in the late 1940s and early 1950s. But Rockefeller wasn't convinced and the new campus was built in the farthest reaches of suburban Amherst.

The decision to build the campus in Amherst has assumed somewhat mythical proportions in the life of the contemporary city, something that virtually everyone, in the conversations Buffalonians love to have about "what's wrong with Buffalo," agrees would have done more to revitalize downtown than any other project that has ever been on any planner's drawing board. And yet, somehow, for reasons that remain mysterious—the source of endless speculation, the topic of term papers, newspaper articles, and cocktail-party conversations almost twenty years later—the new campus was built not downtown, not on the waterfront, but in Amherst. Conspiracy theories abound. University trustees, say some, wanted it in Amherst because they owned tracts of undeveloped land there. Downtown businessmen, say others, didn't want it downtown, didn't want all those disshelved radical students hanging around. (It was, these same people argue, shortly after Erie County Community College, with its large minority student body, was given a downtown location in the early 1980s that merchants in the Main Place Mall had the benches removed from in front of their stores.) Others argue more rationally (though their critics disagree) that there simply was not enough room on the waterfront for the kind of massive, wide-open, "traditional" campus that the trustees of the state university system wanted to build.

The loss of the university to Amherst was a devastating blow to the city and nothing that has happended since has come close to making up for it. The spin-offs from the university have made Amherst the fastest growing area in the state, sought out by businesspeople and entrepreneurs in a seemingly endless cycle of growth prompted by easy access to the "brains" of the community.

Some tried to make the most of a loss that seemed to many irredeemable. Recognizing the importance of tying the body of the community to its brains, of linking the world of work to the world of ideas, a group of citizens consisting of politicians and downtown interests, in the wake of the decision to build the campus in Amherst, began to advocate the construction of a rapid transit line between the new campus and downtown Buffalo. From the beginning they had the highest hopes for the rapid transit system. After all, was it not the rapid transit system that had turned Toronto around?

Since the mid-1960s Buffalo has been living in the shadow of Toronto, exciting, dynamic, energetic, and just ninety miles to the north. Aided by Canada's liberal immigration policies and by the often violent Quebec national movement, which led many of Montreal's financial institutions to move, Toronto, with its glittering downtown skyline, its model waterfront development, its vital ethnic neighborhoods, its vibrant cultural life, and its state-of-the-art rapid transit system, has become one of the world's great urban centers. It wasn't always that way, some Buffalonians say, recalling days when Toronto was a "cow-town" and Torontonians came to Buffalo for weekend sprees of shopping, dining, and entertainment. But for years now it has been the reverse—Toronto is the irresistible lure for sophisticated Buffalonians hungry for the taste of a "real" city.

It is easier to deal with the tangible than with the more abstract and complex aspects of urban growth and development. In their eagerness to understand, if not duplicate "how Toronto did it," Buffalonians, adding to their ever-growing list of "if onlys," have focused on the city's rapid transit system. In the late 1960s and early 1970s the "if only" of a rapid transit system became a distinct possiblity.

The Toronto system, some said at the time, was a faulty model. It was begun in 1954, when population density was still high, long before the suburbs had begun to drain the city of its people. Buffalo, on the other hand, had lost so much of its population before construction of the line began in 1979 (it was originally supposed to have been completed in 1975) that, some argued, a rapid transit system for Buffalo had lost its rationale long before construction was even begun.

False too, some said, was the image of Buffalo's downtown presented in a 1971 report prepared by a Philadelphia consulting firm—tulips planted everywhere, elegant couples promenading up and down a covered pedestrian mall on Main Street, sitting in outdoor cafes as if they were on the boulevards of Paris. Where, people asked, were the bag ladies, the bums in their wool stocking caps, the clusters of teenagers, the wig shops, the stores selling knock-off designer sweatsuits and costume jewelry?

Despite the doubts, support for a Buffalo-Amherst rapid transit line grew. The twelve-mile transit line between Buffalo and Amherst, with its half-billion-dollar budget, its years of work for area construction workers, its promise of a revitalized downtown, seemed too good to all but the most skeptical. Virtually everyone in Buffalo supported the idea of a Buffalo-Amherst rapid transit line. When a state-of-the-art subway car went on display for a week in May 1973, more than thirty-two thousand people went downtown (in their cars) to see it. Rarely has a project received the kind of communitywide bipartisan support that the rapid transit enjoyed in Buffalo during the early 1970s. It was extraordinary: a $500 million windfall, the equivalent of $25 million in outside aide pouring into the city every year for twenty years, dumped in the lap of the community. The hype promised that the project would do for Buffalo what rapid transit had done for Toronto. Everyone wanted it—the downtown business community, the construction unions who were staring at close to ten years of full employment working on the line. Neighborhood groups, too, many of whom had vigorously opposed an original proposal for an overhead system, became its ardent supporters, once they were promised the line would not mar their streets but would be tunneled under Main Street. There were a few doubters, people who argued that rapid transit systems work only in high-density communities—places like New York City, London, Paris, and Toronto, where mass public transit is more convenient and comfortable than private transportation. These critics tweaked the management of the local transportation authority, claiming that for a fraction of the cost they could create the best public transportation system in the country simply by buying buses, vans, and jitneys. But because the rapid transit line had far more to do with jobs and with the illusion of urban revitalization than with the realities of public transportation, a trade-in of rapid transit funds for other, more effective transportation uses was never seriously considered. And, as long as someone else was paying (the federal government and the state), there was no reason, it seemed, not to build the subway.

And so, on April 2, 1979, after more than ten years of delay and a decade of changes that left the line, now officially called the Light Rail Rapid Transit line, a mere shadow of the ambitious, city-suburban system that had been originally planned, construction began. The final plans were humble and much reduced from those envisioned in the early 1970s. The federal Urban Mass Transit Authority refused to fund the full line when construction costs, as a result of inflation and the switch to tunneling, doubled. The final plans called for a line that ran 6.4 miles up and down Main Street instead of the 12.7-mile line originally projected between Amherst and downtown.

Construction of the line proceeded apace for more than six years and Main Street was inaccessible to pedestrian and vehicular traffic for the bulk of that time. When the system finally opened, Main Street's retail core, whose revitalization was the primary purpose of the project, had been all but destroyed by the long, forced hibernation. The central business district the new subway was intended to save, the strip that gave the photograph in the Siegel's car wash so much life and vitality, was gone.

By the mid-1980s the suburbs in general and Amherst in particular had become the preferred place for doing business in the Buffalo metropolitan area. The decision to build UB's new campus in Amherst had made this inevitable. By the end of the 1980s Amherst, with close to 120,000 residents, had become a major corporate center, the site of shopping malls and countless residential developments—condominiums and co-ops, townhouses and high-rise apartment buildings, high-priced residential communities with preposterous and pretentious names like Woodstream Farms and Farm House Estates—as well as industrial parks, hotels, medical centers, and vast, wooded corporate complexes. "It's natural that so much development should occur here," said an Amherst offical proudly in 1987. "Companies tell us they need to be near the university, creating jobs for the twenty-first century." As for the downtown area, said architect David Stieglitz, "It's like asking a body to function without its brain. It can do it, but not for very long."

In addition to suburbanization, downtown renewal was also ham-

pered during the early 1970s by the debate over city planning in general
and downtown revitalization in particular. It became increasingly mired
in bitter conflicts between downtown interests and neighborhood groups.
Given the emphasis that federal community-development programs
placed on citizen participation, it was difficult for the downtown business
community to dominate the urban-renewal agenda. Downtowners, particularly downtown businessmen, the bankers responsible for the creation of the Main Place Mall, the M&T Plaza, and the Marine Midland
Tower, had become suspect as policymakers and politicians suddenly
discovered "the neighborhood."

The conflict between neighborhood and downtown that characterized the 1970s reached a head during the controversy over construction
of a new downtown convention center. As suburban shopping centers
continued to undermine downtown's retail function, planners began to
conceive of a downtown revitalization driven by services catering to
businesspeople and other out-of-town visitors. Mayor Sedita was an
ardent advocate of downtown renewal. Afraid that it would undermine
his efforts to concentrate development efforts downtown, Sedita in 1972
vetoed a Common Council resolution that the City Planning Board,
appointed by the mayor, be replaced with an elected one. He was convinced that a convention center was critical to downtown's survival,
and included an $11 million item for the construction of the facility
in his 1972–73 capital budget. Heady with the rhetoric of the neighborhood movement, the Common Council was critical of the proposal,
insisting that what the people of the city needed was better schools
and services, not a downtown convention center. The mayor strongly
disagreed, arguing that strong neighborhoods depend on a strong and
vibrant downtown. "The downtown area," he said, "is the only place
in the community where additional tax base can be generated so that
the city can continue to provide services. We will have less tax resources
if we don't do something for downtwn. This is the history of cities
that fought decay and won." The *Evening News,* which had just moved
to its brand-new building near the foot of Main Street, agreed, arguing
that that "collapse of downtown will lead to the collapse of neighborhoods." So too did the *Courier Express,* which insisted that the convention center was "a community must."

A lot of Buffalonians disagreed. In late 1972 a coalition of neighborhood groups, led by veterans of Saul Alinsky's Chicago-based Industrial Areas Foundation, formed the Alliance of Consumers and Tax-
payers. ACT opposed the use of public funds for the construction of
the convention center. Much to the shock and anger of Sedita and

the rest of the downtown establishment—the bankers, merchants, hotel owners, and others intrigued by the possibilities of a convention center in the heart of downtown—ACT was successful in securing enough signatures to place the question before voters in a referendum to be held in November 1973.

Throughout the fall the debate raged, a fascinating dialogue between two opposing views of community development, two notions of urban life deeply rooted in the city's nineteenth-century heritage. For downtowners, the convention center was a lynchpin in a planned revitalization of the central business district, a generator of jobs as well as a lever for future development of hotels, office buildings, and even apartment buildings. ACT, on the other hand, rooted in the ideology of the neighborhood movement and convinced that neighborhood residential and commercial revitalization was paramount, seemed unconcerned that downtown was dying. Perversely insisting that somehow the neighborhoods could survive without a strong downtown core, ACT campaigned vigorously and aggressively against the convention center. By casting construction of the convention center in terms that made the "downtown establishment" the issue, ACT successfully appealed to the class-consciousness of Buffalo's white working-class neighborhoods. Said one irate woman about the convention center, "Can I eat there? Can I dress up and go dancing there? Buy lingerie? See a movie? Make a day of it? Get a job and work in it? Walk by it safely at night?" With the exception of the African-American council districts on the East Side (where the development of downtown as a service center offered the promise of jobs) and the middle-class Delaware District, the convention-center proposal was defeated soundly in every section in the city.

In 1973 the Convention Center was built anyway, using county instead of city money. It is an architectural monstrosity in the heart of downtown Buffalo, blatantly violating Joseph Ellicott's eminently workable, early-nineteenth-century street pattern and destroying the surrounding environment, particularly on the Pearl Street side, where a blank, poured-concrete wall has made any street life permanently impossible. In addition, the facility has been a financial dud.

Continued stagnation followed completion of the Convention Center. Hampered by weak leadership, torn apart by the ongoing struggle between downtown and the neighborhoods, and plagued by the fiscal crisis of the mid-1970s, public and private efforts to revitalize downtown came to a complete and sudden halt. Everyone seemed to give up on downtown—except the preservationists.

For years they had watched in horror as one after another of Buffalo's magnificent buildings were demolished. They had never forgotten the destruction of Frank Lloyd Wright's world-renowed Larkin Adminis-tration Building on Seneca Street in downtown Buffalo. The *Evening News* was saddened by the rubble-strewn sight, writing in 1949 that "The city allows the Larkin Building to go to pieces day by day. The area from street to street is carpeted with broken bricks, sticks, rubbish, and waste. The parallel side streets are even more cluttered with fallen plaster, masonry, and rubble. Groups of urchins have fun hurling brick-bats and plaster chunks at one another and at visitors to the struc-ture. . . ." Some, like Councilman Joseph Dudzick, had tried to save the building and in 1950 introduced a resolution in the Common Council recommending that the city pay for its improvement. "The building could be altered to house a basketball and tennis court, gymnasium equip-ment, and facilities for other types of recreation," he said. The resolution and other, later rescue efforts were defeated. In February 1950, despite editorials in newspapers throughout the country, demolition began. "Demolition," wrote Jack Quinan, a historian who had documented the history of the building, "is, after all, a drastic critical comment."

Throughout the 1950s and 1960s urban renewal had eviscerated the hearts of cities thoughout the country. But by the end of the 1960s the tide had begun to turn and in cities everywhere public officials and developers had begun to think about the preservation and renovation of old buildings instead of their demolition. As late as 1969, however, Buffalo was too busy tearing down to stop and think about preserva-tion. An article in the *Evening News* in late 1969, called "The Wreckers," told the story in a way it never intended. "In Buffalo today we watch as our builders fashion a new city. On every side giant new buildings replace the old city we knew. We honor our builders. We should honor our wreckers who made it possible. For in American cities today you cannot build unless you destroy." The writer of this unintentional parody of serious reporting proceeded to interview those she saw as the heroes of this grand reconstruction of tired old Buffalo.

One was Edward E. Gabriel, president of Niagara Wrecking and Lumber Company. Gabriel, the reporter wrote, "figures that he has torn down about 25 percent of the downtown area. He has vanquished such landmarks as the old AM&A's store, the old Erie County Savings Bank, and the Hotel Buffalo, the vanguard of the Statler chain, not to mention the old Family Theater, Fort Porter, and the stockyards." Demolition had for Gabriel become an article of faith, a world view. "Urban renewal is true," he said. "It reflects man's progress in life. We have to be rid of the old to build the new." The reporter asked Gabriel about "the toughest building he had wrecked." Gabriel answered "You can't tell by looking at them. The old Erie County Bank was built like a fortress. But it wasn't as tough as parts of AM&A's. One of the toughest little buildings was an old brewery at Virginia and Washington. The concrete floors were fourteen inches thick: we let the wrecking ball drop and it would bounce back at us."

Another hero in the battle against anachronism was Nelson Reiman, president of Reiman Wreckers. "It's making progress for the city," he told the *News*. "Some of his most interesting projects," said the article, "were the Lehigh Valley Railroad station, the Washington Market, the Vienna Theater, not to mention the Larkin building designed by Frank Lloyd Wright. Reiman says, 'The Larkin Building was the toughest. The floor slabs—twenty-by-twenty-foot pices of Median stone—were tied together with rods. It was like a barrel held together with staves. There were ten stories and we had to take all but the last three down by hand. It took four months.' "

James Williams of Buffalo Demolition told the *News*, "We can do a hundred homes a month now. Today you can put an old house on the ground in a couple of minutes; one pass at it and that's it. It takes about four hours to haul it away." The reporter thrilled to such efficiency. She ended her paean to the new Buffalo stirringly. "The end of this dramatic story cannot be written yet," she wrote, "if indeed there is an end to a city's upreach. . . . So, here's to the sunlight on the top of Buffalo's highest building of the future and the view from it, windows of a city which has become a metropolis."

It is difficult, twenty years later, to believe that anyone would laud "demolishing the environment that has shaped the lives of five generations of Buffalonians." The absence of any response by newspaper readers suggests that Buffalonians accepted the consequences of what they were told was "urban renewal." That this would have been the case ten or even five years before might have been understandable. But by 1969, the kind of wholesale, blockbuster demolition that the *News* enthusiastically described had begun to go out of style. People in cities all over the Western world had begun to think about preserving community heritage. In Buffalo, too, beginning in early 1970, there emerged a small but devoted group of citizens committed to the preservation of the city's wonderful, architecturally significant buildings.

One of these was the Guaranty Building, built by Louis Sullivan in 1896 on Church and Pearl Streets in downtown Buffalo. With its use of structural steel, its terra-cotta exterior, and its bold, vertical emphasis, the Guaranty is an internationally recognized masterpiece of modern architecture. By the early 1970s, however, the "Prudential Building," as many people in Buffalo called it, after the name on the sign that had been on the building for years, had gone to seed. The building had long been neglected, and its tenants were leaving in droves, lured from such old office buildings to the newer and jazzier high-rises—the M&T, the Marine, and the Main Place towers—that urban renewal had helped to build on Main Street.

Soon the Guaranty's owners defaulted on mortgage and tax payments. After a nearly disastrous fire in 1977, the owners' main creditor, a bank in Oklahoma, threatened to tear the Guaranty down. Local preservationists tried to save the building. Their leader, architect John Randall, had come to Buffalo in 1973 specifically to save the Guaranty. He had led a similar struggle to save St. Louis's Wainright Building, another Sullivan masterpiece. Randall's ardor for the Guaranty was persuasive and within months of the fire he had convinced the bank not only to delay demolition but to make him the building's manager. Singlehandedly at first, virtually living in the building that had been almost destroyed by decay and thoughtless, inappropriate remodeling, Randall went to work. He salvaged doorknobs and fixtures, removed dropped celings, revealed long-hidden steel staircases, and saved Sullivan's striking terra cotta.

Following a visit in late 1977, Sen. Patrick Moynihan became an ardent advocate of the building's preservation and by 1981 a creatively packaged financial deal was arranged to buy the building. Combining a federal grant of $2.4 million, a $6 million low-interest loan from the Erie County Industrial Development Agency, and tax shelters for a group of limited partners who invested $4 million, the building was bought in 1981. Under its new owners, one from Cleveland, the other from Connecticut, the Guaranty was carefully, lovingly, and perfectly restored. Following a celebratory reopening in December 1983, a reporter for the *News* described what he called the "poetry" of the building. "The rich ornaments of the Guaranty are more striking than most embellishments. An attentive eye sees in them images of plant life, flowers, seeds, burgeoning vines and branches." Sen. Moynihan was more to the point. It was clear, he said, that historic preservation in Buffalo had become a political force to be reckoned with. Speaking of the Guaranty, he said, "This is what America gave to the world and Buffalo chose to preserve it."

While the efforts to preserve and readapt the Guaranty Building injected a degree of faith and enthusiasm into the general efforts to revitalize downtown, it was the election of Jimmy Griffin as mayor in 1977 that was the crucial turning point. Despite his close identification with Irish South Buffalo and a campaign that smacked of blue-collar, urban populism, it was clear from the beginning that Griffin would be a persuasive and forceful advocate of downtown renewal. The new mayor was eager to regain the power City Hall had lost to the neighborhoods during the 1970s. He began an aggressive program of downtown revitalization that was not only good public policy but increasingly good politics too. Griffin's commitment to downtown resulted in the creation of a host of new and imaginative approaches to revitalization, innovative kinds of public-private partnership that completely changed the urban development process in Buffalo.

The late 1970s were exciting days for downtown revitalization. Everyone in the urban-renewal business was talking about the Harbour Front project in Baltimore and the Quincy Market development in Boston, and how the American Cities Corporation, working with flexible and creative local governments, had remade the downtown sections of those presumably hopeless old cities of the "Rust Belt." The Carter administration, extremely generous to the cities, was pouring hundreds of millions of dollars in block grant money into them. Now, added to the block grants was a new program that handed out "Urban Development Action Grants." Devised by Robert Embry, an undersecretary at the Department of Housing and Urban Development, UDAGs rewrote the rules that had for years defined the relationship between the public and private sectors in the development of the nation's downtowns. Since the Housing Act of 1949 the role of local governments in urban renewal had been limited to land-acquisition and demolition. As a result of federal and local government largesse, private developers in cities throughout the country had received as gifts millions of acres of prime downtown land on which to build their projects. It was through such a partnership that Buffalo's mammoth urban renewal projects of the late 1960s and early 1970s—the M&T Plaza, the Marine Midland Tower, the Main Place Mall, and the Erie County Savings Bank—were built. By the late 1970s, however, despite the fact that more than $100 million in private funding had been poured into these projects, confidence in the country's downtowns had eroded almost beyond repair.

Part of the problem was design. The downtown renewal of the late 1960s and early 1970s produced boring and banal buildings. The façade of the M&T, like the Erie County Savings Bank on the other side of Main Street, is bland and faceless. Both buildings are cookie-cutter, 1960s-style urban-renewal banks, with no reference to either local architecture or the local community. Buildings just like them were built in countless downtowns in countless cities thoughout the nation during what surely will be considered years when the quality of American architecture and urban design was at its nadir. Worst of all is the Marine Midland Tower. The grotesque giganticism of this massive structure (designed by a Buffalo native, Gordon Bunshaft) recalls far more the designs of dictators than it does the context, environment, and community in which it is located. Unlike the M&T building, which, to its credit and our benefit, reaches out to the street in a way that makes possible the creation of one of the more pleasant public spaces in Buffalo, the Marine Tower, like the Convention Center, completely destroys the street.

Bad design hurt downtown, but the urban traumas of the mid-1970s killed it: the fiscal crisis, the quickening collapse of the industrial economy, and the relentless growth of Buffalo's suburbs. These trends overwhelmed the massive infusion of millions of public urban renewal dollars. Still more public action, it seemed, was needed. Thus, Urban Development Action Grants. The UDAG program taught city governments the concept of leverage—the investment of public money in such a way that it multiplies itself in private investment. By the early 1980s the cities themselves were assuming an increasingly entrepreneurial role in the urban development process.

A political outsider with ties to none of the old-line establishment, Mayor Griffin was willing to try a new approach to the problems of downtown revitalization. Notwithstanding a strong penchant for cronyism, Griffin was willing to appoint creative, dynamic, and politically independent people to lead the Office of Community Development, which was responsible for downtown revitalization. One of these people was Larry Quinn.

Raised in Amherst and a graduate of Canisius High School, Quinn came back to Buffalo following his graduation from Notre Dame in 1974. The bottom was falling out of the economy in those days. Bethlehem, everyone knew, was on its last legs and Buffalo's only remaining Fortune 500 companies—Houdaille Industries and National Gypsum—were moving out of the city. In the midst of this crisis, Quinn went to work at the Erie County Industrial Development Agency. Encouraged by the stimulative renewal policies of the Carter administration, the ECIDA had begun to emerge as an effective engine of economic development. It was here that Quinn was introduced to the UDAG program. In 1978 he moved to City Hall and began doing economic development work for Griffin.

Quinn brought the youth, energy, and creativity usually associated with the entrepreneuerial world of the private sector to City Hall. The ninth-floor office of the Department of Community Development became an exciting incubator of development ideas and projects. Casting the city in a brand new role and acting sometimes as broker, sometimes as banker, sometimes as general partner, sometimes as general contractor, Quinn engineered a series of stunning and improbably development deals that not only changed the face of downtown Buffalo but redefined the public role in the development process. The city became the chief catalyst of downtown development, creating and implementing complex deals that brought together a combination of low-interest public loans, grants, union pension-fund investment, and private equity to remake downtown Buffalo.

The first project was a downtown hotel. Using $4 million in low-interest money lent by the city under the UDAG program, San Francisco developer Clement Chen built a Hilton on the waterfront. The completion in 1980 of the first hotel to be built in the city in over fifty years legitimized the city's role as an equal partner with developers in downtown projects. Griffin now shifted his attention to another section of Main Street, the intersection with Genesee Street. Located there since 1902 was the headquarters of the Buffalo Savings Bank. In 1979 the bank had brought in Ross Kenzie as president. A leading officer at Merrill Lynch, the giant stock brokerage, Kenzie saw Buffalo as a place he would be able to exercise "serious" power. Although Kenzie lived in the suburbs, the headquarters of his bank, an imposing, turn-of-the-century building topped by a sparkling gold-leaf dome, was downtown. He appeared to be intrigued by the notion of playing Donald Trump to Jimmy Griffin's Ed Koch, and wanted not only to stay at Main and Genesee but to grow and expand there too. These were the early, heady days of deregulation and the bank business was booming. With a series of bold acquisitions and a name change to "Goldome," in only a few years Kenzie had turned the bank into one of the largest savings institutions in the nation.

Kenzie, known increasingly as "Boss Ross," had big plans for his Main Street headquarters. He began working with Griffin and Quinn to create a plan for the renewal of both sides of the Main Street corridor at Genesee. The project was many-faceted, consisting of a new headquarters for Goldome on one side of the street, and on the other, a new Hyatt Hotel and a new headquarters for the Liberty Bank. The plan was the most elaborate and, at over $123 million, the most expensive ever considered for downtown Buffalo. Only the most adroit fiscal legerdemain could pull it off.

The Hilton project had been a landmark, one of the first UDAGs in the country. It was risky, untried business, with the city lending the developer $4 million at 1 percent interest. The deal had worked, though.

The hotel was built and the payments on the loan were recycled, used to begin the construction of new, owner-occupied homes on the city's East Side. The mayor was pleased and described the role the city was willing to play in the redevelopment process in entrepreneurial terms. "As long as it is not a free lunch we'll gamble some of our own money if they gamble some of theirs," he said of the city's private sector partners.

The city would need a lot more than $4 million for the Main-Genesee project, however. Everyone had to kick in. Because the project would stimulate and sustain the Main Street rapid transit line, Buffalo's congressional delegation prevailed upon the Urban Mass Transit Authority to provide $3 million for land acquisition, tenant relocation, and demolition. Among the Main Street buildings to be torn down was an Art Moderne masterpiece, the W. T. Grant store. HUD provided $16.5 million in the form of a low-interest UDAG. New York State signed up too, granting the city $7.5 million to build a new parking ramp across from the planned Hyatt. Then came equity from the banks, Goldome and Norstar (like the old Buffalo Savings Bank name, "Liberty" no longer suited new management), and from Hyatt.

The hotel was the most difficult and complex part of the deal. By 1980 local developer Sergio Fornasiero had secured a commitment of $2 million from Hyatt for the construction of a new hotel on the corner of Main and Genesee. By the end of the year, however, the deal was unraveling, a victim of the deadly mix of politics, personalities, and large sums of money. Fornasiero, one of the first and only local people willing to back the Main-Genesee project, suddenly pulled out of the deal. So did the Hyatt, which now told Quinn that it was willing to manage the hotel but not own it. With the whole showcase project suddenly on the line, Quinn scrambled for new local investors. Paul Snyder, founder of the Freezer Queen Company, a free-wheeling, risk-taking, first-generation entrepreneur, showed an interest.

Quinn's proposed package was complex and extremely inventive— $3.5 million from accrued interest earned from a $19-million loan; $8 million in low-interest UDAG money with a repayment schedule tied to hotel revenues; $19 million in bonds marketed by the Erie County Industrial Development Agency, bought by local banks (the participation of the ECIDA not only raised huge sums of money for the project but exempted Snyder and the other owners from property taxes); finally, $8.5 million from Snyder and his partners. And then, just as the deal looked all sewn up, Snyder and company began to hedge. Quinn suddenly found himself $4 million short.

Many Buffalonians blame unions for the collapse of the city's economy, but they should know that it was union money that came to the rescue of the Hyatt Hotel project. Quinn went to see Mike Fitzpatrick, president of the Western New York District Council of the Iron Workers. Quinn had heard Fitzpatrick was interested in making "a social investment." They struck a bargain: Quinn arranged to have Fitzpatrick lend Snyder union pension funds at below-market interest rates in return for a promise that only union labor would be used to build the hotel. It was a risky idea, but it paid off.

The opening of the Hyatt Hotel in February 1984 was a critical moment in the effort to revitalize Main Street. A locally conceived, initiated, and executed project, the hotel was far better for having been built by Snyder and the Iron Workers than if it had been built by Hyatt. Convinced that the Genesee Building, a sixty-year-old office building on the corner of Main and Genesee, would have to go, Hyatt had outraged local preservationists. Snyder was willing to consider rehabilitating the Genesee. Stung by charges years before that he had been insensitive to local sentiment when he sold the Buffalo Braves, a professional basketball team, to out-of-towners, Snyder, admittedly under intense pressure from the preservationists, ended up directing his architects to try to save the Genesee Building. They did, and today Buffalo's Hyatt hotel is a jewel on Main Street, ingeniously integrating old and new in one of the most successful adaptive reuses anywhere.

Meanwhile, the growth of the suburbs as a competeting commercial and retail center continued unabated. Shopping malls had been killing off neighborhood commercial streets since the end of the 1950s. The impact on downtown was relentless and not even the millions of public dollars could stem the damage. In 1981 the gargantuan McKinley Mall was completed in Hamburg, due south of downtown Buffalo. Plans were already in the works for an even bigger mall, the Galleria, in Cheektowaga to the east. And, notwithstanding the city's efforts to create the Theater District on Main Street, UB announced in 1981 that it planned to build an arts center with a brand-new theater on the Amherst Campus. In late 1980 Larry Quinn desperately appealed to Erie County Executive Ned Regan to create a "rational, balanced growth policy" for the entire metropolitan area.

What made the growth of Amherst so disturbing was that much of it was being aided and abetted by quasi-public agencies like the Amherst Industrial Development Agency. It is understandable that downtown, desperately struggling against the forces of economic and demographic decline, should use public power and public funds to generate and leverage private development—but why should a booming community like

Amherst, whose growth and development was feeding on the decaying body of downtown, do the same? It was greedy, unfair, and, most significantly, stupid. Nevertheless, throughout the 1980s, as Buffalo struggled against the odds to stay alive, the Town of Amherst and the AIDA dangled incentives that lured business and industry to the town at the fastest rate of any municipality in the sate.

Amherst's growth led not only to the unprecendented destruction of the environment, but to an unnecessary climate of business uncertainty within Amherst itself. Real-estate development has occurred so quickly and so shortsightedly in Amherst that brand-new malls and plazas are filled one year and empty the next as newer, bigger, and more state-of-the-art malls and plazas built nearby lure frightened retail tenants from one place to the next. Amherst became so strangled by unplanned, excessive development that by the end of the 1980s residents finally began to demand a more rational approach to growth.

In downtown Buffalo, city planners continued to search for one. Main Street remained the focus. Following a trend begun in the late 1960s, planners in City Hall at the Niagara Frontier Transportation Authority decided that the lower section of Main Street would become a pedestrian mall, free of all traffic except the rapid transit line, which emerged from underground at Tupper Street. With the Marine Tower at the south end and the Goldome-Hyatt-Norstar complex in the middle, Main Street would once again become the focal point of downtown Buffalo. Needed to anchor the Main Street pedestrian mall at its northern end was what some people were calling a "Theater District."

The moving force behind the Theater District project was Harold Cohen, from 1974 to 1984 the dean of the School of Architecture and Environmental Design at UB. Under the leadership of Cohen the School of Architecture had become one of the more exciting idea-incubators in Buffalo. It had achieved some cachet for having been one of the few departments at UB that did not abandon the city. At the time it occupied one of Buffalo's great industrial buildings, a sleek, turn-of-the-century steel and glass factory on Main Street known as Bethune Hall; the school became an energetic laboratory of city-oriented design projects. Cohen was a strong and dynamic leader who had been able to attract to the school people like Reynhar Banham, Edward Logue, Buckminster Fuller, and other internationally known designers, planners, philosophers, and tinkerers. It was Cohen's inspiration that led Quinn to commission a design for the Theater District. Cohen's response, "The Entertainment District Project Report," called for the creation of a Main Street "Entertainment District." When anchored by a mixture of office, commercial, and residential uses, the report declared, the "Entertainment District" could become "one of the biggest, most innovative, and exciting urban development efforts in the United States."

In the old days, of course, long before the view in the photograph at Siegel's car wash, there had always been a theater district. It was so obvious that nobody called it that. In 1959, the year the Siegels' photograph was taken, Main Street was still bustling, lined with movie theaters. In October of that year the Shea's Buffalo featured *It Started with a Kiss* with Glenn Ford and Debbie Reynolds. Up the street at the Teck, Frank Sinatra and Edward G. Robinson starred in *A Hole in the Head.* The May Britt and Curt Jurgens remake of *Blue Angel* was at the Palace, Richard Burton and Claire Bloom were appearing at the Center in *Look Back in Anger,* Sophia Loren and Tab Hunter were at the Paramount in *That Kind of Woman,* and Vincent Price played in *The Bat* at the Lafayette. No one had to be told that the area where almost a dozen theaters did round-the-clock business on a few densely packed blocks of Main Street was the theater district.

By the time Harold Cohen arrived in Buffalo, there was nothing left. The city had taken ownership of Shea's Buffalo for back taxes. The buildings adjoining it and across Main Street were either boarded up or housing down-in-the-mouth retail tenants trying to hang on. Cohen's charge was to bring them back. The focal point of the Theater District would be the group of historic late-nineteenth- and early-twentieth-century buildings that lined both sides of Main Street between Tupper and Chippewa. Shea's Buffalo was on this block. A magnificent, spacious, incredibly ornate 1920s movie palace with cantilevered balconies and a "Mighty Wurlitzer" that knocked the socks off of generations of Buffalonians, Shea's had just been saved from demolition by the tenacious efforts of a group of preservationists called the Friends of Shea's. Across Main Street from Shea's is the Market Arcade, built in 1892. Intimate in scale, this indoor street was modeled on London's Burlington Arcade. Boarded up and vacant for years, Cohen's plan imagined that the arcade, Shea's, and the turn-of-the-century commercial buildings adjacent to them would be the heart of the new Theater District. The concept was daring, "chutzpadick," said Cohen, who spouted Yiddish freely to both his high-toned following at the School of Architecture and the mayor from South Buffalo. Abandoned by developers, torn up by the seemingly endless chaos caused by the construction of the above-ground rapid transit line, Main Street was a shambles, a sea of mud filled with islands of debris. Cohen's vision seemed preposterous.

But he was ambitious and energetic. A Jew from New York who

privately complained that Buffalo's real problem was that there were "not enough Jews or Jesuits" here, Cohen, speaking with a Jackie Mason-like lilt and intonation, brought intellectual energy and commitment to a project that few had much interest in. For years the university had turned its back on downtown. Now Cohen, who had come to Buffalo from the University of Illinois just three years earlier, was involving his department in one of the most ambitious planning projects the city had undertaken in years. Larry Quinn, meanwhile, was working on the concept of a "Theater Place," a mixed-use residential, commercial, and office development for the two buildings next to the Shea's Theater. He had talked about it to a group of design students at the School of Architecture. The Common Council, he said, had allocated more than $3 million to rehabilitate the two buildings. The problem, Quinn confessed, was that he had no tenant.

A student named Fred Fadel was in the audience listening to Quinn that afternoon, and he did have a tenant. Born and raised in Niagara Falls, Fadel had come to Buffalo in the late 1960s to go to UB. By 1979 he was working as a bartender at the Tralfamadore, a small, funky, smoky, crowded, New York–style jazz club located on Main Street a few miles from UB. The club featured jazz as good as any west of the Hudson, but it had a seating capacity of only two hundred. Ed Lawson, the owner of the "Tralf" and jazz-man par excellence, was looking for a bigger room. Fadel, who was studying planning and urban design at the School of Architecture, immediately approached Lawson about moving the Tralf to Theater Place. Lawson liked the idea, excited about the possibility of bringing jazz back to downtown Buffalo. So did Quinn. The problem was money.

There were other problems too, at least as far as the mayor was concerned. Just a block up Main from the recently renovated Studio Arena Theater was a very popular, sometimes rowdy gay bar known as City Lights. In September 1983 the owners announced their intention to move to new and larger quarters in the Theater District. Soon after, the bar was raided by the Buffalo police. Calling the City Lights clientele "sexual deviates" and "fruits," Mayor Griffin announced his intention to try to deny the bar a liquor license. Refusing to apologize for his comments, Griffin said boastfully, "Where I lived in South Buffalo as a kid we always referred to them as faggots and fruits." Some thought Griffin was wrong to try to prevent City Lights from expanding. Eight members of the thirteen-member Common Council issued a statement calling the mayor's comments a "wholly unjustified attack" and asserting that "the city depends upon the continuing support and contribution of people from every lifestyle."

The mayor's actions were not only homophobic but poor public policy. In cities thoughout the United States gay people have been at the vanguard of urban revitalization. Stifled and oppressed by the homogeneous, family-oriented character of most urban and suburban neighborhoods and willing to take risks that middle-class families would rarely assume, gays have always sought out havens in the discarded sections of our cities, building communities in places straight people have rejected. From Portland, Oregon, to Portland, Maine, gays, along with artists, performers, hippies, punks, and writers, have been our true urban pioneers, paving the way for the gentrifiers and the developers who have invariably followed in their wake.

Fadel worked steadily on the Theater Place project and in early 1981 approached a man who had spoken to one of his classes, a suburban real-estate developer named Alan Dewart. Dewart's development interest consisted of home building and the construction of chain restaurants, but he had once worked for the New York State Urban Development Corporation and had learned how to make money in the increasingly small and narrow cracks that fell between public and private sectors. Dewart was intrigued by Fadel's energy and enthusiasm, and seemed interested in the marriage of the Tralf and Theater Place. With Fadel "playing Cupid," Quinn, Dewart, and Lawson worked out an innovative real-estate deal. It was a risky venture for Dewart and his partners. Happy doing his thing in the suburbs, Dewart often wondered if he wasn't crazy. The city would have to make it worth his while by allowing him and his partners to take advantage of federal real-estate investment tax credits. Quinn agreed. The result was that for a $750,000 investment, Dewart's group assumed ownership of the two old Main Street buildings. The city, meanwhile, held a $3.5 million first mortgage on the project. The terms were easy—a forty-year, low-interest payback, plus a generous federal tax credit. Whatever profits Theater Place earned would be shared with the developers' partner, the City of Buffalo.

Profits were slow in coming. The Tralf was very popular for a while, but the club and Theater Place were losing money. In an effort to protect their investment, Dewart and his partners looked across Main Street to a vacant group of turn-of-the-century commercial buildings next to the Market Arcade. They wanted something spectacular, something that would generate excitement, and, above all, crowds. The Theater District needed people, lots of them, to create the density and resultant synergy that make for vital city districts. Only a movie complex, Dewart and his associates thought, would do the trick.

Cinema complexes built in the suburbs were islands set in vast concrete parking lots. To see movies in the suburbs is to walk hurriedly through parking lots filled with idling automobiles, dodging cars backing in and pulling out, rushing to beat the traffic jams that always follow them. Even the best movies somehow never seem as good in the suburbs as they do in the city. But the companies that built movie theaters thought the audience was in the suburbs, not downtown. By the end of the 1970s there were only a handful of movie theaters, sprinkled sparingly throughout the city. Even the one or two downtown theaters that pitched the sleaze and martial arts films to teenagers had closed.

Dewart and his partners were convinced that an audience existed for downtown theaters. One of the partners, Irving Korn, tried to convince General Cinema Corporation, one of the largest and most successful developers of suburban movie theater complexes in the country, to build one in downtown Buffalo. A General Cinema spokesman in Boston told Korn the company never built movie houses in cities.

Korn had lived in the suburbs for almost forty years, but increasingly his investments drew him closer to the city—particularly his ownership with Dewart of offices in the building at 701 Seneca Street, of unique design and one of Buffalo's largest commercial structures. The million-square-foot, serpentine structure was built at the turn of the century as part of the spectacular complex designed by Frank Lloyd Wright for the Larkin Soap Company. Korn knew the mysterious, cavernous building inside and out. It gave him a sense of pride and place, binding him to the history and architectural legacy of the city. In 1981 Korn moved into an apartment on Delaware Avenue and began his involvement in Theater Place.

Korn was convinced of the viability of a Main Street movie house and thoughout 1984 and 1985 he relentlessly lobbied the people at General Cinema. The company's Buffalo-area manager was impressed by Korn's persistence and soon Korn had persuaded General Cinema executives to come to Buffalo for a day. In a limousine he had rented, Korn drove them though a city that he himself was in the process of discovering. He drove through solid, middle-class neighborhoods that, during his years of suburban isolation, he had never known existed. Between Korn's energy and commitment and the deal-making skills of Fred Fadel, who had recently been appointed commissioner of community development, a financial package was put together that convinced General Cinema to build a complex of eight movie theaters—now called the Market Arcade Cinema—on Main Street in downtown Buffalo.

The deal was clever, a sophisticated arrangement that, depending on one's perspective, was either a brand-new form of capitalism or New Deal public works statism at its best. The cinemas would be managed by Korn and his partners and construction financed completely with a $4.2 million mortgage held by the city. General Cinema was rewarded for its willingness to come to Buffalo with a lease that obliged it to pay no fixed rent but rather a rate based on a percentage of ticket sales. Like the postion it took in the Main-Genesee project, the deal cast the city in a high-risk venture traditionally the domain of speculative private investors. To the protagonists—Mayor Griffin and the young and creative people who served him in the community development department—it was a new and courageous brand of revitalization. Others were concerned, wondering about development that appeared to be forced in the absence of a demonstrated market.

That was not the case on the waterfront, however, which, since the early 1980s, had become increasingly popular for the construction of expensive condominium developments. City planners had had their eyes on Buffalo's waterfront since the turn of the century. In 1904 architect George Cary submitted an elaborate proposal for a vast railroad terminal complex and civic center stretching from Niagara Square to the Erie Basin that would have dwarfed New Yorks' Grand Central and Washington's Union Station. The terminal got mired in political wrangling, and it was never built.

In the late 1930s city planners tried to rid the waterfront of the commercial and manufacturing land-uses that had prevailed there since the founding of the city. The City Planning Board proposed yet another sweeping plan for the area behind City Hall. There would be "neighborhood development," a "yachting harbor," a "passenger boat harbor," an office complex, parking lots, and a "sunken flower garden." Forgotten during the war and in the rush of suburbanization that followed it, the proposal became the outline for ambitious plans proposed by the New York State Urban Development Corporation in the late 1960s. While some of the housing had been built and the Erie Basin Marina, with its magnificent, serpentine path out into the lake, was completed in the 1970s, it was not until the early 1980s, when the Griffin administration made it a priority, that the redevelopment of the waterfront began with direction and vigor. High-priced condominiums and office buildings have replaced the commercial and business uses that filled the area for so long. In recent years the rate of construction has created concern about access to the water and whether the public will still have a place in what is fast becoming an increasingly exclusive enclave.

Near the foot of Michigan Avenue, at the end of a long landfill that juts out into the waters of Lake Erie and was once one of the busiest parts of Buffalo's crowded harbor, is a sophisticated restaurant called Shooters, one of a national chain of restaurants in waterfront cities thoughout the Great Lakes. It is vast, with several levels of indoor eating and drinking areas and outdoor concrete decks, lapped by the waters of the lake and filled with white outdoor tables and chairs. On summer weekends Shooters is packed with a young, well-heeled, largely suburban crowd attracted by the heady, rock'n'roll-filled atmosphere of sex, sun, and liquor. Cars are everywhere, sometimes parked a mile or more away, and huge power boats line up like the grain ships of yore, waiting for a place at the restaurant's crowded slips. The music blasts and a deafening public-address system calls out the names of people waiting to be seated on a line that could be as long as the hold on the *Henry Steinbrenner*. On the wall near the entrance where the line starts to form are three enlarged photographs of the waterfront at the turn of the century. When one is standing amid the excited crush of people for a place at the bar, these views of what once was here— the dense hodgepodge of ships and lumber mills and grain elevators and railroad yards and taverns and boardinghouses, and the shacks and cottages of people who could afford to live no place else—make the past seem particularly distant and removed. The lighthouse, built in 1833, still standing nearby at the Erie Basin Marina, is all that remains. In the wonderful book *Buffalo Architecture: A Guide,* it is called "one of the oldest structures on the Great Lakes. . . . Forming a part of the seal of the city, the lighthouse is sometimes regarded as the symbol of Buffalo."

Other symbols, such as Buffalo's great downtown department stores, disappeared. The final death of downtown as a retail center was signaled in early 1987 when Sibley's department store, originally known as "Hengerer's" and a fixture on Main Street since the beginning of the century, went out of business. Efforts to lure a new store into the building proved fruitless, so the city encouraged its conversion to an office building. Again, public funds were the leverage. In order to induce private developers to undertake the project the city brokered a deal involving HUD, the city, and County Industrial Development Agency. It was a project that was low in risk and rich in reward for the developers. For a relatively small equity investment, the developers, who had made millions in suburban malls, received a package that consisted of $5 million in low-interest government loans, more than $11 million in taxable revenue bonds, and generous abatements of real-estate taxes. But the market was limited and demand slow. The developers went begging for tenants. Finally, by the end of the 1980s, the building's offices began to fill— but only with lawyers, accountants, stock brokers, and the like, lured away from their buildings in a market inundated with empty space.

There were other problems downtown too. The Theater Place project barely stayed afloat. Restaurants came and went and finally its center-piece, the Tralf, closed in October 1987. It reopened a year later as a publicly supported, not-for-profit "Jazz Institute." Plans to rehabilitate the Market Arcade building also found no takers, so the city itself, acting as developer and general contractor, undertook the $7 million project "on spec."

And so, despite hundreds of millions of dollars of public money, despite extensive new construction and rehabilitation, despite years of clever, imaginative, and herculean political and financial legerdemain, the city's vast and ambitious hopes to create a new Main Street have not yet been fully realized. The construction of new buildings, the re-habilitation of old ones, and the opening of the rapid transit line have added a degree of vitality to Main Street envisioned by few even ten years ago, but there is still a real sense of uncertainty about the future. Although it has resumed some of the functions it once had as a regional entertainment center, Main Street has yet to prove that it has a vital and necessary place in the life of the contemporary metropolitan area. Fighting a relentless, uphill battle against suburbs that continued to add extensive commercial, retail, and entertainment functions to their traditional residential ones, downtown Buffalo still has to sell itself, creating marketing as well as financial gimmicks in an effort to build a constituency large enough to keep it afloat.

Downtown's problems, while clearly rooted in powerful economic demographic trends, have been compounded by serious mistakes in conception and design. Planners have for too long been obsessed with the suburban market. From the waterfront to Main Street, revitalization efforts have focused on "bringing back" big-spending suburbanites to downtown. These efforts are very difficult, very expensive, and probably doomed to fail. In order to lure these people back to a place they left in the first place, planners have imposed a sense of scale and design on downtown projects that, while perhaps successful in the glitzy, more artificial ambience of suburbia, simply does not work in a city. The most successful downtowns are those that emerge more organically, in direct response to the daily patterns of the lives of people who live nearby. But, threatened by the flight to suburbia, planners in Buffalo, as in cities thoughout the country, have turned their backs on what they knew in their hearts about the way people lived in the city, opting instead for the fashionable but disastrous blockbuster notions and images of downtown revitalization that did so much to destroy downtown districts to begin wtih. The result has been that many gritty yet lively urban places and spaces have been replaced by ones that, while clearly more sanitized and suburbanized, are far less appealing. While the Convention Center and the Marine Midland Tower are the most glaring examples of this process, other, more recent revitalization efforts have also put image ahead of function. The problems that the Tralfamadore continues to have, for example, are caused not by demographics or economics but rather by design. Forsaking the smoky, cramped, dark, funky, and really "city" feel of the old Tralf, designers opted for what some believe to be the off-putting, cavernous, cold, and suburbanized environment of the new facility. When, despite these extremely expensive efforts, the Tralfamadore continued to fail, it remained easier and some-how more comforting to blame "historical forces"—the flight to the suburbs, the decline of the economy—than to rethink concept and design.

Artificiality of concept and design and an emphasis on image has hampered other efforts to revitalize Main Street. Most of Main Street's most expensive and highly touted projects were made possible by the destruction of the city's retail core: Kobackers and J. N. Adams in the 1960s, W. T. Grant's, Grossmans, and Hens & Kelly in the 1970s, and Hengerer's in the 1980s. If, as the current crop of planners insist, down-town retail is "dead," it is as much the fault of the planners as of the demographic trends they tend to blame. For it was these stores that brought and kept generations of shoppers—Poles, Italians, and African-Americans from the East and West Sides, as well as the more genteel shoppers from the Delaware District—downtown. Now, on the new main Street, lined with banks, a hotel, and shiny buildings with "Class A" office space, there is no place for these people to go. As misguided planners and developers concoct ever-more complex and generous financial packages in a desperate effort to lure high-priced retailers like Brooks Brothers and Ann Taylor downtown, the area's natural constit-uency, the people who live in the city and who crave the exciting and nurturing human environment that they know is possible here, remain frustrated and disappointed.

There are signs, however, that downtown is beginning to change. Increasingly, the people of Buffalo are coming back to Main Street. At year-round festivals—Curtain Up, Winterfest, the Friendship Festival, and others—hundreds of thousands of people descend into downtown, walking up and down Main Street, sampling food, entertainment, and merchandise. Today the Theater District has become a reality, driven by nine legitimate theaters—some repertory, some experimental and avant garde—that cities twice the size of Buffalo would envy. People are flocking to the Market Arcade cinemas and filling Pilot Field, the wonderfully intimate baseball stadium that, though completed in 1988, somehow fits very appropriately in the midst of the turn-of-the-century streetscape that surrounds it. Young people, it seems, particularly like downtown. For it is here, unlike in the suburbs where so many of them were raised, on the old pavement and in the stones of the refurbished buildings, in the dark and cavernous halls of the Hippodrome Billiard Academy and even in the shiny newness of the Market Arcade cinemas across Main Street, that there is a sense of place, of history, and of community that feels good to them and that they, better than their elders, know can only be found on the common ground that is a city.

16

RACE, CLASS, AND ETHNICITY IN CONTEMPORARY BUFFALO

In the waning days of summer, the sun seems to shine particularly brightly on the University District, penetrating its thick, low clusters of trees, casting shadows on the front porches of the small, wooden houses lining its streets. Named for the campus of the University of Buffalo built there after World War I, the University District is vast and varied, encompassing inner-city neighborhoods like St. Bartholomew's parish, where Father Bissonette was killed, in the devastated Fillmore-Leroy neighborhood, and the large, magnificent houses of Huntley Drive and Woodley Road. In between is the bulk of the district, the last and only truly racially balanced neighborhood in Buffalo.

Located on Buffalo's northeast side, the University District was the second home for upwardly mobile first- and second-generation Germans, Italians, and Poles who moved from the East Side. On Olympic Avenue there is still a thriving German restaurant named Troidl's, packed on weekends with people from all over town eating roast duck, potato salad, and sauerkraut. Like so many other neighborhoods, the University District was undermined by the events of the late 1960s and 1970s. Shaken by the tremors of the riots of 1967 and the insidious actions of block-busting real-estate agents, frightened by the sudden movement into the neighborhood of large numbers of African-Americans, whites who had long before fled the Fillmore-Leroy section began to leave the area. The final blow was UB's decision to pull most of its operations off of its Main Street campus. The departure of over twenty-five thousand students and faculty left a gaping hole that by the end of the 1980s had not yet been filled.

But by the mid-1980s the white exodus slowed. By the end of the decade it seemed to have stopped completely and now whole sections of the University District are racially balanced. While the balance clearly remains precarious, there are signs that it is stable.

There are other neighborhoods in Buffalo where African-Americans and whites live together but what makes the University District different is that it is a low-to-middle-income neighborhood where family income of thirty thousand dollars is at the high end. In Parkside, for example, African-Americans—Florence Baugh, Arthur Eve, and former City Court Chief Judge Wilbur Trammell among them—have lived for years, since the early 1960s when Dick Griffin and Jack Anthony organized the Parkside Community Association to ensure the area's smooth transition from a white to an integrated neighborhood. Since then still more blacks have moved into Parkside and today, with its large, elaborately detailed, one- and two-family late-Victorian homes refurbished and restored, its rear gardens and front lawns rich and well-maintained, the neighborhood is one of the most desirable in the city. Unlike the rest of the University District, however, Parkside is now among the more expensive neighborhoods in the city. Its residents are not only more affluent than the average Buffalonian, they are also far better educated, boasting among them many of the professors from UB, as well as from Canisius College and Medaille College, located on the fringes of the neighborhood.

Blacks live in other middle- and upper-income neighborhoods too, on quiet, verdant side-streets in North Buffalo, where Jews and Italians still predominate, and in the Middlesex-Chatham area, where close to a dozen African-American families have moved in recent years. Blacks have been moving in even larger numbers into suburban Amherst where, in homes worth upwards of $150,000, they live scattered comfortably and usually uneventfully among their white neighbors. It is to Amherst's characteristically large, clean new homes that so many of the better-paid African-American public-school teachers and administrators have moved in recent years. Racial problems and incidents, they say, are the exception. But, however infrequently they occur, they always hurt, reminding people like Verna Morton, head of the Board of Education's magnet-school program, how slowly racial attitudes change. Morton's son was visiting her from out of town, she says sadly, when he was stopped by two Town of Amherst police officers while jogging through the streets of the neighborhood late one afternoon in the spring of 1989. They wanted to know, she says in painful disbelief, what he was doing jogging "out here."

Now that more affluent African-Americans have begun to move to Amherst, a kind of melting pot is occurring there, and in the suburbs in general, that was never possible in a city that had been divided for so long by fortress-like enclaves of race and ethnicity. Thus it is in Amherst, as in many American suburbs, that the racial and ethnic barriers have begun to break down as people of all races, colors, and creeds live, albeit only if they can afford to, in the same neighborhoods. While race relations are improving in the increasingly integrated, affluent suburbs, they are, many people sense, deteriorating in the city. The movement of blacks to the suburbs has hurt the poor inner-city neighborhoods, weakening the ability of even the community's strongest institutions to deal with the many problems created by racism and poverty. Rev. Herbert V. Reid, who has been the pastor at Gethsemane Baptist Church on Grape Street in the Fruit Belt since 1963, sees it in his congregation. "When black folks live white," he says, "they tend to church white." Reid recalls his family church in Sanford, Florida, where his principal, his teacher, and his family's doctor were all in the choir. It's not that way today, he says. The white churches, "want my doctors, lawyers, judges, and school teachers. They don't want my welfare mothers."

The racial mix that characterizes much of the University District is different from that in Amherst. It has occurred in a low-to-moderate-income neighborhood that for years suffered terribly as a result of massive white flight. But then suddenly, in the late 1970s and early 1980s, the simple solution of cutting and running were interrupted by the realities of severe economic dislocation. Stagflation—the two-headed monster of unemployment and inflation—ended the flight to the suburbs that had done so much to weaken the city's neighborhoods. Buffalonians, particularly in working-class neighborhoods throughout the city, were no longer able to afford to move. Because it hit in the middle of the vast population upheaval that was sweeping the district, the economic crisis of the late 1970s and early 1980s interrupted a demographic process that most certainly would have led to the creation of an all-black district. What happened instead was that the exodus of whites and the influx of blacks was halted just as it had reached a point of balance. This state of affairs remains unique in the city.

Under the leadership of a bright and hardworking African-American councilman, racial balance has been maintained in the University District while real-estate values, for homes as well as for businesses, have increased. Building on his work as a community coordinator during the halcyon days of citizen participation in the early 1970s, Councilman Archie Amos has augmented the district's political infrastructure with broad-based participation at the grassroots level. There are now more than ninety integrated block clubs in the district and a host of citizen's advisory boards, each of which works with a different sector of the district's economy. Acting as a dynamic broker between his constituents and City Hall, Amos, an aggressive interventionist, has helped to cement the commercial stability of Bailey Avenue, the district's leading commercial strip. In a city where politicians rarely cross ethnic—let alone racial—lines, Amos's greatest skill is his ability to work equally well with both African-Americans and whites. He has had to in order to survive politically. And had he not survived, one suspects, neither would his neighborhood.

While the University District has survived as a result of the collapse of industry, South Buffalo has survived despite it. Lost long ago were the thousands of jobs that generations of South Buffalonians had long held in the Bethlehem and Republic steel mills, the railroad yards, and the grain elevators. But somehow, South Buffalo hung on and indeed, is today thriving. For years the neighborhood was sustained by pride and intense neighborhood loyalty. Rooted in history, geography, ethnicity, and religion, a mulish neighborhood chauvinism has helped to generate South Buffalo's sometimes annoying, but clearly effective, persistance. In addition to a strong sense of neighborhood identity, South Buffalo has always been economically and socially diverse. In addition to a large blue-collar population, there has been in South Buffalo, as in Irish-American neighborhoods in cities throughout the country, a large middle class deeply rooted in politics, the civil service, and other areas of public employment. Since the end of World War II, Irish-American politicians from South Buffalo have exercised extraordinary power in local politics, with an access to patronage jobs unrivaled by any neighborhood in the city. As a result, there has always been a large and influential middle class of public employees from the area—teachers, police officers, firefighters, and mail carriers who provided an economic cushion to the neighborhood that allowed it to survive the collapse of industry.

This cushion has been particularly soft since the election in 1977 of South Buffalo's own, Mayor Jimmy Griffin. Griffin loves South Buffalo and naturally has been extremely kind to it. He has paid lavish attention to the neighborhood's infrastructure, generously supporting loans to its businesspeople and homeowners, repaving and plowing its streets, improving and maintaining its parks. He has been particularly generous to the neighborhood with his patronage and, in a process as old as city government itself, awards it to his family, friends, neighbors, and supporters.

Today South Buffalo's largest employer is not Bethlehem or Republic Steel but Mercy Hospital, and while many of the area's employees are relatively low-paid workers in the health care field, the neighborhood continues to attract higher-paid professionals. Today, in addition to thousands of public employees, South Buffalo contains a growing number of young doctors, lawyers, and bankers, many of whose parents left the neighborhood for the adjacent suburb of West Seneca in the 1960s and 1970s.

The neighborhood looks good, too. Its well-maintained streets and the magnificent Cazenovia Park, yet another Buffalo park designed by Fredrick Law Olmsted, are as nice as any in the city. Today South Buffalo boasts several magnificent residential neighborhoods, rising real-estate values, and a few "good" restaurants. It even boasts a summer colony in Crystal Beach, Ontario, where, in a semicircular enclave with the backs of its small, wooden cottages turned to the world, dozens of South Buffalonians pass the summer, happily drinking Canadian beer.

Yet, there's plenty of poverty in South Buffalo, whole streets filled with the human and physical devastation caused by the decline of industry. But on balance South Buffalo has prospered, and with Mayor Griffin's election to his fourth term, its prospects remain good.

For good or ill, Jimmy Griffin has been the dominant figure in Buffalo since he was first elected in 1977. He is something of a larger-than-life figure, in may ways an anomaly. Shanty Irish from the old First Ward, he drinks beer, swears, has a tendancy to push people around, and stands for "the old values" of factory, neighborhood, and clan. Indeed, it was at the moment that all of these hallowed institutions of urban America were crumbling that Jimmy was elected. And yet, despite an outlook (more than a vision) rooted in the past, it is Griffin more than anyone who has been responsible for leading Buffalo into what many people here feel is a much-improved era in the history of the city.

Griffin not only expends enormous amounts of energy leading the city, but more than once he has put his money where his mouth is. In 1979 Griffin corralled ninety-nine friends and followers and cajoled them into investing a thousand dollars each to buy a Double-A baseball team. The group called the team the Buffalo Bisons and installed it in the ratty 1930s-era War Memorial stadium known affectionately as the "Rockpile." Griffin alone harbored a dream of major-league baseball in the city that he loved. His dream started to come true in 1983 when Bob Rich, Jr., bought the team at ten cents on the dollar. Three years later, the team had been transformed into Triple A and was playing in the brand-new downtown stadium known as Pilot Field.

It was the mayor's fierce local pride that led him to buy stock in Empire of America, a local bank that went public in 1986. Griffin was furious when it declared bankruptcy in late 1989. "I want to tell you that a couple of years of my kids' education went down the drain and I'm sure a lot of people feel the way I do that it could have been done differently," he said at a press conference. He felt the whole community had been betrayed and, in the brash, outspoken way his constituents love, he mocked the bankers responsible. Upon hearing that it had been a female vice president who made the bankruptcy announcement to the stockholders, Griffin was scathing. "I guess all the men up there hid behind the skirts of the women and they couldn't make the announcement on their own."

It is Griffin's feisty, no-nonsense, shoot-from-the-hip cockiness, his gruff, macho, tough-talking persona that accounts for his almost primal appeal throughout Buffalo's white ethnic neighborhoods. Referring to a celebration following Griffin's victory in the 1989 Democratic mayoral primary, a reporter for the *News* wrote, "It was a Jimmy Griffin kind of crowd. Mostly men, a lot of them wearing green pants or green tee shirts, some of them wearing caps with 'Buffalo Bills' or 'Celtics' or 'Thirsty's' and 'Dogherty's' written on them, most of them with a cup of beer in hand. 'Four more years,' one celebrant yelled. 'Four more beers,' said another."

Griffin had triumphed in the primary (and therefore would almost certainly be re-elected to the mayoralty in November) over two opponents who, unfortunately for them, bore no resemblance to the mayor. One was an African-American, Wilbur Trammell, the other a WASP, William B. Hoyt III, a descendant of a family whose history in Buffalo goes back more than a hundred years. Hoyt, concerned that Buffalo's ethnics might be resistant, asked a group of his friends a question clearly not intended to be rhetorical: "Can a WASP be elected mayor of Buffalo?"

Little remains of the power that Buffalo's WASPs once exerted over the city's economy. While there are individuals—a few lawyers and bankers—who still function as power brokers, it is a result not of some WASP *droit du seigneur* but rather of the influence they have acquired as a result of their own work and ambition. While Buffalo's WASPs still tend to be wealthy, their wealth is far less in capital investment than it is in stocks and bonds. Recently however, a handful have shown that they are far from a dying breed and, in the entrepreneurial tradition usually associated with immigrants, it is WASPs who have been involved in more than a few of the area's leveraged buyouts.

The WASP presence is still felt in many areas of the city's life. As a group, WASPs tend to dominate the cultural scene and are the primary donors as well as most active supporters of the Buffalo Philharmonic Orchestra, the Albright-Knox Art Gallery, and the Burchfield Center for the Arts. And, much to the surprise of many out-of-towners, there remains in Buffalo, on the quiet, lovely, still somewhat pristine side-streets between Elmwood and Delaware—Cleveland, Lexington, and Highland Avenues, Tudor Place and St. Catherine's Court—a beautiful and very expensive WASP residential enclave. This, in addition to a few WASP-dominated town clubs, Presbyterian and Episcopalian churches, a few summer colonies on the Canadian and American shores of Lake Erie, comprise a strongly structured WASP community that, despite the denials of its members, resembles Buffalo's other ethnic communities in many ways. But in politics Buffalo's WASPs, as might be expected in a city so overwhelmingly African-American and ethnic Catholic, have played no serious part for years. Hoyt's question was therefore an easy one to answer.

Bill Hoyt began his political career as a councilman from the relatively WASP, silk stocking Delaware District in the early 1970s; soon after he was elected to the State Assembly from a jurisdiction that went well beyond the boundaries of his old council district. As a result, in 1989 Hoyt still had very little recognition on either the black East Side or in Buffalo's blue-collar white ethnic neighborhoods. Griffin couldn't have been more thrilled when the Democratic Selection Committee endorsed Hoyt as their candidate for mayor in the spring of 1989. He was much more worried about Anthony Masiello, another Democrat seeking the endorsement. Unlike Hoyt, Masiello had deep support among blacks and, more significantly for Griffin, also among the white ethnics who had voted him mayor in 1977, 1981, and 1985. While Griffin himself stood no chance of being selected by the committee (endorsed too many times by the Republican, Conservative, and Right-to-Life parties, he was anathema to Democratic Party regulars), several "Griffin people" were on that committee. After several ballots in which neither Hoyt nor Masiello won a majority, insiders say, they threw their support to Hoyt, by far the weaker of the two in a contest with Griffin.

Hoyt's problems grew more serious when, shortly after his endorsement by the Democratic Party, Wilbur Trammell announced that he too was seeking the mayoralty. The mayor gloated. "The more the merrier," he said. Hoyt's candidacy foundered, weakened by his WASPish persona and undermined by the presence of Trammell.

Many blamed Trammell and the black leaders who had created his candidacy. With an instinct for failure that borders on political suicide, the powers that be in Buffalo's African-American political establishment have consistently made the wrong decisions. Three times since 1977 a black candidate has run for mayor, each one losing more badly than the last. Encouraged and supported by most of the city's black leadership, weak and incompetent black candidates with little appeal outside of their own community have run. In doing so they have divided the anti-Griffin white opposition, allowing the mayor to be elected four times. Afraid that black support for a progressive white political leader would undermine their support within the black community, leading African-American politicians, while perpetuating their power, have undermined the creation of a broad-based interracial political coalition.

While it has been easy, even justifiable, to blame "Washington" or "the mayor," the problems of Buffalo's African-Americans have been exacerbated by political difficulties within their community. With their leaders either unable or unwilling to build bridges to the white community and an electorate crippled by very low voter participation, Buffalo's African-Americans, although they make up more than 30 percent of the population, have remained isolated and politically weak. In despair many have turned inward, making still more difficult the efforts that some are still trying to make on behalf of interracial harmony.

WASPs at least, if only through Hoyt, are engaged in the rough and tumble of community life and politics. This tends not to be true of Buffalo's Jewish community. By and large the Jews of Buffalo have turned their back on the city. Although numerically never strong (even when there were approximately twenty-five thousand Jews in Buffalo in 1950, they never constituted more than 3 percent to 4 percent of the population), for years the great majority of them at least lived in the city, particularly on the old East Side where, side by side with the rest of Buffalo's poor, first-generation Buffalonians, they shared a world and a world view created by their common environment. In Buffalo, as in so many American cities, blacks and Jews were particularly close, living next to one another, sharing doubles, attending the same public schools, public parks, and public libraries. Although it may well have

been circumstance more than choice that bound them, the similarity
of their situation and the synergy of their presence on the same turf
led to the creation of a special relationship. It clearly influenced Norman
Goldfarb, who never tired of telling people about the old days on the
integrated streets of Buffalo's Lower East Side. Without the mix that
occurred on the East side of Buffalo and in neighborhoods like it in
cities throughout the Northeast, the strong white support given to the
early civil-rights movement might never have materialized.

   This dynamic relationship unfortunately came to an end in Buffalo
when Jews fled the city in disproportionately large numbers; today more
than 75 percent of the area's Jewish population lives in the suburbs,
mostly Amherst. Rapid suburbanization, combined with the lack of a
Jewish working-class tradition in Buffalo, has resulted in the absence
of the kind of progressive Jewish constituency that has been a force
for so much positive change in so many other cities. Their absence
is particularly felt in the public schools, where Jewish children, parents,
and teachers, normally so active on behalf of excellence in public education, are few and far between. Buffalo's Reform Jewish community
is committed to pluralism and to strengthening ties between the city's
different racial, ethnic and religious groups, but their presence is weak.
The Jewish Federation in particular, by sponsoring programs of dialogue
with Polish and African-American groups and ecumenical, interracial
tours of Israel, has kept the often flickering candle of good will burning.

When the Kensington Expressway was closed down temporarily for repairs
during the summer of 1989, the quickest, most direct route from the
airport to downtown was via Genesee Street. For those whose view of
the inner city is blurred, seen only from the windows of cars moving
fast along the Expressway, the Genesee Street route is an eye opener.
It begins in Cheektowaga, a suburb to Buffalo's east. A typical postwar
"tacky" suburb that was long the subject of derision, Cheektowaga boomed
during the 1950s and 1960s when, stimulated by some of the most powerful
forces in recent American life—the automobile, a desire for new homes
for growing families, and racial fear—thousands of Germans and Poles
from Buffalo's East Side poured into the area. Genesee, once Cheektowaga's prime commercial street, is somewhat shabby now. While there
are still a handful of butcher shops, candy stores, photographers, and
even a few funerary monument showrooms, Genesee, like the other older
commercial strips in the suburbs, has been undermined by two generations
of relentlessly spreading shopping malls. Soon, Cheektowaga becomes
Buffalo, joined by Genesee Street to an old German neighborhood known

as Schiller Park. It still resonates with Germanic character: Kerns, Zelmer, Hagen, and Floss are the names of some of the streets. Scharf's Schiller Park Restaurant and the Deutsches Haus still cater to a largely German clientele and the Schiller Park Senior Citizens Center remains a lively, though lonely, outpost of "Germanness."

The streetscape changes suddenly and dramatically at the intersection of Genesee and Bailey and while the street names—Zenner, Kilhoffer, and Moselle—reveal the neighborhood's past, the streets themselves vividly display the present. It is the landscape of the urban ghetto. Here, Genesee is lined with dilapidated storefronts, many closed, the others— "Price Chopper," "Johnny's Used Furniture, "Scotty's Take-out Steak Sandwiches"—open for business behind grated windows. People of all ages are everywhere, standing against the rickety wooden buildings, sitting on old kitchen chairs or on couches, too old and ratty for the living room, that have been pulled out onto shaky porches. Genesee-Moselle, as the neighborhood is called, is a dangerous place crippled by the social pathology that plagues neighborhoods like it in cities throughout America. There are signs, however, that people do care and are trying. One of them is the headquarters of CRUCIAL, an African-American community group that has been trying to organize the community against the drug blight.

Further down Genesee, in the heart of the black community, near Martin Luther King Park, is the fortress-like, soaring, turn-of-the century church of St. Mary of Sorrow. Built as a German parish church in 1891, it had twelve thousand parishioners immediately after World War II, during the neighborhood's heyday. Now it hovers over the decrepit intersection of Genesee and Rich Streets like a massive stone ruin. Inside is a food pantry, a thrift shop, and offices for two social workers assigned by Catholic Charities. But today St. Mary's is being rehabilitated and soon, as the Martin Luther King Urban Life Center, it will house the offices of a small liberal arts college known as Houghton as well as the offices of the Preservation Coalition of Erie County.

While much effort has gone into explaining the persistence of the problems that are destroying this community, the suggestions usually offered—racism, ignorance, failed public policy—somehow fall short, paling beside the overwhelming bleakness and devastation of the reality of a physical environment that seems to have no explanation. Even the decline of industry, the most dramatic and sweeping change in the city's memory, does not completely explain the degradation that has occurred in Buffalo's inner-city neighborhoods, though it certainly has taken its toll. Because they tend to make up a proportionally greater percentage of the industrial work force, blacks were particularly hurt by plant closings, particularly at Bethlehem and Republic. Close to a thousand of the 7,500 people laid off at Bethlehem in 1982 were African-American, and between two hundred and three hundred lost their jobs at Republic that same year. The closing of factories with central city locations—Trico, for example—hurt too. Trico drew most of its workers, black and white, from surrounding neighborhoods. According to a 1986 survey by Buffalo State College, its closing, announced in late 1985, would mean a loss of $7 million in salaries paid annually to people living in the Fillmore, Ellicott, Lovejoy, and Masten districts.

The impact of the loss of industrial jobs was devastating to the black community (approximately four thousand blacks have lost industrial jobs in the area since the mid-1970s), and is extremely important in understanding the plight of the African-American community today. Not only were the jobs good but those who worked them were their community's most serious citizens, homeowners, active in their churches and schools, important as role models to neighborhood children. This collateral damage to the fabric of the community, as much as the jobs and dollars lost, was a blow that Buffalo's black community has barely begun to get over.

The blue-collar middle class has been shrinking all over the city, as has the real income of industrial workers regardless of race, color, or creed. The impact of industrial decline, therefore, was not significantly different in blue-collar white communities like Lovejoy, Black Rock, Riverside, and South Buffalo. What made it somewhat more difficult for Buffalo's African-American community was the small size of the city's black middle and professional class. Economic security, even prosperity, for blacks in Buffalo always came through industry, particularly those sectors of the industrial economy where labor unions were strong. The Chevrolet, Ford, Bethlehem, Republic, and American Brass plants produced several generations of prosperous blacks, men who owned their own homes, whose wives were school teachers and principals, whose children went to college, and whose families contributed to the health and stability of their community. With the exception of a handful of black businesspeople, the sum and substance of black prosperity and economic security was dependent completely on industry. Unlike other industrial cities like Cleveland and Detroit, where a black middle class based on civil service and the professions is everywhere apparent, the black middle class in Buffalo has remained relatively invisible. In these other cities large numbers of blacks have assimilated into the world of the professional middle classes. Blacks in Buffalo, generally speaking, have not. While there has always been a small number of black professionals in Buffalo—doctors, dentists, and lawyers and the like—serving the needs of a mainly black clientele, there have been very few African-Americans in the broader business or professional world, in downtown law and accounting firms, for example. Until very recently the visible signs of a black middle class (particularly a male one) were few and far between. The majority of blacks in Buffalo lack the accoutrements that mark black middle-class communities in other cities.

This is less true of black women who, far more than black men, historically have been much more exposed to the workings of the white middle-classes, particularly in the Buffalo public schools. While many of their husbands worked in back-breaking but well-paying industrial jobs, black women, now in their fifties and sixties, people like Mildred Stallings, Evelyn Cooper, Erma Robinson, and many of Buffalo's other principals and teachers, went to college and graduate school, making their way into the world of middle-class success and behavior. The younger generation of such African-American women married professionals. As a result Buffalo's African-American women appear to be more adept than their male counterparts at coping with the adjustment problems of the post-industrial age. Thus the majority of Buffalo's whites continue to see blacks, particularly black men, in the most traditional work roles. As a result racial stereotypes persist and prophecies continue to be self-fulfilling.

Because of the small size of Buffalo's African-American middle and professional class the city has nurtured few educated and polished black political leaders, people like Andrew Young in Atlanta, David Dinkins in New York, Doug Wilder in Virginia, and Norman Rice in Seattle, who, speaking the language of the middle class, can reach out beyond the confines of a narrow ghetto constituency and build city-wide coalitions. When such figures do emerge in Buffalo, they are suspect in their own community. This was one of Wilbur Trammell's major problems when he ran for mayor in 1989. Trammell is a black Horatio Alger, a very wealthy businessman, a lawyer, and, until he resigned to run for mayor, chief judge of the City Court. Trammell lives in the Parkside section. He is well-known throughout the white community, and is not identified with the grassroots black community. For these reasons, which have far more to do with lifestyle than with politics, Trammell lacked a base of support among blacks.

Clifford Bell, an African-American councilman-at-large, like Councilman Amos and Councilman James Pitts, from the University District, is one of the few black politicians who do manage to straddle the color line. Bell grew up on Monroe Street on the East Side, one of six brothers. His father was a Bethlehem steel worker for thirty-eight years and because of that, Bell says, his family enjoyed a strength and stability that many others in his community lacked. In the mid-1950s Bell and three of his brothers opened a laundry on Jefferson Avenue, the heart of the Black East Side. Over the years the business expanded, becoming one of the more successful African-American enterprises in Buffalo. While Bell never considered working at Bethlehem, he recognizes its significance, like that of the other factories in the area, in the life of his community. If nothing else, he says, it offered young people a start. For those who stuck with it, big-industry factory work offered a sound, steady, if dangerous and unimaginative, job. Even had these plants not closed it is unlikely that Clifford Bell's children, or the children of Buffalo's other middle-class African-Americans, would have worked in them either. Indeed, like many of the college-educated young people born and raised in Buffalo, the Bell children had left the area altogether.

The opportunities for educated, middle-class African-Americans are limited in Buffalo and many of them, like their white counterparts, are leaving, to greener pastures in Boston, New York City, Washington D.C., and, more so in the case of blacks, to Atlanta. Nevertheless, the expansion of the service sector, combined with affirmative action programs, even when less aggressively pursued than many would like, has begun to create a growing number of middle-class opportunities for African-Americans in Buffalo that were rarely available a generation ago and that have, to a certain extent, compensated for the loss of jobs in industry. While less apparant here than in some other cities, the number of blacks in middle-class work, particularly in the professions, is growing steadily, if slowly. An interesting by-product of school desegregation in general and of Judge Curtin's 1980 hiring order in particular, is that the number of minority professional staff working in the public schools has nearly doubled since 1975, from 492 that year to 823 in 1988. While there is certainly not a direct correlation between those who lost their old jobs as a result of industrial decline and those who gained new ones because of school integration, the latter could not have come at a better time in the life of the African-American community, for just as one sector of the economy critical to the welfare of the black community collapsed, another one, perhaps more significant in the long term was opening up. At the same time, similar orders issued from Curtin's court led to the creation of close to three hundred new jobs in the police and fire departments. While Curtin's decisions could not have come at a better time for Buffalo's blacks, the timing could not have been worse for the city's whites. Now, added to the hurt of losing their factory jobs was the anger of being denied a civil service job because of affirmative action. Ironically, Vince Suitt of the Urban League had warned against this in 1963. Arguing against employment quotas, Suitt said that they were a "very dangerous and poisonous influence in the whole community structure, particularly when there is high unemployment."

Meanwhile, the private sector too, according to the U.S. Equal Employment Opportunity Commission, was becoming more receptive. Between 1986 and 1987, the commission reported, there was an increase of 158 African-Americans in managerial and professional jobs within local corporations.

Added to this are the approximately ten thousand blacks who still work in manufacturing jobs in the area (a hundred thousand area jobs in manufacturing multiplied by the commission's figure of 10 percent black manufacturing employment). The result is the existance in Buffalo of a substantial and significant, though still largely hidden, African-American blue- and white-collar middle class.

While many have moved to Amherst and Williamsville, many more members of Buffalo's expanding black middle-classes live in the city, between Main Street and Humboldt Parkway on Eastwood Place, Meech Street, and Blaine and Oakgrove Avenues and in the old Humboldt neighborhood, on Hamlin Road, Brunswick Boulevard and Goulding Avenue. These are, all of them, well-maintained, lovely side streets, filled with houses occupied by owners committed to and concerned about the health and well-being of their neighborhoods. A city-state partnership recently built 167 brand-new single homes in the Pratt-Willert area of the black East Side. Cited in 1989 by the Urban Land Institute as an "outstanding model of urban revitalization for all American cities," the program has encouraged the purchase of affordable homes by middle-class blacks and whites in a neighborhood they had abandoned. Forty percent of the homes are owned by whites, according to Commissioner of Inspections and Community Revitalization Joe Schollard. The move of middle-class blacks into the area has encouraged people concerned about positive role models for the African-American children of this long-distressed neighborhood.

With the exception of small pockets here and there, conditions on the black East Side are, clearly and obviously, serious. As in African-American neighborhoods all over the country, whole communities are plagued by a pervasive and insidious social disintegratoin that gets worse every day. Although still lower than in other cities of similar and larger size, drug-related violent crime is growing at a rate that is frightening to people throughout the community. Some, searching desperately for excuses, blame it on Buffalo's location. Recently, Buffalo has become a major distribution center for heroin, cocaine and marijuana leaving and entering the country across the Peace Bridge. It is a tradition that goes back to Prohibition. The Peace Bridge was built in 1927 and immediately became a primary point of entry for illegal alcohol beverages. Now, some say, the Peace Bridge performs the same role for drugs. There are other explanations too. Gangs, some from Jamaica, others from Los Angeles, are reportedly moving into the city. A fall 1989 story in the *News* reported that, "There's a lot of concern on the street about the California dealers moving in." A police investigator said, "They are bringing in cheaper, better cocaine and trying to undercut the Buffalo dealers." The story also reported that, "On Kehr Street and several other East Side locations police recently noticed graffiti trumpeting the arrival in Buffalo of 'The Crips' and 'The Bloods,' two Los Angeles–based drug gangs. One sign painted on an abandoned building in the area lists the name of six men described in the graffiti as 'the baddest Crips from L.A.' " Whatever the cause, drugs are destroying the lives of growing numbers of Buffalo's African-American children, caught innocently in the machinations of drug-dealing killers.

In the meantime, poverty gnaws away at other neighborhoods throughout the city, the old ethnic neighborhoods which used to symbolize family, stability and right-living to their inhabitants. The change is particularly poignant on Vermont and Connecticut Streets, and Massachusetts and Rhode Island Avenues, named for the states whence came the original settlers of this neighborhood, and where later proud first- and second-generation Italians recreated the tight-knit, village-like communities they had always known. Most of them have moved away now, but they have held on to their old, wooden homes, and now, as absentee landlords (synonymous in Buffalo, where home ownership is so deeply valued, with "slum lords") are renting them to the poorest of the poor: welfare tenants. With their rent paid directly to the landlord by the county, these tenants, it often seems, are unable, unwilling, or both, to maintain their homes. On warm summer nights the streets and porches are filled with half-dressed, mostly obese young men and women, some white, some black, some Hispanic, just hanging out, smoking endless cigarettes, drinking endless amounts of beer, endlessly working on the dilapidated cars that seem to litter the streets. And everywhere are the children.

The public schools in these neighborhoods are filled with the children of the poor. In fact, according to Superintendent Reville, over 60 percent of the children in the city's schools in early 1989 came from families that lived in poverty. Reville arrived at the number by dividing the number of children in the system into the number of those who qualified for free lunches. While that figure may be somewhat exaggerated to justify large spending requests, public education in Buffalo is saddled with crippling problems of poverty. Buffalo is poor in comparison to most urban areas (Buffalo's average 1985 personal income of $8,840 placed it sixty-sixth among seventy-five cities in the country and almost $3,000 below the national average.) Other data supports this view of the relative poverty of Buffalonians. A smaller percentage of the area's population live in the suburbs or have college educations than the national average. While among the lowest in per-capita income, Buffalo is among the highest in percentage of people receiving public assistance. Caught between a decline in real income and an increase in housing costs, the number of the poor, the hungry and the homeless have grown too. The City Mission has been serving more meals than ever before. "This is the busiest summer that we've had in the history of the mission," said the facility's director in late September 1989. "We served twelve thousand more meals during July as compared to last July, and I am sure that when the final figures are in, it will be even worse for August and September." The Friends of Night People, meanwhile, was serving two thousand meals per month to working people.

Poverty then, was a critical, debilitating problem for teachers and administrators in schools in the city's poorest neighborhoods. "Some of these kids," says Marilyn Reich, a kindergarten teacher at School 31 on Stanton Street, "deserve awards just for getting to school." Regardless of where they are—on Sears Street on the Polish East Side, on Normal Avenue on the West Side, on Hertel Avenue in Black Rock, on Stanton Street on the African-American East Side or on West Delavan Avenue on the Upper West Side—the problems, transiency, drop-out rates, single-parent families, too-little participation by parents, too much television, are typical of public schools in poor neighborhoods in cities throughout the country. For in these neighborhoods, where it is hard enough just getting through the week, schools and schooling have an unfortunately low priority. By the end of the 1980s many began to sense that schools in these neighborhoods had become dumping grounds for the poor. The best and the brightest kids in the neighborhood schools, unfortunately labelled "generic schools," were being skimmed off by the magnet schools, creating a growing division along class lines within the public school system that had never before existed.

The difficulty has been exacerbated by a perennial school funding crisis. Dominated by Catholic politicians with deep loyalties to parochial education, Buffalo has always spent far less per pupil on public education than any city in the State—$515 less than the state average in 1989. The gap has grown greater since Jimmy Griffin's advent to the mayoralty. Griffin's enthusiasm for the widely recognized achievements of the Buffalo public schools has been lukewarm and his support for them reluctant at best. Unlike other cities, where local funding of public schools has remained steady while state funding has increased, Buffalo's contribution has dropped from 34 percent of its budget in 1977 to 16 percent in 1989. While the costs of public education in the city, where disproportionately large numbers of students are in expensive vocational and special educational programs, are far greater than they are in the suburbs, Buffalo spends far less per pupil than its suburban neighbors. As a result, parents and children in Buffalo's highly praised, much-copied public school system are, at the beginning of the 1990s, waiting and watching, wondering how long what took so long to achieve will unravel.

17

THE BUFFALO PLAN IN TROUBLE

The twilight view from the eighth floor of City Hall is breathtaking. Early one Wednesday evening in August 1989, as the Board of Education met there, shimmering rays cast long streaks of light, glistening and dancing on the surface of the sparkling waters of Lake Erie. The sun had been high and bright in the sky throughout that clear, cool day, and now it was setting gently down, behind the distant horizon. On the nearby shoreline of Canada, where beaches are nestled among the trees, long shadows loomed across the water and the puffy-blue sky was filled with fiery streaks of orange and red. Not everyone saw it, certainly none of the nine board members. Most had their backs turned; they were hudding around a long table, arguing, debating, making motions, and shuffling papers. But from where he sat Joe Murray, associate superintendent for instructional services, could see the lake tableaux, and for a moment or two his mind wandered.

By the end of 1989 Joe Murray had begun to think about retiring. He'd been with the Buffalo public schools for close to thirty years, working as a teacher, a principal, and then, since 1975, as Eugene Reville's right-hand man, the "brains," some people said, behind the desegregation plan, the "architect" of it, said others. Relied on by Judge Curtin, indispensable to Reville, few people questioned the judgment or vision of Joe Murray, known respectfully as "Mr. Murray" to thousands of parents, teachers, and administrators throughout the system. Murray was a policeman's son from Riverside, the product, like so many key figures in the school case, of his local parish school, Canisius High School, and Canisius College. Murray, like Reville, was a liberal, devoted to the principles and goals of the civil-rights movement, and he welcomed Judge Curtin's desegregation orders as the chance not only to implement a vision he believed in, but to improve the quality of public education in Buffalo in the process. Indeed, under the leadership of Reville and Murray and a Board of Education willing to follow their direction, Buffalo's public schools had, by the middle of the 1980s, achieved a level of racial integration and educational excellence that was the envy of cities throughout the United States. People came from everywhere to see for themselves how Buffalo had done what no other city had been able to do. The man they sought out, time and time again, was Joe Murray.

Despite his origins in Riverside, Murray, like Reville, had long before shed the cultural and behavioral trappings associated with the area. Both had moved out of their native communities and now lived around the corner from each other in one of the city's nicest residential neighborhoods. They were both well-educated, thoughtful, and extremely articulate in dealing with the public and with politicians. Open-minded, fair-thinking, and daring in their approach to one of the thorniest, most intractable problems in American life, Reville, Murray, and John Curtin had all appealed, like Robert F. Kennedy and Martin Luther King, to the best instincts of their community, challenging and pushing the people of Buffalo to reach beyond the boundaries of their parochial experiences to achieve something great and unique in the annals of contemporary urban life.

By the end of the 1980s, however, the work they had done to so dramatically alter and improve Buffalo's public schools was threatened. The backlash against liberalism unleashed during the Reagan years and heightened during the Bush campaign of 1988 was felt in Buffalo. There, as in the rest of the nation, racial discord and divisiveness was growing. White resentment toward certain aspects of the desegregation program had long been smoldering. In May 1989 the people of Buffalo elected a Board of Education in which, for the first time, a majority of the members were opposed to the goals and objectives for which Reville, Murray, and Curtin had been working since 1976.

Throughout most of the 1980s Reville and Murray had enjoyed the support of a liberal majority consisting of a Jewish man and five women—one WASP, one Catholic, and three African-American. They worked closely with Reville and Murray, setting and controlling the agenda of the board, regularly overriding the dissident voices of three Catholic men—two from Irish South Buffalo, one from the predominantly Polish East Side. Following the elections of May 1989, however, the tables were turned. Reville had resigned after fifteen years as superintendent to become the "super superintendent" of a merged city-suburban school system in Little Rock, Arkansas. (They had been making progress in Little Rock, the city that Gov. Orville Faubus made famous for its resistance to integration, when, in March 1990, Eugene Reville was killed in an automobile accident. Mourned for days in his native city, where he had lived and worked for fifty-seven years, Reville was sorely missed in Little Rock, too. "It's been chaos down here since Gene died," wrote one observer.) And the new majority was created when two more Catholic men, both outspoken in their antipathy to the reforms of the Reville-Murray era, were elected. Joined by Mayor Griffin, long hostile to public education, the board began to dismantle the programs that had been so painstakingly created.

The change on the board revived visions of Buffalo's ancient legacy of interethnic conflict. Despite the willingness of the majority of ethnics living in Buffalo's old white neighborhoods to participate in the school desegregation program, white resentment was growing against what many felt was preferential treatment for minorities, particularly blacks. While many of their grievances were genuine and poignant, they became frightened and exaggerated when used successfully by the five candidates in their campaign for election to the Board of Education in the spring of 1989. Particularly volatile was the issue of teacher tests, the source, like all race-specific hiring programs, of the most bitter backlash.

In the spring of 1985 the Board of Education decided to reinstate the basic teacher competency test that it had suspended several years earlier in response to Judge Curtin's affirmative action ruling on staffing patterns in the Board of Education. In 1979 Curtin had ruled that 21 percent of all job categories in the schools—administrative, teaching, and engineering—be filled with black and Hispanic minorities. In order for teachers to reach that percentage, Curtin had insisted that for every white person hired as a permanent teacher, a black or Hispanic be hired too.

Superintendent Reville, like most of the board members, was in favor of administering the test to candidates who had received a bachelor's degree and were certified to teach in New York State. "A teacher, in order to be successful, has to have these skills in arithmetic and language," he said. The test in question was a general competency test for basic arithmetic, grammar, and writing skills. It would count for 30 percent of a candidate's "point rating" in the hiring process. A subject-area test would be worth 25 percent, and a personal interview before an integrated panel counted for 45 percent of the score.

The civil rights community opposed the test. Leroy Coles, president of the Urban League, said it was "injurious to the black and minority teachers." Dan Acker of the NAACP and Frank Mesiah, two of the original plaintiffs in the school desegregation case, agreed. They said the test had far more to do with "keeping blacks from entering the teaching profession" than it did with measuring the education of people applying for teaching jobs.

Not all blacks agreed. Indeed, Florence Baugh, perhaps the most influential board member, a woman with great credibility among blacks as well as whites, agreed with Reville. She had received calls from dozens of black teachers, who were incensed by the suggestion that they couldn't pass the test. "In all my years I've never seen incompetency come in colors," she said. "Either you're incompetent or you're not. I don't want to see anyone in the classroom who doesn't belong there." Most people agreed. Jeremy Finn, a professor of educational psychology at UB and, like Coles and Acker, an advisor to Reville on the teacher-test question, had selected and recommended the test. "We spent several months looking for a test that would measure the most basic teaching requisite—minimal literacy on the part of the teacher," he said. "As models and as instructors our teachers should read well, write clearly, and perform simple arithmetic." Like Baugh, Finn saw no inconsistency between the teacher test and Judge Curtin's one-for-one hiring order. Neither did the U.S. Equal Opportunity Commission, charged with monitoring affirmative action programs. It approved teacher tests that covered material considered essential to the performance of a job.

Under pressure from Acker, Mesiah, Coles, and a group called the Black Leadership Forum, Reville wavered at first; but then, on instructions from the board, he ordered that the teacher competency test be given. In May 1985 eighteen hundred people took it. Among them was a reporter for the *News,* a former teacher, eager to see what the fuss was all about. "To put it bluntly," he wrote after taking it, "the test was designed to weed out incompetents lacking the basic skills."

If he was right, the results, released reluctantly by Reville in mid-August, were frightening: 13 percent—143—of the whites and 38 percent—114—of the blacks and Hispanics who took the test failed. In January 1986 it was revealed, to everyone's shock, that the actual number of blacks and Hispanics who had failed was 65 percent. Compliance with Judge Curtin's ruling suddenly became a difficult problem.

Legally, the board knew it had no choice. While several members had opposed Curtin's quota, they never considered resisting it. The problem, though, was far more political than it was legal. If it abided by the test results and hired only those minorities who had passed, the board would be out of compliance with the court's order. If, on the other hand, it hired those who had failed, the board would comply with Curtin's quotas but at a cost that few people in the city were willing to pay. In late September 1985, after intense debate, the board made a decision to hire as temporary teachers 111 minority people who had failed the exam. (In the best Orwellian "newspeak" tradition, they were taken from what was called the "Qualified Applicant List.") Oscar Smukler, one of the several board members who opposed the action, insisted angrily, "I don't think that Judge Curtin's order required us to hire unqualified applicants." Baugh, meanwhile, had changed her mind. She now supported the hiring because of "shortages" of teachers. "The classrooms have to be staffed," she said. Baugh was not alone. Indeed, it was the reluctance of any black political or community leader to oppose the hiring of the teachers who had failed the test that contributed to the growing division along racial lines that the issue of teacher testing had encouraged.

Racial lines had begun to form immediately following the issuance of Curtin's original one-for-one hiring rule. From the beginning the ruling had created hardship among Buffalo's white teachers. Not only had the judge imposed a hiring quota, but his policy regarding layoffs was strict and, in the eyes of white teachers, punitive. Race, not seniority, Curtin said, must guide the board in the event of layoffs. Therefore, white teachers with greater seniority would have to go before more recently hired minority teachers. While Curtin's lay-off policy disturbed senior teachers, his hiring quota disrupted the careers of beginning teachers. As it became clearer that whites, despite having passed the test, were not being hired, they began to bristle about the test requirement. One associate superintendent, Albert Thompson, could offer little solace. Using the increasingly convoluted language of affirmative action, he said, "If a nonminority asked me personally what their chances of getting hired were, I'd have to tell them 'very slim.' But I can't discourage people from taking the test . . . that would be discrimination and that's what we're trying to avoid." Since no white could receive a probationary position (the first step toward a permanent position) until a minority received one too, more than four hundred white teachers, all of whom had passed the exam and who therefore were, according to the terms of their union contract, entitled to probationary status, were hired merely as temporaries. Known as "Curtin temps," these men and women had, since the judge's 1979 order, been working on a year-to-year basis with no benefits, no seniority, and, worse still, no knowledge of when and if they would be replaced by a minority who may well have failed the same test they had passed. (The Buffalo Teacher's Federation appealed Curtin's ruling to the Supreme Court, where it was sustained in 1984. In 1988, however, Curtin, recognizing their hardship, allowed them to count their temporary time toward probationary status. The result was that by early 1989 almost all had achieved permanent status.)

Meanwhile, the board, in a desperate effort to comply with Curtin's 21 percent quota, launched an elaborate campaign to recruit black and Hispanic teachers to Buffalo. Board officials visited recruitment fairs and black colleges throughout the South and a nine-week advertising blitz was launched in Puerto Rico. Board promotional materials called Buffalo "The Apple of Your Eye for a Lifetime of Opportunity."

But nothing disturbed people more than the fact that the Board of Education had hired teachers who had failed the competency test. The damage done by this decision was devastating and long-lasting. By singling out for preferential treatment blacks and Hispanics who had failed the same test that whites passed, the board unleashed a torrent of anger and resentment that is just now beginning to peak. The decision reinforced white stereotypes, undermined confidence in the school system, and insulted and demeaned the many blacks and Hispanics who had become teachers without the alleged benefits of "preferential" treatment. It seemed no one could benefit from the hiring of teachers who had failed—not the children, not their parents, and neither the black and Hispanic teachers who had made it on their own nor those hired with questionable credentials. The decision severely damaged the delicate but much improved climate of race relations that had prevailed in Buffalo since the remedy phase of the school desegregation case began in 1976.

Black leaders were as much to blame for this state of affairs as the new breed of rabble-rousing conservative politicians who have controlled Buffalo's Board of Education since mid-1989. For by defending—indeed, encouraging—the hiring of minorities who failed this simple, objectively arrived-at test of professional competency, they failed their constituents by insulting them. Competency, as Florence Baugh had said, should not be a question of color. But by making it one, the city's black leadership helped to turn the debate not into a discussion of academic competence and excellence but rather into a bilious argument cast in ugly racial terms. From this unfortunate development, the city has yet to reap what will surely be a bitter harvest.

The teacher-test question was one of several issues that by the end of the 1980s were damaging race relations in the city. There were other, similar concerns tied to the sense that Buffalo's black and Hispanic minorities were the beneficiaries of preferential treatment. Buffalo public school teachers had all come up the hard way. The first- and second-generation children of Italian, Polish, Irish, and Jewish immigrants, they were raised poor, worked hard, and, as a result, were often the first in their families to graduate from college. They came of age in the 1940s and 1950s, when poverty was the motivation for hard work and success. Their parents, many of whom spoke no English, worked hard and so did they, particularly in school, for they knew that education was their only way out. While sympathetic, they are not impressed by excuses or by talk of poverty. Given this background, it is understandable that many of these teachers, men and women in their forties and fifties, were losing patience with an attitude that was shifting responsibility away from the child and parent to the school system. As a result, many of them argued, failure was being rewarded. When black and the Hispanic candidates failed the teacher test and and the principal's test, the official reaction was first to discount the tests, saying that they were "culturally biased," and then to abandon them altogether. When a high percentage of black and Hispanic children failed and dropped out, officials introduced the concept of "social promotion," whereby a child could only be held back once in elementary school and once in high school. The curriculum was changed too; when bilingual education and an African-American infusion program were introduced many whites reacted with hostility. When larger numbers of blacks were suspended or sent to special education classes for antisocial behavior, the teachers who sent them were accused of being racist, memos were sent, and the practice was curtailed.

These approaches to the problems that many black and Hispanic children were having in the city's schools seemed to be doing little for the children and still less for everyone else. Indeed, more than anything, they were a significant cause of the growing racial friction that was threatening the city of Buffalo. For by specifically targeting minorities for compensatory treatment these programs incurred the resentment of both minorities and whites for whom success was the deserved fruit of hard work. In addition these programs undermined the sense of pride and achievement to which all people are entitled when they succeed. Many considered race-targeted approaches insulting and condescending. They demeaned the minorities they were supposed to help, alienated whites, and in the process helped to divide the community.

Despite passionate and genuine concerns about these programs, the increasing tension could have been defused by political leaders dedicated more to conciliation than to division. Under the leadership of the new majority on the Board of Education, however, opportunities to exploit and exacerbate interracial tensions through appointments, promotions, and racially charged rhetoric were rarely missed. Feelings throughout the community hardened and the extraordinary progress that school desegregation had achieved was threatened. People were concerned that the members of the new majority were involved more with their own political agenda than with educational matters.

Understandably concerned with budgetary accountability, the new majority wielded an ax where a scalpel was called for. While railing against budgetary excess, they showed little knowledge of or concern for the educational needs of the children of Buffalo. People also worried about the new majority's close ties to Mayor Griffin, the favoritism they seemed to show South Buffalo, and their apparent disdain for the demands of the African-American community.

Griffin had been an effective but highly divisive major since he was first elected in 1977. Building on a solid base of support in South Buffalo, he had been re-elected three times without ever turning to the support of African-American voters. Indeed, it seemed the more he antagonized the city's blacks, the better he did at the ballot. He seemed to be a bitter and obstreperous opponent of the efforts of Curtin, Murray, and Reville to improve and integrate Buffalo's public schools. Annually he had turned down board requests for funds and annually he had been lectured in the matter. But in May 1989 the tide turned in the mayor's favor when the new majority was elected. The board appeared eager to implement his budget and his agenda, and, perhaps more significantly, to appoint his supporters to positions at all levels of Buffalo's public school system. For years the mayor had been extending his political reach, tentacle-like, first throughout City Hall, then into the Fire and Police Departments where, it was said, every appointment and promotion was personally approved by the mayor. Griffin had built a political machine of unparalled strength and now the Board of Education, some people feared, was becoming another one of its cogs.

Joe Murray seemed tired and sad as he occasionally glanced out the window at the breathtakingly beautiful sunset that August evening in 1989. Since 1976 he had been working to create the high quality, integrated urban public school system that had become the envy of the nation. Now it seemed there was little he could do, as the Board's new majority whittled away through out the summer and fall of 1989 at the programs he had been so instrumental in building. But Murray, people said, was a scrapper, the type you'd want on your side in a fight. And in the fall of 1989, a fight was looming in Buffalo. As the board, under the firm control of a new and arrogant majority, swiped away at programs that had been so painstakingly created, parents, children, and teachers throughout the city, increasingly horrified by the scale of the damage, began to organize and resist. Joe Murray was there to help them.

So too was John T. Curtin. From the beginning of the case Curtin had not only encouraged the participation of the community in the development of the remedy, he'd required it. He knew from the start that the legacy of racial isolation in the Buffalo public schools could never be overcome without the willingness of all parties involved to work together. Curtin's deep commitment to the democratic process was rooted in his faith in the ability of the people of his community to solve their own problems if given the chance. Recognizing that the carrot does better than the stick if you are willing to wait a bit longer for the results, Curtin was always patient with Reville, Murray, and the Board of Education, allowing them, much to the frustrated dismay of the plaintiffs, to gradually phase in their plans. Curtin knew well that if he wasn't patient the school case, won in the courts, would be lost in the streets.

Curtin had given the parents a sense of ownership of the schools, and now they were turning to him for help. Beginning in late October 1989 letters began to pour in to the judge's chambers documenting the extent of the board's cuts and their impact on the programs that had kept so many of the schools integrated. Art and music, jazz bands and marching bands, concerts and assemblies, field trips and enrichment programs were being slashed with what the parents felt was a heartless disregard for education and integration.

One of the first letters came from a woman on the far East Side named Marlies Webb Wesolowski, president of the Olmsted Home School Association. She had come to Buffalo from England with her parents in 1969. Because her father worked as a designer at the old Birge Wallpaper factory on Niagara Street (today the factory is gone, replaced by a McDonald's), they lived on the Lower West Side, where Marlies attended Grover Cleveland High School. A newly arrived immigrant, she witnessed first hand the conflict between white ethnics and African-Americans that has for too many years pock-marked the history of this country. She watched as tough, swaggering Italian teenage boys gathered 'round a yellow school bus filled with black kids bused in from the East Side, rocking it in rhythm to chants of "Nigger, go home."

She was also there when the "Three M" gangs invaded the school. At the end of the year her family moved to Depew and Marlies graduated from that suburb's largely Polish-American high school.

When Marlies Webb married Richard Wesolowski, she moved to the East Side, on Crossman Street off Genesee, around the corner from the Scharf House, perhaps Buffalo's best traditional German restaurant. The neighborhood was pleasant, the homes reasonably priced and just a short drive from Sierra Research Co., where Richard worked as an engineer's aide. The Wesolowskis sent their two boys to the parish school in their old neighborhood in Depew. But by the mid-1980s they had begun to hear good things about the Buffalo public school magnet program, specifically about the Gifted and Talented Program at the Olmsted School, old School 56 on Delevan Avenue on the West Side.

It was a difficult change for the family when the boys were enrolled. The bus ride was a long one for the children and it was hard for the parents to get to the school on a regular basis. The Wesolowskis ended up liking the school, however. Four years later they still liked it and Wesolowski, the new president of the Home School Association felt particularly threatened by the heavy-handed budget cuts imposed by the new Board of Education. Frustrated in her efforts to reach the members of the board or the Common Council, Wesolowski decided to write Curtin. In a long and poignant letter she outlined the impact of the cuts on her school. Saying she felt that she and the other parents were "left out in the cold with no solution," she expressed her hope that there was something Judge Curtin could do. Wesolowski thought it was a long shot, and that though Curtin was not likely to respond, she would at least get her anger and disappointment off her chest.

Five days later, however, on October 14, 1989, Wesolowski went to her mailbox and found a copy of a court order signed by U.S. District Judge John T. Curtin. In no uncertain terms it ordered the parties in the school case to respond to him about the concerns outlined in the letter of Marlies Wesolowski. She was overcome with disbelief, unable at first to grasp the implications of what had happened: a federal judge with the power, as Gene Reville once reminded a South Buffalo audience, to call out the 101st Airborne Division, had issued a court order in response to a letter that she, a parent from Crossman Street in East Buffalo, had written. Wesolowski sensed it was a special event, unique to the democratic process. Others had difficulty grasping it too. In an interview, even one of Curtin's clerks said it wasn't true. A federal judge simply did not issue court orders in response to letters from citizens. He might write back, he might even call it to the attention of the lawyers, but no, he wouldn't issue a court order. Even Curtin somehow failed to appreciate the significance of the event. When asked about it he responed in his casual, disheveled way, scratching his head as he prepared to leave his chambers for a noontime run: "Yes. It seemed to have merit and I thought a court order was appropriate."

And so at the beginning of the new decade the Buffalo school desegregation case was back to where it started. However, those who care about maintaining and strengthening the quality of democratic life in the city are breathing easier because of the continued vigilence of Judge John T. Curtin. Far more than public education is at stake in the battle that looms ahead. For during the late 1970s and early 1980s, as the people of Buffalo wrestled with the challenge of school desegregation, a new sense of community had begun to emerge, one in which the traditional bonds of race, class, and ethnicity were beginning to break down. While sometimes a source of strength and security, these ancient ties often functioned as barriers. Under the judicious vision of John Curtin; the relentless prodding of the plaintiffs led by the intrepid Norman Goldfarb; the inspired leadership of administrators like Gene Reville, Joe Murray, and Evelyn Cooper; the dedication of citizens like Theresa Muschat and Carol Holtz; and the goodwill and faith of thousands of teachers, parents, and children throughout the city, the old gates of the city were crumbling and new ones had begun to appear.

18

NEW GATES FOR THE OLD CITY

Every city has its gates, which need not be of stone. Nor need soldiers be upon them or watchers over them. At first, when cities were jewels in a dark and mysterious world, they tended to be round and they had protective walls. To enter, one had to pass through gates, the reward for which was shelter from the overwhelming forests and seas, the merciless and taxing expanse of greens, whites, and blues—wild and free—that stopped at the city walls.

In time the ramparts became higher and the gates more massive, until they simply disappeared and were replaced by barriers, subtler than stone, that girded every city like a crown and held in its spirit. Some claim that the barriers don't exist, and disparage them. Although they themselves can penetrate the new walls with no effort, their spirits (which, also, they claim do not exist) cannot, and are left like orphans around the periphery.

To enter a city intact it is necessary to pass through one of the new gates. They are far more difficult to find than their solid predecessors, for they are tests, mechanisms, devices, and implementations of justice. There once was a map, now long gone, one of the ancient charts upon which colorful animals sleep or rage. Those who saw it said that in its illuminations were figures and symbols of the gates. The east gate was that of acceptance of responsibility, the south gate that of desire to explore, the west gate that of devotion to beauty, and the north gate that of selfless love. But they were not believed. It was said that a city with entryways like these could not exist, because it was too wonderful. Those who decide such things decided that whoever has seen the map had only imagined it, and the entire matter was forgotten, treated as if it were a dream and ignored. This of course freed it to live forever.

Mark Helprin, Winter's Tale

Neighborhood schools were comfortable, familiar. Families had gone to them for generations and everyone knew the names of teachers and principals going back years. Like the parish church, neighborhood schools were extensions of the home, an important part of the primal, intricate, and tightly knit fabric that helped hold the city together. But then, following Judge Curtin's 1976 ruling, things began to change and the neighborhood school as people had known it for so long began to vanish. Some were closed. Some were paired with other neighborhood schools in distant corners of the city. Some were changed into magnet schools, which drew students from all over the city. Some people bemoaned the loss of the neighborhood school as yet another sign of the erosion of neighborhood community life. Others, however, seeing the dynamic mix that was occurring at the magnet schools, the confluence of children from all of Buffalo's long separate neighborhood nooks and crannies, hailed the change and rejoiced that a new and far more pluralistic understanding of community life was being created at these new gates to the old city.

As a result of the magnet schools, fifteen thousand children in 1989 (35 percent of the student population) have discovered that there exists a whole world beyond the confines of the gates of their old neighborhoods. And while many of them no longer have as many friends on the block, they now have them everywhere else throughout the city. On weekends, parents drive their children to birthday parties and sleep-over dates in places they themselves, the products of a more parochial upbringing, have long forgotten about or have never seen before. As they get older, Buffalo's children begin riding the buses and the subway from one end of town to the other. Rich kids and poor ones, white kids and minorities are all going here one day, there the next, continuing to nurture on weekends and vacations the democratic process of cross-fertilization that begins in the magnet schools of the city.

Admission to the magnet schools is through application and lottery. It is a process that, unlike simply packing your child off to the local neighborhood schools, requires effort, intelligence, information, and commitment on the part of parents. For this reason the magnets have been criticized as elitist, benefiting only the best and the brightest. While there may be some truth to the charge, the fact is that without the magnets, "that something special at the end of the bus ride," as Joe Murray said, Buffalo would not have been able to integrate its public schools. It is because of the magnets that in Buffalo—unlike in New York, Cleveland, Boston, Detroit, or Chicago—middle-class residents of all colors and creeds have maintained faith and confidence in their public school system. "Parents' nights" at the magnets are filled with a true cross-section of men and women from all walks of life and work drawn together not by their race, color, or neighborhood background but by their hopes and expectations for their children's future. By engaging parents in the process of their children's education, the magnet schools have touched them where they are most sensitive and responsive, laying the foundation for still greater involvement in the affairs of their community, building new gates for the old city. As a result of the magnet schools, many of these people have rediscoverd Buffalo not only as a place but as a process where there exists the promise of creating a community that is both interracial and pluralistic. At a time when urban public school systems have become the dumping grounds for the poor, the racial and class mix that exists within the magnet schools of Buffalo is an example to people everywhere concerned about the state of democratic pluralism in contemporary American urban life. Walking through the new gates of their old city, the people of Buffalo are becoming neighbors.

On the lower West Side, Buffalo's most eclectic neighborhood, people of different races have been neighbors for years. The Lower West Side has always welcomed strangers—maybe because it is so close to Canada; maybe because it is here, near the waterfront, for so long the center of the city's commercial life, that housing has always been cheap. Whatever the reason, the Lower West Side remains as friendly and as hospitable today as it always has been.

For years the Lower West Side was predominantly Italian. But the patterns of migration, encouraged by urban renewal, changed all that and today the Lower West Side—indeed much of the rest of the West Side—is Hispanic. There are over thirty thousand Hispanics, most of them Puerto Rican, living between the Niagara River on the west, Elmwood Avenue on the east, City Hall on the south, and Porter Avenue on the north. Like minority communities everywhere, the Puerto Rican Lower West Side has been severely damaged by the decline of industry. While it struggles with the usual litany of problems endemic to all poor, inner-city neighborhoods, its community leaders remain energetic and morale is high. The community is increasingly well-organized, with its own newspaper, boys' club, senior citizens' group, political clubs, community organizations, and a host of locally owned stores and small business. Ever more vocal and visible, Buffalo's Puerto Ricans are sure to become increasingly prominent and significant in the life of the city.

The focal point of Puerto Rican life and culture in the area is School 76, the Herman Badillo Bi-Lingual Academy, located on South Elmwood Avenue. Seventy percent of the school's 560 kids are Puerto Rican, and 60 percent of its 44 faculty members are Hispanic. The school bubbles with excitement, vitality, great energy, and enthusiasm. Its Puerto Rican principal, David Caban, believes that "you can't isolate self-concept from education. What you are is good. What your parents are is good and your language and your culture are good, too." Kids at the school graduate proficient in two languages, Caban says proudly. "They can make it in the world because their sense of who they are has been strengthened at our school. We don't want them to forget that."

Nor does John Elm, the principal of School 19, want the Native American children of the West Side to forget their heritage. School 19 on West Delevan, the only Native American magnet school in the country, is dedicated to the preservation of the distinctive heritage of the nearly 200 Native Americans enrolled in the program. Founded in 1978, the school is the only one in the state where children can study the Mohawk and Seneca languages, earning Regents credit for foreign-language study. Working with Native American cultural resource people, Elm, himself born on the Onondaga reservation near Syracuse, offers daily presentations on Indian culture, traditions, life, values, and language. The program seems to be working. While the number of Native Americans graduating from high school remains low, the percentage has increased dramatically since the school was founded.

Despite the predominance of Puerto Ricans on the Lower West Side, the neighborhood is polyglot, an exciting melting pot of people struggling to build a community for themselves in this strange and fascinating city. It all comes together on Niagara Street, where Puerto Rican stores and restaurants, a Vietnamese grocery, and several Italian luncheonettes, bakeries, and grocery stores share the fertile turf. Nothing better reflects the ethnic diversity of the neighborhood than Tops Supermarket on Niagara Street. Here, where the parking lot is always empty because people in this neighborhood tend to walk or use public transportation, the aisles are filled with people and products from di-

292 City on the Lake

verse lands and cultures.

Equally diverse are the students who populate the halls of Grover Cleveland High School on Jersey Street, the neighborhood high school. Directly across Porter Avenue from Kleinhan's Music Hall, one of the world's great concert halls, Grover Cleveland, a "generic" school, is alive with the energy of diverse cultures. It has always been a neighborhood school, and throughout most of the century it, like the neighborhood, was primarily Italian. Now the most pluralistic school in Buffalo, it offers a promise and potential that few other schools in the city can match. The kids at Grover speak fourteen different primary languages, including Russian, Japanese, several variants of Chinese, Spanish, Arabic, Vietnamese, Cambodian, Thai, Turkish, and Laotian.

One third of the school is Puerto Rican, another third African-American. Today there is none of the interracial friction, let alone violence, that so frightened Marlies Wesolowski almost twenty years ago. And while struggling to improve their academic performance, the "students are learning about one another, about life," said one teacher. They are all building new gates for the old city.

There are other schools in the neighborhood where the children of the Lower West Side come together. At School 38 on Vermont, renamed the Frank A. Sedita Community School, there are 27 Native Americans, 11 Asians, 212 African-Americans, 258 whites, and 84 Hispanics. At School 45 on Hoyt Street there are 22 Native Americans, 86 Asians, 369 African-Americans, 428 whites, and 114 Hispanics. The children of the Lower West Side meet in churches too, at Immaculate Conception on Elmwood and at Holy Cross on Niagara Street, where there are daily masses in English and Spanish. Down Niagara Street at St. Anthony of Padua, the oldest Italian parish in Buffalo, Father Secondo Cassarotta says a weekly mass in Italian. Founded in 1892, St. Anthony's barely survived the havoc brought to the parish by urban renewal in the late 1960s and early 1970s. Today it is fitting that the parish, founded in 1892 by the Scalabrini fathers, protectors of migrants, is more than half Hispanic with a growing number of Vietnamese. Cassarotta, himself born in Italy, is dedicated to strengthening the heritage of his Italian parishioners. He feels that their ethnic heritage has been undermined by assimilationist tendencies among his people as well as pressures from without. Since he came to Buffalo in 1980 Padre Secondo, as he is called, has revived the traditional Sicilian saints-day celebrations and instituted Italian culture and language courses and a particularly festive "Festa di Sant'Antonio" every June—dozens of the church's parishioners take to the streets, proudly parading statues of their patron saint, just as it was done at the turn of the century.

Ever mindful of the Scalabrini mission, Cassarotta is particularly eager to strengthen the ties of his church to its diverse parishioners. Spanish masses are offered regularly and an annual celebration of Vietnamese New Year's Day has been instituted. Last March, at their annual St. Joseph's Day Table, the parishioners of St. Anthony raised twenty-five hundred dollars for the Scalabrini Refuge Center in Tijuana, Mexico. Called "La Casa del Migrante," the shelter takes care of thousands of homeless Mexicans who are trying to enter the United States. Cassarotta wants his parishioners to be neighbors; he too is building new gates for the old city.

So are Anna Cottone and Lucy Falzone. One Puerto Rican, the other Italian-American, the two women had been neighbors on the Lower West Side for years and never knew it. Cottone, a community activist on behalf of all of her people, is the founder of Los Tainos, a Hispanic senior-citizens group located on Hudson Street. Around the corner on Seventh Street, in a community center named for Father Vincent Belle, a popular priest from Holy Cross murdered in the parking lot of his church on New Year's Day, 1959, Falzone presides over an Italian senior citizens group known as the "Father Belle Swingers." By the end of the 1980s Los Tainos, despite a membership of more than two hundred, faced serious financial problems and the prospect of losing its center. Then, in the summer of 1989, when the collapse of Los Tainos seemed all but certain, Lucy Falzone and the "Belle Swingers" opened their arms. With the help of the Urban League, Cottone and Falzone negotiated an agreement to share the large common dining room in the Father Belle Center. Every day, at long tables arranged in rows in a bright second floor room overlooking the small frame homes below and the fast-moving waters of the Niagara River beyond, several hundred senior citizens from very different cultural backgrounds share common ground on Buffalo's Lower West Side. Los Tainos, the Belle Swingers, the Father Belle Center, and the whole Lower West Side have been strengthened by this union.

The energy of the melting pot on the Lower West Side has spilled over into the adjacent Allentown district, creating a truly democratic mixture of people in this historic neighborhood. Allentown, a small, century-old network of streets within walking distance of downtown, has had a special cachet since the early 1960s when a group of its residents, Buffalo's first real preservationists, formed a neighborhood association to protect its architectural integrity and to nurture its development as the "Greenwich Village" of Buffalo. Allentown's side streets—Park Street,

Mariner Street, Irving Place, Days Park, and Arlington Park, where
the late-nineteenth-century homes border small, lushly landscaped ovals
of green—have a lovely, genteel, distinctly village-like atmosphere. There
is nothing genteel, however, about Allen Street itself, with its mix of
gin mills, submarine shops, antique stores, and one or two gourmet
food stores. Allentown has never been an ethnic neighborhood exactly,
attracting instead a mixture of people who like the area's slightly tawdry
yet funky urban-ness.

Allentown's focal point—indeed, something of a magnet for people
from all over the city (suburbanites tend to shy away from its gritty
reality)—is the Towne Restaurant. Family owned and operated, the
Towne is open twenty-four hours a day and serves the whole rainbow
of people who make up the city. It thrives on diversity. Dusty, paint-
splattered contractors on break, business people meeting for breakfast
or lunch, neighborhood street people, gays, musicians, society ladies
from the Allentown Association, neighborhood artists and shopkeepers,
and well-dressed couples on their way to a Philharmonic concert at
Kleinhan's all seem comfortable in the no-questions-asked ambience of
this wonderful restaurant, an institution really, where the food is good,
the portions large, the service excellent, and the price right. The crowded
community bulletin board in the vestibule proclaims that the Towne
belongs to everyone. Ads, posters, and announcements crowd it: Black
letters on orange poster board announce "Nightmare on Allen Street,"
a Halloween rock 'n' roll jam to be held at Nietzsche's, the best live
music bar in Buffalo located just down the street. A beautifully printed,
silk-screened poster invites the public to a lecture on "The English Country
House" at St. John's Grace Episcopal Church, sponsored by the Preservation Coalition of Erie County. Under a richly detailed pen drawing,
another sign says that there is a one-bedroom apartment available in
the historic Tifft Row Houses, a group of early Victorian brick homes
across the street from the Towne. Still another sign announces that
two films will be shown next week at the Polish Community Center—
one is called "Polonia Lives: A look at the efforts of Polish and Black
residents resisting plans to destroy their neighborhood to make way
for an auto plant in Detroit." In the polyglot community that is the
Towne, everyone is a neighbor. Here too they are building new gates
for the old city.

If you follow Virginia Street, just a block below Allen, across Main
to the East Side (the route that the Lower West Side Arterial was
scheduled to take) you end up in the Fruit Belt, a small, wooded
community where the streets are named Grape, Lemon, Rose, Cherry,

Mulberry, Locust, and Orange, and the small, old, wooden homes are set gently into the side of a gently, slow-rising hill. The area has an easy, quiet, relaxed feel to it that belies its location smack between the Kensington Expressway and a giant complex of hospital and medical buildings. Settled long before the Civil War by the city's earliest German immigrants, the Fruit Belt still bears witness to its origins. The community's main streets—Virginia, High, and Carlton Streets—are still lined with the old two- and three-story cast-iron-and-brick buildings typical of the nineteenth-century streetscape: stores downstairs, apartments up. Some of the old churches are still here too: an elaborate Victorian vision of brick and wood, built in 1883 on High and Mulberry Street as the Third German Church; around the corner on Grape Street, a smaller, but equally magnificent red-brick church built, a keystone in the façade tells us, as St. Paul's German Evangelical in 1874. There was another, even older German church, St. Boniface on Locust Street, built in 1849. It's gone now, demolished years ago. But its convent, a lovely and intimate three-story building with delicate, rounded windows and a rounded, welcoming doorway, still stands, a gentle and friendly reminder of what used to be.

The German exodus from the Fruit Belt was sudden. The changes that occurred in this staid, steady, and peaceful neighborhood—the construction of Kensington Expressway, the large and sudden influx of African-Americans—were too much, too soon, and the people panicked and fled. By the mid-1960s all but a few of the old German residents had left. The African-American community in the Fruit Belt has built a sound new neighborhood structure on the old foundations. The shadows cast by the past figure prominently in the present. In the cavernous sanctuary of what used to be the Third German Church on High Street is the Promised Land Baptist Church. The small, pristine church that once housed the German Evangelicals on Grape has since 1963 been the home of the Gethsemane Baptist Church. Led since then by the Rev. Herbert V. Reid, one of Buffalo's most prominent African-American citizens, Gethsemane Baptist plays an extremely important role in the social, cultural, political, and spiritual life of this community.

The past, present, and future are also fused around the corner on Orange Street, in the small and humble headquarters of the oldest settlement house in the city, the Buffalo Federation of Neighborhood Houses. Descended directly from Westminster House and Neighborhood House, both founded in 1893, one by Presbyterians, the other by Unitarians, the federation is a vital center of life in the Fruit Belt community, serving close to four hundred people every day, infants and mothers, teenagers and seniors, helping them all to become stronger and more effective members of their community.

Around the corner on Locust Street, in the old St. Boniface nunnery, is one of Buffalo's most inspiring institutions. Known as the Molly-Olga Neighborhood Art Classes, it has been offering free art classes to people from all over the city since it opened in 1971. It started in Molly Bethel's kitchen on Maple Street. Word got out around the neighborhood that Bethel was a painter and soon some neighborhood kids approached her, half joking, asking if she could teach them how to paint. She could and she did, at a makeshift workbench set up in her kitchen. Word spread, the numbers grew and in 1959, Bethel was given space for her classes at St. Phillip's Church on Goodell Street. Soon she was joined by Olga Lownie, a Ukranian refugee who had come to Buffalo with her parents after World War II. An art student at Buffalo State, Olga began working with Molly as a volunteer and in 1961 joined her as a co-director of what had become a community program. When St. Phillip's was demolished as part of an urban renewal project in the Elm-Oak area in 1971, Molly-Olga, as it had come to be known, moved back to the Fruit Belt, renting space from the nuns at St. Boniface in the Locust Street convent. Three years later, their church gone, the nuns moved out. Using funds raised in the community and privately, the Molly-Olga School bought the lovely building.

Today, more than thirty years after its founding, Molly-Olga offers instruction and work space to more than four hundred children, teenagers, and adults studying painting, sculpture, and photography. Supported by public grants and private donations, the school is extremely casual and friendly, the old building warm and slightly disheveled. Teenagers from the suburbs, down-and-out artists staying at the City Mission, school teachers and nurses, social workers and nuns, they all come to take classes or to work on their own. Downstairs are children, some from the neighborhood who have walked over from other streets in the Fruit Belt, others from neighborhoods all over the city and the suburbs too. Upstairs is studio space for the more accomplished artists, whose work is displayed throughout the building. On one wall are the large, poignant paintings of migrant workers done by Juan Cavazos, who comes to Molly-Olga to paint when not working in the fields of Western New York. On a table in the middle of one room is the passionate wooden sculpture of Peruvian artist Robert Pacheco, who works and teaches at the school. On the wall above are the neighborhood views of Curtiss Robinson, a skilled Fruit Belt primitive painter with a keen and humorous eye for the day-to-day reality of life in this most interesting of neighborhoods. On yet another wall is the Governor's Arts Award, given to the School in 1985 in recognition for Molly-Olga's "contribution to the cultural life of this state." Where love of art and of children transcend race, color, and creed, Molly-Olga is building bridges, creating new gates for this old neighborhood.

So too are the schools in the Fruit Belt, some of the best and most interesting in the city. At the north end of the neighborhood, on East North Street, is City Honors, "the school on the hill." Located in a fabulous turn-of-the-century building filled with carefully sculpted marble; elegantly carved woodwork; high, inspiring ceilings; and long halls lined with oak cabinets packed with ancient silver trophies, this wonderful school, once known as Fosdick-Masten, was almost closed before the Buffalo Plan gave it a new life in 1979 as Buffalo's academic honors school for children from grades five through twelve. Pulsing with the energy and vitality of academically motivated children from neighborhoods throughout the city, City Honors is one of the great landmarks in the life of contemporary Buffalo.

At the south end of the Fruit Belt are two more magnet schools, which, like City Honors and Molly-Olga, have succeeded in infusing this long-isolated African-American neighborhood with children from all over the area. Every day they come—Irish kids from South Buffalo, Italians from the West Side, Poles from the East Side, Slavs from Black Rock and Riverside, and neighborhood kids from the Fruit Belt—some to the Martin Luther King Multicultural Institute, old School 39 on Carlton; others to the Futures Academy, the school that Evelyn Cooper created at old School 37 down the street. M.L.K is devoted to pluralism, and here kids from kindergarten through eighth grade study French, Italian, and Spanish. Then, every spring, with money they raise themselves, honors students in the fifth and eighth grades travel to a different country in Europe. At Futures, in a fanciful Art Deco structure built by the federal Works Progress Administration in 1934, the emphasis is on preparing the children in this school, cited by President Reagan as one of the finest of its kind, for the world that awaits them beyond the confines of their neighborhood and their city. Thus, enriched by schools whose dynamic present has been built on the foundations of a rich past, new bridges have been built to the Fruit Belt and new gates now join it to the rest of the city.

It is through new gates too that hundreds of new immigrants are coming to settle in this old city on the lake. Many of them are helped by two organizations located near each other on Delaware Avenue. Until the end of the World War II, Delaware Avenue was one of the truly grand residential streets of the country, lined with the ornate, architecturally extraordinary mansions of the city's wealthiest citizens. Many of them have been preserved and new uses have been found for buildings that otherwise would have been demolished. One of them, an 1898 Georgian Revival mansion with staggering marble floors, staircases, and fireplaces, has since 1973 been the headquarters of the International Institute. With a Polish, Italian, Arab, Dutch, Panamanian, and Chinese staff, the International Institute works feverishly with the rush of new settlers, providing a wide range of legal, housing, vocational, and personal counseling, helping people from all over the world who are settling in Buffalo to become better citizens. Working in cooperation with the Board of Education, the institute offers free English classes and free citizenship classes to any immigrant, legal or not, eager to learn the language and the ways of their new community. Downstairs one day, in a particularly ornate room that once served as the dining room in this fantastic mansion, an Iranian newspaper editor, a Colombian housewife, an illegal Salvadoran, young men from Greece and Hungary, and two Chinese women in their early twenties are studying English, taught by Gloria Guice, an African-American teacher from the Buffalo public schools. Upstairs, in a small office that was once a maid's room, Mohammad Hamouche, from Lebanon, works on the roster of the institute's soccer team. Called the "Legal Aliens," the team, with players from Mexico, El Salvador, Greece, Hungary, Romania, the Soviet Union, Laos, and Italy, dominates their league.

Across Delaware Avenue in yet another of Buffalo's architectural landmarks, a temple with stained glass windows designed by the great painter Ben Shawn, is Jewish Family Services, which since the early 1970s has been helping Russian Jewish immigrants settle in Buffalo. Since early 1989 they have been coming in growing numbers. Helped by the Hebrew Immigrant Aid Society and supported by local sponsors, more than 240 of the immigrants, young and old, families and friends, have settled in Buffalo. Although entitled to automatic welfare payments, the immigrants rely instead on the generosity of their brothers and sisters in the Jewish community. Through a program called "Project Rescue," people and institutions throughout the Jewish community have raised enough money to support every Russian family with food, shelter, and clothing for four months. As a result of the response of a people with a vivid understanding of the immigrant experience, the new gates to the city for these new residents are warm and welcoming.

Equally so are the new gates erected by Catholic Charities for political refugees coming to Buffalo from Latin America, Asia, and Eastern Europe. "I was a stranger in a strange land and you took me in," says the quotation from the Book of Matthew displayed prominently in the Sidway Building offices of Catholic Charities' Refugee Resettlement Program. In 1989 more than 220 people, refugees from places where they faced imprisonment, torture, and even death, have come to Buffalo in a program that Catholic Charities has been sponsoring since the late 1960s. Milling around the halls are a group of men, women, and teenagers, some Poles, some Ukranians, some Laotians, some Vietnamese. Like the Russian Jews at Jewish Family Services and the "Legal Aliens" at the International Institute, they have passed through new gates built in this old city and now are waiting for their classes to begin so that they can learn a new language and a new way of life in their new home in Buffalo, New York. As they do the city waits for them.

On one July evening each summer, more than a hundred thousand people, at least a third of the city's total population, gather on Buffalo's waterfront to commemorate the birthday of the United States of America. And each year there is a strong and warm sense of community spirit and good will in the city on the lake. The full panoply of the city's ethnic groups is there: African-Americans, Hispanics, Native Americans, Hungarians, Irish, Italians, Jews, Poles, Russians, Ukranians, Africans, Arabs, Indians, and Asians. Young and old, rich and poor, they come from everywhere, emptying out neighborhoods all over the city: the Fruit Belt and Seneca-Babcock, Cazenovia Park and Mineral Springs, Cold Springs and Grant and Ferry, Kaisertown and the Valley, the West Side and the East Side, North Buffalo and South Buffalo. Cars are banned for some distance and the people come on foot, long lines of them—couples, families, alone, and in groups—walking quickly, eagerly down Porter Avenue to LaSalle Park, where the celebration is held. Some arrive on bicycles. Some, mostly suburbanites, curious yet cautious about this large gathering, come on boats. In a marine procession that bears a faint resemblance to a Guardi view of ducal Venice, dozens of them—cruisers, sailboats, speedboats, and motorboats—fill the narrow bottleneck that joins the Niagara River and Lake Erie. It is a gigantic birthday party.

The program is consistently wonderful and the crowd loves it. First comes the music, usually from a pop celebrity, often an upbeat, extended medley of folk songs, patriotic melodies, and popular tunes that quickly become a community sing-along. The finale is a glorious and spectacular display of fireworks that fills the clear, early summer sky with bright, colored lights. The show ends a little after eleven o'clock. Slowly and happily the people fold up their blankets and chairs and begin peacefully and quietly to walk or ride back to their neighborhoods.

The Fourth of July celebration is always an inspirational event, a shining moment in the life of this city that brings out the finer civic qualities of the people of the community. In a way it recalls Woodstock, that great gathering of people in upstate New York in the 1960s, when peace, good will, friendliness, and trust characterized the assembled mass. But unlike the white, young, middle-class crowd gathered at Woodstock, the Fourth of July celebration at Lasalle Park is always interracial, interethnic, and intergenerational, representing a cross-section of the diverse community that is Buffalo. Perhaps such an event would not have been possible in 1969, a time of terrible polarization, when the old and young of many ethnic groups were frightened of one another. But at Buffalo's Fourth of July celebration, anyway, things are different. People are friendly. Buffalo looks beautiful, and the weather always seems to cooperate; the skyline is lit first by the light of the slowly setting sun, later by the brilliance of the fireworks. Enjoying the company of family, friends, and strangers, the city seems together and at peace with itself.

19

BUFFALO: FACING THE FUTURE

In the fall of 1989 Joe Murray expressed his concerns about the fate of Buffalo in the 1990s. In an interview he said, "It is simply not possible to deal with the city's economy or its schools or to make any long-term policy decisions about any aspect of life in this city without first achieving a stable social base that relies on a sense of community and the willingness of people of different races, backgrounds, and levels of wealth to live, work, and function together." But many people wondered, What do we do? How do we do it? James Hillman, a Jungian psychologist, suggested one approach in a talk before a group of Buffalonians in 1983. "The City of the Psyche builds the actual cities we live in," he said. "So it is of first importance to attend to our notions and our fantasies, our dreams and our words before we consciously actualize them in our streets, neighborhoods, and schools." What follows is this Buffalonian's "City of the Psyche," a blueprint for the creation of a new and stronger sense of community in Buffalo.

We must begin by expanding our notion of community so that it includes the whole metropolitan area. Separate municipalities must not be annexed, but they should be strongly encouraged to recognize that it is only as a united area, in which the burdens and blessings of urban life are shared, that we will be able to deal with the social, economic, educational, and environmental problems facing us all.

The decline of the U.S. industrial economy has had a disastrous effect on standards of living in our community as in our nation. Given the critical importance of a strong and diverse industrial economy for the health and welfare of our city, we must continue to support the economic work of all levels of government, forging the kinds of partnerships that in recent years have led to a strengthening and broadening of our economic base. We must continue to recognize the critical role and function of the public sector in the economic life of the community and continue to support the participation of such groups as the Erie County Industrial Development Agency and the Western New York Economic Development Corporation in the economic affairs of our community. When not actually participating as partners in local buy-backs and other forms of investment, public agencies can, through such programs as WNYEDC's Industrial Effectivensss Program, play a critical role in improving the quality of local management. While we should continue to encourage the transfer of companies to well-qualified, well-capitalized local ownership, we must recognize that who owns a company is not as important as who manages it and how.

Because of the importance of owner-occupied housing to the health and well-being of our neighborhoods, we must expand on programs like those in the East Side's Pratt-Willert and Riverside's Rebecca Park, which involve public-private partnership in the creation of new and affordable owner-occupied housing. It is critical that surrounding suburbs be involved in these efforts so that new and affordable homes will be made available throughout the metropolitan area.

Steps must be taken that will ensure that absentee landlords do not become slum landlords. We must encourage the adoption throughout the city of programs like the East Buffalo Community Ownership Program. EBCOP is a community land trust based on the concept that the land beneath a community is its most important asset, and that only through controlling its land can a community prevent the intrusion of slum landlords. Under this kind of program, community groups acquire land through purchase or donation and retain title to the land in perpetuity. This removes the land from the open market. Community groups then determine appropriate uses and lease the land to families, other community groups, or businesses, or use it for public purposes. Such a program would not only prevent the sale of homes to slumlords but would help ensure that an interested and active base of residents is retained in the neighborhood.

The success of downtown Buffalo as a commercial and retail center depends on the creation of a regional policy of planned and balanced economic development. Economic development needs to be more

Buffalo: Facing the Future 303

equitably spread throughout the area in order to prevent the kind of skewed development that has overdeveloped Amherst while undermining downtown Buffalo. Balanced regional development would provide the rationale for a truly regional public transit system, which does not currently exist in the metropolitan area. Once assured that development will be spread evenly, the public will recognize that rapid transit is vital to the whole area, and people will prove willing to provide the kind of support necessary for its creation and maintenance.

Without meaningful public transportation there will never be a truly vital downtown. There will be buildings and parking lots, perhaps a ghastly reflection of suburbia in the inner city, but the sense of place and clustering that makes downtown "downtown" will not exist without good public transportation—and public transportation will exist only where density is high. In addition to encouraging clustered, high-density, mixed-use commercial, retail, and residential developments, the community must make a total commitment to subsidizing public rather than private vehicular transportation. Torn between their desire on the one hand to strengthen rapid transit and its fear on the other to do anything that interferes with the use of private transportation, politicians and planners have long been pursuing contradictory transportation policies. While we spend hundreds of millions of public dollars building a rapid transit line, we continue to spend still more public money subsidizing and encouraging the use of private vehicles in the downtown area. As a result, it is far easier and in some cases even cheaper for a motorist to drive downtown and park at an all-day parking lot than to ride the subway. There are few views more preposterous than the sight of automobiles speeding up and down the two streets that parallel the rapid transit line far more quickly than the trains beneath them; of street-level parking lots adjacent to Metro stops; of a newly built, high-rise muncipal parking ramp hidden behind post-modern architectural gimmicks just steps away from the Metro stop at Lafayette Square. Things did not have to be this way. When Toronto's Dominion Centre was built on Yonge Street shortly after its subway opened in the late 1960s, developers pushed to build a below-ground parking ramp. The city refused, saying it would undermine the viability of the rapid transit line.

While it is perhaps ill-advised to make a hit list of buildings that have been so destructive to the city that they themselves should be destroyed (at the top of almost everyone's list would be the Buffalo Convention Center), it is absolutely necessary that strong steps be taken to improve the quality of Buffalo's urban design. We must recognize that the function of urban design is to deal with the physical environment in human terms and to reinforce the public and communal aspects of the physical environment, to give it, in other words, a "social conscience." A city with a good sense of the role and function of urban design can do much to overcome even the most damaging economic and demographic trends.

Of all the components of a city none has more social impact than the street. It is on the streets and sidewalks of a city that there exists the possibility of enhancing public life and in the process strengthening the sense of community that makes urban life special. For years planners forgot that Buffalonians not only love their streets but need them as well, and that like city dwellers everywhere, we do not appreciate the destruction of our streets by plans that benefit cars more than pedestrians. By allowing drive-in service stations and convenient marts and drive-through fast-food restaurants and banks to invade the streets and sidewalks of our city we have gravely harmed the pedestrian use of some of our best streets—witness Elmwood Avenue. Far too many of our city's streets have been permanently impaired because we have allowed them to be treated as if they were suburban shopping strips and not the intimate pathways so important to the way we live our daily lives. If suburbanites want to see their sidewalks turned into streets, that is their business. But in the city the place for cars is the street, not the sidewalk.

There is nothing wrong with cars. In fact, their presence enhances pedestrian traffic by contributing to the prosperity and vitality of the city's streets. Indeed, one of the primary problems with downtown Main Street today is that private vehicles have been banned from it. The most successful city streets are those that are shared by pedestrians, public transportation, and private cars. Nothing—not a new hotel, a new office building, or even a new apartment development—would more quickly stimulate the revival of Main Street than bringing back cars, which would, as always, be allowed to park on the street.

Urban design with a social conscience must inform the construction of all new buildings in Buffalo. When new structures are built, be they on the waterfront or within one of the neighborhoods, careful and sensitive attention must be paid to their natural and historical contexts. There must be thematic as well as aesthetic continuity, so that the future complements the present as well as the past. The past must be kept with us and we must continue to protect, strengthen, and restore the city's architectural legacy by creating new preservation districts based on themes as much as on individual structures.

We must recognize that the strength of a democratic, egalitarian, and pluralistic society is nurtured in its public schools. If we lose these characteristics in our public schools we will lose them in our society. Recognizing that public education is vital to the health of a democratic society, we must make it a priority for the whole community. The problems confronting public schools in the big cities of this country are so great that only total, community-wide efforts will be able to affect significant improvements. The problems are complex and varied. Much would be accomplished by creating one unified, city-suburban "super district" for schools similar to the kind Eugene Reville led in Little Rock, Arkansas, during the last year of his life. Not only would this end the current unconscionable disparity between the wealthier suburban and poorer urban school districts, it would also create, once and for all, a truly integrated public school system for the whole area. More than anything else suburbanization has cleaved the social classes of our community, widening the gap that separates the rich from the poor, the African-American from the Hispanic from the white. By joining the separate school districts of our area we could, in one giant, courageous step, create the strong social base that Joe Murray thought essential to making progress against the problems that beset our community.

Under such a scenario, the schools of the area will be for everyone; and there will be no schools for the poor. But until that day, large numbers of the poor will remain concentrated within the Buffalo district. As long as this is so we will have to waste precious resources mitigating the impact of poverty on children and their families in our community. In the meantime, schools will have to intervene more intensively and more effectively in the lives of the poor, providing a range of services and activities that go beyond the role and function that schools have traditionally played in the life of the community. This has already begun to happen, as, for example, at the Buffalo Public Schools' Parent-Child Center. Given the difficulty so many poor families have in coping with the problems of poverty, it is the responsibility of the rest of us to broaden the mission of the public schools so that the children of the poor can receive the support and the services that their families are unable to provide. If we are to ever win the war on poverty, the public schools of our nation must become one of our forward armies.

The disparity between rich and poor in our community is a disgrace. Admittedly, this is a national problem that requires national solutions, but there are things that we can begin to do locally to ease the problem. Again, beginning to think in more metropolitan terms would help. The creation of one metropolitan-wide tax system would mean that tax revenues would be distributed throughout the region based on need. This would end the barriers that currently separate and isolate the more affluent suburban residents of the area from the problems of poverty that weaken and undermine the lives of so many residents of Buffalo. The continued existence of huge disparities of wealth in our region, as in the country as a whole, insults our democratic heritage and threatens our hope for a democratic future.

We must continue to insist that state and federal governments not only develop clear and strict guidelines for environmental health, but also enforce them, so that our community's priceless treasures of air and water are forever sustained and preserved.

We must demand leaders whose vision of the good and healthy community is broad, egalitarian, and pluralistic. We need leaders willing to build bridges of conciliation and cooperation to all residents of the city, including those who oppose them in elections. We must insist that all of our political leaders work to overcome their hostility to working together for a more harmonious, interracial community. From the African-American community, Buffalo needs more leaders who are not afraid to stress that it is achievement and example that create success. From the white community, Buffalo needs leaders who recognize the importance of providing equal opportunity for everyone regardless of race or ethnic background.

In order to create leadership with a broader vision, the city should move away from representation in the Common Council by district toward a system where all members are elected at large. Such a system would engender broader vision on the part of our representatives, leading them to develop programs that address the problems and concerns of neighborhoods throughout the city, not just in their own backyards. To encourage fresh leadership, Buffalo should limit the tenure of the mayor to one six-year term.

Nothing undermines people's willingness to take the risks necessary to build a pluralistic community than the fear of crime. If we are ever to build the kind of community for which we are striving we must get serious about crime, making people understand that the community will harshly punish those whose behavior destroys its peace and stability. People of all ages must feel safe and protected in their schools, streets, neighborhoods, and parks. City law enforcement needs to be more effective, the administration of justice swifter and more certain, and punishment more severe. At the same time, the community must understand that a great deal of criminal behavior is nurtured in an environment of poverty and that we must therefore be willing to create economic alternatives for the residents of our poorest communities.

Lesser anti-social behavior must also be punished. Vehicular anarchy—speeding, running red lights, and so on—is becoming endemic in our community, undermining our confidence in the streets in particular and in the external environment in general. This kind of anti-social behavior is almost as destructive of community-building efforts as criminal behavior and must, through stricter enforcement of traffic laws, be stopped. Littering laws, too, must be more seriously enforced, so that those who do not cherish a clean, attractive, and healthy environment will not be allowed to spoil it for those of us who do.

In order to encourage the development of community-oriented values among our citizens, public-school children should be required to perform a certain amount of public and community service, for which they would receive school credit. In addition, the city, working with the county, state, and federal officials, should create public works programs similar to the Depression-era Civilian Conservation Corps, programs that would enable high-school students to continue their public service in a paid capacity upon graduation. In order to strengthen community values among the rest of the population, certain specific public functions currently performed by government should be turned over to neighborhood groups. The city should be divided into planning districts similar to those outlined by Louise McMillan in her 1974 proposal to Mayor Sedita. Residents within these areas, using resources and materials provided by the city, would be responsible for such neighborhood-based concerns as beautification, snow removal, garbage pickup, recycling, and activities supportive of the local police precinct. By turning over appropriate and specific functions to neighborhood-based groups, citizen participation and responsibility would improve and the democratic basis of the society would become stronger.

We need to keep the borders of our country and the gates to our city open. People are our ultimate resource and more immigration is far better than less immigration. Because people tend to immigrate when they are young, immigrants are an asset to any community. Generally hard-working, with a faith in the American dream that many Americans have lost, immigrants bring energy, productivity, and creativity to our city and our nation. We must, therefore, do more to help and encourage immigration.

To encourage the citizen participation and to draw ideas and inspiration from the broadest possible base, contests like the Invention Convention sponsored by the Buffalo public schools should be held regularly and prizes awarded to those who propose the most inventive solutions to the problems of everyday life in the city. Citizen participation should be reinstituted as a routine feature of the development of public policy in all areas of community life. Only in this way will the people of Buffalo offer up their hopes, dreams, and visions for their city, so that our future will be one that we ourselves can control.

EPILOGUE

Winter is beautiful in Buffalo. In Delaware Park snow blankets the long expanse of Olmsted's sweeping meadow. Giant old trees like skeletons, their leaves months ago fallen from their branches, stand in lonely, statuesque clusters. In the distance their tops seem puffy as if, like upended dusters, they are brushing up against the sky. In the distance, over the lake, the sky is often dark and foreboding, filled with black and grey swirling clouds. It is a sky that changes quickly and dramatically. From time to time the clouds are suddenly penetrated by long, orange shafts of sunlight. Long, eerie shadows race across the great breadth of the magnificent fields in Delaware Park as the sunlight comes and goes. At the same time, the sky can be completely different above the meadow. Sometimes it is gentle and blue, with soft pastel pink, blue, and white clouds. It is often empty and silent here, particularly in the middle of the meadow, where, standing alone, surrounded by a field of freshly fallen snow, one can hear nothing but the birds and the crunching footfalls of occasional solitary runners.

It is a bit warmer by the lake. When there is no wind on the lake shore there is no sound but that of ducks paddling through the cold, dark water, and the sonorous regularity of distant, gently muffled foghorns. Stanley Swisher works as supervisor of grounds for the city's engineering department. Swisher is thin and wiry, with red hair, blue eyes, and ruddy cheeks, his face permanently tanned from working outdoors at the Erie Basin Marina. Reached by a long and gently curving road that stretches out into Lake Erie, the Erie Basin Marina, built with slag from the old Bethlehem Steel mill, has sweeping views of the lake and its long, slow, dramatic sunsets. Since its completion in 1974 the Erie Basin Marina has become one of the most beautiful and popular public places in Western New York. Here, on Buffalo's windswept waterfront, within view of the long shadows cast by the grain elevators and the ghost-like ruins of Bethlehem and Republic Steel, Stanley Swisher has created one of the best rose gardens in the United States.

Swisher grew up in Friendship, New York, a tiny town about thirty-five miles southeast of Buffalo. After a two-year stint in the service, Swisher came to Buffalo to go to college at U.B. He'd been a medic in the Navy and after graduating he taught kids at the Association for Retarded Children. He loved teaching but found himself drawn to Buffalo's waterfront. In 1970 he began working for the harbor master of the city of Buffalo.

Swisher's parents owned a greenhouse in Friendship and Swisher, raised among flowers, began to try his hand at horticulture on the windswept shores of Lake Erie. With seeds bought from Stokes Seeds in Buffalo he started with a petunia bed in front of the Hatch, the Erie Basin Marina's restaurant. Every year he added another bed of perennials. Today Swisher's handiwork adds up to more than fourteen thousand tulips; a bed of marigolds; two beds of zinnias; several beds of mixed tiger, hybrid and Asiatic lilies; a bed of summer bulbs with shrubs; some strawberries and ornamental kale; tuberous begonias; hibiscus; and drawf orange, tangerine, lemon, lime, and grapefruit trees.

Most of all Swisher loved roses and to learn more about them he enrolled in the horticulture program at McKinley, one of Buffalo's public vocational schools. In 1982 he planted his first roses at the Erie Basin Marina. In 1987 Swisher's rose garden was selected by the American Rose Society as one of the nation's several hundred "Display Gardens." In 1989 Swisher's rose garden was selected as one of the nation's forty "Demostration Gardens." Soon, Swisher hopes, his rose garden will be chosen as one of America's thirteen "Test Gardens." It wouldn't be the first time for Buffalo. Back in the late 1940s and early 1950s, Swisher says, the Humboldt Rose Garden in Humboldt Park was one of the best in the country.

"People thought I was nuts," he says. " 'It's too windy and cold down here,' they told me. But they were wrong. The wind is good for the roses. It blows away the fungus and disease. Besides, it's a great micro-climate down here. Spring comes a bit later and fall lasts a bit longer."

There are more than fifteen hundred rose bushes in Stanley Swisher's rose garden at the Erie Basin Marina. Their names—Loving Touch, Dream Glo, Make Believe, Cinderella, Red Love, Fragrant Cloud, High Spirits—suggest romance, promise, mystery, and love.

ACKNOWLEDGMENTS

I would like to thank the following people for their contributions to this book.

In the schools: Gene Reville, Joe Murray, Kathy Shriver, Ken Echols, Nancy Graziano, Jim Gallagher, Carol Holtz, Theresa Muschat, Donald Beck, Priscilla Niedermeyer, Marva Daniels, James Heck, Willie Evans, David Kelly, Oscar Smukler, Florence Baugh, Mozella Richardson, Joan Downey, Jim Cawley, Richard Marotta, Rocco Lamparelli, Bill Bennet, Joann Skorka, Michael Annelli, Judith Fischer, Michael Casserly, Michael Ryan, Anthony Palano, Ben Randle, Nancy Miesczak, Pat Clemens, Helen Becker, Marilyn Reich, Marion Canedo, Linda Smolen, Mildred Stallings, Sal Andolina, Erma Robinson, Daniel Manley, Donna Kogler, Elizabeth Burgos, John Davis, Killian Kozminski, Guy Outlaw, Joyce Harrington, Fran Hill, Verna Morton, Mrs. Pinero, David Caban, Lydia Wright, Phil Rumore, Charlie Kam, Evelyn Cooper

In the community: Rev. Herbert V. Reid, Leroy Coles, David Perry, Greg Olma, Jim Pierakos, Sergio Fornasiero, Louis Rodriquez, Otto and Lilly Popper, Bess and Sylvian Ozarin, Ethel Baras, Seymour Berkoff, Peter Morrow III, Debora Maccagnano, Elwin Powell, Paul Knab, Bruce Beyer, Jim Mang, Sally Hamlin, Fr. Joe Schuster, Dennis Woods, Karl Kronberg, Michael Margulis, Tony Dutton, Audrey Mang, Fr. Secondo Cassarotto, Claire Silverman, Mary Bell, Yvonne Foote, Bill Seiner, Robert Gower, Fr. Walter Kerns, Fr. Bill Stanton, Sally Schlarth, Dick

Miller, Larry Quinn, Harold Cohen, Shonnie Finnegan, Anne Brittain, Heinke Boot, Ewa Sokolowski, Lucy Cullerer, Olga Lownie, Molly Bethel, Matthew Shuman, Milton and Marjorie Friedman, Irving and Mildred Levick, Robert T. Coles, Dean Sallack, Mark Hursty, Judith Kossey, Louise MacMillan, Joe Ryan, Jim Miletello, Will Clarkson, Robert Fernbach, Ruth Lampe, Ray Bissonette, Fr. Allan Bryan, Andrew Golobiewski, Lew Harriman, Alan Dewart, Irv Korn, Fred Fadel, Gordon J. Thompson, Leland Jones, Alan Marquardt, Norm Harper, Lou Jean Fleron, Jack Williams, Joe Godell, David Campbell, Donald Quinlan, Irving Sanes, Frank Palumbero, Margaret Strassner, Bill Falkowski, Fr. Dave Gallivan, Fr. Antonio Rodriquez, Charlie Livermore, Cleon Service, Fr. Jack Weimer, Mike Vogel, Sue McCartney, Scott Field, Mark Norton, Alan Abels, Dan Cunningham, Roberta Drapanas, George Sax, Jan Peters, Andrew Rudnick, Catherine F. Goldman, Robert Wilmers, Allison Des Forges, Marliss Wesolowski, Linda Pieri, Hubert Gerstman, Glenda Cadwallader, Anna Cotton, Lucy Falzone, Sam Cooper, George Smyntek, Mary Jo Gianbelluca, Ann Markusen

In the government: James D. Griffin, Clifford Bell, James Pitts, Norm Bakos, Archie Amos, Joe Schollard, David Franczyk, Jim Keane, Daniel Higgins, Gene Fahey, Dave Rutecki, Joel Giambra, Michael Mulderig, Michael Fitzpatrick, Joe Tanzella, Frank Manuele, Harry Hoffer, Bill Price, Frankie Perez, Paul Barrick, Stanley Swisher, Sal Galuzzo, Jose Pizarro

At the Bar: John T. Curtin, Bob White, Michael Brady, Pat Martin, Marilyn Hochfield, Dick Griffin, Willie Schoellkopf, Ray Chambers, Jan Curry, David Jay, Kathy McDonnough, Vincent Doyle

For any others who I may have fogotten, thanks too.

Name Index

Dupont Co., 171
Dutton, Anthony, 137
D'Youville College, 61, 97

East Buffalo Community Ownership Program, 302
East High School, 101, 108, 137
Eastman Machine Co., 168
East Side, 190
East Side Arterial, 31
Eastwood Place, 273
Echols, Kenneth, 147
Economou, Peter Gust, 97
Edwards, Floyd, 111, 113
Efner Street, 28
Elam Place, 47
Ellicott, Joseph, 14, 241
Ellicott District, 17, 19, 20, 22, 36, 101, 194
Ellicott Housing Projects, 74, 112
Ellicott Urban Renewal Project, 20, 21, 22, 139
Elm, John, 291
Elm-Oak Arterial, 31
Elmwood Avenue, 128, 129, 290, 304
Erie Basin Marina, 128, 255, 310
Erie County Bar Association, 147
Erie County Industrial Development Agency, 220, 222, 233, 244, 248, 300
Erie County Savings Bank, 245
Erie Downs Country Club, 132
Esser Street, 195
Evans, Dr. Frank, 12, 24, 104
Eve, Arthur O., 73, 132, 165, 166, 261

Fadel, Fred, 252, 253
Falkowski, Bill, 51–56
Falzone, Lucy, 293
Father Belle Community Center, 293
Father Belle Swingers, 293
Federal Bulldozer, The, 29
Federation of South Buffalo Community Organizations, 180
Felicetta, Frank, 112, 113
Fenian Movement, 59
Fenice, Msgr. Carl J., 21
Fillmore Avenue, 39, 53
Fillmore-Leroy, 40, 41, 46, 197, 260
Fillmore-Leroy Community Development Corporation (FLARE), 43
Finger, John, 142, 143
Finn, Jeremy, 280
Fisher-Price Co., 213
Fitzpatrick, Michael A., 62, 231, 249
Fleischmann, Manly, 118

Floss Street, 269
Ford Motor Company, 172, 219
Fornasiero, Sergio, 248
Foschio, Leslie, 135, 136, 165
Fosdick, John S., 95
Fosdick-Masten High School, 74, 106, 257
Fox Street, 23
Frank A. Sedita Community School, 292
Franklin Street Theater, 234
Freezer Queen Co., 223, 224, 233
Friendship Festival, 258
Friends of Night People, 275
Fruit Belt, 189, 294
Fuller, R. Buckminster, 250
Futures Academy, 192, 193, 196, 209, 297

Gabriel, Edward E., 242
Gadsden, Ala., 175
Gaitor, William, 115, 142, 190
Galleria Mall, 249
Gallivan, Fr. David., 36, 92
Galuzzo, Salvatore J., 27
Gardenville, N.Y., 195
Gardner, Arnold, 124
Garrity, Arthur O., 131
General Cinema Corporation, 254
General Electric Co., 216
General Mills Co., 170, 225
General Motors Co., 171, 227
Genesee Building, 165, 249
Genesee-Moselle, 41, 46, 269
Genesee Street, 268
Gethsemane Baptist Church, 262, 295
Gibraltar Steel Corp., 220
Gifted and Talented Program, 286
Goldfarb, Norman, 72, 93, 107, 108, 115, 123, 127, 131, 132, 134, 141, 142, 181, 183, 186, 199, 207, 208, 287
Goldome Bank, 230
Goodyear family, 229
Goulding Avenue, 23, 105, 273
Grable, James W., 86
Grand Metropolitan Co., 226, 227
Grant and Ferry, 39
Grant Street, 203
Grant's, W. T., 258
Grape Street, 294
Graphic Controls Corp., 222, 227, 228
Greater Buffalo Opera Company, 235
Gregory, Anthony, 149
Griffin, James D., 58, 63, 64, 72, 97, 164, 166, 173, 181, 184, 186, 193, 200, 206, 207, 245, 246, 252, 263, 264, 279, 284

Tanzella, Joseph J., 20
Teacher Competancy Test, 279
Ted's Restaurant, 128
Textron Corp., 220
Theater District, 235, 250
Theater Place, 253
Theatre of Youth, 234
Third German Church, 295
Thompson, Albert, 281
Timon, John, 62
Tonawanda, N.Y., 27
Toolan, Fr. Dave, 86
Tops Supermarket, 291
Toronto, Ontario, 237, 238
Tosh Collins Community Center, 128, 196
Towne Restaurant, 294
Townshend Street, 53
Tralfamadore Cafe, 252, 257, 258
Trammell, Wilbur, 261, 265, 267, 271
Transfiguration R.C. Church, 14, 53
Trico Company, 171, 212, 215
Trocaire College, 60, 89
Troidl's Restaurant, 260
Trollope, Anthony, 169
Tudor Place, 266
Tuscarora Street, 60

Ummiker, Edward, 34
Unia Polski, 53
Unitarian Universalist Church, 83
United Auto Workers, 171
United Auto Workers, Local 2100, 214
United Electrical Motor Co., 216
U.S. Commission on Civil Rights, 105
U.S. Environmental Protection Agency, 38
U.S. Second Court of Appeals, 198
United Way, 227
University District, 44, 260
Urban Development Action Grants (UDAGs), 245, 246, 247
Urban Mass Transit Authority, 239, 248

Vanadium Co., 168
Vandalia Street, 58
Vermont Street, 274
Vietnam, 83
Vine Alley, 94
Vine Alley Colored School, 14, 94, 95
Virginia Street, 27, 294, 295
Virginia Street festival, 36
Visitation R.C. Church, 101
Vulcan Street, 202

Walden-Bailey, 41
Walker, James, 173
Wallace, George, 121
Wardwell, George S., 95
Wardynski Sausage Company, 54
Washington v. Davis, 149
Waterfront School, 158, 159, 196
Watson Street, 162
Waverly Beach, 128
Weimer, Fr. Jack, 79, 90, 91, 133
Weimer's Grove, 79
Wesolowski, Marlies W., 285, 286
Wesolowski, Richard, 286
West Delavan Ave., 275
Western Electric Co., 168
Western New York District Council of Iron Workers, 249
Western New York Economic Development Corporation, 221, 222, 302
Western Savings Bank, 170
West Hertel Middle School, 18
Westinghouse Electric Co., 168, 216
Westminster House, 295
West Seneca, N.Y., 27, 264
West Side Arterial, 31, 33, 203
West Side Times, 72
Willax, Paul, 171
Williams, Carol, 126
Williams, J. H., Co., 195, 202
Williams, James, 157
Williams, Walter, 174
William Street, 14, 111, 112
Williamsville, N.Y., 133, 273
Willis, Benjamin, 100
Wilmers, Robert G., 227
Winterfest, 258
Wolf, Richard, 213
Woltz Street, 54
Wood and Brooks Co., 195, 202
Woodlawn Jr. High School, 102-103, 105-106, 136, 137, 157
Woodley Road, 260
Woods, Dennis, 90
Woodward Avenue, 50
Worthington Pump Co., 168
Wright, Frank Lloyd, 48
Wright, Dr. Lydia, 104, 105, 110

Yonge Street, 303

Zelmer Street, 269